SEA DETAIL

A Naval Officer's Voyage

VICE ADMIRAL
WILLIAM D. SULLIVAN
UNITED STATES NAVY (RETIRED)

D1535135

PUBLISHED BY

F🛡RTIS

A NONFICTION IMPRINT FROM ADDUCENT

WWW.ADDUCENT.CO
WWW.ADDUCENTINC.COM

TITLES DISTRIBUTED IN
NORTH AMERICA
UNITED KINGDOM
WESTERN EUROPE
SOUTH AMERICA
AUSTRALIA

SEA DETAIL

A Naval Officer's Voyage

VICE ADMIRAL
WILLIAM D. SULLIVAN
UNITED STATES NAVY (RETIRED)

Sea Detail: A Naval Officer's Voyage

William D. Sullivan

ISBN 9781937592608 (hardback)
ISBN 9781937592660 (paperback)

Published by Fortis (a nonfiction imprint from Adducent)
Jacksonville, Florida
www.Adducent.co
www.AdducentInc.com

Published in the United States of America

TABLE OF CONTENTS

PART I: BEGINNINGS

Chapter 1	Prologue	1
Chapter 2	Taking The Oath	4
Chapter 3	Greenhorn Ensign	19
Chapter 4	Join the Navy and See the World	33
Chapter 5	Destroyer Navy	46
Chapter 6	Middle East Force	71

PART II: COLD WAR NAVY

Chapter 7	Department Head	98
Chapter 8	Staff Puke	118
Chapter 9	*Challenger*	139
Chapter 10	Back to the Persian Gulf	147
Chapter 11	East Coast Sailors	160
Chapter 12	Assignment Pentagon	169

PART III: DESERT SHIELD / DESERT STORM

Chapter 13	First Command	179
Chapter 14	Déjà Vu in the Suez Canal	192
Chapter 15	Stop, Board, and Search	199
Chapter 16	NATO Ops	214

Chapter 17   The Mediterranean and Beyond   224

PART IV: NEITHER WAR NOR PEACE

Chapter 18   Getting Purpled   267
Chapter 19   Cruiser Command   281
Chapter 20   (Near) Collision at Sea   304
Chapter 21   Welcome Aboard Ladies!   314
Chapter 22   Flotilla Commander   328
Chapter 23   Striking Back at Terrorism   357
Chapter 24   Homeward Bound   373

PART V: REACHING FOR THE STARS

Chapter 25   Ready to Fight Tonight   398
Chapter 26   9/11 and the Pacific   415
Chapter 27   Iraq, Iraq, Iraq   435
Chapter 28   NATO   464
Chapter 29   Going Ashore   506

FOREWORD

I began these memoirs for my family and perhaps a few close friends who might be interested enough to read what I say about them. I wanted a record, for my children and for my grandchildren, of my experiences in the Navy. As I was growing up with my father a career naval aviator, I paid little attention to exactly what he was doing. I knew his rank, I knew where he had been stationed, and I knew that he was a Navy pilot. But I really didn't know much about his experiences. At family gatherings, particularly our Thanksgiving get together, he would regale us with sea stories of his adventures flying off of aircraft carriers. These stories were always fun to listen to, but, although we heard many of the same stories over and over again, it was hard to construct a chronological narrative. Some time ago, I asked my father to take the time to write it down; to tell his story. He did. Much of what is recounted here about him comes directly from that account. My father died in 2014 at the age of 91 and I will forever be glad that I asked him to tell his story.

Likewise, my wife Iris's father had a remarkable Army Air Corps and United States Air Force career of his own. He had been a prisoner of war in Germany in World War II and, later as an Air Force officer, seconded to the CIA as a liaison officer. He had spent his last year on active duty in Saigon at the Military Assistance Command, Vietnam. He had a tale to tell as well. After my father had written his account, Iris and I implored her Dad to do the same thing. He began recounting his adventures, also hand written, but had not finished before he died of a heart attack in 2007. Iris's mother had died the year before. We found his unfinished autobiography, handwritten on a lined legal pad, when going through his personal effects. Sadly, he was far from finished when he passed away.

I resolved that I would not let my time pass without leaving a record for our children, Chris and Amy, and our grandchildren, Peyton, George, and Merritt, and perhaps for whoever follows them. It hit me when my daughter Amy commented on the fact that she never really knew, growing up, exactly what I was doing in the Navy.

In one of my cleverer decisions, I began a simple log, not a diary, on the day I was commissioned in September 1972. I kept that log going for almost 37 years; recording every time a ship I was on got underway, came into port, or passed through a significant geographical point. If we got underway and went to sea in the morning only to return to port in the afternoon, I logged it. When we crossed the Equator or the Arctic Circle, or transited the Suez Canal or Panama Canal, I put it in the log. The Strait of Gibraltar, the Strait of Hormuz, the Straits of Messina, the Malacca Strait, I recorded them all. For that reason, all of the dates and places in this narrative are accurate. While commanding *USS COWPENS (CG-63)*, I kept more of a diary as well as the log. That diary provides more detail for that command than I had for the others. Navy ships normally publish "cruise books" to record events during major deployments; much like a class yearbook. The cruise books I have were very helpful in remembering names. If I am inconsistent in the use of first names, it is because those first names were not included in the respective cruise book.

Not everyone I worked with or for in my Navy career was wonderful. Far and away, most were. I have thought hard about how to recount some of those formative, but less pleasant relationships without doing harm. I learned as much from poor leaders as I did from the good. The reader will have to judge whether or not I have succeeded in carefully dancing around the negative influences in my life without causing undue harm to reputations or feelings. Likewise, I have been careful not to impugn the character, or harm the reputations of my juniors. If they failed me in a way that was worth recounting, I have tried to obscure their identities. My own failures, at least the ones I'm willing to confess, are described.

"Sea detail" describes both an active evolution, and a specific state of readiness in a Navy ship. Setting the Special Sea and Anchor Detail is the process of manning special watch stations for a ship that will be transiting in restricted waters where there is danger (normally of grounding). Special stations are manned for navigation, ship handling, engineering readiness, and a heightened state of readiness to rapidly respond to unforeseen circumstances. Setting the "special sea and anchor detail" results in a condition known as being "at sea detail." I chose this title for the special thrill, the knot in the stomach, and the adventure of hearing those words passed over the ship's loudspeaker system.

I considered whether or not to end this story with my final sea assignment, command of *USS COWPENS (CG-63)*. The succession of shore assignments that followed included only incidental sea details. But, as things worked out, I served 11 more years wearing the uniform of an admiral; almost a third of my 37 years commissioned service. My experiences as a flag officer, working in the "joint world," experiencing world events from the Joint Staff at the Pentagon, at North Atlantic Treaty Organization (NATO) Headquarters, and in the Pacific theater, gave me a perspective and experiences I thought worth sharing.

In addition to leaving a record, I hope this memoir inspires the reader to recognize potential in the young and immature. Many of the early episodes recorded are typical of junior officers (and other young people) everywhere—not what you would expect of someone destined to rise to flag rank. Actually, destined is the wrong word. How about, "who somehow manages to" become a three-star admiral. The best advice my father gave me, and he repeated it often, was, "No matter what crappy job they give you, do your best and it will be recognized." I'd like to think that, in the aggregate, I did that.

Finally, this is the story of two lives, mine and my wife Iris. Married while still in college, there is not a day in my Navy career that she was not by my side; in spirit if not physically. It may sound trite, but I would not have achieved the success I did without her support and wise counsel - she was and is my best asset and I love her dearly.

"Now, Station the Special Sea and Anchor Detail."

CHAPTER 1

Prologue

The Aegis guided missile cruiser *USS COWPENS (CG-63)* sliced through the calm waters of the North Arabian Sea at 20 knots. All radars were silent and no external communications left the ship except via satellite. Her running lights were off; she was a ghost, silently moving to a point in the vast ocean while avoiding the commercial sea lanes bringing shipping to and from the warm waters of the Persian Gulf. Her eyes and ears were in the SH-60B Light Airborne Multipurpose System (LAMPS) helicopter patrolling 50 miles ahead of the ship and transmitting radar data back via a one-degree pencil beam known as Hawklink. It was the night of the 19th of August 1998 and *USS COWPENS* was on a secret mission.

The Captain picked up the ship's announcing system microphone, the 1MC, on the bridge, paused for a second to gather his thoughts, and then began: "Good evening Thundering Herd, this is the Captain speaking. As you all know we went through Hormuz last night and secured all radars so as to keep our position secret. We're now about 200 miles south of Pakistan where we'll stay until tomorrow evening when we close the coast and enter our launch basket for a Tomahawk strike on a terrorist training camp in Afghanistan. Many of you saw the news on closed circuit TV this evening about the embassy bombings in Kenya and Tanzania on the 7th of August. The United States believes that the terrorist Osama bin Laden was responsible for those attacks, which killed hundreds, including Americans. Tomorrow we expect to try to take him out. I will keep you informed. Nothing is going to happen tonight so those of you not on watch get a good night's sleep. The ship is ready and I know you are ready. This is why we are here." The Captain then went on to briefly describe what was known about bin Laden and his past terrorist activities and signed off.

Eleven days earlier *COWPENS* had transited the winding channel into Sitra Harbor, tied up at Mina Sulman pier in Bahrain, and the Captain had traveled to Commander 5th Fleet headquarters to pay a call on the 5th Fleet Commander, a three-star admiral he knew personally from a previous assignment.

He spent an enjoyable three hours sitting in the admiral's office, swapping sea stories and catching up on old times, while the admiral directed the efforts of his staff, which was organizing a team to go to Nairobi. At one point, the admiral said, "We think this guy Osama bin Laden is responsible for this. We think we know where he is and if we can tie it to him, we're going to go after him." He went on to say that bin Laden had a terrorist camp in Afghanistan and if retaliation was ordered, the United States would attack the camp with a Tomahawk strike.

The admiral then said, "If we get the go ahead, you'll be one of the shooters. This is real close hold; you can't tell anybody."

Now the ship was at sea, steaming towards a point in the ocean from which the Tomahawk strike would be launched in concert with other ships of the United States 5th Fleet. In the days leading up to August 19th, the 5th Fleet staff had been quietly repositioning the Tomahawk capable ships in theater to position them for possible strike operations. *COWPENS* transit of the Strait of Hormuz the previous night had been the final piece of that repositioning. Until this evening the Captain had been instructed not to reveal the details of the ship's mission to the entire crew. This is what he had just finished doing. Coincidentally, that evening on the SITE TV system the evening news was from August 7th, the day of the embassy attacks (ships at sea are routinely updated with movies, television programs and sporting events by replenishment ships whenever the opportunity arises). All three major news networks led with the story, showing video of the destruction and of the dead and injured. Other reporting showed President Clinton vowing revenge. Everything reinforced what the Captain had told the crew on the 1MC.

Confident that the bridge and Combat Information Center (CIC) watch had things well in hand, the Captain went one deck below to his cabin and sat down with the night orders which would provide his guidance to the Tactical Action Officers (TAOs) and Officers of the Deck (OODs) who would be on watch through the night. He was looking forward to a good night's sleep himself, as the ship's track would be avoiding the major shipping lanes to minimize the possibility of a chance encounter. With any luck he would get few calls from the watch officers during the night.

After sending the night orders to CIC, the Captain sat back in his chair and thought about the coming events. Above his desk, digital displays showed him the ship's radar picture (dark this night with radars secured), course, and speed. He was a Navy captain, in command of an Aegis cruiser, the top of the line surface combatant in the United States Navy, and, if nothing changed, tomorrow he would be responsible for his own ship's launch of ten Tomahawk missiles. As the senior Commanding Officer (CO) among all the firing ships, he was designated Launch Area Coordinator, responsible for the execution of operations by the other three cruisers and destroyers also launching missiles. He would be personally responsible for executing the desires of the national leadership in responding to terrorism. Perfect execution was the only acceptable outcome.

48 years old, he had been in the Navy as a commissioned officer for almost 26 years. He leaned back and thought about the events that had brought him to this time and place. Maybe he wouldn't sleep so well that night after all.

I was that ship Captain and this is my story.

CHAPTER 2

Taking the Oath

O n June 26, 1971, I reported to Naval Station Newport Rhode Island to begin the first summer of Officer Candidate School (OCS) as a Reserve Officer Candidate, or ROC. I had been steered into the ROC program by my father, himself a Navy captain. The ROC program allowed officer candidates to break OCS into two summers, the first after the junior year of college, and the second following graduation. There were several advantages to the ROC program of which I was only vaguely aware at the time. Most notably, a ROC began to accrue time for pay purposes from the day he was sworn into the Navy as an officer candidate. ROCs did not get paid while in college, but did get pay while on active duty for training at OCS. While at OCS that first summer I would therefore have a summer job paying me as an E-5 (an enlisted paygrade) with one dependent. That came to $431.90 per month for the two months and one week of that first ROC summer. I had married my college sweetheart, Iris Stutzer, only one week earlier on June 19th. Our "honeymoon" consisted of driving from Winter Park, Florida to Newport. I had taken Iris to Boston that morning to fly to Honolulu and spend the summer with her mother. Her father, an Air Force lieutenant colonel, was in Vietnam.

Raised in a Navy family, I had never really considered joining the Navy while growing up. It wasn't until 1970, while I was a student at Florida State University, that my father recommended I apply for Officer Candidate School. He was in the twilight of his own remarkable 30-year career and was in his last assignment as Commanding Officer of the Naval Reserve Training Center in Orlando, Florida. He was a full captain and naval aviator who had enlisted after Pearl Harbor in his hometown of Boston,

4

Massachusetts, having dropped out of high school, and become one of the Navy's first sonarmen. While in the Canal Zone at Rodman, Panama, he heard about the Enlisted Pilot program, applied, and was accepted. He earned his wings and a commission after the war and progressed through the ranks as a TAR officer (Training and Administration, Reserves) and Navy pilot.

After being accepted into the enlisted pilot program, Dad, now a sonarman third class, left Panama in November 1943 to begin flight training which took two years and transferred him all over the country. During this period the war in the Pacific was proceeding better than anticipated when it came to pilot attrition rates. Consequently, the Navy pilot training pipeline was overloaded with students and wholesale washouts were the order of the day. Students had to fly continuous error-free flights to avoid washing out.

1944 was spent in Pensacola, Florida flying the SNJ Texan and Douglas Dauntless dive bombers of Battle of Midway fame. Dad carrier qualified in SNJ's aboard *USS RANGER (CV-4)*. He received his Navy wings in December 1945 as a First Class Aviation Pilot (AP1C), applied for a commission, and was promoted to ensign in February 1946.

Dad then went to Naval Air Station Fort Lauderdale for advanced training in the Grumman TBM torpedo bomber before orders to VT-11 flying TBM's in San Diego. When the air group was assigned to *USS VALLEY FORGE (CV-45)* for an around the world cruise, all of the reserve pilots were transferred out of the squadron and Dad ended up in VRF-2, a ferry squadron, flying all types of different Navy aircraft throughout the country for maintenance and delivery from the factory.

In the post-World War II Reduction in Force, or RIF, Dad was released from the Navy in February 1948, returned to Boston, and signed up with the reserve TBM squadron at Naval Air Station Squantum in Boston Harbor. At a wedding of mutual friends in 1948 he reconnected with my mother who had been a high school classmate although Dad had dropped out of high school his senior year. He was recalled to active duty in October 1948 and he and Mom were married May 14, 1949.

He received orders to Naval Air Station, Corpus Christi, Texas where he became a flight instructor in Advanced Operational Training, qualifying new ensign student pilots in the F-4U Corsair, the AD-1 Skyraider, and TBMs. I was born in Corpus Christi on March 29, 1950 and Dad, who had just been promoted to lieutenant (junior grade) was RIF'd again in April. Rather than leave Corpus Christi, Dad took a job flying Stearmans for an aerial crop spraying company until the Korean War broke out in June. When he heard there was a shortage of Navy pilots, he wrote the Bureau of Naval Personnel (BuPers) requesting a recall to active duty. By August he had heard nothing, so he put me and Mom on an airplane to Boston and drove to Washington where he parked himself on the right desk in BuPers until he was ordered back to active duty in September 1950.

Once re-activated, Dad was assigned to VA-15 at Naval Air Station Jacksonville, Florida flying the AD-4 Skyraider. He ultimately made five overseas deployments and, before his carrier flying days were over, had taken off and landed on the carriers *RANGER (CV-4), VALLEY FORGE (CV-45), ORISKANY (CV-34), WASP (CV-18), LAKE CHAMPLAIN (CV-39), CORAL SEA (CVB-43), LEYTE (CV-32)* and *ROOSEVELT (CVB-42)*.

Dad went on to have a 30-year career and retire as a Captain on July 1, 1971 despite never really graduating from high school. His high school in Boston sent him a diploma in 1942 after he joined the Navy, but we think it was because they wanted to be sure he wouldn't come back after the war. He never really stopped flying and continued a career in civil aviation until his mid-eighties. He flew after retiring from the Navy for individuals with private airplanes and became a fully qualified instructor pilot and president of the local aero club in Orlando. He flew his last flight as pilot-in-command at the age of 83. In 2008 he received the Wright Brothers Award from the Federal Aviation Administration for 10,000 accident free hours.

I am the oldest of five children; four boys and a girl. Eighteen months separate me from my brother Frank, and another 18 months between Frank and son number three, Steve. Dad used to brag that during his active flying days he fathered a child approximately nine months after each deployment. Son number four, Paul, came along six years after Steve, and sister Patty two years later.

Frank, Steve and I did a lot together growing up because only about three years in age separated us. My father beat into my head that since I was the oldest, I was responsible for whatever collective calamity occurred, often reminding me that "the Captain of the ship is always responsible for whatever happens."

Dad was a strict disciplinarian, particularly to we three oldest sons. I think he slacked off a little when Paul and Patty were old enough to start getting in trouble. He insisted on respect for adults and forgetting to say "Yes Ma'am" or "No Sir" would earn a quick rebuke or a smack on the back of the head. This training stood us in good stead with the parents of our friends, who were impressed by the polite little Sullivan boys. When I was in high school I ended up briefly behind bars along with three of my wrestling team buddies following a skip school and go drinking day that went off the tracks. My pal Mark Kennedy told me that his parents put him on restriction and forbade him to hang around with the other two culprits, but "Billy Sullivan was OK."

In 1970, the Vietnam War was in full swing and the nation was about to initiate the first draft lottery. I was a sophomore at Florida State University in Tallahassee and muddling through college without a specific career plan. The lottery, based on birthdates, was intended to inject fairness into the draft process. Too many of the "privileged" were using influence to avoid being drafted and the bulk of the draft fell on the poor. Dad told me that serving in any branch of the service was dangerous, but at least as a Navy officer if you died on duty you would have slept on clean sheets the night before and eaten a decent meal at a table with a tablecloth and silverware; the alternative being a can of C-rations and a muddy foxhole. I thought that was pretty good advice, and besides, I was a mediocre student, majoring in Criminology at Florida State and not knowing what I wanted to do with my life.

On October 17, 1970, my Dad swore me in to the ROC program at his Reserve Center in Orlando. This was after I had taken the basic exam and completed all the required paperwork. To this day, I am convinced that the chief yeoman who administered the exam, and worked for my Dad, spent the afternoon after the test erasing my wrong answers and penciling in the right ones. Years later, as a Navy Recruiter, I did the same thing for those applicants we really liked but who had fallen a few answers short. In fact, I did it for my younger brother Steve.

As a ROC, I would be going to OCS in Newport, Rhode Island for nine weeks the summer after my junior year at FSU and then again in the summer of 1972 for ten more weeks after graduation. The kicker was that if I flunked out of school or fell too far behind, the Navy would grab me and I would begin my career as Seaman Recruit Sullivan. That provided plenty of incentive to graduate. It also caused me to firmly decide on Criminology as a major in order to graduate on time. I was planning to marry Iris and having a job after graduation sounded like a good plan. When I told Iris what I was considering, she was all for it. In addition to being the daughter of a career Air Force officer and familiar with military life, she realized that I would at least have a job after graduation.

When the draft lottery rolled around, we bought a keg of beer at the Sigma Nu Fraternity house and drank while the numbers came out of the basket. Because I was already committed to the Navy the result was of little consequence to me, but this was high drama for many of my frat brothers. Several had low numbers and faced certain draftee status if they didn't quickly take action and enlist in the service of their choice. My number came out two from the end: 363. I would have never been drafted. I don't regret for a minute enlisting in the Navy when I did.

Iris and I were married on June 19, 1971, in Winter Park, Florida where my family lived. At the time, Iris's father, Lieutenant Colonel Norman Stutzer, U.S. Air Force, was in Saigon at the

Military Assistance Command, Vietnam (MACV), on a one-year tour. Her mother, Mae, was living in an apartment in Honolulu. Before his assignment in Vietnam, Lieutenant Colonel Stutzer had been on the Pacific Air Forces staff (PACAF), at Hickam Air Force Base on the island of Oahu. Although I had corresponded with Iris's father in the past, I had not met her parents until the day before the wedding–exciting!

That first ROC summer at OCS I was part of class 7110 and assigned to C Company, "Charlie Company" in the ubiquitous military phonetic alphabet. In 1971, OCS consisted of about 450 officer candidates at various stages of their progression through the program, divided into 20 companies of roughly 25 officer candidates each. Each company had a lieutenant or lieutenant (junior grade) company officer and the officer candidates closest to graduation assumed leadership roles within their respective companies and within the brigade at large. Most were not ROCs and attending OCS after graduation for 19 weeks straight through. We were the modern equivalent of the "90-day wonders" of World War II fame, there to augment the supply of freshly minted naval officers produced by the Naval Academy and the Reserve Officer Training Corps (ROTC) programs. In 1971, OCS was not co-ed, future women officers were trained in an entirely separate program, also at Newport, called, imaginatively enough, Women's OCS. Because no women were serving at sea then, their curriculum was very different from the men's program. All women officer graduates would fill billets ashore after graduation.

Once issued uniforms and given regulation haircuts we were subjected to a vigorous indoctrination week known as "Hell Week" followed by a routine weekly curriculum of professional military classwork, physical fitness, and learning how to march and properly wear a uniform. I was one of the do-gooders who checked in with a fresh haircut and shined shoes, but many of my classmates did not feel so inclined and reported with shoulder length hair, blue jeans, and tie-dyed tee shirts. These were many who had joined the Navy so as not to be drafted and were making a statement about not being lifers and, in many cases, not supporting the Vietnam War. It didn't seem to matter to those in charge as we soon all looked alike. We new officer candidates were restricted to the OCS area for the first four weeks which meant no trips out in town or to other areas of the naval station except on official duties. Courses included basic Navy organization and leadership, navigation, tactics, engineering, rules of the road, naval law, weapons systems, and so forth. In the tactics class we were taught how to work the Maneuvering Board and had training in a Combat Information Center (CIC) and bridge mock-up where at-sea situations could be simulated.

A great deal of emphasis was placed on maneuvering board, which is a method for converting relative motion, as seen on a radar scope, into true motion, as it happens on the ocean surface. Using maneuvering board, one can figure out a radar contact's actual course and speed, how close that ship will come to your own ship, how to maneuver to avoid that ship by a specific distance, what the true wind is, and what course and speed to steer to obtain a desired wind over the deck for helicopter operations, and so forth.

Maneuvering board (Mo-Board) was considered pretty important at OCS and on the day before my last day that summer, I got in trouble for gaffing it off. I was in tactics class and it was the last day before all the ROCs were to go back to their college campuses and finish their degrees. In the next class period I had a navigation final exam. When the lieutenant running the tactics class gave us some mo-board problems to work to kill time, I studied for the navigation test. Maybe he saw me, I don't know, but he called on me for the answer to the first problem and I was totally unprepared. When he asked me what I was doing, I confessed that I had been studying for the navigation final. I got sent to the Principal's Office—actually the head of the Tactics Department, a lieutenant commander.

This guy really chewed my ass—I thought he was going to throw me out of OCS. He laid into me about how many sailors were killed on the *USS HOBSON (DMS-26)* in 1952 when she was cut in half by the aircraft carrier *USS WASP (CV-18)* because some shit-head JO like me on the bridge didn't work the mo-board. I didn't know it at the time, but my father had been on the *WASP* when that collision had occurred. He finally let me go and I was glad to get out of the office with my budding career still intact.

On Friday evenings after classes, the entire battalion assembled on the parade ground for something called pass-in-review. This was followed by "sports night" where each of the companies fielded teams and competed in a variety of athletic events. At Pass-in-Review the entire brigade formed up on the parade field in front of King Hall, the band played marching music, and we paraded in front of the Commanding Officer of Naval Education and Training Center Newport rendering the proper salutes. The company officers carried swords and did all the sword salute maneuvers and the rest of us marched with our M-1's. Family members and local interested civilians were invited to watch. We were graded, by company, on our precision.

Charlie Company was awful. We were a mongrel mix of tall guys, short guys, plump guys (at least initially), skinny guys, and one black guy who was taller than everybody else and really stood out. My second summer, in 1972, when Iris was in Newport with me, she said Charlie Company looked like a piston engine going by with heads going up and down all out of sequence and guys shuffle-hopping to get back in step. We never won Pass-in-Review. At Sports Night there were runs, swimming, basketball, soccer, obstacle course and volleyball. I was pretty good on the obstacle course and usually did that and then went to the pool to swim in the relay. Again, each company was in competition with all of the other companies.

As part of our training we had the opportunity to go out in Narragansett Bay in the YPs. YP stood for Yard Patrol Craft. OCS had eight YPs, old wooden-hulled, diesel-powered patrol boats that didn't go very fast and had no weapons, but were good for teaching officer candidates a little about shiphandling, piloting, visual signaling, and formation steaming. It was fun to get out of the classroom and go for a boat ride on the bay.

One of the watches we had to stand was a security watch on the YP's while they were tied up at the piers down by the Officer's

Club. One night I had the midwatch (midnight to 4:00 AM) along with one of my company mates. When we were dropped off at the pier to relieve our predecessors, there was a commotion with some officers standing around and a base fire truck on the scene. We walked up to find out what was happening and discovered the base Command Duty Officer (CDO), a lieutenant commander, was chewing out the two officer candidate watchstanders. It turned out that these two landlubbers had panicked and called for help because they thought the YP they were on was sinking. What really happened was that the tide was going out and the YP started getting lower next to the pier.

One Friday night during Sports Night, I swam in the relay races at the pool doing the butterfly. Later, when I got back to the barracks and was in my room, I realized that I had lost my wedding ring. I figured it had slid off my finger while I was thrashing my way to a last place finish. It was about 9:00, but I worried that if I waited until morning or got permission from somebody in authority, I might never find it. I sneaked out of the barracks with my Navy-issue swim trunks on under my uniform and went to the indoor pool which was deserted but unlocked. I starting diving down to the deepest point near the drain, which was about 15 feet below the surface. It was right under the 20-foot tower so the pool had to be deep enough to handle jumpers from that height. And I found it. Ever since then, I never wear it while swimming or doing anything athletic. I also never wore any rings aboard ship because I had heard the horror stories about guys slipping going down ladders, grabbing for a hatch coaming, getting the ring caught on the edge, and ripping their finger off when they continued to fall.

After four weeks in OCS, my group was finally allowed to go on liberty from Saturday morning until Sunday at 6:00 PM. Three or four of us went into downtown Newport for beers every Saturday night. In 1971, Newport was not the upscale tourist town that it is today. Thames Street was very seedy and populated with a series of bars that were frequented by the local lobster fishermen, dockworkers, and a generally rough crowd. We adopted a place called the Skippers Dock, and would go there to drink long neck

Narragansett beers for about 35 cents each. We never had any trouble in these places, but traveling in a pack was a good idea. Many of the clientele were ex-Navy and probably not too fond of officers or officer wannabes.

Finally, my first summer in OCS was over. Having successfully escaped despite the mo-board incident, I drove to Virginia to pick up Iris and then on to Tallahassee for my senior year at Florida State. I felt like the summer in Newport had changed me and given me a better perspective on what was important. I was going back as my fraternity's president but about to relinquish those duties because, now married, I had other responsibilities and the president was required to live in the fraternity house. I felt that many of the fraternity issues that I had wrestled with as president the previous spring were really trivial when compared to real life–or at least "real life" as I then perceived it–who knew how important mo-board was? The fraternity experience however, taught me a lot about group dynamics and leadership.

After an academic quarter in an apartment across the street from the Sigma Nu house (much to Iris's chagrin) we moved into student housing in Alumni Village. On December 27, 1971, Christopher Michael Sullivan came into the world at Tallahassee Memorial Hospital. Chris was born the evening of the first Fiesta Bowl, then a minor bowl, and Florida State was playing Arizona State. It was a great game, with the scoring going back and forth as we watched it on our 8" black and white TV with rabbit ear antennas. Near the end of the third quarter, Iris said she was feeling really uncomfortable and thought maybe this was it. If I remember, the game was tied 28–28 at the time.

"OK, OK, we'll go pretty soon. Yeah, first down!"

We watched the whole game, which ended in a 45-38 Arizona State win, and then raced to the hospital. Chris was born about an hour later. Today he is a huge Florida State football fan and I think it began when he watched the fourth quarter of that first Fiesta Bowl, albeit upside down.

In May of 1972, nearing graduation from FSU, Iris and I prepared to make the trip from Tallahassee, Florida to Newport, Rhode Island for my final 10 weeks of OCS and eventual commissioning as Ensign, United States Navy Reserve. We now had 5 ½ month old Chris and he and Iris would be living in Newport although I would still be required to live in the barracks on base.

As luck would have it, one of my Sigma Nu fraternity brothers, Henry Cuadra, had enlisted in the Navy in 1971 after he graduated from FSU and was assigned as a yeoman third class in the Chaplain's Office at Commander, Cruiser-Destroyer Force, U.S. Atlantic Fleet (CRUDESLANT), Newport, Rhode Island. I had called Henry for advice on where Iris and Chris could live while I finished OCS. Boy did Henry come through! The CRUDESLANT Chaplain at the time was Captain John J. O'Connor, later to become an admiral, the Navy Chief of Chaplains and, after retirement from the Navy, Cardinal O'Connor of New York. Father O'Connor had arranged for a Navy couple to live in a very large house on Bellevue Avenue that had been a convent and still belonged to the Archdiocese of Providence under the name St. Joseph's. The couple was Commander Noel Petree, Jr. and his wife Ruth Ann and their four young children. Commander Petree was deployed as Commanding Officer of *USS WARRINGTON (DD-843)*, having taken command that June in Pearl Harbor while the ship was on the way to Vietnam. Through the good offices of Father O'Connor, the Petree's, a good Catholic family, were living in St. Joseph's as caretakers while waiting to get into Navy housing. *WARRINGTON* was homeported in Newport. Henry explained our plight to Father O'Connor who in turn asked the Petree's if they would mind some boarders. The Petree's graciously agreed. Ruth Ann Petree could not have been nicer and she and Iris became very close.

When I checked back into OCS I asked for, and was assigned to Charlie Company—so did most of my ROC buddies from the year before who were also now finished with college and back for the final 10 weeks. There was a bit of a reunion of the Charlie Company ROC's, but the rest of the crowd was all new. Coming in with nine weeks behind us we were not treated as new recruits, and soon were responsible for running the company. That summer was pretty routine. On weekends I could go to St. Joseph's and be with Iris and Chris. In the final three weeks I could go home most week nights as well, but had to sleep in Nimitz Hall.

On July 16th, things at St. Joseph's suddenly became more interesting. Ruth Ann was visited by Lieutenant Commander Phil Quast, the Operations Officer at the destroyer squadron which was the parent command of *WARRINGTON*. It was July 17th in the South China Sea and *WARRINGTON* had hit a mine.

Thus began an odyssey for Ruth Ann and a real learning experience for Iris and me as we watched how the Navy handled this crisis and how Ruth Ann handled it as the wife of the captain of the ship. There were casualties, but no fatalities, and the ship had to be towed to Subic Bay in the Philippines to assess the damage. Commander Petree had only been in his first command for less than a month. There was speculation that the ship had missed a message and had steamed through an area where U.S. carrier aircraft were jettisoning mines that had not been delivered but could not safely be brought back aboard the carrier. Apparently *WARRINGTON* had hit one of our own mines. Ultimately, the damage to *WARRINGTON* was judged to be so severe as to not be worth the cost of repairs. The ship was decommissioned in Subic Bay on September 30, 1972, and the crew broken up and sent to other ships or returned home to Newport. Noel Petree was later given a second command of another destroyer homeported in Norfolk.

In August, I received my orders. I was to report to the Naval Justice School Non-Lawyer Course in Newport, Rhode Island on the Monday following our Friday graduation. After six weeks of the Non-Lawyer Course, I was to report to the heavy cruiser *USS NEWPORT NEWS (CA-148)* for duty as the Legal Officer. At the time, *NEWPORT NEWS* was deployed to Vietnam providing naval gunfire support to forces ashore. I was initially disappointed with my orders but I shouldn't have been. I had my heart set on an *ADAMS* class guided missile destroyer (DDG) as I had seen them in Narragansett Bay and knew from my studies that these were pretty slick ships. In 1972, they were second only to the DLG's (Destroyer Leader, Guided Missile), a bigger class with longer range missiles, as the hottest ships in the surface Navy. The *SPRUANCE* class was coming, but not yet operational. By the late summer of 1972, the Vietnam War was beginning to wind down. President Nixon had made the decision to begin the "Vietnamization" process, essentially abandoning the South Vietnamese as a lost cause, and therefore many of my classmates were not getting shipboard assignments. I should have been happy just to be going to sea, but at the time did not realize how lucky I was. I also didn't appreciate what an advantage it was to be going to a big ship with a big wardroom as a brand new ensign. I had no idea why I was being sent as the Legal Officer and actually thought it might have had something to do with my criminology major at Florida State. I should have known that the Navy was nowhere near that clever.

Roughly two weeks before commissioning, Iris and I planned a trip for me to go to Norfolk, where *NEWPORT NEWS* was homeported, and find a place for us to live. At the time, my next younger brother, Frank, was stationed at Naval Air Station Norfolk as a Second Class Aviation Mechanic and living in the barracks at the naval air station. Dressed in my finest Officer Candidate Summer White uniform, I caught a flight to Norfolk and was met by Petty Officer Frank Sullivan in his Triumph TR-6. We proceeded to go out on the town and rolled into his barracks about midnight where I was going to sleep in his room to cut down on expenses. I created quite a sensation in my uniform–Frank's fellow residents thought I was a real officer roaming the barracks on a surprise inspection. I suspect many joints went down the toilets or sailing out the windows once the word got around.

On September 22, 1972, I stood with about 350 other brand new ensigns as we were commissioned by the Commanding Officer of Naval Education and Training Center, Newport, Captain Robert L. Scott, and guest speaker Vice Admiral Fred G. Bennett. I noticed in Admiral Bennett's biography that at one time he had been Commanding Officer of *NEWPORT NEWS*. Thirty-four years later, in 2006, I addressed the Rotary Club of Tallahassee as a rear admiral at my brother Paul's invitation and Captain Scott, long since retired, was in the audience. He came up to me after my presentation and said, "Based on your biography, I'd say you graduated from OCS in 1972."

I said, "Yes sir, that's right."

He handed me a card, and said, "Do you remember me?"

I looked down at the card, and in a moment of rare inspiration said, "Yes sir, you were the CO who commissioned me."

He said, "I'm glad to see somebody in that class made it!"

Iris and Ruth Ann Petree were in the audience at commissioning but not my mother and father. I was disappointed but not surprised. Traveling for something like that was not in their genes and I'm not sure my father, just retired himself as a captain, held out much hope that I would amount to anything in the U.S. Navy—particularly as a "Black Shoe" and not a Naval Aviator.

On the 1st of October 1972, *USS NEWPORT NEWS* suffered an in-bore explosion in one of the 8" guns in Turret 2 while firing a naval gunfire support mission off the coast of Vietnam. 20 sailors were killed and the accident was big news in the Navy town of Newport, Rhode Island. I took in the news from a position of relative ignorance and wondered whether or not it would affect my orders.

After Naval Justice School, we moved into our townhouse style apartment in Virginia Beach and I reported to the Cruiser-Destroyer Flotilla Headquarters which was embarked in a destroyer tender, *USS SIERRA (AD-18)*. *NEWPORT NEWS* was scheduled to return from Vietnam so the plan was for me to be "stashed" on the staff and join the ship on return. Within a few days that plan changed, the ship was indefinitely extended, and I received orders to fly to the Philippines and join her there.

After a long flight in a charter DC-8 hopscotching across the Pacific via Hawaii, Wake Island, and Guam, I arrived at Clark Air

Force Base north of Manila and was bused to Subic Bay Naval Station. I checked into the BOQ and went to Base Operations where I was told *NEWPORT NEWS* was on the gunline off Vietnam and they would look for a ride to get me out to the South China Sea to join the ship.

CHAPTER 3

Greenhorn Ensign

USS NEWPORT NEWS (CA-148) was at the tail end of an eight month deployment to Vietnam which had been recently extended, resulting in my trip. Commissioned in 1949, *NEWPORT NEWS* was the last of the *DES MOINES* class eight-inch gun cruisers with three triple gun turrets. She also boasted six twin 5-inch/38 gun mounts. Her eight-inch guns could fire a 335-pound high explosive projectile up to 20 miles. In full rapid fire mode with all three turrets, she could put 90 rounds in the air before the first projectiles impacted. 717 feet in length and displacing 21,000 tons, she was the first air-conditioned surface ship in the U.S. Navy and the last all gun heavy cruiser in the world. Powered by four boilers and four propellers, the ship was capable of speeds in excess of 30 knots. Heavily armored, the design of the ship reflected the World War II era in which the class was built. The 8" gun turrets featured an 8" armor face of the turret on the theory that while slugging it out with the Japanese in a gun battle, the turrets would be pointed at the enemy ships. In addition, the hull featured a 6" armor belt at the waterline and there was an armored "citadel" inside the pilothouse where the captain and bridge team would be afforded extra protection in an engagement. In October 1962, *NEWPORT NEWS* had been the Atlantic Fleet flagship in the Caribbean during the Cuban Missile Crisis.

Beginning my duties as Legal Officer, I was replacing an ensign who had been fired for doing nothing except the bare minimum in order not to get court-martialed. These were the days of rampant drug use, draftees in the Navy to avoid the Army, racial tensions in the fleet and Chief of Naval Operations Admiral Elmo Zumwalt. In October of that year a race riot had occurred on the aircraft carrier *USS KITTY HAWK (CV-63)* during which almost 50 sailors were injured, some requiring medical evacuation. There was plenty of business for the Legal Officer.

In retrospect, it was a good place for me to cut my teeth as an officer and gain experience. In a wardroom of 60 officers, about 30 being ensigns or lieutenants (junior grade), responsibilities were more dispersed and a brand new, inexperienced officer could make some mistakes while learning. I certainly made my share, in fact, although I was never told that was the case, I was fired as First Division Officer in 1973–more on that later.

When I joined *NEWPORT NEWS* the ship was returning from a gunline period about one month after having suffered that in-bore explosion in the center gun of Turret Two. The ship was firing naval gunfire support missions for the Marines in South Vietnam at one o'clock in the morning on October 1st when a faulty base detonating fuse in one of the rounds exploded in the breech the instant the firing charge was initiated. The resulting explosion instantly killed everyone in the turret. Secondary explosions of the powders in the ammunition handling hoists killed the entire magazine crew as well.

I joined the ship in Subic Bay after an unsuccessful attempt to rendezvous with *NEWPORT NEWS* onboard *USS PASSUMPSIC (AO-107)*, an old oiler (commissioned in 1946) which I had been ordered to embark for the ride to the Gulf of Tonkin. *PASSUMPSIC* had arrived in the operating area full of fuel to replenish the fleet only to suffer a main feed pump failure which necessitated a return to Subic Bay for repairs.

I had quite the adventure while attached to *PASSUMPSIC* while in Subic. Our return coincided with the birthday of the Commanding Officer and a wardroom party was planned in Olongapo just outside the gates of the Subic Bay Naval Base. I had become friendly with a lieutenant (junior grade) in the wardroom and was included in the festivities. We crossed the creek separating the base from the town of Olongapo and took over a small bar to celebrate the CO's birthday. The creek, the Magsaysay River, was famously known as the Shit River and the bridge was widely known as the Shit River Bridge. The name was appropriate, as raw sewage flowed freely from the town of Olongapo down the Magsaysay River and into Subic Bay. Sadly, there were always young Filipino boys in dugout canoes who would dive into the river for pennies or Philippine pesos, thrown off the bridge by sailors and Marines who perversely enjoyed the spectacle of these desperate children willingly diving into sewage in order to survive.

We had a semi-wild party for the CO, until it was time to return to the ship. The party-killing issue was that there was a curfew in effect in Olongapo in 1972. In September of that year Philippine President Marcos had declared martial law and the Navy was complying with the mandate. Everybody had to be back across the bridge and on base by midnight or be put on report. Our party broke up and we joined the throng of sailors and Marines, many drunk and making lots of noise, surging toward the bridge to beat the deadline. I was walking next to my buddy in a tightly packed crowd and we were about halfway across the bridge when, suddenly, his head disappeared to be replaced by a big, beefy forearm and fist. A big Marine had positioned himself in the middle of the bridge and was randomly punching out anybody who came within range. If I had been two feet to the right, it would have been me. The surging crowd gave him a target rich environment, like a grizzly bear spearing salmon swimming upstream, that just kept coming of its own momentum. There was no way to stop.

I knelt down as my buddy lay on his back, conscious, but holding his nose with both hands and blood gushing through his fingers. Two other victims lay close by. Before I could help him to his feet to get through the gate, whistles blew and the Shore Patrol showed up en masse, grabbing everybody who was on the bridge, regardless of whether they were punch-ees or punch-ers. This included the two of us. There were about eight paddy wagons on the other side of the bridge inside the gate and we were all loaded in and a deadbolt dropped through the outside door latch.

I sat on a bench inside the paddy wagon with about 15 others, all of whom were complaining that they had done nothing wrong and didn't know what they were doing in a paddy wagon. We began moving, rumbled along for about five minutes, and then pulled into a paved parking lot in a semi-circle with the back doors facing a small building. We watched all the Shore Patrol leave the paddy wagons and go into the building, presumably to confer over what to do with the approximately 100 prisoners out in the parking lot.

I was looking through the mesh screen wondering what was going to happen, and how much trouble I was going to be in, when someone came running out of the bushes next to the parking lot and began running behind each paddy wagon pulling the deadbolt pins and throwing them into the bushes. As each door was unlocked the prisoners piled out the back, many falling down drunk, getting up and sprinting as best they could into the darkness. When he got to our paddy wagon we joined the stampede. Amid many obscene shouts the entire prison population escaped into the night. I think the Shore Patrol was just as happy not to have to process this crowd and nobody gave chase. We couldn't be sure, so we ran all the way back to the piers and clambered up the brow of *PASSUMPSIC* to the safety of our staterooms.

The next morning *NEWPORT NEWS* steamed into Subic Bay and tied up to an adjacent pier. I packed my bags, bade farewell to the officers and the Captain and reported aboard for duty. I got lucky and was assigned to a two-man stateroom. Because *NEWPORT NEWS* had some junior officer bunkrooms with as many as eight racks in them, being a brand new ensign assigned to a two-man stateroom was a good deal. Sleeping was tough in the junior officer bunkrooms because somebody was always getting up or coming in throughout the night as people rotated on and off watch. The snoring was multiplied as well. All of us in midships officer's country shared a gang head and shower down the passageway.

I was escorted to the Legal Office which was all the way forward in the forecastle area of the ship and two decks down. This, I was to learn, was a less than ideal location as when the ship got into a seaway, the pitching up in the bow area was greatly exaggerated. I had been warned that my predecessor, who had been kicked off the ship the last time in Subic, was completely incompetent, did the bare minimum of his assigned duties, slept most of the day, and was rarely out of his stateroom except to eat and stand watches. Like many others, he was a naval officer as a preferable alternative to being drafted. My rationale for attending OCS was not much different, but I was resolved to do the best job I could, whatever that job was. When I later had my meeting with Captain Walter F. "Zeke" Zartman, he asked me if I had received any "special" treatment at the Non-Lawyer Naval Justice Course in Newport after receiving my commission. I honestly did not feel like I had, but apparently he had sent a nasty letter back to the school on the performance of their previous graduate and he wondered if the school had paid extra attention to the next ensign on his way to *NEWPORT NEWS*.

We got underway for the gunline again on the morning of December 2nd, not knowing how much longer this cruise was going to last. The ship had been hurriedly deployed to Vietnam from Norfolk on April 13th, due to a need for additional naval gunfire support as operations heated up in early 1972. It was an open-ended deployment with no return home date published. The ship had only been notified on April 10th that they would be leaving on deployment a mere three days later.

After dinner in the wardroom I wandered out on deck to watch the sunset and savor the fact that I was a naval officer aboard a major combatant ship and sailing off to war. It was heady stuff. I was also such a rookie that it didn't dawn on me that as we sailed toward the Gulf of Tonkin the sun should have been setting in front of the ship, not behind it. It didn't hit me until Captain Zartman came on the 1MC:

"Men of Thunder, this is the Captain speaking. For the past one and a half hours we have been sailing towards a new foreign port, Norfolk, Virginia."

A cheer went up throughout the ship. This crew had been gone eight months, had worked hard, fired thousands of rounds, been shot at, and lost 20 shipmates in a turret explosion. They were ready. I just turned and looked aft at the setting sun and kicked myself for not being savvy enough to realize we were headed east.

NEWPORT NEWS made a high speed transit of the Pacific without stopping until Rodman, The Canal Zone, on December 20th to transit the Panama Canal. During the 18 days underway to Rodman, I settled into my job and got to know the officers and crew. Knowing the entire crew was nearly impossible with a complement of roughly 1,100 men. As I performed my duties during the run to Panama, I quickly learned about discipline and lack thereof, in the 1972 Vietnam Navy. We had Captain's Mast every single day for two weeks with about five sailors at a time lined up to see the Captain for a wide variety of minor offenses. Many of them had occurred during the three days in port in Subic Bay. The Legal Office team was kept busy and I attended every single Mast.

When I look back today at my cruisebook from that 1972 cruise, I am reminded of how far our Navy and our military has come since those days. In the Zumwalt era, beards and long hair were tolerated, and standards for appearance on a ship working around the clock in a war zone were loosely enforced. In the tropical heat of the South China Sea, tee shirts and dirty dungarees were the order of the day. Only on the bridge was any semblance of decorum observed, with ballcaps and dungaree shirts required. By today's standards the crew looked like a bunch of pirates, yet at the same time they worked long, hard hours to get the ship's mission accomplished. Today's all volunteer force and highly technical Navy is a far cry from what I experienced in 1972.

We met an oiler north of Hawaii to refuel in order to save time and refueled again in Rodman for what was to be a high speed run through the Caribbean and the Gulf of Mexico, the Florida Straits, and up the east coast to Norfolk. The goal: arrive home on Christmas Eve. On December 21st we began the canal transit and, having no sea detail station assigned, I was free all day to sightsee and take in the spectacular beauty of Panama and the Panama Canal. Once again my sense of direction proved unreliable as leaving the Pacific on the western side and heading towards the Caribbean on the eastern side, one actually travels northwest. The rising sun was behind us off the starboard quarter. As it turns out, the way the Isthmus of Panama bends back on itself where the canal was built between 1904 and 1914, ships traveling east actually travel west and vice versa. In fact, the eastern end of the canal on the Caribbean side, is actually a third of a degree of longitude west of the western end of the canal on the Pacific side. This is a good one for winning bets in bars, but be prepared to prove it. The Panama Canal turns a 14,000-mile trip between New York and San Francisco around South America and Cape Horn into a 5,900-mile trip.

Once we entered the Caribbean the evening of the 21st, we began a full power trial for the engineering plant and raced across the Caribbean at over 30 knots with all four boilers on the line. Achieving the stated goal, we pulled alongside Pier 12, Naval Station Norfolk the morning of Sunday, December 24, 1972. It was a cold and dreary day, but spirits were high among the crew. It was a neat Christmas present. Many of the crew were seeing new babies for the first time. I manned the rail with the rest of the Admin Department and quickly spotted Iris on the pier with our son Chris, three days' shy of his first birthday.

I felt like a little bit of an imposter returning to this hero's welcome. I had been gone only five weeks, while most of the rest of the crew had been gone over eight months, had suffered some real hardships, and had been involved in combat operations in the war zone. When the decision had been made to ship me out to the Philippines to meet the ship, this Christmas Eve return was not anticipated. When I had left Iris behind in our apartment in Virginia Beach to travel to the Pacific, I did not know when I would be coming home.

As 1972 turned into 1973, I settled into a routine on the ship and began to strike up some friendships, including with Ensign Rob Hofmann who would someday become the God Father of my as yet unborn daughter. Rob was the Third Division Officer, one of the deck divisions, responsible for the fantail and flight deck area. Rob was a 1972 graduate of Villanova Naval ROTC and an accomplished golfer. In his senior year he won the NCAA East Regionals and was invited to play in the NCAA championships. *NEWPORT NEWS* was permanently assigned as the Second Fleet Flagship and when underway carried a small helicopter detachment and an SH-2 Seasprite helo for ferrying the Second Fleet Commander around the force. As Third Division Officer, Rob was responsible for the flight deck and the crane equipment on the fantail.

Another close friend was Ensign Gary Lankenau, a Supply Corps Officer and 1972 Naval ROTC graduate from the University of Colorado. Rob and Gary were both bachelors and the three of us became close friends and liberty buddies when out of homeport. As a Supply Corps Officer, Gary did not stand watches underway so, when on watch, Rob and I would delight in making bogus calls to his stateroom in the middle of the night, pretending to be somebody in one of the firerooms trying to reach the Oil Lab or the Pipe Shop.

On February 5, 1973, we left Norfolk for an overnight transit to Charleston, South Carolina for an exercise to be conducted inport featuring our Second Fleet Commander, Vice Admiral Jake Finneran, and his staff. We were to be in Charleston for a week and then do some underway training before returning to Norfolk. We sailed into Charleston Harbor past Fort Sumter and up the Cooper River in a bitter cold sea detail and tied up the ship at the Charleston Naval Base. That night it began to snow and it didn't stop until Charleston was completely immobilized under 13 inches of snow–a rare storm for that part of the country. The snowstorm had paralyzed the area and most roads were closed all week so there was no chance to go into town and sample antebellum Charleston. The O'Club, however, was within walking distance and became a regular gathering place. On Friday night the Charleston O'Club held a happy hour featuring nickel beers. This was a management decision they soon regretted as the combination of the presence of ships from other ports, the paralyzing snowstorm, and Friday night, resulted in an unexpectedly exuberant crowd.

In March, I was given the opportunity to relinquish my duties as Legal Officer and was moved to the Weapons Department where I became the First Division Officer, responsible for a division of about 25 Boatswain Mates and Deck Seamen, the ship's forecastle and anchoring tackle, and the ceremonial quarterdeck area. Coincident with this I was sent to Landing Signal Officer (LSO) School at Naval Air Station Norfolk and to spotter school at Naval Base Dam Neck, Virginia. Each was a Monday to Friday weeklong school. Spotter school was in preparation for my new General Quarters assignment as a MK-37 Director Officer, controlling the ship's five inch guns. LSO school would qualify me to direct flight deck operations on the fantail as the ship operated helicopters.

Through March and April of 1973, we were underway for several short periods in preparation for a major exercise to be held in the Puerto Rican operating areas in May. I became accustomed to my new duties as First Division Officer and familiar with my division, which was led by Boatswain Mate Chief Orville Wise. Chief Wise was as salty as they come; a burly, mean looking guy, covered with tattoos. He had fouled anchors on each earlobe, tattoos on his neck, all over his arms, and when he occasionally raised his trousers to get his pocket knife from his ankle sheath, I saw tattoos down there too. I really didn't want to know where else he had them.

On Tuesday, May 29, 1973, we were underway for LANTREADEX 3-73, my first real fleet exercise. I stood watches in CIC and my General Quarters Station in Director 1, callsign on the sound-powered circuit "Sky One." Being a big gun heavy cruiser, naval gunfire was a major part of the exercise for *NEWPORT NEWS*, callsign "Thunder." We bombarded the island of Vieques with 8" and 5-inch and I had the opportunity to put my naval gunfire spotters training to use in Sky 1. The 8" were impressive. I could follow the flight of the rounds coming out of Turret 1 through my binoculars and watch them all the way to impact on the island. *NEWPORT NEWS* had a Marine Detachment on board and the detachment CO and XO were the spotters in the fire control directors for the 8" guns. We also fired the 5-inch and I proved adept at calling the rounds on to the targets on the island. I particularly enjoyed the SEPTAR shoot. A SEPTAR is a remote controlled fiberglass boat about 25 feet long mounted with a radar reflector, making it easier to track on the surface search and fire control radars. For this exercise, Sky 1 was given control of Mount 51 forward, Mounts 53 and 55 on the starboard side, and Mount 56 aft. These were twin barrel 5-inch/38 rapid fire gun mounts. Rapid fire was a relative term because the rate of fire was dependent on the crew in the mount who had to physically handle the 70 pound projectiles and 50 pound powders as they came up the ammunition hoists and load them into the trays to be rammed into the breech. As soon as the breech block closed the round would fire if the firing key was closed, either in gun plot, the director, or in manual mode inside the mount itself. For this exercise I would be controlling the firing key on my director handle bars in Sky 1. As we engaged the SEPTAR with all four gun mounts, the Marines proved to be the fastest mount crew, spurred on by their no nonsense gunnery sergeant.

On the 6th of June, we pulled in to Roosevelt Roads, Puerto Rico; the first of many stops for me over the years in this beautiful part of the world. Roosevelt Roads, Puerto Rico is known as "Rosy Roads." Because it was only a one-night stop and we had been underway working hard for a week, everybody not in the duty section hustled ashore as soon as liberty call went down and headed for the clubs. In 1973, the Officer's Club at Rosy Roads was at the top of a hill up the road from the piers and an easy walk. With all the exercise ships in port, the O' Club bar was jumping and the more the drinks flowed, the louder and more raucous it became. Around 7:00 PM some of the local base officers and their wives began to show up at the club for Wednesday night steak night. The bar was off to the side of the dining room, and we were the recipients of many annoyed glances from the dinner patrons. The two *NEWPORT NEWS* helicopter pilots who operated the SH-2 for Admiral Finneran, sneaked into the kitchen, hid around a corner, handed their clothes to an accomplice with instructions to meet them outside, and then burst naked through the kitchen doors into the dining room, streaking all the couples having dinner, and bolting out the front door of the club before the stunned patrons could react. Alerted to this event, the entire bar gathered in the doorway to watch the reactions of the diners. About 15 minutes later the base CDO showed up and closed the bar. Nobody could identify the streakers; as one wag said, "They weren't wearing nametags, sir."

The next morning, we were underway early in a cold rain for the half day transit up the coast to San Juan and a three-day port visit. On Saturday, June 9th, I had duty and was assigned as Shore Patrol Officer for a ship's party that was to take place on the beach near San Juan. I put on my Tropical White Long uniform with "SP" armband and along with two sailors, one of them Boatswain Mate Second Class Craig Baird from my division, went to the site of the party and hung around on the alert for trouble. It beat being stuck on the ship and there was lots of good eyeball liberty at the beach besides *NEWPORT NEWS* sailors. The crew was having a good time drinking, swimming, sunbathing, playing volleyball, touch football, and so forth.

Naturally, as the afternoon wore on and the beer kept being consumed, touch football turned into tackle football and volleyball became a lot more physical. Eventually, a fight broke out and, being a novice Shore Patrol Officer, I leaped into it along with my two enlisted SPs as we pulled the combatants apart and told everybody to settle down. When it was over, Petty Officer Baird pulled me aside and said, "Sir, you stay out of the fights; that's our job. Your job is to stay out of the way and write people up. Let us handle the fighters." Good advice. Fortunately, that was the only fight we saw that day.

We left San Juan on June 11th and sailed north to New York City, arriving on the 15th. Admiral Finneran was a native New Yorker and while commanding the Second Fleet, he made it a point to schedule the flagship for a visit to New York each year. As First Division Officer responsible for the forecastle and ceremonial quarterdeck, I was responsible for rigging the canvas awnings for the big reception planned for the night of the 16th. With 18 month old Chris at home, Iris could not make the trip to New York to join me. The reception was a big success and the local Navy League had arranged for a group of young ladies from a local nursing college to be invited to add some color and variety to the crowd. We junior officers were tasked with escorting a nurse, although we were elbowed out of the picture by some of the more senior members of the wardroom.

We left New York on the 18th of June and returned home to Norfolk on the 22nd. The next event on the schedule was for the ship to go to Bethlehem Steel Shipyard in Baltimore for a three week drydocking period to clean and repaint the hull. We transited the Chesapeake Bay on July 17th and entered the shipyard for the drydocking period.

Two of the projects for First Division while in drydock were to roust out the anchors and anchor chain, sandblast and paint them, and to clean out and reorganize the sail locker where all the canvas was stored that we had used in New York. When we had pulled it out for the New York reception, it became obvious that the sail locker was badly in need of preservation and the canvas needed to be better organized. The shipyard would handle the job on the ground tackle, but the sail locker project fell to First Division.

In 1973, racial tensions were still an issue in the fleet and the Black Power movement served as a rallying point for many blacks. First Division was about 50-50 black and white sailors and one of the black petty officers, Boatswain Mate Third Class Williams, was put in charge of the sail locker project. All the canvas was pulled out, staged on deck, labeled as to where it went when rigged, and the crew went to work on preserving and painting the sail locker. I learned a valuable lesson about being involved more intimately with projects like this one.

Petty Officer Williams reported to me that the painting and preservation were complete and we were ready to stow the canvas below. He proudly reported that they had configured the sail locker so it would be readily apparent where the various sections of canvas went. "Show me," I said. We climbed down the ladder to the sail locker, which was a big space about 20 feet long and 15 feet wide, two decks below the main deck. It had not been painted in accordance with the Naval Ship's Technical Manual, which called for Formula 24 White. Instead, the overhead featured a large wide black stripe running down the middle, with the port side painted red and the starboard side painted green. Very clever. Red is the color for the port running lights and green the color for starboard. I was savvy enough to know that the unofficial Black Power flag was red over black over green horizontal stripes.

"What's this?" I asked.

"Don't you see, we put all the canvas that goes to port under the red, all the canvas that goes to starboard under the green, and the centerline sections under the black."

"Williams, do you think I'm stupid? Paint it all white like it's supposed to be and stencil it for the canvas sections." Then I went looking for Chief Wise who should have known what was going on. I have no idea how many coats of white Formula 24 it took to cover the red, black and green Striping.

My tenure as First Division Officer was about to come to an untimely end although I didn't know it the morning of the 9th of August when we left the shipyard and sailed back down the Chesapeake to Norfolk. We arrived in Hampton Roads around 3:00 PM that afternoon and anchored the ship in the harbor. As First Division Officer I had two responsibilities; anchoring the ship and making sure the accommodation ladder was rigged at the quarterdeck to receive boats; most notably the Second Fleet Barge which would be bringing Admiral Finneran out to his flagship.

My boatswain mates were struggling with the accommodation ladder, trying to get it rigged while two miles away across the harbor we saw the Admiral's Barge headed our way. Captain Ron Kelly was there hovering over my accommodation ladder crew and looking unhappy. I, sensing the danger, busied myself with the anchor detail, overseeing the passing of the pelican hooks and all the details coincident with securing the anchor. Captain Kelly looked over at me several times while the boatswain mates flailed with the accommodation ladder with a decidedly agitated look on his face. At the last minute, the ladder was rigged sufficiently for the admiral to come aboard and Captain Kelly hustled him off to the flag spaces with a backwards scowl at me on the forecastle. Two days later I was notified that I was now the Weapons Department Administrative Officer. I was slow to realize it, but it was pretty obvious to me that I had been fired as First Division Officer. Nobody ever said it, and it was not specifically mentioned in my next fitness report, but I did get a low grade, a D, in "Forcefulness."

CHAPTER 4

Join the Navy and See the World

O ther than Puerto Rico, the Panama Canal, and the Philippines, the Navy had not yet really taken me to see the world. That was all to change in September 1973 as *NEWPORT NEWS* crossed the Atlantic for what would be a most enjoyable two-month cruise to Northern Europe with Commander Second Fleet embarked. We left Norfolk on September 18th and headed across the Atlantic for a combination NATO exercise and "show the flag" tour of NATO ally countries. I was now the Weapons Administrative Officer which included duties as the Preventive Maintenance System (PMS) officer for the Weapons Department. I was being given the chance to redeem myself after First Division. I remained the Sky 1 Director Officer at GQ and having qualified as a CIC Watch Officer had moved to the bridge to stand watches as Junior Officer of the Deck (JOOD) in order to train up for eventual OOD qualification. I had noted however, that no ensigns in *NEWPORT NEWS* were qualified as OODs. It seemed there was an unwritten rule that until you made lieutenant (junior grade) you weren't sufficiently seasoned to be an OOD. I enjoyed the bridge watches and enjoyed "driving" the ship.

Our first port of call after crossing the Atlantic was Portsmouth, England, the United Kingdom's main naval base. We arrived to full military honors and a gun salute in honor of Admiral Finneran who had a NATO "hat" as Commander, Striking Fleet, Atlantic. Following an enjoyable port visit including a side trip to London, we were underway the morning of September 29th for "Exercise Swift Move" in the North Sea with an armada of U.S. and other NATO-nation ships. The exercise lasted ten days and was the only serious operational tasking for the rest of the cruise. From here on in we were to hop from port to port beginning with Oslo,

Norway. In each port the admiral and his staff and Captain Kelly had representational duties with our hosts, but the junior officers were far removed from these responsibilities. Our biggest challenge was affording all this time in European ports. In 1973, my monthly pay before taxes was $712.50. Added to this was $141.60 for "married with dependents Basic Allowance for Quarters."

On the 6th of October *NEWPORT NEWS* crossed the Arctic Circle and we officially joined the Royal Order of the Blue Nose. The junior ensign in the ship, the "George" ensign, Bill Saller, was detailed to paint the bullnose blue and did so appropriately garbed in a jockstrap, boondockers, kapok lifejacket, and blue hardhat. Before painting the bullnose, he was required to stand watch on the forecastle in that same outfit with a pair of binoculars and sound-powered phones to be on the lookout for the Arctic Circle which would presumably be visible on the surface of the sea. At the same time, he manned "Forward Steering" consisting of one of the anchor windlass brake wheels. From the bridge he would be ordered "right standard rudder" over the sound-powered phones. As he turned the brake wheel, the helmsman on the bridge turned the ship. All seemed to be going well until he was given a left turn order and the helmsman deliberately turned the ship right. This resulted in a serious ass chewing over the sound-powered phones much to the amusement of the spectators on the bridge.

Also on the 6th of October, a coalition of Arab countries, led by Egypt and Syria, launched a surprise attack on Israel. The 6th was the Jewish holy day of Yom Kippur and the attack achieved complete surprise and initial success in the Sinai Peninsula and the Golan Heights, both of which had been under Israeli control since the 1967 six-day war. Both the United States and the Soviet Union mounted massive resupply efforts, the U.S. in support of Israel and the Soviets in support of the Arabs. This opposing support increased tensions between the U.S. and the Soviet Union causing the United States to raise the DEFCON Level from Four to Three. DEFCON stands for "Defense Readiness Condition" and represents a scale of readiness from DEFCON Five, meaning normal readiness to DEFCON One, meaning nuclear war is imminent. The system had been put in place in 1959 and the United States had only gone as high as DEFCON Two once, during the Cuban Missile Crisis in 1962. None of this seemed to have any bearing on our port visit schedule, however. I thought that perhaps we would have been ordered to steam towards the Mediterranean in a show of force, but we were not. By the end of the fighting, the Israelis had regained the upper hand and pushed as close as 25 miles from Damascus and 60 miles from Cairo. Under the terms of the cease fire, Israel returned to the post-1967 war borders, except for losing control of the Sinai, as it remains today.

On Wednesday, October 10th, after exiting the North Sea through the Skagerrak which serves as the gateway to the Baltic Sea, we steamed up the Oslo Fjord to enter Oslo. I climbed up Princess 1 to sightsee as we proceeded up the fjord. The scenery was spectacular with the steep sides of the fjord rising almost straight up from the water which was hundreds of feet deep. There was snow on the ground and in the fir trees and the entire scene was like a postcard.

NEWPORT NEWS' saluting batteries were located on the 01 level forward of the bridge. As we were to once again exchange a gun salute with the Norwegians as we entered Oslo Harbor, the starboard side gun was being test-fired while we were still well down the fjord. Something wasn't working properly so one of the gunners called down to another on the main deck for a screwdriver. A heavy 10" screwdriver was tossed up and landed in the box of saluting charges causing an explosion. Saluting batteries use a percussion firing pin to explode the charges resulting in a loud bang and a puff of smoke. Staged next to the saluting battery was a box of 24 charges, nose down, percussion cap up. Several charges went off, sending shrapnel flying and injuring the Weapons Officer and a senior gunners mate standing nearby. Because Turret 2 had suffered the in-bore explosion on October 1st the year before, the crew began to talk about *NEWPORT NEWS* being jinxed in October.

We pulled into Oslo and tied the ship up at a large cruise ship pier which sits right below the spectacular Akershus castle in downtown Oslo which dates to around 1300. From our berth we could see the famous Holmenkollbakken ski jump, site of the ski jumping competition in the 1952 Winter Olympics and many other ski jump events.

The first event was to be a visit by King Olav V, King of Norway. We assembled the Honors Sideboys on the quarterdeck, the Second Fleet Band which was to play Ruffles and Flourishes and the national anthems of both countries, and all of the Second Fleet staff and wardroom officers. Full honors would be rendered to the King on his arrival. Admiral Finneran was on deck personally making sure that everything was in order for the King's visit. The Boatswain Mate of the Watch, Boatswain Mate Second Class Tom Timmons, was given the script for what he should say over the 1MC once eight bells had been rung and before the King walked through the Sideboys. On his cheat sheet was written, **"Eight Bells, Olav V arriving."**

Just then a large black sedan pulled onto the pier, unexpectedly early, and everybody hustled into position, including Admiral Finneran. Eight bells were rung, the band raised their instruments, and Petty Officer Timmons announced over the 1MC, "Olav the Fifth, arriving!"

A bewildered gentleman in a coat and tie got out of the car, looked at all the hoopla and waved. The XO ran down to the pier and determined that this was the businessman with the garbage contract who had come to make arrangements with the Supply Officer. The XO told him to beat feet and come back later; King Olav was due any minute.

Everybody in the quarterdeck area relaxed and we waited for the real king to show up. In the meantime, Petty Officer Timmons left his station to make a head call, handing the script over to Boatswain Mate Second Class Craig Baird to back him up.

Shortly thereafter the King's entourage pulled onto the pier and everybody once again squared themselves away and got ready for the grand arrival. The XO gave a nod to the OOD, eight bells were sounded, and Petty Officer Baird announced over the 1MC, "Olav the Vee, arriving!"

Heads snapped around, especially Admiral Finneran and Captain Kelly, and stared at Baird. He had a confused look on his face at all the attention. No harm was done, the King probably didn't even hear it, but the ranks of wardroom junior officers were shaking with suppressed laughter.

The King had the good sense to bring Miss Norway with him and she was the hit of the whole event. In fact, when the cruisebook was published you would not have known the King was even there; but there were plenty of pictures of Miss Norway.

On October 15th we departed Oslo back down the fjord for a one-night transit through the Skagerrak and the Kattegat to arrive in Copenhagen, Denmark the morning of October 16th. We tied the ship up in Copenhagen just a few yards from the famous Little Mermaid statue in Copenhagen Harbor.

We departed Copenhagen on Iris's 23rd birthday, October 20th. I had been buying gifts in each port with what little money I had but had failed pretty miserably in both Oslo and Copenhagen. We sailed once again through the Kattegat and the Skagerrak out into the North Sea and down the coast of Denmark and the Netherlands to enter Rotterdam, The Netherlands through the Nieuwe Waterweg which provides ocean-going vessels access to the largest port in Europe and in 1973 the busiest port in the world. Rotterdam was formed by a dam built on the Rotte River in 1270 and because it sits at the mouth of the Rhine-Meuse-Scheldt Delta it has always been the sea gateway to Europe.

Leaving Rotterdam on Friday the 26th of October, we headed for our next stop in Lisbon, Portugal. Lisbon was to be our last port of call on this pleasure cruise. Transiting the English Channel on October 27th we entered the Tagus River to sail upstream to Lisbon. There was no suitable berthing for the ship so we were to anchor out in the Tagus and utilize contracted water taxis to get ashore. The first night in, the Portuguese rear admiral who commanded

COMIBERLANT (Commander Iberian Atlantic) hosted a large reception for Admiral Finneran and his staff and the officers from *NEWPORT NEWS*. Anyone not on duty was required to attend in Service Dress Blue uniform. COMIBERLANT was subordinate in the NATO command structure to Supreme Allied Commander Atlantic, a U.S. Navy four-star in Norfolk and to Admiral Finneran in his NATO hat as Commander, Striking Fleet Atlantic.

There were busses to take us to COMIBERLANT headquarters for the reception but I missed the bus along with five other junior officers. The Beach Guard Officer at Fleet Landing directed us to an 8 passenger van driven by a Portuguese man in civilian clothes who drove us to the reception. When we got out and thanked him he said, "I will wait for you here." Rob Hoffman said, "What do you mean?" He said, "I am yours for the evening."

The reception was a lavish affair with copious amounts of food on a huge buffet table, unlimited supplies of wine and beer and many beautiful Portuguese women wandering about in evening dress. The van group stuck together and stayed around long enough to get credit for being present, fed, and lubricated for the events to come. At about 9:00 PM we went outside, found our van and asked the driver for advice on a good place to go. He recommended Estoril which was a resort town further west along the coast. We all piled into the van.

First we needed something to drink so we asked him where we could get something for the ride to Estoril. He thought for a second, put the van in gear and off we went through the streets of Lisbon. He pulled up in an alley behind a restaurant somewhere in the city, shut off the van, got out, went to the back door of the restaurant, and went inside. We all waited in the van.

In a few seconds he poked his head out the door and waved us in. Exchanging curious glances, we climbed out of the van and went through the back door. We were in a very busy restaurant kitchen, full of Portuguese men all wearing checked chef-style pants and chef smocks. There were also a number of dishwashers and other general help in dirty white aprons, tee shirts, blue jeans and tennis shoes. We were treated like conquering heroes, especially by the younger dishwashers. They were pointing at our ribbons and giving us exaggerated salutes. They broke out two jugs of white wine, about a half-gallon each and handed them over. We said "How much?" to the driver and he said, "Nothing."

Someone got the idea to take off his ribbons and pin them on the apron of one of the dishwashers. He beamed and gave another big salute, so we all removed our ribbons and had an impromptu awards ceremony in that hot, steamy kitchen, pinning all our ribbons on dishwasher aprons and chef smocks. Amid much hand shaking and saluting we grabbed the wine, exited the back door and piled into the van. The trip to Estoril was unsuccessful in that we couldn't find anything productive to do besides finish the wine on the ride back to the ship.

We left Lisbon on November 2nd and sailed straight across the Atlantic to Norfolk, arriving on the 8th of November. It had been a fun 51-day cruise, visiting five countries and hopping from port to port like a cruise ship with the exception of the Swift Move exercise after Portsmouth. I couldn't believe they were paying me to do this.

After two and a half weeks inport, *NEWPORT NEWS* was underway again on November 26, 1973 for another Second Fleet exercise in the Puerto Rican operating areas; LANTREADEX 2-74. On one of the days during the exercise we were at General Quarters and we Director Officers were in our directors in the hot sun with nothing to shoot at. I was in Sky 1, Rob Hofmann, who had moved to 5th Division and now was the 5-inch/38 gun division officer, was in Sky 2, Ensign Bill Saller, who had replaced Rob as 3rd Division Officer, was in Sky 3, and Lieutenant (junior grade) Lorne Hunt was in Sky 4. On the circuit in Gun Plot was the Fire Control Officer, Lieutenant (junior grade) Hugh Redding, a crusty Limited Duty Officer, or LDO. Since we had completed all our movement checks and were bored, Rob and I, without planning it, decided to have some fun at Saller's expense. Bill Saller had an annoying, nasally, distinctive New Jersey accent. On the sound-powered circuit, no one could tell who was talking unless they identified themselves or you could recognize their voices.

I started it.

"Gun Plot, Sky 3, what's going on?" In a nasally Saller voice imitation.

"Sky 3, standby."

Saller says nothing, probably figuring someone just identified themselves incorrectly.

After a few minutes I hear Rob come on, "Gun Plot, Sky 3, what's the status?" in an imitation Saller voice.

"Sky 3, Gun Plot, knock it off, you'll know when we know!" Agitated Hugh Redding voice.

"Gun Plot, Sky 3, that wasn't me."

"All Stations, Gun Plot, silence on the line!" Pissed off sounding Hugh Redding.

Some snickering which cannot be traced to Sky 1 or 2.

A few minutes later I chime in imitating Saller, "Gun Plot, Sky 3, how much longer do we have to stay up here?"

"Goddamit Saller, stay off the line! You'll come down when we secure from GQ dammit!"

"Hey, that's not me, it's somebody else!"

"Shut up dammit!"

After GQ Saller found Rob and me in the wardroom and said, "Hey, I know it was you assholes doing that."

After a couple of days inport Roosevelt Roads, we returned to Norfolk on the 12th of December and stayed in port through the Christmas holidays and into the New Year. I was home for Christmas for the second year in a row and for Chris's second birthday; a record I would manage for 18 years until Operation Desert Shield in 1990.

As 1974 began, I looked forward to making lieutenant (junior grade) in September but also wondered what was in store for me in the Navy. I was still the Weapons Admin Officer, but Lieutenant Commander Paul Brouer, the Weapons Officer was looking for a new job for me in the Weapons Department; it looked like I was in line to be 2nd Division Officer, or Main Battery Officer, in charge of the 8"/55 gun turrets. I was excited about this possibility but had other career things on my mind. *NEWPORT NEWS*, now 25 years old and ill-suited for the missile and submarine threat posed by the Soviet Navy, was scheduled to be decommissioned in August 1975. My obligation from OCS was only three years which meant my obligated time would be up one month after the ship left active service. The Vietnam War was over and a lot of junior officers brought in during the peak would no longer be needed. This was great news for all those who were only in to avoid the draft, but I was less certain about whether I wanted to get out and start a new career so soon. I had a wife and a child to consider; most of the others were single. I was also enjoying what I was doing.

I knew there was a program called "augmentation" for those officers who received a reserve commission, like me, to request augmentation to the regular Navy. In 1972, when I was commissioned at OCS, only Naval Academy officers received a regular commission or "USN" designation. OCS and ROTC graduates were commissioned "USNR" in the reserves. There was no additional obligation for transferring to the Regular Navy, and you were less likely to be tossed aside if there was a Reduction in Force, or RIF. Given all this, I wrote a simple letter to the Bureau of Naval Personnel and requested augmentation to the regular Navy. It would be some time before I received a response.

In the meantime, we were underway again on January 18, 1974 and sailed up the coast to Newport, Rhode Island where Commander Second Fleet and his staff would participate in a war game at the Naval War College. We arrived the next day and began a weeklong visit to Newport. In February *NEWPORT NEWS* visited Fort Lauderdale, Florida and Roosevelt Roads, Puerto Rico to renew our naval gunfire support qualification. I was notified on the transit home that I would be replacing Lieutenant (junior grade) Bill Blaine as the Main Battery Officer in charge of the 8" gun mounts and to begin turning over duties with him on the transit home. Bill was leaving the ship to cross-deck to *USS BARNEY (DDG-6)*, an *ADAMS* class guided missile destroyer.

I asked Bill how he had received these orders and he told me that he had simply written a letter to the Bureau of Naval Personnel and requested something called a "split tour."

"Can I see your letter? I might want to do the same thing," I said. He gave it to me and I wrote one word for word just like it; short and simple.

When Bill Blaine left the ship I took up my new responsibilities as 2nd Division and Main Battery Officer, determined to do better than I had as 1st Division Officer. I was happy to remain in the Weapons Department and not to have been snagged by the Chief Engineer to become Boilers Officer.

Second Division was run by Gunner's Mate Chief Rodriguez, a Puerto Rican who was very professional and a great mentor to Ensign Sullivan. The division itself now only had two operational 8" gun turrets because of the explosion in 1972, but was still responsible for maintaining the outward appearance of Turret 2. After the explosion, the destroyed barrel had been removed and a large steel plate placed over the center gun area. The entire turret from the turret itself down to the ammunition and powder handling rooms had been somewhat cleaned up but left unrepaired, torn and mangled from the explosion. It was spooky to go inside and see the destruction and imagine what it must have been like for those unfortunate souls who died. The only saving grace, at least for those in the turret itself, is that they died instantly, never knowing what happened. Those further down in the handling rooms had a second or two longer to live and wonder what was happening. Only one got out alive and he later died of smoke inhalation.

My division consisted of about two dozen gunners mates and non-rated seamen. In addition to Chief Rodriguez, Gunners Mate

Second Class Johnson was responsible for Turret 1 and Gunner's Mate First Class Myers for Turret 3. Myers would later make Chief and move over to 5th Division under Rob Hoffman on the 5-inch guns. The division was a tight knit group, although in 1974 appearances were still a little shabby, with hair too long by today's standards; Afros for the black guys and a fair number of beards, mutton-chop sideburns, mustaches and goatees.

Chief Rodriguez was well organized and we established a good working relationship. As the Division Officer I was responsible for conducting certain pre-fire checks before we fired the guns which were required to be observed by an officer. He was very good at taking me by myself into the turrets and showing me what to do so that when I did it the first time with the turret captains watching I would look like I knew what I was doing.

One day in the summer of 1974 while we were inport Norfolk, I was lying in my rack in my stateroom late in the morning. This was not very professional but it was not uncommon for officers to sneak off and get a little rack time during the day, especially nooners after lunch. All of a sudden bang, bang, bang on my stateroom door and I hear the Chief Master-at-Arms shout, "XO's inspection of officer's staterooms!" and his master key set begin rattling in the doorknob.

I leaped out of my top bunk where I had been lying in my khaki's and was hopping around on one foot trying to get my boots on with my shirt half un-tucked and rack tracks on my face when the Master-at-Arms and XO Commander Briner strode into the stateroom. Busted.

"Morning, Bill," said the XO.

"Morning sir," I sheepishly replied while finishing my tuck.

The XO looked around, "Rack not made," he said. The chief wrote it down.

On the forward bulkhead of the stateroom I had a dart board with an 8x10 picture of the previous XO, Captain Bob Leverone, taped to it. It had so many dart holes in the face that he was hardly recognizable.

The XO looked at it, looked at me, and said, "Take that down," and turned to walk out. Just then my alarm went off which I had set to get up in time for lunch. XO Briner just looked at me and walked out of the stateroom. Major league busted.

In July, Vice Admiral Stansfield Turner relieved Vice Admiral Finneran as Commander, Second Fleet in a ceremony aboard *NEWPORT NEWS*. Admiral Turner went on to become Director of the CIA after leaving Second Fleet. Also in July I received the response to my split tour request with orders to *USS SEMMES (DDG-18)* an *ADAMS* class guided missile destroyer homeported in Charleston, South Carolina. My orders instructed me to detach from *NEWPORT NEWS* in August and report to *SEMMES* in September with 30 days leave authorized. I was thrilled. I was getting off *NEWPORT NEWS* before she really began to wind down for decommissioning the following year; I was going to a guided missile destroyer, what I had always wanted; and Iris and I would be moving out of Norfolk and closer to family, all of whom were living in Florida.

Iris had never really been happy in Norfolk. We had a baby, we lived in a small townhouse style apartment in the London Bridge area of Virginia Beach, and we had only one car. I had been carpooling to the ship and when it was my turn to drive Iris was stuck home with Chris. We also found out in May that Iris was pregnant with child number two on the way.

On the 30th of August I officially detached from *NEWPORT NEWS* to execute my orders to *SEMMES*. I received a pretty good detaching fitness report, the obligatory plaque and send off at the quarterdeck and nothing else. Although I thought I was one of the best bridge watchstanders, I was still not a qualified underway officer of the deck, the unwritten "no ensigns" rule apparently still in effect.

The transition from *NEWPORT NEWS* to *SEMMES* obligated me to an additional 18 months on active duty, carrying me beyond the three-year obligation I had incurred at commissioning. I was not concerned by this detail, in fact my motivation for augmenting to the regular Navy had been to protect against being involuntarily asked to leave before I was ready. With Iris pregnant with child number two I was also motivated by a certain level of job security and a steady paycheck. Finally, I was enjoying the adventure and the challenge of going to sea in a warship and visiting foreign ports.

CHAPTER 5

Destroyer Navy

W e moved to Charleston and I planned my report aboard to occur on Wednesday, September 24, 1974. In one of my smarter moves as a junior officer, I did this so I could report aboard as a lieutenant (junior grade) and not an ensign. My two years' time in grade to jay-gee occurred on Sunday, September 22nd and I naively thought that since promotion to lieutenant (junior grade) was virtually automatic, I could just go ahead and promote myself. It was automatic, right?

I reported for duty in *USS SEMMES (DDG-18)* in the Charleston Naval Shipyard where I met the CO, Commander John Nyquist. John Nyquist would prove to be one of the more inspirational leaders in my Navy career. My new boss as Weapons Officer was Lieutenant Gil Lauzon, a bachelor who had received his commission after graduating from Tufts. Gil lived aboard the ship which was still in the shipyard, but out of drydock and in the water. I was assigned to the forward-most stateroom on the main deck level, just aft of the wardroom to room with Lieutenant (junior grade) Don Ramage, the Communications Officer. This stateroom would turn out to have some drawbacks as cockroaches were a serious problem due to the proximity to the wardroom galley across the passageway.

My "self-promotion" paid dividends as I walked aboard a ship that had several junior officers who had never been to sea due to the shipyard period and there was a shortage of qualified OODs. After a brief indoctrination and a couple of inport OOD watches, I was designated a Command Duty Officer, or CDO. The CDO is the officer in charge of the ship on his inport duty day, and responsible for everything after normal working hours and overnight when the CO, XO and department heads go home for the evening.

Normally the CDO must be a qualified underway OOD because one of the requirements is the ability to get the ship underway in an emergency without the presence of the CO, XO, or any of the senior officers. Because we were in the shipyard in a cold-iron status with the boilers laid up we couldn't get underway except under tow, so the CO decided it would be safe to let me, with my recent operational experience, stand CDO. Besides, I had a few ribbons from my *NEWPORT NEWS* assignment, including a Vietnam Service Medal and a Navy Unit Commendation Ribbon, so I looked saltier than I was.

First Division was led by Chief Boatswain Mate Larry Ellis who was widely regarded as one of the top chiefs in the Chief's Mess. Boatswain Mate First Class William Wright, was the Leading Petty Officer; a good sailor who was somewhat overshadowed by Chief Ellis. There were a collection of solid petty officers and some good seamen as well as a couple of troublemakers.

I enjoyed my role as First Lieutenant, responsible for the entire topside appearance of the ship, for the boats and davits, the ground tackle, the ship's life rafts, and for seamanship evolutions such as underway replenishment, helicopter operations, towing, tying up the ship, and anchoring. I had learned a few things in *NEWPORT NEWS* and fell comfortably into my new job.

SEMMES was an *ADAMS* class guided missile destroyer, or DDG; the class of ship I had always wanted. Commissioned in 1962, *SEMMES* was the 17th ship of the class. By today's standards she bristled with weapons and radars, looking like a real destroyer should. The *ADAMS* class sported two 5-inch/54 caliber gun mounts, a MK-11 or MK-13 guided missile launcher, Anti-Submarine Rocket (ASROC) launcher, and MK-32 torpedo tubes forward under the bridge. Her radars included the SPS-10 surface search radar, SPS-40 air search radar, and SPS-39 three dimensional air search radar. Her fire control radars included two SPG-51 guided missile fire control radars and one SPG-53 gun fire control radar. For anti-submarine warfare she had the SQQ-23 PAIR hull mounted sonar which had some passive detection capability. The ship was 437 feet in length and displaced 4,500 tons. Powered by four Babcock and Wilcox superheated 1,200 psi boilers and twin screws, she was capable of over 30 knots. She was a real greyhound.

The first two weeks of January 1975 saw *SEMMES* conducting sea trials in the Charleston Operating Areas to work the bugs out of the engineering plant. Despite the cold weather, the firerooms were unbearably hot, exceeding standards. Something was wrong with the ventilation and we needed to get it fixed before operating in the warmer climes down south at Guantanamo Bay, Cuba and in the Middle East the following year.

Iris was due to have the baby around the 25th of January, the same time that the ship was scheduled to be doing anti-submarine warfare (ASW) training at the Atlantic Fleet Underwater Test Complex (AUTEC) in the Tongue of the Ocean; very deep water near Andros Island in the Bahamas. I did something that I would never again do, and asked the XO if I could stay behind while Iris had the baby. He said yes. On January 27th, Iris went into labor and our daughter Amy Christine was born at Naval Hospital Charleston. Amy came into the world the day before *SEMMES* returned to port and I was glad that Iris had been able to squeeze her out while the ship was still gone since I had missed the underway period.

The shipyard period was typically onerous and we were all anxious to get the ship out and start operating. One of the things I became familiar with that was new to me from *NEWPORT NEWS* days was the capability for *SEMMES* to carry nuclear depth charges which could be delivered from our Anti-Submarine Rocket (ASROC) system—a weapons system *NEWPORT NEWS* did not have. With the ability to carry nuclear weapons came a very rigorous program to ensure the security of these weapons, including a Personnel Reliability Program (PRP) for all personnel involved in the handling, employment and security of the weapons. While in the shipyard we had no nukes on board, but in order to keep our skills up we acted like we did as the yard period began to wind down. For the CDO this meant a daily "Security Alert Drill" in port to test the reaction of the security alert teams to respond to a threat to the security of the weapons. As CDO I was responsible for the drill on my duty days. We often had unplanned drills because the Roving Patrol was periodically late getting back to the quarterdeck every half hour to report "all secure." When that happened, no matter what time of the day or night, a security alert was called away and everyone not on the security team had to freeze in place while the security team rushed to the armory to draw weapons and then to the ASROC magazine to ensure the security of the weapons. There was a maximum time to respond and failure to meet the standards could fail the ship when the inspection team came aboard. Often one of the sensors on the ASROC magazine door would malfunction and an alarm would sound on the quarterdeck, the bridge and in Damage Control Central, kicking off another drill. There were some days, and nights, when, for various reasons, we had two or three security alerts.

Near the end of the overhaul we had a wardroom meeting and Operations Officer Lieutenant Bernie Hollenbeck handed out the Personnel Qualification Standards (PQS) for Surface Warfare Officers to all the junior officers. A few years earlier the surface Navy had decided that we needed a formal qualification process and a device to wear on our uniforms identifying us as Surface Warfare Officers (SWO). The aviators had long had wings and the submariners had their gold dolphins. Up until that point in time each ship handled these qualifications in their own way and the standards were not standards at all. The Navy had recognized the need to professionalize the qualification process for Surface Warriors.

I recalled this initiative from my time in *NEWPORT NEWS* when it was announced. A Navy-wide contest was held to design the recognition pin. When this notice was posted on the bulletin board in the *NEWPORT NEWS* wardroom, many creative designs were drawn in; the most popular being the "cock and balls" device. Eventually the SWO pin design was approved and the pins manufactured. They featured a stylized ship's bow with crossed swords and wave-like wings. This was pretty clever and someone even came up with the idea of calling them "swords" for Surface Warfare Officer Recognition Device. That never caught on and they simply became known as the "SWO Pin." Qualification as a SWO required complete knowledge of your ship from stem to stern; engineering plant, weapons systems and tactics, navigation, seamanship, damage control, communications and so forth. Any officer who had achieved OOD Underway qualification was to be grandfathered into the program and receive the SWO recognition pin without having to do the PQS.

Also around this time, my chief Boatswain Mate, Chief Ellis was transferred to shore duty to become an instructor at Great Lakes Naval Training Center, leaving me without a chief in First Division. I was comfortable with Petty Officer Wright, a black first class petty officer who had been an effective leading petty officer and with whom I had a good working relationship. BMC Ellis later sent a card to the Chief's Mess which our Command Master Chief, Sonarman Master Chief Henderson, showed me. It said;

"All settled in here at Great Lakes. Already stung me a WAVE. How is LTJG 'Super' Sullivan doing?" I felt pretty good about the "super" part.

We loaded out ammunition and missiles in early February and on the 5th of March set sail for the Caribbean for Missile Systems Qualification Trials in the Roosevelt Roads area Atlantic Fleet Weapons Training Facility, or AFWTF. I was standing watches as JOOD underway and as the Condition 1AS JOOD/Conning Officer. Condition 1AS was the most ready condition for engaging an enemy submarine.

We were in Rosy Roads for one day of range safety briefings and underway for two days of surface to air and surface to surface missile firing exercises with our Standard Missile 1, TARTAR guided missile system and MK13 single arm launcher. It was exciting to see the missiles scream off the launcher against drone air targets. We also did a surface to surface shot against an unmanned SEPTAR target. I was on the bridge and watched as we launched against the SEPTAR at about 10 miles range just as a rain squall blew through the area obscuring the target from visual sight. When the squall passed there was a smoking hulk on the horizon from a direct hit.

During our transit down to the Caribbean we had been tasked with conducting a burial at sea, not the last time I would be involved in such an event. It is possible for Navy veterans or their families to request a burial at sea. The Navy takes these assignments very seriously and there are specific requirements for the conduct of the ceremony. Sometimes family members are allowed to observe from aboard ship, but most often they are not present because it is simply not practical. The ship is responsible for putting together a package to mail to the family after the ceremony which includes a nautical chart pinpointing the location of the burial, empty cartridge cases from the 21 gun salute, pictures, and the American flag used to cover the casket if it is a body. They get a properly folded flag regardless, including after a ceremony involving cremains.

There was a famous horror story of a ship that failed to properly weight the casket to ensure it sunk and it bobbed alongside the ship after being slid into the sea. The CO had ordered the gunners to take it under fire with small arms and sink it, which took many rounds and ended up splintering the casket and its contents into many pieces. When word got back to headquarters with the details of what had happened, the CO was fired.

Captain Nyquist wanted to avoid that fate so he instructed the XO to make sure the casket sunk when it slid into the sea. The XO told the Weapons Officer to put two 5-inch/54 inert rounds into the casket to take it to the bottom. Each round weighed about 70 pounds. All of these preparations were made and the very proper and somber ceremony took place on the fantail while the ship hove to in a calm sea with beautiful clear blue-green water.

When the platform board was tilted up to let the casket slide into the sea, things began to quickly go wrong. First, we all heard the projectiles slide the length of the casket when it was tilted up. No one had made sure they were placed at the foot of the casket or tied down. And then, before the casket hit the water, both projectiles rocketed through the end of the casket and splashed into the water. Not only had they been placed near the head of the casket, but they were also pointy end down and smashed right through the foot of the fiberglass casket.

John Nyquist's face was ashen as he watched this unfold, unable to do anything. Fortunately, however, the two 5-inch diameter holes at the end of the casket let in enough water that it sank very quickly.

Ever the cool customer, Captain Nyquist turned to the XO and said, "Secure from burial detail."

Following the missile trials which were successful, we had a couple of days in Roosevelt Roads before setting sail for Guantanamo Bay, Cuba and Refresher Training or REFTRA. As we transited from Rosy Roads across the Caribbean to Cuba, we had an all officers meeting in the Wardroom to do two things: lay out the ground rules for REFTRA in GITMO and officially promote me to lieutenant (junior grade). Whoops! The paperwork had finally come in after the list of who knows how many ensigns were promoted to lieutenant (junior grade) and my name was on it. John Nyquist had a knowing look on his face as he read the official notification. There was no pinning ceremony as I had been wearing the silver bars since I reported aboard six months earlier having frocked myself. Captain Nyquist never said anything, but I knew he knew what a stunt I had pulled and I think he and the XO secretly thought it was pretty slick.

I had also recently received notification that my request to augment to the regular Navy had been approved and my designator was changed from 1105 (USNR) to 1100 (USN). I was now officially "regular Navy," not a reservist on active duty. This was a big deal because I now would be more likely to be able to stay in the Navy if that's what I wanted. I was a mere 6 months away from the end of my obligated service following commissioning at OCS and I was enjoying what I was doing; especially on *SEMMES*.

On the subject of the game plan for REFTRA the CO and XO laid out the ground rules. REFTRA was an intentionally difficult qualification period, lasting six weeks, and was designed to run a ship through all its paces; engineering, damage control, ASW, gunnery, seamanship, communications and navigation. All ships coming out of the shipyard were required to successfully complete REFTRA before moving on to fleet operations and eventual overseas deployment. The XO, Lieutenant Commander Jim Greene, announced that the ship would be in three section duty and that because of their many responsibilities, the department heads would not stand inport duty. Three CDO's were designated, me, Lieutenant (junior grade) Dave Miller, the ASW Officer, and Lieutenant (junior grade) Bob Hardy, the CIC Officer.

The routine for GITMO was to get underway early every morning, around 6:00 AM, spend the whole day at sea conducting exercises and drills under the watchful eye of the REFTRA instructors, and return to port in the early evening so the instructors, living at Guantanamo Bay Naval Base, could go home for the night. One of the more onerous, and remarkably difficult tasks was to achieve the proper setting of Material Condition Yoke before the ship got underway each morning. Material Condition Yoke required that certain hatches, scuttles and ventilation outlets were securely closed. It was explained to us that many ships failed to properly set Yoke even after four or five weeks at GITMO. Ships had been extended beyond six weeks because they couldn't pass the inspection by the instructors who knew exactly where to look for violations. For that reason, the XO announced that every morning at 4:00 AM, the ship would hold reveille and division officers would personally set Yoke on all the Yoke-designated hatches in their respective spaces.

One of the beauties of GITMO is that it is on the southeastern tip of Cuba, has a large natural harbor which provides good protection, and the water outside the harbor immediately drops off to great depths so that deep, blue water operations could safely be conducted quickly after passing the sea buoy. GITMO has a naval air station as well as the harbor, and aircraft operated out of it to simulate attacks on the ships, tow targets, and so forth. My younger brother Frank, who had enlisted in the Navy after high school in 1970, had been designated an aircraft mechanic and assigned to GITMO where he was a plane captain on S-2 Tracker aircraft towing aerial targets for the ships and assisting in ASW exercises. The United States assumed territorial control over the southern part of the bay under the 1903 Cuban- American Treaty which granted it a perpetual lease of the area. The Castro government of Cuba has always maintained that this U.S. presence is illegal and was achieved by the threat of force which is in violation of international law. The naval base was established in 1898 when the U.S. took control of the bay following the Spanish-American War. After Fidel Castro came to power following the Cuban Revolution in 1959, President Eisenhower declared that the status of the naval base would remain unchanged.

We pulled into GITMO on March 21st, tied up the ship and received a large party of inspectors in the wardroom, led by a full captain, to make introductions and brief us on our training syllabus. Early the next morning, 4:00 AM to be exact, word was passed over the 1MC, "Division Officers, check the setting of Material Condition Yoke."

For three weeks we were underway every morning early and back in the evening after a full day of drills and inspections. It was hard, tiring work, but we also had a little fun. On Sundays we had a day of rest and occasionally during the week those not on duty would go to the Officer's Club for a few drinks.

One of the wardroom pass arounds over the past several weeks had been a Dan Jenkins novel called *Dead Solid Perfect*, a funny book with a wide variety of crazy characters centered on the adventures of a professional golfer. Among the characters was the Needham family, a bunch of Texas bad-asses led by oldest brother Waylon. We all read and enjoyed the book, including Captain Nyquist and Lieutenant Commander Greene. John Nyquist was a good tennis player and we initiated a wardroom tennis tournament called the Waylon Needham Invitational which John Nyquist eventually won. Since I had introduced the book to the wardroom he began calling me Waylon when he was in a particularly good mood or if I did something he liked.

One of those occasions occurred when we were conducting an ASW exercise and simulating the hunt for a Soviet *FOXTROT* class diesel submarine. I was the Condition 1AS conning officer, which meant I drove the ship while wearing a set of sound-powered phones and taking instructions from the Tactical Action Officer (TAO), Bernie Hollenbeck, in CIC.

One of our instructors was a real prick of a lieutenant whose name I do not recall but who we all hated and referred to as Instructor Asshole. He had a very obnoxious, arrogant, holier-than-thou air about him which nobody, not even good old John Nyquist, could stand.

He was on the bridge for this exercise as we simulated our location, tracking and attack on this "*FOXTROT*" submarine.

He turned to me and said, "Do you know what a *FOXTROT* looks like? Could you identify it if it surfaced out there?"

"Sure." I said. I didn't have a clue.

"Here, draw me one." He pushed a piece of mo-board paper and a pencil in front of me. John Nyquist was sitting in his Captain's Chair on the bridge and watching.

I started with what I figured was a pretty safe beginning, a straight line representing the forward hull of a submarine followed by the front of the sail. Then I acted like I was busy on the sound-powered phones and whispered to Bernie in CIC, "Bernie, get out the AFNICM, tell me what a fucking *FOXTROT* looks like."

The AFNICM was an intelligence manual that had pictures and descriptions of all potential enemy naval ships, submarines and aircraft.

John Nyquist picked up his sound-powered handset, dialed the right circuit and listened in. I started the top of the sail but stopped and gave some orders to the helm to stall for time.

Bernie came back on, "OK, it's got some kind of bump coming up at the front of the hull on the main deck."

I added a little box-like structure at the front of my hull and then rounded it off to the waterline for the bow.

"The sail is kind of elongated, sloping aft and it's got an exhaust pipe looking thing at the top rear which kind of points aft."

I drew a sloping rear part of the sail and added a little pipe-like thing sticking out at the back of the sail. I added a periscope and a small mast. The instructor was leaning a little too close so I busied myself with an order to the status board keeper and moved away. Nyquist was trying hard to look away and not give away the game. The instructor began nodding his head approvingly.

"At the stern of the hull there's something sticking up that looks kinda like a fin."

I added the fin, capped it off with some waves along the water line and a little wake and pushed it towards Instructor Asshole. He looked at it, said, "Not bad," and went over to the Captain and said, "That's the first time someone has gotten it right."

Nyquist nodded sagely and looked over at me and said, "Good job Waylon."

One evening after returning to port Weapons Officer Gil Lauzon came up to my stateroom and said, "I've got something to tell you." I thought I might be in trouble for something.

"Tomorrow you're the OOD, the Captain is signing the letter right now."

Finally, I was going to be the OOD. In my mind I had been acquitting myself well on the bridge all along so it was an overdue qualification. I still had to do my Surface Warfare qualifications though, not being in the grandfather program, and had been working on them diligently. Engineering was the sticking point. I'd never served in the Engineering Department and my steam cycle knowledge was not what it should have been. Once while I was on watch on the bridge Captain Nyquist had asked me where the main condenser was and I had told him I thought it was under the boiler. He got a really worried look on his face at that answer.

My deck gang was extremely busy throughout REFTRA. There were the daily evolutions of mooring and getting underway which entailed all the line handling; there was precision anchoring in the harbor; and there was underway replenishment training, man overboard drills, vertical replenishment, boat operations, low visibility details using the leadline, and so forth. They were a tired bunch.

Among other tasks, we were required to demonstrate our ability to re-arm missiles at sea from the ammunition ship (AE). An oiler was in GITMO and was detailed to send over the rig to simulate the AE delivering missiles to *SEMMES*. In order to do this, we had to rig a kingpost aft on the O1 level deck forward of the MK13 missile launcher. The kingpost was a 15-foot steel post about 6 inches in diameter which was configured with all the necessary fittings at the top to take a spanwire under tension from the ammunition ship and all the inhaul and outhaul lines and blocks to transfer the 15-foot-long 1,500-pound missile from one ship to the other while underway. We rigged the kingpost and came alongside the oiler. They passed the messenger and then the rig. As the padeye came across attached to the spanwire, the trick became to get this heavy load up the kingpost, over the pelican hook, secured into place and ready for the oiler to put tension on the spanwire. Unlike a standard underway replenishment station, there was simply no way to get several men around the shackle at the top of the kingpost and muscle it into place. Because of the way the padeye had been rigged by the oiler, the inhaul lines would not pass any further through the snatch block.

We had a seaman in First Division named Tucker, a big, strong black kid who was one of the better seamen in the division. Petty Officer Wright and I made eye contact.

"See if Tucker can get up there and connect it," I said.

What followed was a remarkable feat of strength as Seaman Tucker climbed the kingpost, and hanging on with his left arm reached out with his right, grabbed the padeye on the end of the spanwire, and muscled it the last foot to the pelican hook. Then, still wrapping his left arm around the top of the kingpost, he used his left hand to slide the jaws of the pelican hook through the padeye so it could take the strain. He inserted the safety cotter pin and, exhausted, climbed down. He had saved the day. I would reward Tucker later that year back in Charleston when I discovered what his family situation was.

After three weeks of REFTRA and a grueling schedule, we were granted a five-day break and a port visit to Montego Bay, Jamaica. The XO announced at Officer's Call that the three GITMO CDO's, me, Bob Hardy, and Dave Miller, would not have to stand any duty throughout the visit. The department heads would stand CDO for us.

We pulled into Montego Bay the next morning and anchored in the harbor, there being no suitable pier. We had arranged to set up a wardroom "admin" at the local Holiday Inn and the XO put me in charge of it. That was fine with me as I got to leave the ship on the first liberty boat, stock up on beer and soda, and secure the room. I didn't plan on coming back to the ship until it was time to get underway in four days. We set up camp at the Holiday Inn and spent the next four days lounging around the pool, drinking, reading and just generally relaxing. We all had a chance to call home, something that today is done almost daily, including underway in the open ocean, but in 1975 was seldom done. Letters, with the inherent delays, were the primary means of communication.

On the morning of Saturday, April 19th, we cleaned up the admin and I went to the front desk to pay for the room with a check cut from the wardroom mess. They wouldn't take the check. The ship was due to get underway pretty soon and I had no time to go back and get cash, so I pulled out my VISA and paid the $250 bill. $250 for a room in Montego Bay for four nights is a pretty good deal by today's standards, but in 1975 on lieutenant junior grade pay it was a lot of money. I had no time or way to call Iris and warn her and we weren't due home for another month. I wrote her a letter once back on the ship but she didn't receive it until after the VISA bill showed up in the mail with my $250 Holiday Inn charge on it. She later told me she wondered just what the hell I was up to.

As April drew to a close we prepared for our final battle problem which we knew was going to be a challenge. The engineering plant had struggled, especially with the warm tropical weather and temperatures in the boiler rooms and engine rooms were unbearably hot. Heat stress was a real concern and the Chief Engineer was forced to rotate his watchstanders out of the engineering spaces on a much more frequent than normal basis. The fact that we kept steam up overnight inport didn't help matters.

On the 30th of April, the same day that Saigon fell to the Communist North Vietnamese, we sailed out of GITMO harbor for our final battle problem with a full complement of inspectors aboard, including the captain senior inspector. It was a complex, multi-warfare exercise which we successfully completed and were granted a passing grade by the inspection team. We sailed out of GITMO on the morning of the 1st of May and headed back to Roosevelt Roads after a celebratory night at the O'Club. Next up was Naval Gunfire Support qualification at Vieques Island.

SEMMES pulled into Roosevelt Roads on the 5th of May for an overnight stay and briefings and meetings with the Naval Gunfire Support (NGFS) range personnel. We were underway the next morning and soon arrived on the range off the island of Vieques which lies about 10 miles east of the Puerto Rican mainland. The 21-mile-long island is inhabited, but in 1975 the eastern half was used as a live fire range for Navy ships and aircraft.

I was quite familiar with Vieques having fired on the range several times while aboard *NEWPORT NEWS*.

Things did not go well on two fronts over the next two days. The engineering spaces continued to experience excessive ambient temperatures due to problems with the space ventilation which had been modified during the overhaul period. Secondly, the fire control system was malfunctioning and we were consistently experiencing difficulties with rounds on target. After a return to Roosevelt Roads we headed home to Charleston with our two-and-a-half-month shakedown training cruise having been only partially successful. Missile qualifications and Refresher Training at GITMO had been successfully completed but the engineering difficulties and our failure to pass NGFS qualifications were both major disappointments.

On the 10th of June we re-entered Charleston Naval Shipyard to have warranty work performed on the engineering plant to correct our high heat problems. At the same time, our gunnery fire control system was given a groom to determine the cause of our problems at Vieques. The big sweat however was our upcoming Operational Propulsion Plant Examination or OPPE. OPPE was another of the required examinations and certifications which had to be successfully completed in order to certify the ship ready for fleet operations and eventual deployment which, for *SEMMES*, was scheduled a mere six months away in January 1976.

OPPE was a relatively new development in the surface Navy in 1975. During the Vietnam War our surface ships had been run hard and not maintained in a manner that would ensure long life and engineering plant safety. It was recognized that the surface force needed to learn some lessons from the submarine force which necessarily operated its nuclear propulsion plants to very exacting standards. The surface Navy had been relatively sloppy in this regard. It was not uncommon for the chief or first class boiler tender in a steamship to light off the plant from memory or with personally written notes from the greasy "wheelbook" in his back pocket. Bringing up steam in a 1200 psi boiler and operating a plant that relies on a precise balance of air, fuel and water to function efficiently and safely is a complex operation requiring all systems and valves to be aligned properly and in the proper sequence. 1200-pound steam is also a deadly killer and the Navy had learned the hard way, through loss of life, that operating these steam plants required exacting professional standards.

Recognizing all this, the Navy introduced the OPPE in the early 70s and it quickly became one of the most demanding inspections required of a surface ship. The Engineering Department had to demonstrate its ability for three duty sections to properly operate the plant, respond to engineering casualties, perform required maintenance, properly document all activities and respond to emergencies. The damage control activities involved the entire crew as damage control parties were made up of crewmembers from every department. Bridge watchstanders such as myself had to demonstrate an understanding of the engineering plant and had to know how to immediately respond to a given engineering casualty or emergency and what the limits were to ship maneuverability in each case. The OPPE rivaled the nuclear weapons safety inspection as the most difficult. The fact that *SEMMES* had entered the shipyard to correct known engineering problems a mere seven weeks before the OPPE added to the pressure on the crew.

June and July were pressure packed months as we remained in the shipyard and ran countless drills to train up for the OPPE. In the Weapons Department we were likewise gearing up for our own nuclear weapons safety inspection and follow-on attempt to achieve the naval gunfire support qualifications we had failed at Vieques.

We had one nice diversion during this period for Bob Hardy's wedding in July. Bob's father was the Chief Master Sergeant of the Air Force, the Air Force's most senior enlisted man and the principal enlisted advisor to the Air Force Chief of Staff, General David C. Jones. This was a very big deal, the equivalent of the Master Chief Petty Officer of the Navy.

Bob's dad went out with a bunch of us in the wardroom for Bob's bachelor party the night before the wedding. We went to a topless bar in North Charleston that featured a dancer with huge breasts; callsign/stage name "Bambi." After her performance, and knowing that we were a bachelor party, she came over and sat with us. Nobody knew quite what to say until Bernie Hollenbeck broke the ice saying, "I cried during the forest fire in your movie." I'm not sure Bambi got it.

On the 3rd of August we were underway with the OPPE team aboard and headed out the Cooper River for the Charleston Operating Areas to conduct our OPPE. We passed the exam and returned to Charleston on the 6th much relieved. The heat problems in the engineering spaces had been corrected during the yard period and, despite the hot August temperatures the spaces remained within normal temperature limits.

Rather than send *SEMMES* back to Vieques to complete our NGFS qualification, we were sent to Bloodsworth Island in the Chesapeake Bay where there was an active Navy range often used by naval aircraft from Patuxent River Naval Air Station or Naval Air Station Oceana in Virginia Beach. It no longer exists as a range, but back then the Navy fired on it and bombed it regularly. It was a challenging three days with lots of concerns about merchant traffic up and down the Chesapeake and numerous crabbers and fishing boats threatening to foul the range. For three days we bombarded the island and on the 17th of August returned to Charleston to prepare for an upcoming pre-deployment exercise in the Virginia Capes operating areas.

I had been assigned the collateral duty as Public Affairs Officer (PAO) in *SEMMES*, responsible for recording events and writing articles for the base newspaper. There was an unofficial competition between the ships to get recognition for our sailors in the paper and especially between *SEMMES* and *USS SELLERS (DDG-11)* as the two *ADAMS* class DDGs in Charleston. I had a Polaroid camera to take pictures of promotion and award ceremonies which I would enclose with a typed up story of the event and mail in to the base newspaper.

On this day we were in the wardroom waiting for a promotion ceremony for a couple of the crew and I snapped a test picture of our Navigator, Ensign Steve Avery, and Command Master Chief, Master Chief Sonarman Henderson. After the ceremony I went back to my stateroom to take care of the article about the promotion and I looked at the picture of Avery and Henderson and thought to myself, "What can I do with this?" Steve Avery was a Naval Academy grad and a bit of a pretty boy. Master Chief Henderson was a wheeler-dealer master chief well-known around the Charleston waterfront.

I sat down and typed out a caption for the picture for the base newspaper:

Father and Son Team Reunited on USS SELLERS

Ensign Steve Henderson has joined his father, Master Chief Robert Henderson, aboard USS SELLERS (DDG-11). Ensign Henderson, a recent graduate of the U. S. Naval Academy, is serving as the ship's navigator. Master Chief Henderson is SELLERS' Command Master Chief.

I didn't think much about it for a week or so until one day I was having lunch at the Officers Club with our Gunnery Officer because we were away from the ship at a nuclear weapons safety course. I had picked up a base newspaper from the rack on the way in. At the bottom of the front page was the picture of Avery and Henderson with my caption. Uh, oh.

In the meantime, our Chief Engineer, Lieutenant Commander Andy Dowd, had been over on the tender, *USS SIERRA (AD-18)*, and also picked up a copy. He got back to *SEMMES* in time for lunch and burst into the wardroom waving the paper and showed it to Captain Nyquist and the XO. Everybody thought it was funny, but the CO and XO kept their composure and didn't demonstrate any open delight in my prank. Captain Nyquist was friends with Captain Flannery of *SELLERS* and he didn't want my little joke to stir up any bad blood.

That afternoon, back in class at the nuclear safety course, I was summoned from the classroom to take a call from Lieutenant Gil Lauzon, my boss.

"Hey Willy (he liked to call me that), you coming back to the ship after the course?"

"Yessir."

"Go see the Captain when you get back; he wants to see you."

That afternoon a little after 4:30 I walked aboard *SEMMES* and went straight to the CO's cabin and knocked.

"Come in."

"You wanted to see me sir?"

He turned around from his desk, looked at me, and then held up the newspaper.

"You do this?"

Gulp, "Yessir."

He just looked at me with the hint of a smile on his face and a twinkle in his eye, and then gathered himself and said, "Don't do it again."

"Aye, aye, sir."

He was losing control of his smile as I left. I later learned that he and the XO secretly thought it was great and that it had really energized the wardroom. I also found out that Master Chief Henderson was treated like a hero at the Chief's Club that afternoon. I was never told, but I suspect that John Nyquist called Commander Flannery and filled him in. I suspect he thought it was funny too.

On the 4th of September, we departed Charleston to participate in COMPTUEX 4-76 in the Virginia Capes Operating Areas. This would be *SEMMES'* graduation exercise before deploying to the Middle East in January. COMPTUEX stood for Comprehensive Training Unit Exercise and would involve the aircraft carrier *USS AMERICA (CV-66)* and various cruiser, destroyer and auxiliary ships from the Atlantic Fleet. This would be the first time since the overhaul that *SEMMES* would operate in a fleet steaming environment with an aircraft carrier and numerous other ships.

We were seeing some changes in the wardroom at this time as well as some changes in First Division. Our Operations Officer, Lieutenant Bernie Hollenbeck, was transferred and replaced by Lieutenant Herb Fauth. Iris and I lost our good friends and next door neighbors, the Hollenbecks, but only temporarily as our paths would cross again in the years to come. We also had a change of command ceremony to prepare for as in December, Commander John Nyquist would be departing for duty in Washington to be replaced by Commander Fred Williamson. We did not look forward to losing our beloved Captain Nyquist, the "Silver Fox." We had some new additions in First Division as the Bureau of Naval Personnel, realizing we were a deployer, began manning the ship to its full complement.

One morning in Charleston I had gone down into First Division Berthing and discovered a tall, thin black guy standing in the compartment talking to some of the other seamen. He had on an ankle-length, red suede double-breasted coat, a big floppy red felt hat, stacked heel red pointy toe shoes, and greasy slicked back hair; he looked like a pimp.

I said, "Who are you?"

"Fox," he said.

One of the petty officers said, "He's new on board, a seaman, his luggage got lost."

I said, "OK Seaman Fox, go find your luggage, put on a uniform, and we'll get you checked in. Welcome Aboard."

I later reviewed his record and found out his name was Washington–"Fox" is just what he called himself. I also saw him out in town once out of uniform and realized why he kept his hair all slicked down. He had an Afro as big as a beach ball once he got all the gunk out of his hair. He would have gone up in a huge ball of flames if he got anywhere near a fire aboard ship. But he turned out to be a pretty good performer in First Division.

During this same period, I was also exposed to the tough life some of our young enlisted men had in the early 70s Navy. Seaman Tucker, he of the one-handed connection of the spanwire on the kingpost during REFTRA, was having some difficulties at home which he was reluctant to talk about. When I couldn't find him one day I asked Petty Officer Wright where he was.

"I sent him home to take care of some things."

"What's up?"

"I don't know; he's not himself. I think he's got money problems."

I went back to my stateroom and looked him up in my Division Officer Notebook. Married, four kids, no home phone; but an address in North Charleston.

I got in my car and went to visit him. He was shocked and embarrassed when he answered the door in gym shorts, no shoes and a tee shirt. I said I wanted to talk to him and see if there was anything he needed. I liked Tucker. He was a good, hard-working sailor and a leader among the non-rated deck seamen. Reluctantly he let me in and introduced me to his wife and the four young kids, perhaps only one of school age. The place was dingy and dark, only one room and a door to what must have been a bathroom. There was almost no furniture. Instead, a loft had been built at one end of the room and it appeared the whole family slept together up in the loft. I quickly realized why the place was so dark. There on the floor was a 20 gallon can of Navy-issue red lead primer. The whole inside, walls, loft and even the ceiling had been painted with red lead. It was pretty obvious that Tucker had stolen the primer from the paint locker on the ship, or perhaps from the shipyard.

I let the primer theft go and talked to him about how he was getting by on $437 dollars a month E-3 pay with six mouths to feed and he told me he was struggling. We talked about Navy Relief and how he could get a loan and set up an allotment to make sure the family had money coming in while we were deployed. He really appreciated my concern and my advice, even though we were both probably the same age, and I earned his loyalty forever. Another lesson learned; this time a good one.

The exercise went fine and we returned to Charleston on the 18th of September. During this period inport, as part of my collateral duty PAO assignment, I had arranged for a fellow named Dave Rosenberg to come to Charleston from the Morale Welfare and Recreation (MWR) department in Norfolk for two days to give the crew a preview of the cultures of the Middle East in the base auditorium as part of our preparations for deployment. He was somewhat famous for introducing Navy crews to the various cultures in the areas of the world to which they would be deploying. He put on an entertaining show and made sure everyone understood the protocols for dealing with the Arab culture. He warned against staring at the women, touching someone or waving with your left hand (reserved for wiping your ass) and showing the soles of your feet (an insult). One of the bogus recommendations though had to do with Coca-Cola. He told us that the Arabs hate the Jews and Coca-Cola was a Jewish-owned company so Coca-Cola products were verboten in the Arab world. We stocked the ship with Pepsi products based on his recommendation only to get over there and find Coke signs and Coca-Cola trucks everywhere. I think the guy owned stock in Pepsi.

We were back to sea again on the 8th of November to provide escort services for *USS AMERICA (CV-66)* in the Virginia Capes operating areas. *AMERICA* had a number of tests and trials to run as part of her own preparations for deployment and it was Atlantic Fleet policy that a surface combatant be present at all times as a "shotgun." It was more good experience for we bridge and CIC watchstanders to operate in close proximity to an aircraft carrier. Carriers are dangerous beasts, especially at night. They have so many lights that it's often difficult to tell what target angle you see because the normal stern, side, range and masthead lights are washed out by flight deck lights, hangar bay lights and all sorts of extraneous lights that can obscure standard navigation lights. They are also so big that one hand often doesn't know what the other is doing. They are commanded by aviators who worry more about the wind and the airplanes than a destroyer not clever enough to stay out of the way. It was a longstanding and proven in blood axiom that you always turn away from an aircraft carrier if you have to make a turn; no matter how far away he is.

One night I had the watch as OOD on the bridge for the 20-24 (8:00 PM–Midnight) watch. We were keeping our distance while *AMERICA* spun circles around a buoy in the OPAREA to calibrate radar equipment. Around 10:30 she finished and signaled us by flashing light that she was setting up a north-south night steaming line and drills were complete for the night. I called Captain Nyquist in his cabin and he said, "OK, take up station 500 yards astern and follow him through the night." At least that's what I *thought* he said.

I was feeling pretty good that the Captain trusted me enough to not come up to the bridge himself and keep an eye on things as most CO's would. I ordered up some speed and worked out an intercept course to fall in 500 yards astern of the carrier.

About a half an hour later I called him up again; this time I think he was in the rack.

"Captain, we're on station, 500 yards astern, on course 180, speed seven knots."

"500 YARDS! I SAID 5,000 YARDS!" Oops.

"Uh... Sorry sir, I thought you said 500."

Silence for a few seconds.

"OK, ease back to 5,000, call me when you get there. How much further before she turns north?"

Then he thought about it a second and said, "Change that, drop back to 1,000."

"Aye, aye sir. Sorry about that."

I knew what he was thinking, better to be closer astern when she reversed course; she'd be less likely to come all the way around and hit us going the opposite direction than if we were two and a half miles astern when she started the 180 degree turn.

We returned to Charleston the 16th of November and went upriver to the Charleston Naval Weapons Station near Goose Creek, South Carolina on the 12th of December to load ammunition, including missiles and nuclear depth charges for our upcoming deployment. This was to be Captain Nyquist's final ship move in command of *SEMMES* as Fred Williamson was scheduled to relieve him a week later.

I had been diligently working on my SWO PQS throughout this time and I was going to be the first in *SEMMES* to go before a SWO Qualification Board. Today, the CO of a ship is empowered to qualify the officers in his wardroom following completion of the PQS and successful completion of an oral board, normally including himself, the XO and department heads. The rules in 1975 mandated that an officer had to be boarded by two or more CO's from other ships. After a thorough quizzing by a murder board consisting of the CO, XO and *SEMMES* department heads, I was sent to *USS SELLERS (DDG-11)* for a board by her CO, Commander Gerard J. Flannery, and the CO of a fleet tug whose name I don't remember. This was a big deal because I was not only the first officer in *SEMMES* to go through the official PQS program and the board, I was the first officer in the squadron and quite possibly the first officer on the east coast. I wondered if Captain Flannery had made the connection between me and the bogus newspaper article. We held the board in the Captain's cabin and the two CO's did their best to make me comfortable. That afternoon, December 16, 1975, I was pinned with my gold SWO pin in a simple ceremony in Captain Nyquist's cabin with a lot of hearty congratulations from my fellow officers. I do not know if I was the first in the Navy to qualify under the new standard SWO PQS program, but I was one of the first.

As PAO I was also responsible for the change of command programs and I prided myself on getting ahead of the game and getting a draft approved and all the programs printed, without mistakes, and delivered to the ship five days before the ceremony. I stored them in my stateroom for safekeeping.

On the 19th of December Commander Fred Williamson relieved Commander John Nyquist as CO of *USS SEMMES (DDG-18)*. The ceremony went smoothly and Captain Nyquist walked off the ship wearing the four stripes of a Navy captain, having been selected for promotion but not allowed to wear it until he gave up command. We hated to see him go. He was a great CO and I credit him as a major factor in my decision to stay in the Navy. As he left the ship, many of we JO's were of the opinion that he would never make admiral because he was too nice a guy. He eventually retired as a three-star vice admiral.

As First Lieutenant I was responsible for the appearance of the ship and she looked good for the ceremony. As PAO I was responsible for much of the preparations including publicity, invitations, and the programs. XO Jim Greene came up to me on the quarterdeck and shook my hand and told me I'd done a good job.

I then went back to my stateroom and saw the two boxes of programs sitting on my rack. I went aft to the XO's stateroom and found Jim Greene changing out of his blues and sheepishly told him we/me hadn't handed out the programs. He gave me a "you gotta be shitting me" look and then smiled and said, "Let's don't tell the Captain."

CHAPTER 6

Middle East Force

O n the 13th of January 1976 *SEMMES* sailed out of Charleston for a six month deployment to the Middle East Force in the Persian Gulf. This was a single ship deployment as we were to augment the standing force in the Gulf. The Middle East Force was established in August 1949 following World War II. It had begun as a task force immediately following the war as numerous U.S. oilers, Navy and civilian, were plying the waters of the Persian Gulf to transport oil. There has been a permanent U.S. Navy presence in the Gulf, on a rotating basis, since 1947. When the Kingdom of Bahrain achieved full independence from British protectorate status in 1971, the United States entered into a lease treaty with Bahrain for the use of the harbor and land for a U.S. Navy facility. A one-star admiral was designated as Commander, Middle East Force (COMIDEASTFOR) and in 1972 the converted *RALEIGH* class LPD, *USS LASALLE (AGF-3)* became the COMIDEASTFOR flagship, permanently based in Bahrain. *LASALLE* was painted all white to ward off the heat and became known as "The Great White Ghost of the Arabian Coast."

Although this was to be a 6-month deployment for SEMMES, it was to be a 3-month deployment for me. In the fall of 1975, I had been talking to Captain Nyquist about what I should do for shore duty which was next for me after *SEMMES*. The United States had ended the draft in 1973 following the unpopularity of the Vietnam War and the inequities of the draft system. We had moved to an all-volunteer force which meant we needed to attract and recruit people into all branches of the military. There was a push to get volunteers for recruiting duty and Captain Nyquist had recommended that I consider it. However, it came about, I had orders to detach from *SEMMES* in March 1976 and report to the Navy Recruiting District in Atlanta, Georgia as an officer recruiter.

We hit an oiler for fuel halfway across the Atlantic and pulled into Rota, Spain on the 20th of January to refuel again and take on stores. We left Rota the next day, transited the Strait of Gibraltar at night and I entered the Mediterranean for the first time. I had the bridge watch as we transited the Strait and was able to look to port and see Gibraltar and the lights of Europe and to starboard and see the lights of Tangiers, Morocco and the continent of Africa. We then stopped for one night in Naples, Italy where I was able to leave the ship and call Iris at home in Charleston. I was going to miss Amy's first birthday in another four days. The first of many significant events in her life I would miss, although at the age of one, I doubted she would miss me.

Next stop was Port Said, Egypt and what was to be my first, and a very eventful, transit of the Suez Canal. As we transited the Med towards Port Said I witnessed one of those rare meteorological events that I have never again seen; St. Elmo's Fire. I had the 20–24 watch on the bridge as OOD in the eastern Med on a night when there were thunderstorms and lightning in the area, although it was not raining at our location. As I looked forward through the bridge window I saw what looked like lightning dancing all over the HF antenna atop Mount 51. This was a cross-shaped antenna mounted on top of the gun mount and the entire antenna, both the vertical main post and the horizontal cross bar, was lit up with a bluish-yellow light dancing all over. It almost looked like it was on fire although these were clearly not flames. St. Elmo's Fire is a weather phenomenon in which luminous plasma is created by a coronal discharge from a grounded object in an electric field in the atmosphere, such as near thunderstorms or even volcanoes. Sometimes it is accompanied by a buzzing sound, although I heard nothing that night. It lasted about five minutes and I dutifully made a log entry in the deck log.

On the 28th of January, we made the approach to Port Said harbor for that night's transit of the Suez Canal. The Suez Canal is approximately one hundred miles in length and connects the

Mediterranean Sea with the Red Sea via the Gulf of Suez. The canal is controlled by Egypt and handles roughly one hundred ships per day in convoys traveling both north and south. Southbound convoys anchor in the Great Bitter Lake at midday to permit the northbound ships to pass before continuing south to Port Suez.

The canal is somewhat unique in that it was built without locks despite an elevation change between the Mediterranean and the Red Sea. The Great Bitter Lake in the middle of the canal serves as a lock of sorts, balancing the flow of water from either end. Built between 1859 and 1869 by the French engineer Ferdinand de Lesseps, the canal was acquired by Great Britain in 1875 and nationalized by Egypt in 1956. The canal was closed to Israeli shipping by the Egyptians from 1948 to 1975, and closed to all shipping from 1967 to 1975 following the 1967 Arab-Israeli War. In 1975 the canal was cleared of wreckage resulting from the Six Day War and was expanded in 1976 to permit larger ships safe passage.

The canal presents a number of challenges, not the least of which is dealing with the Egyptian canal pilots whose use is required of all ships. From a navigational standpoint, the biggest challenge occurs at either end of the canal when ships are required to anchor to await the formation of the convoy. The southbound transit is the more challenging of the two because it begins in the dead of night. Ships anchoring outside Port Said, Egypt must navigate at night to the canal entrance where they are met by the pilot boat bearing the canal pilot. Port Said is a city of a half a million people and the city is a sea of lights at night, making navigational aids difficult to pick out against the brightly lit backdrop. Add to this an outer anchorage filled with hundreds of ships anchored helter-skelter awaiting their turn to enter the canal. There is a considerable language barrier which comes into play during this adventure as well. Bridge-to-bridge VHF radios are used to coordinate the form-up of the convoy and give directions to entering ships. English is the international language of the sea, as it is in the air, and English speaking skills vary widely among the port authorities and the master's of ships of all nationalities.

There is a weather phenomenon which routinely occurs in and around the Suez Canal; a ground fog which forms as the result of high humidity and cool night desert air. This ground fog would play a major role in this particular canal transit as well as another transit many years later. As First Lieutenant, I was responsible for all of the ship's ground tackle, mooring gear, and ship's boats, consisting of a 26' motor whaleboat in the portside davits and a 26' Captain's Gig in the starboard side davits. There were requirements to ensure that all of this equipment was made ready for use throughout the transit.

On this canal transit, *SEMMES* was ordered to the inner harbor by the Port Said authorities when we arrived the afternoon of January 28th. As the only military ship in the southbound convoy, we would lead the approximately 50 merchant vessels of all sizes through the canal. Anchoring in the inner harbor was a benefit as it meant that we would enter Port Said in daylight and the pilot would board the ship while we were at anchor later that night. We were avoiding the midnight approach to the canal entrance through the outer anchorage. It also meant that we would be swarmed by dozens of "bum boats" carrying Egyptian merchants hoping to sell everything from rugs to brass pots to the crew. In the pre-*USS COLE* days this was routine in these third world ports and one of the reasons that in October of 2000 the approach of the small boat on *USS COLE (DDG-67)* in the harbor at Aden, Yemen aroused no suspicion.

There is a bureaucratic ritual to a canal transit, which keeps the ship's officers and crew busy from the afternoon arrival until the midnight beginning of the canal transit itself. The net result is that the key leadership in the ship gets very little sleep before beginning the canal transit around midnight. By the time the ship exits the canal at Port Suez around sunset the next day, the CO, XO, key officers, and crew are pretty tired. What lies ahead the next night is an all-night transit of the Gulf of Suez in company with the 50 or so ships headed south at various speeds and the 50 or so ship's headed north from the Red Sea to Port Suez for the next day's northbound transit. As First Lieutenant, my sea detail station for the transit was as supervisor and safety officer on the forecastle. We had plans to rotate this assignment among the various Weapons Department officers throughout the transit and I took the first leg.

The transit had begun at about midnight on a cool, humid, night as we sailed south through Port Said and into the barren reaches of the Egyptian desert which extended to the dark horizon on both sides of the canal. Behind us at intervals of a little over a quarter of a nautical mile were 50 some commercial ships of all shapes and sizes; all of them bigger than the 4,500 ton *SEMMES*. Once south of Port Said and into the desert, the canal straightens out for a long 20 nautical mile stretch on a due south base course ending a few miles north of the city of Ismailia.

At about 2:30 on the morning of the 29th as *SEMMES* was steaming south on the long straight leg of the canal north of Ismailia, I noticed that fog was beginning to set in. Very quickly visibility dropped sharply and soon the banks of the canal, some 200–300 feet distant, were indistinguishable. The canal is marked by a series of lighted poles, red to the east (port when headed south) and green to the west, which marks the left and right edges of the channel. These markers are spaced at intervals of about 1,000 yards. Ahead of the ship I could see nothing as there were no ships ahead to provide a reference. Looking straight up I could see the stars, so this was a low lying ground fog. Looking back up at the bridge, I could see the CO and bridge watch team silhouetted in the bridge windows by the low backlight from the bridge status boards. Looking back towards the canal, I saw that the ship was passing between two of the lighted canal markers to port and starboard and noted that we appeared to be a left of center of the canal. At about this time I also sensed the ship slowing from about 12 knots to something less than 10–perhaps 7 to 8 knots.

At about this time the 1JV phone talker who was in communication with the bridge called out, "Bridge says to put someone in the eyes of the ship." At about that time my walkie-talkie crackled to life and the XO, Jim Greene, said, "Bill, go up to the bullnose and tell me what you can see." I heard the forced draft blowers change pitch, indicating lower steam demand and a further slowing of the ship. As I reached the bullnose, I looked down over the port side in time to see one of the red lighted channel markers pass almost directly under me. We were on the far left side of the canal and I quickly radioed this information to the XO on the bridge.

The sound-powered phone talker then said, "Stand by the anchor;" an order from the bridge indicating we were about to drop the anchor. As we scrambled to make the starboard anchor ready to drop, the activity level on the bridge picked up and I could hear the bridge-to-bridge radio; probably the Egyptian pilot warning the ships astern that we had slowed down and might be stopping completely. Fifty-some ships in line behind us would have to react to the lead ship stopping–there was no room to safely pass.

As I looked aft, thinking the channel marker would hit the ship, I felt a shudder indicating a backing bell and noticed that the stern of the ship was now cocked to the port side, toward the east bank of the canal. Suddenly, everything just stopped. The ship was cocked at an angle with the bow pointing towards the canal center and the port quarter towards the east bank. From where I stood it looked like the stern was resting against the canal's east bank. We had not been given the order to drop the anchor but stood ready to do so. Over the walkie-talkie the XO told me to meet Lieutenant Gil Lauzon, the Weapons Officer, on the fantail. Walking aft on the port side of the ship, it became obvious that the port quarter of the ship was touching the canal bank.

ADAMS class DDG's were twin screw ships which delivered great power and maneuverability. Each 13-foot manganese bronze screw protruded about two feet beyond the side of the ship's outer hull. That is the reason for the screw guards on the side of the ship's hull over the area where the screws protrude. These screw guards, six-inch diameter steel bumpers not unlike a football helmet face mask, are designed to hold the ship far enough off a quay wall or pier piling to prevent the screws from striking the obstruction and getting damaged during a docking or undocking maneuver.

As Gil and I surveyed the situation from the fantail it was obvious we were stuck against the side of the Suez Canal. I looked north up the canal in the darkness and could see the lights of the next ship behind us, apparently holding its position, but also directly behind us and not out in the middle of the canal. I didn't have time to reflect on this, as the XO came over the walkie-talkie again and told me to get back up to the forecastle and lower the starboard anchor. Having realized we were indeed stuck, the Captain had decided we better get the anchor down to at least hold the bow of the ship out in the channel. I supervised the fo'csle detail in lowering the anchor, leaving the wildcat engaged so that we could quickly raise it if necessary. The ship was now fairly securely positioned with the port quarter against the bank and the bow held by the anchor some 100 feet from the east bank and perhaps 500 feet from the west bank. Now what? Call for tugs from Ismaila to come pull us off perhaps? How much damage had been done to the port screw, port shaft and hull when we hit the bank?

We later determined that the port screw had dug itself into the bank underneath a stone interface that runs from above the water at the canal's edge to about 10 feet below the surface. From there, the stone gives way to the natural sand and mud sides and bottom of the canal as it gently curves down to a depth of about 60 feet in the center. The screws on the *ADAMS* class DDG turned in opposite directions with the port screw turning counterclockwise (when viewed from astern) and the starboard screw turning clockwise when the ship was moving ahead. This arrangement eliminates side torque when both screws are moving ahead or astern together, and maximizes side torque when it is most desired when twisting the ship with one screw moving the ship forward and the other driving her astern. Unlike modern ships with Controllable Reversible Pitch Propeller systems, where blade pitch is hydraulically reversed but the shaft continues to turn in the same direction, *SEMMES* was required to change the direction of shaft rotation in order to move from ahead to astern. In our case, when the Captain reversed the port engine to stop the ship, the port screw began rotating in a clockwise direction when viewed from astern.

The screw dug itself into the mud/sand wall of the canal below the stone interface and then up under the stone facing.

The Suez Canal is not a still body of water. As we moved south that night we were pushed along by about a two knot southerly current. As a ship slows with a following current, the rudder becomes less effective as the flow of water across the rudder is relatively less. In our case, when the ship slowed, the current began to push the stern to port. With literally no flow across the rudders, they became useless.

Returning to the fantail after we lowered the starboard anchor, I again began discussing options with Gil Lauzon. Meanwhile on the bridge, the CO and XO were doing the same. The Egyptian pilot had successfully stopped the convoy behind us and was calling the canal authorities in Ismailia to report our predicament and muster some tugs for assistance. Captain Williamson was also sending a report to our new boss, COMIDEASTFOR aboard his flagship, *USS LASALLE (AGF-3)* in Bahrain. At the XO's behest, I went with Gil to the bridge. It was now about 3:00 in the morning and the fog was still heavy.

When we got to the bridge, Captain Williamson asked if we thought we could get the ship out of the mud by ourselves. One of the cardinal rules in a grounding situation is to not try to drive the ship off with the engines. Typically, that will do more damage to the ship's drive train and make matters worse. Best to sit tight and wait for help or a tidal change which might float the ship free.

Working through the English language difficulties with the pilot, we learned how the merchant ships behind us in the convoy were able to stop without suffering our fate. The canal designers had built bollards along both sides of the canal so that ships could tie themselves up while stopped along the sides. These bollards, large, well anchored metal posts designed to accommodate a ship's mooring lines, were positioned every 500 feet along those portions of the canal with a favorable bank for mooring a ship. Single propeller merchant ships could lie against the canal bank without digging into the mud.

This knowledge gave us an idea. If we could run our mooring lines across the canal to the west bank bollards, we might be able to warp ourselves free of the mud using the two ship's capstans, one on the forecastle and one on the fantail. There was a problem however. The ship's number one and number six mooring lines were each 600 feet long. Lines two through five were each 300 feet in length. In order to run lines from the bow and stern to the bollards on the opposite bank, we would need close to 1,000 feet of line aft and about 900 feet forward in order to have enough line to work around the capstans and be handled by the ship's deck hands.

The obvious answer was to connect two or more lines together, and using the ship's boats, run the lines to the opposite bank. Petty Officer Wright astutely advised that we couldn't tie the lines together or we'd never get the knots untied after putting enough strain on them to pull the ship free of the bank. We solved this problem by breaking out some large metal shackles from the bo'sun's locker which were big enough to connect the eyes of two mooring lines together. As this plan began to take shape, we energized the Weapons Department and began hauling the ship's mooring lines out on deck, shackling them together and faking them out to run to the opposite bank.

We put our ASW Officer, Lieutenant (junior grade) Jim Babbitt, and a six-man crew into the Captain's Gig and lowered it into the Suez Canal. The motor whaleboat on the port side could not be lowered into the water because of the canal bank. With all three after mooring lines shackled together on the fantail, we lowered the eye of line 6 into the gig, had the crew tie it off to a cleat and began feeding line to the gig as it headed across the canal to look for a bollard on the opposite bank. As the gig disappeared into the fog, Jim kept us updated on his progress by walkie-talkie. As we watched the first shackle pay out over the side, 600 feet of line now between the ship and the gig, a new problem became apparent. 600 feet of wet five-inch nylon gets heavy in a hurry. Jim reported that the gig was really struggling to pull it. On top of that, he was worried about the cleat pulling out of the deck under the strain. We also began to wonder how Jim and his boat crew of six sailors were going to haul this line up the side of the canal bank and place the eye over the bollard, if they found one. Nylon line floats but we needed to get this done before it got waterlogged and even more difficult to handle.

Reaching the far bank, Jim radioed that there was no bollard where they had landed. The XO told him to get out of the gig, climb the bank, and look for one. Jim was a little nervous about this. It was 3:30 AM, we had been told that the Egyptian Army patrolled the canal, and we wondered if any soldiers in this area had any idea what was going on. Jim thought he might get shot by some trigger-happy sentry spotting him clambering over the bank. It was less than three years since the last Arab-Israeli War and who knew what the rules of engagement were for a Suez Canal sentry?

Walking first south, Jim found a bollard about 200 feet from where the gig had made its landing. We thought this would be good, as the angle of pull would seem to help, given the ship's position. Summoning the gig forward, Jim and the boat crew managed with a superhuman effort to haul the eye of the line up the bank and slide it over the bollard. With the gig headed to the forecastle to take the bow line across, we took a tentative strain on the line aft with the after capstan. Nylon mooring lines can be very dangerous under strain and the situation we were in made it even more so. A nylon line will stretch and if it then parts it will snap back like a big rubber band. Sailors had lost arms and legs or been killed by a parting nylon line. On the forecastle Petty Officer Wright had just completed feeding the mooring line down to Jim Babbitt and the gig crew for the trip across the canal. Jim and his crew easily found the next southernmost bollard and again were able to put the line in place.

It was now almost 4:30 and the fog was beginning to lift. We could see across the canal and could also see astern where the remainder of the convoy sat tied up to the east bank. Gil Lauzon informed me that the Egyptians were sending two tugs north from Ismailia to pull us off the bank. The canal authorities had a vested interest in getting our convoy moving again as the northbound convoy was due to get underway in about an hour from Port Suez.

We had to be anchored in the Great Bitter Lake by the time that convoy reached the southern end of the lake so that they could pass by and enter the section of the canal we now had now blocked up. Except for the Great Bitter Lake, the Suez Canal was a one-way street in 1976. Today there are two channels at the Mediterranean end for the first 9 miles or so.

From this point on began a delicately coordinated effort to warp the ship free of the bank using the lines and the capstans. The technique we developed was to put as much tension as we dared on the lines with the capstans and then sit and let the line's natural tendency to want to return to its original shape move the ship. The pause also allowed the capstan motors to cool. We were concerned about the motors overheating and failing.

At about 6:00 when the sun was just beginning to peek over the desert horizon and the fog was almost completely dissipated, the ship pulled free of the bank with a sucking sound and began drifting towards the center of the canal. Things started happening fast at this point as a number of things had to occur at once. We had to get the lines off the bollards and back on board as quickly as possible. We also had to get the anchor off the bottom. We couldn't do both at once up forward because although the capstan operated freely with the wildcat disengaged, it was slaved to it when engaged. The stern was swinging towards the middle of the channel now and I had visions of the ship going perpendicular to the channel and hitting the bank on the other side, or even swinging around with the southerly flowing current, pivoting on the anchor, and ending up pointed north, facing the convoy.

It was imperative that we get the after line out of the water as quickly as possible so as not to foul the ship's screws now that we were swinging to starboard. The CO would be afraid to use the engines with all that line floating loose in the water back aft. On the forecastle, we began heaving around on the anchor. We were slowly taking in line at the same time, but only at the pace the anchor was coming up. However, and for whatever reason, the ship's bow started moving to starboard as soon as the anchor was clear of the bottom. Whatever forces were at work on the ship were somehow working out in our favor. The movement across the canal slowed and it looked like we were in less danger of drifting across to the opposite bank.

When all lines were clear the captain began to slowly move the ship forward. He immediately received a report of heavy vibrations on the port shaft from the Chief Engineer. In the *ADAMS* class DDG's the port shaft is the short shaft, running some 75 feet from the after engine room to the port screw. When ships sit in port in a cold-iron status, a device called a jacking gear is engaged and a small electric motor very slowly turns the shaft and screw to prevent the turbine rotors from sagging under their own weight. We had been sitting for four hours with the port screw securely stuck in the canal bank but with steam up to move the ship when we were finally freed. A bowed rotor was a near certainty. Running the shaft under these conditions ran the risk of tearing up the bearings and seals on the steam turbine and the main shaft bearings.

Once we were moving south, the gig fell in astern and followed us. We still had to get to the Great Bitter Lake before the northbound convoy. Within minutes of getting underway on our own power the two tugs from Ismailia appeared around a bend in the canal. They also fell in astern in case *SEMMES* encountered more difficulty on the journey south. While continuing south we recovered the gig.

Everyone was pretty tired. It had been four hours of tension and frenzied activity. But there was also a great feeling of satisfaction among the deck gang for getting the ship unstuck. We were proud of what we had done under pressure and of the fact that we hadn't suffered the humiliation of having the Egyptian tugs pull a mighty U.S. warship out of the mud.

As we moved south the vibrations in the port drive train gradually eased. Ultimately they disappeared completely and no repairs were required. When the ship reached Bahrain, divers were sent over and reported no damage to the screw blades or the running gear. Perhaps because of the lack of damage and the circumstances of our grounding, Captain Fred Williamson escaped any formal censure by the chain of command.

Our first stop after transiting the canal and Gulf of Suez and entering the Red Sea was Jeddah, Saudi Arabia on the 2nd of February for a two-day visit. Jeddah sits on the Red Sea coast about halfway between the Sinai Pensinsula in the north and the Bab al Mandeb Strait and the Indian Ocean to the south. It is the largest port on the Red Sea and the second largest city in Saudi Arabia after Riyadh.

I had CDO duty the first day in but on the second day was able to participate in an event sponsored by the Americans in Jeddah on behalf of the crew. There was nothing to do in Jeddah itself and Saudi Arabia is a dry country so the crew couldn't go into town to hit the bars–there weren't any. There were some open air markets, souqs, for shopping but not much to buy. The Americans lived in an expatriate compound that was walled off and a virtual American city within the city. Within the American compound the rules were different. There were two kinds of booze served at a ship's party hosted by the American ex-pats, "clear" and "brown." Both tasted exactly the same. It was all moonshine and had a pretty good kick. Fortunately, nobody went blind.

On the 4th, we left Jeddah and sailed south to the port of Djibouti in the French Territory of the Afars and Isahs on the Horn of Africa. We passed through the Bab al Mandeb Strait through which the Red Sea empties into the Gulf of Aden and then on to the Indian Ocean. The Gulf of Aden separates the Arabian Peninsula from the African continent, as does the Red Sea. In 1976 Djibouti was a French territory which had at one time been called French Somaliland. In 1967 it had changed its name to the French Territory of the Afars and Isahs (FTAI) after a treaty deal with France. Djibouti was also where the French Navy based its Red Sea Fleet.

On the 6th of February we pulled into Djibouti for what was to be a three-day visit to resupply and refuel. That evening the wardroom was invited to a cocktail reception by the French Rear Admiral who commanded the Red Sea Fleet, but because I had CDO duty I missed the fun. The next day, after I had turned over CDO to Lieutenant Herb Fauth, the Ops Officer, I grabbed my tennis gear and piled into a car with several other officers to go to the French Officer's Club where we planned to play tennis, go to the pool, and relax for the day.

We got to the club which was in the middle of a desert area and immediately ordered some Heinekens. They had a pet cheetah on a chain and collar tied up out behind the club near the tennis courts. I had taken about two sips of my Heineken when we got word that everybody had to hurry back to the ship; liberty was cancelled.

We got back on board and discovered that that morning an FTAI busload of children had been kidnapped near the border with Somalia and taken across the border. Tensions were high between FTAI and Somalia and COMIDEASTFOR wanted everybody aboard ship in case there was trouble. That night the word came down from COMIDEASTFOR that we were to sail in the morning because the U.S. State Department wanted us out of town so it wouldn't appear that we favored one side or the other in the dispute.

We left Djibouti the morning of the 8th and sailed out of the Gulf of Aden and entered the Indian Ocean on the way south to Mombasa, Kenya for an exercise with the Kenyan Navy. That night I was once again standing the midwatch when I saw another rare phenomenon that I also have not seen since. Around 2:00 AM I saw a glow of light pass down the starboard side close aboard as we were sailing along at 16 knots. I ran out to the bridge wing thinking we had just missed or perhaps run over a small fishing boat. Instead I saw a patch of snow-white water that looked like there was a big searchlight under the surface shining up.

Turning forward I saw another patch, further away. It looked like we were about to enter a fog bank. It was not fog but a very large area, perhaps two football fields in size, of this same white, glowing water. We sailed through it and I realized it was bioluminescence in the water. It is normal, especially in tropical waters, for the ship to stir up bioluminescence as it moves through the water and disturbs plankton and other tiny creatures, but I had never seen the ocean glow like this before.

I later learned that what I had seen was a phenomenon called "milky seas effect," or a "white sea;" a condition in the open ocean where large areas of seawater are filled with bioluminescent bacteria, causing the ocean to uniformly glow an eerie blue at night. I learned that there had only been 235 documented sightings of milky seas since 1915–mostly concentrated in the northwestern Indian Ocean which is exactly where we were. I made the appropriate log entry as I had done after the St. Elmo's Fire incident, but I'm sure my sighting never made it into the scientific journals.

We sailed south down the coast of Somalia enroute Mombasa and in so doing we were to cross the Equator on the 14th of February. All we Pollywogs would be indoctrinated into the realm of Davy Jones and King Neptune in a traditional Crossing the Line Ceremony. The ceremony of Crossing the Line is an initiation rite that commemorates a sailor's first crossing of the equator. Originally the tradition was created as a test for seasoned sailors to ensure their new shipmates were capable of handling long, rough times at sea. Sailors who have already crossed the equator are Trusty Shellbacks and those who have not are Slimy Pollywogs. It's a two-day event, one evening and the next day, in which the Trusty Shellbacks are organized into a "Court of Neptune" to indoctrinate the Slimy Pollywogs into "the Mysteries of the Deep."

In 1976, these were still pretty rough events with all male crews and less political correctness than we have today. It began in the evening with a visit by King Neptune and his Court on the forecastle and with a beauty contest to elect the fairest of the fair. I was amazed at the outfits and props these guys came up with; skimpy panties, bras, wigs, balloons for oversized breasts, high heeled shoes, elbow-length gloves. Where the hell was all this stuff being kept before today? It looked like we had a fair number of closet cross-dressers in the crew. Some of these guys looked pretty damn good!

That night was the Wog Rebellion where the Pollywogs ran wild and generally tried to make life miserable for the Shellbacks. We paid the price the next morning with 4:00 AM reveille and a special breakfast of eggs with all kinds of nasty ingredients and copious amounts of hot sauce. We were required to assemble on the forecastle in skivvies and boondockers on our hands and knees while the Shellbacks whacked us with cut off sections of firehose, called shillelaghs, and hosed us down with firemain. An obstacle course was set up down the port side of the ship to the fantail where the Royal Court awaited.

Captain Williamson was a Pollywog and like a good sport he suffered the humiliation like the rest of us, but I didn't see him getting too many shillelagh whacks. XO Greene was a Shellback and kept an eye on things from the bridge.

The obstacle course included dunking pools and chutes to crawl through filled with food scraps from yesterday's meals, egg shells and other unpleasant things. The worst part was crawling the length of the ship on hands and bare knees on the non-skid and periodically getting whacked on the ass with the firehose sections. On the fantail there was a set of wooden stocks everybody had to spend some time in while soft tomatoes were pushed into our faces. We had to kiss the belly of the Royal Baby who was the fattest Shellback on the ship, sitting in a chair in a diaper with gun grease smeared all over his belly. The Royal Baby made sure he pulled your nose deep into his bellybutton when it was time for the kiss. It was pretty gross. At the end, King Neptune blessed each Pollywog with the Captain's sword and from then on we were Shellbacks. A saltwater shower rounded out the initiation. Each new Shellback was given a service record entry and a card to prove he had been initiated. This is something you always wanted to make sure was documented; otherwise you might have to be initiated all over again on your next ship. Naturally there were a handful of sailors who didn't want to go through it and they were allowed to stand watches and not be involved. I believe when it was all over they regretted their decision.

We arrived off the coast of Mombasa, Kenya on February 28th and conducted two days of exercises with the Kenyan "Navy." All they had were a couple of small patrol boats so we did some very basic maneuvering, communications and seamanship drills. It was of little value to us but all part of showing the flag and helping developing nations improve their capabilities. We did not go into port which was a big disappointment to everyone.

On March 2nd, we headed east for a port visit in the Seychelles, a tropical paradise in the Indian Ocean. The Seychelles is a small group of islands about 1,000 miles east of Kenya. As we were visiting, the islands were a crown colony of the United Kingdom but they were to gain their independence later that year.

As we were communicating with the husbanding agent and the British Consulate in Mahé, on the island of Victoria where we were to visit, an invitation was received for us to participate in a "boxing exhibition" to be held the second night in. We canvassed the crew and found three black sailors, one of them mine, Seaman Goode, who thought they were pretty tough and would represent *SEMMES* in the exhibition. They began spending their free time sparring, jumping rope, lifting weights, and generally posturing and strutting around trying to look tough on the ASROC deck.

On the day before we were to pull into the Seychelles, the XO had scheduled an awards ceremony and the ship's Navigator, Ensign Steve Avery, who was also the Admin Officer, was busy for the day and a half before the ceremony getting everything ready. Consequently, he was not paying enough attention to the navigation of the ship.

Navigation in 1976 was pretty rudimentary by today's standards. We didn't have GPS and our electronic navigation was limited to LORAN, which is only available in certain parts of the world, not to include the Indian Ocean, and Omega. Omega was notoriously inaccurate and quartermasters were equally as notorious for fudging their fixes so that the Omega fix plotted more or less on top of the Dead Reckoning (DR) fix. The Omega system used a very low frequency radio signal that could be read over two thousand miles. By comparing the time difference between signals received from different transmitting stations, the navigator could determine his position using a special graph.

Steve Avery had been preoccupied with his awards ceremony preparations so for two days the ship had been merrily DR-ing its way toward the Seychelles with the quartermasters dutifully plotting Omega fixes which miraculously landed on top of our DR.

On the 4th of March, Lieutenant Herb Fauth had the Deck for the 0800-1200 watch. In accordance with the ship's routine, we called away sweepers at 11:30 and my deck gang was topside sweeping down the main deck when a couple of seamen looked over the side from the forecastle and saw the bottom. They relayed this information to the bridge and it was reported to Herb Fauth. Herb looked over the starboard bridge wing and saw the same thing; lots of pretty coral formations and interesting shapes and colors and thought nothing of it. The idea to check the chart to see how deep the water should have been where we thought we were never crossed his mind. That "should have been" depth was over a mile.

Herb was relieved by Jim Babbit and nobody bothered to tell Jim that they were watching the bottom go by. Herb went down to the wardroom where we were having lunch, reported to the Captain that he had been properly relieved by Lieutenant (junior grade) Babbit and sat down to eat. He then casually mentioned that there were some really pretty coral formations visible from the bridge.

Captain Williamson and the XO shot out of their chairs and sprinted out of the wardroom for the bridge with Steve Avery in hot pursuit.

When the CO got to the bridge, he took a quick look over the side, and screamed, "ALL ENGINES STOP!" Then, "All engines back full, rudder amidships."

With the ship stopped, we tried to figure out where we were. We were too far from land to have radar contact. The Leading Quartermaster was now on the bridge frantically trying to get an Omega fix, but the Omega transmissions were 10 minutes apart so it was taking some time. We started trying to back down our wake when somebody had the idea to light off the SPS-40 air search radar and see if we could see anything with its 200 nautical mile range. Sure enough we started getting a return from what we assumed were the mountain tops from the Seychelles islands. From the bearing we figured we were way south of where we thought we were. Looking at the charts, the CO, XO and Navigator determined that we were in a section of coral reefs that in some places were only ten feet beneath the surface. *SEMMES* drew 25 feet.

We gingerly backed down until the bottom was no longer visible, then turned around and steamed west for an hour and then due north to get around the reefs. Steve Avery broke out the *Sailing Directions* and sure enough, they warned of a very strong southerly current in that part of the Indian Ocean. I couldn't help thinking about if it had been at night when we entered that area. We would have run aground in the middle of the Indian Ocean. We went ahead with our awards ceremony that afternoon and needless to say, Herb Fauth was not one of the awardees.

On the 5th of March, we sailed into the harbor of Victoria, on the island of Mahé in the Seychelles. It was an absolutely beautiful tropical paradise with lush green mountains rising straight out of the crystal clear waters of the Indian Ocean. Temperatures were in the mid-eighties with light, tropical breezes. The next night was the invitational boxing match to which we had been challenged by the local police force. A bunch of us went to support our three pugilists expecting to go to a high school gym or something like that. Instead we found ourselves in an open air stadium in the middle of Victoria with about two thousand excited fans. We got a look at the police boxers warming up and immediately knew that this was going to be a slaughter. They were like professionals; fit, mean, and jumping around and punching the air with lightning quick jabs. Our three guys were looking positively terrified. But they had guts and went ahead with the plan.

First we watched a three round match between two of the local islanders and it was obvious that these guys knew what they were doing and trained hard. First up from *SEMMES* was a sturdy young kid from Boilers Division who lasted almost 15 seconds before he was down for the count. The people of the Seychelles are black as were all three of our volunteers. The second match featured another seaman, this one from the Operations Department. Having the advantage of watching the first match, he managed to run around the ring for over a minute before his opponent caught him and knocked him down for the count.

Next up was Seaman Goode, from my First Division. Goode was not very big and it looked like the guy he was up against outweighed him by at least ten pounds, all of it muscle.

A few weeks earlier I had been standing the 20-24 watch on the bridge underway and Seaman Goode was back on the fantail as After Lookout near the end of the watch. He had called up to the bridge to the phone talker on the sound-powered phones saying "something was back there." The phone talker told me he sounded scared.

I picked up the handset and said, "Seaman Goode, what's the matter?"

"I don't know, something's back here. I keep seeing it."

"You see another ship, a light?" We had nothing on radar.

"No, I don't know what it is, but something's here."

"OK, hold on, I'll send Miller back." Petty Officer Third Class Miller was Boatswain Mate of the Watch and responsible for rotating the lookouts and phone talkers. Miller came back about five minutes later.

"Sir, I didn't see anything but Goode is scared shitless. He thinks it's a ghost or something."

Shortly thereafter my relief came to the bridge and relieved me for the midwatch. Normally the OOD would be the last in his section to go below but I asked him to go ahead and take the deck so I could go check on Goode. It was a little before midnight as I walked back to the fantail myself. It was an overcast night in the Indian Ocean and the stars were not out. I came around the missile magazine and there was Goode, standing in the middle of the fantail with his sound-powered phones on, his binoculars hanging around his neck, and holding a broom up in the air by the handle with both hands. Every few seconds or so he would dodge left or right and swing the broom through the air while looking up and aft like he was in a sword fight with a giant.

I soon saw what he saw. A big seagull was following the ship and every few seconds it would pass through the illumination of the stern light, just barely ghosting through and only visible for a split second before disappearing into the darkness. Then it would drift through again. It *was* kind of spooky.

I went up and tapped Goode on the shoulder and he almost clobbered me with the broom when he spun around, wild-eyed.

"Goode, it's just a seagull, he's following the ship. He won't hurt you."

"You sure?"

"Yeah, nothing to worry about. You gonna be OK until your relief gets here?" The rest of the watch was in the process of turning over.

"I don't know. I don't like it."

I stayed back there a few minutes more until Goode's relief showed up and we told him what to watch for.

So this was the Seaman Goode who stepped into the ring for *SEMMES* boxing match number three. He had the same look on his face as when the seagull was scaring him. After watching what had happened to his two shipmates, Goode had a plan. The crowd was screaming for blood. Goode went out to the middle, tapped gloves with his opponent and then bounced back into a crouch with both gloves up in front of his face. His opponent shot out a jab, just to see what would happen, and Goode went down in a heap. Fight over. New record. Five, maybe six second knockout.

The next night, our last in the Seychelles, the British Royal Navy contingent on the island hosted the wardroom for a little party at the club which was to be my farewell party. I would be leaving the ship in the Persian Gulf and it was thought that we should do it now when we had a good opportunity rather than wait.

We left the Seychelles on the 8th of March and sailed north through the Indian Ocean and North Arabian Sea to the Strait of Hormuz. In 1976, the Iranian Revolution was three years away and Iran, under the Shah, Mohammad Reza Shah Pahlavi, was a staunch ally of the United States. Iran purchased military equipment from the United States and sent its officers to be trained at U.S. military schools and institutions. The engineering schools of the finest colleges and universities in America were full of Iranian students. Iran played an important role in the geo-strategic game, as a buffer between the Soviet Union to the north and its long held desire to have access to a warm weather port. Iran, Pakistan, Afghanistan and India lay between the Soviet Union and access to the warm waters of the Persian Gulf, North Arabian Sea and Indian Ocean.

Our first stop was in Bandar Abbas, the main Iranian naval port just north of the Strait of Hormuz. We tied up at a pier in the naval base and the Captain made all the standard official calls on the senior Iranian naval officers. Later that day, the Captain, XO and Operations Officer attended a briefing for an exercise we would begin the next day with the Iranian Navy.

That night we were taken by bus to a reception ashore at an elaborate officer's club off the base for a cocktail reception. I remember looking out the bus window at the great amount of construction of modern looking buildings and facilities surrounded by dingy brown undeveloped land and shanty-like mud huts, and thinking to myself that Iran was buying its way into the 20th century with oil money. The juxtaposition of horse or donkey-drawn carts and modern, fancy, cars, trucks and busses made for a strange picture. Many of the structures were elaborate monuments that served no obvious function other than as a grandiose symbol of the affluence of the Iranian regime.

The reception was elaborate, with lots of food and free-flowing wine and beer. Although Iran is a Muslim country, the rules were not as strictly enforced among the officer elite as they were in Saudi Arabia. This was particularly true of the Iranian Navy which had modeled itself after the British Royal Navy, right down to the uniforms and rank insignia. We chatted casually with the Iranian naval officers who included among them their frigate, corvette, patrol boat and oiler officers as well as pilots from their F-4 Phantom, F-14 Tomcat, and P-3 Orion squadrons.

The next morning, we set sail along with a small flotilla of Iranian ships including their *SABALAN* class frigates, small missile patrol boats and their oiler for an exercise in the Persian Gulf. This was to be my last underway aboard *SEMMES* as I was scheduled to depart the ship during our next port of call in Bushehr, Iran. We sailed north, finishing the Hormuz transit up past Qeshm Island, the Tunb Islands and Abu Musa and Sirri Islands and out into the central gulf. We conducted maneuvering drills and gunnery using the U.S. ATP-1A Signal Book. The Iranians were professional and good, aggressive, shiphandlers.

The evening of March 14th, the commodore of the Iranian flotilla came to *SEMMES* in his flagship's Zodiac boat to have dinner in the wardroom. He was dressed in a blue uniform with a British-style Navy sweater featuring captain's rank shoulder boards in the British Royal Navy style. During dinner he was very engaging and told us that he was a distant nephew of the Shah. After dinner he went back to the fantail to board the Zodiac, and instead of taking the pilot ladder we had rigged and climbing down, he threw his legs over the lifelines and jumped the 12 feet into the Zodiac! He landed in a sitting position on the air filled cross-seat amidships, gave a big smile and a wave and they took off back to his ship. We were shaking our heads at this display of bravado.

That night we took on fuel from the Iranian oiler and again they were very professional on the rigs for an alongside refueling evolution which included a 90-degree course change while the refueling rigs were hooked up. They executed this difficult maneuver as well as any U.S. Navy ship would have. All of the signals and procedures were in strict accordance with the U.S. Navy way of doing things. It was obvious that years of training with the U.S. Navy had paid off.

On the morning of the 15th, we pulled into Bushehr, Iran for a two-day port visit where I was scheduled to leave the ship to return to the states for my next assignment as an officer recruiter at Navy Recruiting District, Atlanta. Bushehr was a crummy looking city and the harbor area was particularly dingy despite being the chief commercial seaport in Iran. As we approached the pier we saw a dead camel floating in the harbor.

To meet the ship, in addition to the normal foreign port bureaucrats, was the Naval Attaché from the U.S. Embassy in Tehran, Commander Norm Haack. His job for the day, once the formalities with the Captain and XO were complete, was to get me clearance to leave the country and return to the states. It sounded simple enough but turned out not to be the case. I will always be grateful to him for what he went through that day. The issue was that in order to clear customs in Tehran I had to have an entry stamp in my passport for coming into the country. Otherwise I could be deemed to have entered the country illegally when I tried to leave. It sounded simple since it was no secret that I was entering on a U.S. Navy ship. It was anything but. Commander Haack and I, both dressed in Service Dress Blue uniform, spent the entire day going from government building to government building trying to get someone to take responsibility for stamping my passport for entry into the country. Nobody would do it. We kept getting directed to yet another office where we were told the right person worked. All the Iranians spoke English, so I could follow the conversation except when Commander Haack had to resort to Farsi. Nobody seemed willing to make the bold move of checking me into the country by stamping my passport.

Finally, about 4 o'clock in the afternoon we ended up back in the port about a quarter-mile from the ship. We entered a dingy office on one of the piers that was right out of a spaghetti western. Adobe walls, a shabby roof, very drab inside with a slowly turning ceiling fan and a single light bulb hanging from the ceiling on a wire. One or two small windows let in a little light. A dumpy looking official in some kind of police-type uniform with a great big bushy mustache stood up behind the single desk in the middle of the room when we entered. Commander Haack said something to him in Farsi, there was a brief back and forth, and the guy reached into a desk drawer, pulled out the stamp and stamped my passport. I was officially in Iran.

I spent my last night on *SEMMES* packing my two suitcases and saying goodbye to all my shipmates. I was issued my airline tickets which had been arranged through the Embassy and paid for by the Navy, and on March 16th was driven to the Bushehr airport and put on an Air Iran flight to Tehran. We landed once in Esfahan about halfway between Bushehr and Tehran to let off and pick up passengers and refuel and then continued on to Tehran. I was traveling in my Service Dress Blue Uniform, as I would the next day in accordance with the instructions from the Embassy. I felt a little conspicuous but nobody bothered me.

We landed in Tehran at Mehrabad International Airport about 4:00 PM and I took a taxi to the hotel which had been arranged by the Embassy. I don't remember what I paid, but the next morning when I took another taxi back to the airport I realized that the first driver had gouged me, charging twice what it cost to go back to the airport. As in Bandar Abbas, Tehran had lots of construction underway and many modern buildings and grandiose statues and monuments. We passed through Shahr Park which had a very large St. Louis Arch-looking monument in the center. The streets were thronging with people who seemed to be in a celebratory mood. I asked the driver what was going on and he told me it was the Persian New Year. When we arrived at the hotel and I checked in, the streets were full of people and I heard the occasional explosion outside which I assumed were firecrackers but could have been gunshots–who knew? I stayed in my room that night and ordered a sandwich and a beer for dinner.

The next morning, I put the uniform on again and caught the half-price taxi back to the airport. I was booked on an Aer Lingus flight to Heathrow in London followed by an American Airlines flight to New York JFK, then down to Charleston where Iris, Chris and Amy would be waiting for me. There was some kind of problem with the flights that day and my flight was delayed. The terminal was very crowded and I found a group of Americans, mostly expatriate oil workers, and hung around with them until the flight was called. I saw my first close up of Soviet Army soldiers in the terminal, dressed in heavy khaki-colored overcoats and their ridiculously large flying-saucer looking hats. The rest of the trip was uneventful. Arriving in Charleston on the 18th, I rejoined the family to pack out and move to Atlanta for my recruiting duty tour.

I had spent three and half years on sea duty on two ships and seen a lot of the world already. I had also been fairly lucky in terms of not spending long periods away from home. Despite an active underway schedule on both *NEWPORT NEWS* and *SEMMES*, I had caught only the tail end of the Vietnam deployment, done a short Northern Europe cruise in *NEWPORT NEWS,* and only the first half of a six-month Middle East Force deployment in *SEMMES*. Now I was headed for two years of shore duty in Atlanta. I still did not know how much longer I would stay in the Navy, but I did know that I was enjoying what I was doing. I found the adventure of sailing at sea and visiting foreign ports to be both exciting and fun, and experienced a great deal of satisfaction in doing my duties well and working with and leading sailors. Some decisions lay ahead. I had fulfilled my contractual obligation to the Navy and could resign any time I wanted. By accepting the orders to Navy Recruiting District Atlanta, I had committed to two more years on active duty. I would play it by ear and decide what to do later.

CHAPTER 7

Department Head

My assignment to Navy Recruiting District (NRD) Atlanta began with a three week Recruiting Officer Management Orientation (ROMO) course conducted at Naval Air Station Pensacola. Iris's parents, Norm and Mae Stutzer, had retired to Pensacola in a house that Norm had very astutely built on a lot on Perdido Bay that he bought in the 60s while stationed at Eglin Air Force Base in the Florida panhandle. Norm had retired in 1972 as an Air Force lieutenant colonel after 30 years in the Army Air Corps during World War II and then the U.S. Air Force after it was created in 1947. A World War II B-17 bombardier-navigator, Norm had been shot down on his 13th mission over Germany, on February 4, 1944. He spent the last 15 months of the war in a German POW camp, Stalag Luft One, before being liberated by the Soviet Army.

I joined NRD Atlanta in the Officer Programs Office and served for three years of enjoyable shore duty. I was responsible for recruiting college graduates into the Nuclear Power, Surface Warfare, Supply Corps, and Civil Engineer Corps programs. Having screened for department head, I knew that at the end of this tour I would be returning to sea duty as a department head on a destroyer or frigate class ship. While recruiting I managed to get my younger brother Steve selected for the Aviation Officer Candidate program after making sure he passed the test. Steve went on to fly the A-7 Corsair and F/A-18 Hornet before leaving the Navy and being hired by Northwest Airlines. It was during those three years in Atlanta that Iris and I discussed my leaving the Navy to pursue a civilian career. Although there were temptations, including the potential for a salary greater than the $15,000 a year I earned as a lieutenant, in the end we agreed I should continue in the Navy. I missed the excitement of going to sea. I ended up serving over three years at NRD Atlanta and for the last year was the Officer Programs Officer, or OPO, with the other officers reporting to me. We sold our house and left Atlanta in July of 1979 to move to Newport, Rhode Island where I would begin Department Head training in Class 63.

I checked into the Surface Warfare Officer's School (SWOS) on the 4th of September 1979, and we moved into base housing in the Melville Housing area up the Narragansett Bay from the Naval Education and Training Center. When class began on the 24th, I was assigned to Section 3 of Class 63, a group of about 30 officers, mostly lieutenants, with one lieutenant (junior grade) and one lieutenant commander in the class. Several of my classmates would become career-long and lifelong friends and our paths would cross many times over the years. In this overall class of 100 officers, only two of us would make it to flag rank. We soon nicknamed our section "The Leper Colony" after the misfits in the movie *12 O'Clock High* which we were required to watch as part of our leadership training.

A number of significant world events occurred during our time in Newport which would have a lasting impact on our lives in the years to come. On December 24, 1979, the Soviet 40th Army invaded Afghanistan, ostensibly to support the Marxist-Leninist government of the Democratic Republic of Afghanistan against the Afghan Mujahedeen guerilla movement and foreign "Afghan-Arab" volunteers. Although it meant little to us in Newport, the invasion and nine-year Soviet occupation would have far reaching implications and was one of the keys to the eventual downfall of the Soviet Union and the end of the Cold War.

On the morning of Friday, April 25, 1980, I awoke to the radio alarm clock and realized that something significant was happening. Instead of the usual music or local weather and traffic reports, a serious voice was describing a tragedy somewhere. Listening, I learned that an attempt to rescue the 52 American hostages held at the U.S. Embassy in Tehran had failed and that lives had been lost. The details came out slowly as the day wore on and the magnitude of what had happened was the topic of conversation throughout the next several days. The Shah of Iran had fled into exile in January 1979 in what was known as the Iranian Revolution. Within two weeks, the Ayatollah Ruhollah Khomeini, a powerful Muslim cleric, returned from exile as the leader of the revolution. By February 11th, troops loyal to the Shah had been overwhelmed. On April 1, 1979 Iran voted by national referendum to become an Islamic Republic. On November 4, 1979, the American Embassy in Tehran had been overrun and 52 Americans were being held hostage. This rescue attempt, Operation Eagle Claw, was a bold move on the part of the Carter Administration, and had it succeeded, the presidency of Jimmy Carter might have been judged altogether differently.

I thought about my time in Iran and about the naval officers with whom we had socialized ashore and operated at sea, particularly the commodore who had been a distant nephew of the Shah. How many of them had survived? How many had gone over to the other side?

In February of 1980, Class 63 received our Navy orders. This was a highly charged event. Up until then, we all took the same courses, but once we knew whether we were going to be either a Chief Engineer, Weapons Officer, or Operations officer on our next ship, we were divided into specialty tracks. As important as which job we were assigned was what kind of ship and where was it homeported. In keeping with my "dream sheet" philosophy, I had requested, in order, homeporting in Mayport, Florida; San Diego, California; and Pearl Harbor, Hawaii. I had asked for either a Weapons Officer or Operations Officer billet, not wanting to be a Chief Engineer. Likewise running for the comfort of what I knew best, I asked for, in order, *ADAMS* class guided missile destroyer, *SPRUANCE* class destroyer, and *OLIVER HAZARD PERRY* class guided missile frigate.

In 1980, the newest and most capable surface ships were *SPRUANCE* class destroyers and *OLIVER HAZARD PERRY* class frigates. There were also four *KIDD* class guided missile destroyers. These were four of the *SPRUANCE* class that had been specially built for Iran before the Shah fell. In addition to the normal complement of weapons, the *KIDD* class had MK-26 guided missile launchers which made them the top of the line destroyer of the day. All of us in 1980 would go to destroyers or frigates. My combined first choices came out to be an *ADAMS* class DDG out of Mayport, Florida as Weapons Officer and that was exactly where I was assigned in *USS TATTNALL (DDG-19)*. I was comfortable with that class of ship and with the Weapons Department from my time in *SEMMES*. I had also wanted to get to Mayport for the good weather and to be closer to family for both Iris and myself. I was happy.

I departed Jacksonville the 3rd of September 1980 on a commercial air flight to join *TATTNALL* when she was scheduled to pull into Roosevelt Roads, Puerto Rico. On the 5th of September I was standing on the pier when *TATTNALL* sailed into the harbor. Commander Paul Tobin was my new CO and he became a mentor and supporter throughout my career. As Weapons Officer I was responsible for all the combat systems, the TARTAR guided missiles and MK-13 single arm launcher, the two 5-inch/54 gun mounts, the ASROC launcher and associated ASROC and nuclear depth charges, the MK-32 anti-submarine torpedoes and launchers, the ship's SQS-23 sonar system and of course the gun and missile fire control directors and computers. I was also responsible for the Deck Gang and all the seamanship equipment; anchors, mooring gear, underway replenishment gear, life rafts, and ship's boats.

The next day we had an officers versus chiefs softball game which we won in a close contest, and where I was introduced to Electrician's Mate Chief Charles "Skipper" Deas. I mention Skipper Deas because he became a lifelong friend and was at every major event in my Navy career over the years. From Winter Haven, Florida, he was a dedicated Florida Gator fan, but I turned him into a Florida State Seminole fan; one of my better recruiting efforts. The success of the Seminoles under coach Bobby Bowden might have also had something to do with his conversion.

TATTNALL spent the remaining three months of 1980 in work-up training for a Middle East Force deployment scheduled for early January 1981. We were in and out of port all fall, including a port visit to Fort Lauderdale, ASW training in the Tongue of the

Ocean at Andros Island in the Bahamas, and local Jacksonville Operations Area evolutions as we checked off the pre-deployment events. I was enjoying the ship and the crew and Paul Tobin was a good boss.

In early December, we headed south to Roosevelt Roads again for COMPTUEX 1-81 (Comprehensive Training Unit Exercise) which was our graduation event before deploying in January. The Officer Conducting the Exercise (OCE) was Rear Admiral Hank Mustin, Commander Cruiser-Destroyer Group 2, a hard charging Surface Warfare Officer from a famous naval family. The key event for *TATTNALL* was to be a missile shoot on the Atlantic Fleet Weapons Training Facility (AFWTF) range against radio controlled drone targets. All of our missiles had live warheads and telemetry gear installed so that the shots could be reconstructed and evaluated as to whether they were successes or failures. Obviously, a shot down drone was a success, but it took the telemetry data to determine which ship scored the hit when several were shooting at the same target. *TATTNALL* was allocated six missiles that day; a high number.

Admiral Mustin put six ships in a column at 500 yards spacing and ordered up 25 knots; his goal was to make this missile shoot as realistic as possible. In a real engagement against enemy aircraft or missiles, nobody would be poking around at five knots. We had a great day on the range, with five of six of our missiles being evaluated as successful shots. The one failure was caused by a faulty seeker head slew. When the seeker head slewed to the position that the fire control computer told it to look for the return from the fire control director, it slewed to the wrong angle. Receiving no homing signal from the director, it flew stupidly until the self-destruct criteria were achieved and it blew up. In a couple of cases our missile arrived after somebody else's, but the telemetry data showed ours would have knocked out the target had it arrived a split second earlier. The last shot was at night and Paul Tobin allowed the fire controlmen responsible for the SPG-51 fire control directors to pull the trigger in casualty mode from the radar room. I thought this was a gutsy thing to do with all the ships being evaluated on their performance, but it was great for morale among the crew.

On the 5th of December, the Chief Engineer reported bad vibrations on the starboard shaft which required a return to Roosevelt Roads so that divers could go down the next day and see if they could find the problem; it was believed we might have run through a fishing net which was fouled on the screw and throwing it out of balance. We made the approach on the harbor after dark and I was on the fantail to oversee mooring back aft. Somehow the navigation team and bridge watch became confused and steamed right by the harbor entrance, missing the 90-degree port turn up the channel. I first heard one of the tugs waiting in the channel frantically sounding its whistle, and then I felt the ship begin bouncing and churning as Captain Tobin ordered up an emergency backing bell. We had almost steamed up onto the rocks at 15 knots. The Navigator was subsequently relieved and those duties officially turned over to Lieutenant Commander Denny Zveare, the XO. From that day on I became the permanent Sea Detail OOD.

This was an unexpected port visit and all hands not in the duty section wasted no time going ashore. I was the CDO so stayed aboard. It became a wild night as the crew returned to the ship from the various clubs. I spent a lot of time on the quarterdeck making sure everyone who needed help, got help to get into their racks. Around midnight I was walking up the portside and I noticed two of the monkey lines from the motor whaleboat hanging over the side into the harbor. We were tied up starboard side to the pier. Without thinking about why this had happened, I climbed up into the motor whaleboat and hauled the lines up and coiled them in the bottom of the boat as they should have been. I guess it was my First Lieutenant training kicking in.

About a half an hour later, the word was passed, "Man overboard, port side, away the man overboard detail!" I ran to the port side and looked down into the water. There were two sailors in the harbor alongside the ship, right under the motor whaleboat. Aha, the monkey lines were their planned way of getting back aboard undetected after a midnight swim and I had inadvertently disrupted the plan.

A quick thinking chief grabbed a fire hose from a fire station and lowered it over the side and we hauled them both aboard. They were both completely naked. One of them, Operations Specialist Second Class Badley, tried to run for it up the port side, even though we all knew who he was and there was no place to go. The Chief Master-at-Arms started to chase him up the deck but I grabbed him and said, "Let him go, it's Badley, we know where he lives."

Later when we were back in Mayport, Captain Tobin held Captain's Mast for the two nude midnight swimmers and when he turned to me for my report on the incident I had a hell of a time keeping a straight face.

The next day the divers determined that the starboard fairwater, a metal collar that fits around the shaft where it exits the hull of the ship, had worked its way loose and shimmied down the shaft to ride against the shaft strut which supports the shaft just before the propeller. They removed it and we were back underway that afternoon to rejoin the exercise. We had the fairwater replaced back in Mayport.

On January 12, 1981, *TATTNALL* sailed out of Mayport to begin a six-month Middle East Force deployment to the Persian Gulf. It was a cold, windy day and not many families braved the weather to stand on the pier and wave goodbye. Securing from sea detail and setting the normal underway watch, we headed east to rendezvous with *USS BLAKELY (FF-1072)* a *KNOX* class frigate coming out of Charleston, South Carolina. Iris was on the pier to send me off but both Chris and Amy were in school; we had said our goodbyes the night before. At 9 and 5 respectively, neither one of them seemed particularly upset that Dad was leaving for six months. Because they had been so much younger the last time I had deployed and because I had not been gone a full six months, I don't think they yet fully appreciated how long it would be and what I would miss; beginning with Amy's sixth birthday in a little over two weeks.

We were heading to the Persian Gulf during a tense time in that part of the world. The American hostages were still being held at the American Embassy in Tehran, Iran, having been captured almost two years earlier. Iraq had invaded Iran on September 22, 1980 over a border dispute and fears of a Shia Islam insurgency among Iraq's long suppressed Shia majority, possibly inspired by the Iranian Revolution of 1979. Thus far the war had been largely a land war between the two neighboring countries, but the other Gulf Cooperation Council countries, particularly Saudi Arabia, Bahrain, and Kuwait, were nervous. Saudi Arabia and Bahrain in particular were U.S. allies and feared that the hatred the Iranian government had for the United States could spill over in their direction because of the U.S. Navy presence in Bahrain and the close ties to Saudi Arabia.

After refueling stops in Bermuda and Ponta Delgada in the Azores, we pulled into Rota, Spain for one night and to again refuel and take on stores before entering the Mediterranean Sea. We sailed through the Strait of Gibraltar on January 24th and crossed the Med to arrive at Port Said, Egypt on January 30th to prepare for our Suez Canal transit the next day. While we were refueling in Ponta Delgada on January 20th, we learned that the Iranians had released the 52 American hostages who had been held for 444 days. Of course January 20th was also the day that Ronald Reagan was inaugurated as the 40th President of the United States.

Unlike the first time I had transited the Suez, for this transit we would anchor in the outer harbor and then approach the canal and the city of Port Said around midnight as the lead ship in the convoy. Paul Tobin was senior to the CO of *BLAKELY*, Commander Norm Pattarozzi, so *BLAKELY* would follow astern of us.

I was the sea detail OOD as we approached the anchorage in daylight with the wind blowing about 40 knots and a sandstorm making visibility almost zero. We carefully picked our way through the forest of anchored merchant ships, using radar to avoid ships we couldn't see a mere 300 yards away, and to navigate, which was difficult due to the low, flat coast of Egypt. Because *TATTNALL* would be the lead ship in the southbound convoy we carefully picked our way through the anchorage to a position close to the canal entrance.

Once safely anchored, a boat delivered Vice Admiral William N. Small, Commander, 6th Fleet, responsible for the Mediterranean, who was to ride us through the canal so he could experience what his ships went through during transit. He was to disembark two days later in Sharm el-Sheikh, Egypt, at the foot of the Sinai Peninsula. Admiral Small was very friendly and low maintenance, embarking with only one officer, his Flag Lieutenant, so as not to be too disruptive. I thought to myself that I hoped this transit would go smoother than the one five years earlier in *SEMMES*. Drawing on that experience I made sure that the Weapons Department was ready with the mooring lines, shackles and ready motor whaleboat. I had previously described to Captain Tobin what had happened in *SEMMES*.

Our transit on the night of the 30th and early morning of the 31st was uneventful and about mid-morning the convoy anchored in the Great Bitter Lake to let the northbound convoy pass. Paul Tobin did not get to take the usual two-hour power nap while anchored because he had to entertain Admiral Small at lunch. Consequently, when we exited at Port Suez at the south end of the canal around sunset, he had not slept for about 24 hours and faced an all-night transit south through the Gulf of Suez to the Red Sea in company with a great many ships going both north and south through the narrow Gulf.

He asked me to take the midnight to 0600 watch as OOD for the transit south through the Gulf of Suez and over to Sharm el-Sheikh to drop off Admiral Small. He told me not to wake him unless it was a *real emergency,* just do what I had to do, and gave me permission to sit in his chair as long as I didn't fall asleep. Of course I had been up as long as Captain Tobin so by the time my watch was over I would have been awake for 48 hours with only a couple of catnaps in between. I made it through the night without calling him until 0600 despite having to make a few maneuvers to avoid shipping and cut across the northbound traffic to get to Sharm el-Sheikh. I bet he heard the forced draft blowers change pitch as we speeded up or slowed down, but he stayed in the rack all night and never came to the bridge. I took full advantage of his permission to occupy the Captain's or Executive Officer's chair. Although I can honestly say that I did not sleep, there were several times that my head snapped up after dropping to my chest while I sat in the chair.

One of the amusing events of the canal transit involved one of the Egyptian canal pilots, which all ships are required to use so the government of Egypt can add to the bill. This particular fellow was very garrulous and loved to talk. His favorite topic was the TV show *Dallas* and "who shot JR?" We all knew the answer because the show aired in November 1980, but that episode had not yet aired in Egypt. He correctly guessed it was Kristin but we didn't confirm his guess so as not to ruin the first episode of the next season.

We conducted a Brief Stop for Fuel (BSF) in Djibouti on February 3rd and then headed out to the Indian Ocean towards the tiny coral atoll of Diego Garcia, British Indian Ocean Territories. Djibouti was now an independent country, having been granted independence by France in 1976, shortly after I had last visited on *SEMMES* when we were forced to leave early due to the Somali kidnapping of a school bus.

On the 11th of February, we crossed the equator for my second time. This time I was a Trusty Shellback and not a Slimy Pollywog. Our ceremony in *TATTNALL* was a little tamer than the one on *SEMMES*, but we were still an all-male crew in 1981 and the usual hi-jinks occurred, including the beauty contest. I was once again amazed at the "beauty" of the contestants and the elaborate outfits that had been assembled to impress Davey Jones and his Royal Court.

On the 12th of February, we entered the lagoon at Diego Garcia, a beautiful coral atoll, with crystal clear deep water and a white sand, palm tree-lined shoreline. Since the beginning of the Iran-Iraq war, this part of the Indian Ocean had taken on new importance. In 1981, we were still not operating our aircraft carriers inside the Persian Gulf. The conventional wisdom was that it was too easy to get them bottled up inside the Gulf if something happened to close the Strait of Hormuz. In addition, the restricted waters of the Gulf left little room to fall back in the event of an attack by Iranian forces. Reaction times to high performance aircraft or missiles launched from the Iranian coast would be short and a surprise attack could very well be successful. The United States had equipped the Iranian Air Force in particular with modern aircraft when the Shah was in power; F-4 Phantoms and F-14 Tomcats, as well as P-3 Orion patrol aircraft and SH-3 Sea King helicopters. We had kept an aircraft carrier in the vicinity in the North Arabian Sea since the Iranian hostage crisis at the U.S. Embassy in Tehran had begun. The anchor point, or "MODLOC" was at a point in the North Arabian Sea not so affectionately referred to as "Gonzo Station." It was Groundhog Day almost every day on Gonzo Station. Aircraft were in striking distance of key military facilities in Iran from the North Arabian Sea, particularly the main naval facilities at Bandar Abbas and the airfield at Cha Bahar on the Gulf of Oman.

We tied up alongside the repair ship *USS JASON (AR-8)* anchored in the middle of the lagoon. Alongside *JASON* we could get some repair work done which, in my case, was important because we had a missile shoot in three days for an exercise to be called "Indy Weapons Week" in the waters around Diego Garcia. "Indy" referred to the aircraft carrier *USS INDEPENDENCE (CV-62)* who would participate in the exercise with her airwing. One of our SPG-51 fire control director train amplidyne motors had shorted out and needed to be rewound. In one of the more questionable design decisions, the *ADAMS* class DDGs had the train amplidyne motors in the shaft alleys which were notoriously damp and moist; not the ideal location for electric motors. Chief Electrician's Mate Skipper Deas rose to the occasion and worked tirelessly with the electrical re-wind shop on *JASON* to get the motor rewound and reinstalled in time for us to sail for the exercise.

I really appreciated his efforts and wrote him up for a Navy Achievement Medal in recognition. I think that is where our friendship began to blossom even though he remained a rabid Florida Gator fan.

While visiting *JASON* on business I noticed a picture on the quarterdeck intended to discourage the crew from swimming in the lagoon. The picture had been taken from the quarterdeck at night with the accommodation ladder rigged and a bright spotlight shining down on the lower platform from the main deck. Tied up to the accommodation ladder platform was a 26-foot motor whaleboat. Silhouetted under the motor whaleboat was a giant hammerhead shark, caught in the spotlight from the deck. His head protruded beyond one end of the motor whaleboat and his tail beyond the other. He had to be 28-30 feet long. There was no Photoshop in those days so I had to think it was real.

We sailed on the 15th for Indy Weapons Week and that afternoon we had two successful missile shots against a drone target launched from the deck of another ship. The SPG-51's and train amplidyne motors worked just fine. The next day we received word that two aircraft from *INDEPENDENCE* had collided in midair and we were directed to the area for a search and rescue mission. We came into an area with a film of aviation fuel on the water and the smell that accompanied it along with small pieces of debris. Captain Tobin stopped the ship and ordered the motor whaleboat lowered to pick up whatever debris we could find for the investigation while the ship maneuvered in the vicinity to look for survivors. I was not on watch at the time so I hopped in the motor whaleboat as the Boat Officer, along with Boatswain Mate First Class Teddy Skalecki as the senior enlisted.

We were informed by the carrier that an F-4 Phantom and A-7 Corsair, both from *INDEPENDENCE,* had collided, the F-4 flying up into the underside of the A-7. The A-7 pilot had parachuted to safety and been picked up by another ship. We weren't sure whether we were in the vicinity of where the A-7 went in or the F-4. Some grizzly body parts began to float to the surface; small pieces of human flesh no bigger than my hand. We scooped them out of the water and bagged them. Then we found a piece of a flight suit with "VF" on a torn patch so we knew it was the F-4. The squadron number had been torn away.

I ended up out in the motor whaleboat for about three hours picking up what we could until it began to get dark. The search was called off and the crew of the F-4, a pilot and Radar Intercept Officer, or RIO, were presumed killed. The A-7 pilot had seen no parachutes on his way down and it was assumed that the F-4 had come up under the A-7 cockpit to belly.

Three weeks later when we arrived in Bahrain for the first time and picked up mail, I received a letter from Iris in which she told me that one of the guys in my brother Steve's Aviation Officer Candidate School class, an F-4 RIO named Mike Dellamorretta, had been killed in a midair collision in the Indian Ocean and Steve was going to go to Norfolk for the memorial service. Steve was at the time assigned to VA-82, flying A-7's at NAS Cecil Field in Jacksonville. Mike Dellamorretta had eaten Thanksgiving dinner at our house the previous November. He was probably only about 26 years old. I was really shaken for a while, thinking through the fact that I had been out in the middle of the Indian Ocean picking up body parts of someone I had known and who had been a guest at my house. What had been only unpleasant became emotionally disturbing.

We spent three days after Indy Weapons Week at Gonzo Station in the North Arabian Sea, escorting *INDEPENDENCE*, and then detached to enter the Persian Gulf, transiting the Strait of Hormuz on February 28th. We proceeded directly to something called "Radar Picket Station" in the central Persian Gulf. The Middle East Force had established the Radar Picket Station to reassure the Saudis and Bahrainis that we were there to support them against a potential attack from Iran.

A guided missile ship assigned to radar picket duty had two primary functions. The Persian Gulf is about 600 miles long and runs northwest at the Iran - Iraq border to southeast at the Strait of Hormuz. Middle East Force had set up a steaming line about 50 miles long running along that northwest to southeast axis between two points labeled "Surf" to the north and "Turf" to the south. Surf and Turf were centered between Bahrain and Iran which provided coverage to both Bahrain and Saudi Arabia. The two main jobs of the picket ship were to be ready to shoot down an Iranian jet making an attack on either Bahrain or Saudi Arabia, and to provide electronic warfare identification of Iranian aircraft operating over Iran or the Gulf and provide it to the U.S. Air Force Airborne Warning and Control System (AWACS) flying an orbit over Saudi territory. Both the United States and Saudi Arabia had AWACS aircraft and the missions were flown by a mixed crew of U.S. and Saudi airmen. The AWACS has a sophisticated air search radar mounted on top of a Boeing 707 airframe, but in 1981 it had no Electronic Warfare (EW) gear to identify the radar targets it detected. *TATTNALL* and other Navy combatant ships were equipped with the SLQ-32 Electronic Warfare system which was loaded with a library of radar characteristics to enable the operator to identify a radar contact by correlating the radar signal from the contact with the radar picture in the AWACS or own ship radars.

The Radar Picket Ship mission called for steaming slowly back and forth between Surf and Turf, watching the Iranian air activity to the east, and correlating the EW information with the AWACS flying the orbit. We stood six hour watches as TAO in CIC. Typically, the AWACS, flying at 20,000 feet, would spot an air track as soon as it left the ground, normally in Bushehr, and we would pick up the electronic signature and identify it as an F-4, F-14, P-3, or commercial aircraft and pass that information to the AWACS. *TATTNALL* was not equipped with the Naval Tactical Data System (NTDS) data link so all of this was done by voice over secure radio circuits.

I got a kick out of the fact that our Operations Specialists doing all the talking with the AWACS were typically seamen or junior petty officers while the Air Force officers in the AWACS were mostly captains and majors. On slow nights short conversations would sometimes occur and the Air Force officers were surprised that they were dealing so professionally with junior enlisted Navy sailors.

The rest of March we performed radar picket duty broken only by brief stops for fuel at Sitrah Anchorage in Bahrain. On April 12th we learned of the first space shuttle launch, *COLUMBIA*, from Cape Canaveral. In those days there was no way to get live video so it was several weeks later that we received the tapes which showed *COLUMBIA* blasting off into the Florida sky; it was impressive. This event would come to have some significance for us later in the cruise.

Following a two-week maintenance period in Bahrain we sailed up the coast on May 10th to Dammam, Saudi Arabia, a major commercial port just 40 miles to the north. On the 12th of May the local American expatriates, mainly working in the oil industry, threw a party for the wardroom which reminded me of the party in Jeddah I had attended when on *SEMMES*; complete with the moonshine "clear" and "brown" liquor. We were back underway the next day for more picket duty but nearing the end of our time in the Gulf. We stopped for fuel in Bahrain one more time and then headed for the southern Gulf and a transit of the Strait of Hormuz. The night of the 17th, as we were steaming toward Hormuz, my roommate, Lieutenant Paul Susalla, and I sat on the ASROC deck on the weight benches and smoked cigars while we watched the oil rigs in the gulf slip by, the flames from the burn-off lighting the night sky. It was nice to think that we were heading home. *TATTNALL* sailed down the eastern coast of the Arabian Peninsula, through the Gulf of Aden and into Djibouti again to refuel on May 22nd and then north through the Red Sea and Gulf of Suez to arrive at Port Suez, Egypt on the 25th for the Suez Canal transit the next day.

We transited the Suez Canal uneventfully until we entered the new eastern channel that covers the last 9 miles before the Mediterranean and avoids the city of Port Said. As we were sailing along in the middle of the channel we felt a "thump." The Chief Engineer called the Captain on the bridge and reported vibrations on the starboard shaft. I was not on watch so I went down to after steering and listened. The screw was making a weird swishing sound that I had never heard before from after steering. We checked the fathometer trace and sure enough, we had apparently hit something lying on the bottom in the middle of the channel; our track showed that we had not strayed outside the channel. We guessed that we had either hit something like a large container that had fallen off a ship, or more likely, a large cement block used to anchor the channel marker buoys that possibly had moved into the channel during a storm. Whatever it was, it was big enough to show up on the fathometer trace and solid enough to damage a propeller.

Captain Tobin reported the incident to the staff at 6th Fleet as, having cleared the Suez Canal and entered the Mediterranean, we had shifted operational commanders from COMIDEASTFOR to 6th Fleet. Shortly thereafter we received an action message from 6th Fleet which directed the ship to bypass our one homeward bound, or OUTCHOP, port visit in Malaga, Spain, and proceed to Naples, Italy where divers would inspect for damage. Paul Tobin successfully fought this direction, maintaining that the crew had not had one decent liberty port the entire cruise (Bahrain was OK, but it *was* the Middle East) and we deserved the visit in Malaga. Finally, 6th Fleet agreed to send the divers to Malaga and look at the damage there.

On Monday the 1st of June, we pulled into the picturesque port of Malaga on the southern coast of Spain, the Costa del Sol, for a one-week liberty port visit. We entered the well-protected but tight harbor with its stone seawall and tied up at a pier. Waiting for the ship were Iris and Lynne Tobin who had flown over from Jacksonville to meet the ship. This was the first time Iris had the opportunity to come visit me on a cruise. Iris's parents, Norm and Mae Stutzer, had come over from Pensacola to Jacksonville to stay with Chris, 9, and Amy, 6.

We had a wonderful week touring the southern Spanish coast and seeing the sights of Malaga. We sampled the Spanish cuisine and wines and I put my high school Spanish to use in ordering, "Dos cervezas, muy frio, por favor." We spent some good times with Paul and Lynne Tobin who loaned us their rental car for one day to cruise down the coastal road to Marbella. In those days on lieutenant pay (I was a frocked lieutenant commander) a rental car was stretching the budget a bit too much. While we were in Malaga, the 6th Fleet staff dispatched the *USS EDENTON (ATS-1)* with her divers to inspect the starboard screw where they found a big bend at the tip of one of the blades. Using underwater cutting torches, they cut the bent over section off and smoothed it out as best they could. The ship would be entering the Philadelphia Naval Shipyard for a Complex Overhaul in the fall and the propeller was planned to be replaced then. The additional ship noise, undesirable in an ASW environment, would be of little consequence for the trip across the Atlantic and the limited operations between this cruise and the arrival in the shipyard.

We said goodbye to Iris and Lynne and sailed out of Malaga on the 7th of June, through the Strait of Gibraltar and into the Atlantic that evening in company with *USS BLAKELY* who had visited Barcelona. Also on the 7th of June we learned of an Israeli air attack on the Osirak nuclear power plant in Iraq. We wondered if this was going to ratchet up tensions in the Mediterranean and whether we might be turned around as a show of support to Israel. That did not happen as, publicly, the United States condemned the "unprovoked" attack while secretly approving of it.

We stopped again at Ponta Delgada in the Azores to refuel and then headed to our next stop in Bermuda some 2,200 miles to the west. About two hundred miles west of the Azores, we came across a huge tank-like object floating end-up in the ocean. We stopped the ship and put the motor whaleboat in the water to investigate. The Boat Officer radioed back that this big cylinder was about 15 feet in diameter and although about ten feet was sticking out of the water, he couldn't tell how long it was because it disappeared into the depths. We guessed that it might be a liquefied natural gas container, or some other topside tank that had washed off a ship in a storm.

Captain Tobin called Captain Patarozzi on *BLAKELY* and said, "Let's sink it, it's a hazard to navigation." We recovered the motor whaleboat, manned gunnery stations, put *BLAKELY* in column astern of us and sailed by this thing at about a mile to take it under fire with 5-inch guns. Hitting a target one mile away on such a low trajectory while it is bobbing up and down on the ocean swells is harder than it sounds. We fired about 40 rounds of live ammunition, landing all around it before we hit it. Usually we overshot, the round passing overhead as the tank dropped into a trough. When we did hit it, BOOM! it disappeared.

Years later I was working for Paul Tobin in the Pentagon when he was a rear admiral and I was a commander and he said, "You remember that big tank we sunk in the Atlantic?"

"Of course."

"Well, I think I figured out what it was. It could have been one of the solid rocket fuel boosters from the space shuttle that drops off into the Atlantic after launch from Cape Canaveral."

It made sense. They don't always recover them; sometimes they are destroyed on impact and sink. One could have survived, half filled with water, and drifted two-thirds of the way across the Atlantic.

On the 18th of June we returned to Mayport and homecoming with the families. Of course Iris had been with me in Malaga so it wasn't as though we hadn't seen each other for six months; but it was great to be home for a while with Chris and Amy.

On July 10, 1981, Commander Paul Tobin was relieved of command of *TATTNALL* by Commander Pete Deutermann. Paul Tobin had been a great CO, demanding but fair, and willing to have a little fun when the time was right. I learned a great deal from him about how to probe for details when the officers, chief petty officers, and petty officers were trying to explain something or lobby for a certain course of action. He asked good questions without demeaning the person making his case or implying a lack of trust. I tried to use his leadership style as an example throughout the rest of my career. The new CO and the XO who had taken over in the Gulf would take the ship through our upcoming complex overhaul at Philadelphia Naval Shipyard.

This was to be a 15-month Complex Overhaul during which *TATTNALL* would become one of only three *ADAMS* class destroyers with the Naval Tactical Data System (NTDS) which allows for the real time sharing of radar pictures among all ships in the link. We would also have the Harpoon surface to surface missile system installed. It was a permanent change of station move so all the married personnel in the crew were authorized to move their families to Philadelphia at government expense. I was under orders to detach at the end of February 1982 and return to Mayport where I would be the Combat Systems Officer at Destroyer Squadron 8. For that reason, Iris and the kids would remain in our house in Jacksonville while I was in Philadelphia. That six months of separation while only 850 miles away up the coast would prove to be worse than a six-month deployment 7,000 miles away in the Persian Gulf.

I moved into the BOQ which was old and rundown and although I had my own room, I shared a bathroom with an officer in the next room who was on the aircraft carrier *USS SARATOGA (CV-60)*, also in drydock. On duty nights I slept on the berthing barge with the rest of the duty section as well as the poor young sailors who were single or geographical bachelors and had no place else to live.

The shipyard environment is unpleasant. It is dirty and noisy, the ship is being torn apart and is crawling with civilian shipyard workers. The ship's crew has to maintain responsibility for the work in their spaces and keep up with the overall progress of the overhaul. While many of the sailors enjoy the fact that they aren't getting underway, morale normally dips in the shipyard. *TATTNALL* was no exception.

Early on in the yard period I was informed that the Weapons Department and the Operations Department were to be merged into the Combat Systems Department for the duration of the overhaul and I was to be the Combat Systems Officer. Over half the crew and two-thirds of the ship would be my responsibility. The Operations Officer would be assigned as the Overhaul Coordinator. The Ops Officer took it pretty hard as he was losing his Operations

Officer responsibilities. The NTDS installation was important and required a major rip-out and rebuild of CIC as well as the installation of a new computer system. All of that would normally be the Operations Officer's responsibility. Now it was mine and he was in charge of mounds of paperwork keeping track of overhaul progress.

During my time in the shipyard I completed studying for and passed the Command Qualification Examination, one of the steps required in order to qualify for command of a U.S. Navy ship. It was a four hour, timed exam and I took it in the Captain's cabin on the berthing barge. The exam was then mailed off to BuPers with the CO certifying that he had proctored the test. I found out some weeks later that I had passed. Also, on October 1, 1981, I was officially promoted to lieutenant commander and began drawing O-4 pay.

CHAPTER 8

Staff Puke

O n the 25ᵗʰ of March, 1982, I reported to the Destroyer Squadron 8 staff to relieve Lieutenant Commander Jimmy Jackson as Combat Systems Officer, or CSO. This was my department head "split" tour and a job for which I had actively campaigned. My orders were helped along by Paul Tobin who had recommended me to the detailing shop and sung my praises to the incoming Commodore, Captain Mike Kalleres.

COMDESRON 8 was a relatively new organization, Jimmy Jackson was the first CSO, stood up to serve as the Readiness Squadron for the new class of *OLIVER HAZARD PERRY (FFG-7)* guided missile frigates. This assignment was positive from a family standpoint. It meant we could stay in the house we had purchased two years earlier, and it gave Iris and the kids some stability when it came to friends and school.

DESRON 8 was a growing squadron as new *PERRY* class frigates came off the building ways and entered the fleet. When I arrived in March of 1982, we had responsibility for eight ships; by the time I left almost two years later we had 16. The *PERRY* class frigates were the Navy's newest class of surface warships and therefore highly desirable for command and other officer positions. They were single screw, LM2500 gas turbine powered, had a guided missile system with the SM-1 surface to air missile, Harpoon anti-ship cruise missiles, MK-32 anti-submarine torpedoes, a 76mm Oto Melara gun, and the Vulcan Phalanx Close-In Weapon System (CIWS) for anti-missile defense. They were NTDS equipped and carried helicopters. The earliest versions were built with a helicopter deck that could not handle the bigger SH-60B Seahawk Light Airborne Multipurpose System (LAMPS) helicopters which were being introduced to the fleet, carrying the older SH-2 Seasprite LAMPS helos. Many *PERRY* class frigates were later backfitted with the elongated flight deck that could handle the bigger SH-60s. This modification was expensive and pretty dumb when you consider that the new ship class and the new helicopter class were being developed at the same time and somehow the designers and decision-makers did not make sure the helos would fit on the ships from day one.

The *OLIVER HAZARD PERRY* class ships were also the result of a school of thought that our Navy could afford to build two different levels of surface combatants; high-end, complex and expensive cruisers and guided missile destroyers, and low end, less capable, but also less expensive, guided missile frigates. The so called Hi-Lo Mix. This decision came at a time when the Navy was aspiring to a goal of 600 frontline ships. With a fleet of that size, the Navy could afford a sizable number of less capable, but also less expensive, surface combatants. Ultimately, the United States Navy built 54 *OLIVER HAZARD PERRY* class frigates with four of that number going to the Australian Navy. As I write this, the Navy seems to be returning to this basic concept for many of the same reasons. The introduction of the Littoral Combat Ship (LCS) mirrors the idea of the need for a less capable, less expensive, lightly armed and minimum-manned surface combatant to augment the top of the line Aegis class destroyers. Fast and shallow draft, the LCS is intended to operate in the littorals and to provide a more size and capability compatible counterpart to the many small, coastal navies with which the U.S. Navy routinely trains and operates.

DESRON 8's responsibilities were several. As the east coast squadron responsible for the fleet introduction of the *PERRY* class, we were charged with refining the processes for maintaining these ships and for accumulating data concerning the effectiveness of the maintenance concept which relied more heavily on shore support than with earlier ship classes. The *PERRY* class had small crews by destroyer-frigate standards and, consequently, much of the maintenance was intentionally planned to be supported by Shore

Intermediate Maintenance Activities (SIMAs). Additionally, for the new ships, we conducted crew certification inspections which were required before they could sail out of the building yard and begin operations. I personally disliked being one of the so called experts to come aboard and help run the ship through its paces. We also conducted the routine administrative inspections required to be done by an outside entity. I generally did my combat systems inspections with the ship CSOs over a cup of coffee in the wardroom. Recalling how I hated some knucklehead staff puke from the squadron coming over to *TATTNALL* and inspecting me, I was determined to be more user-friendly.

The Commodore at DESRON 8 was Captain Mike Kalleres, a real character, but also a fun boss who worked hard to foster high morale on the staff and among the squadron ships. Shortly after I reported aboard, our new Chief Staff Officer, Commander John Berg, checked in. John, a Naval Academy graduate, had been CO of *USS MCINERNEY (FFG-8)*, one of the squadron ships. Commodore Kalleres self-identified himself as the "Lead Husky." The premise was that we were all sled dogs, including the ships in the squadron, and he was leading the way. He had developed a list of "Husky Codes" which were affixed to virtually every message that he sent out to the ships of the squadron. Each ship was required to have a copy of the Husky Codes so that they could break them upon receipt and learn the message, good or bad, that the code conveyed.

My Combat Systems team consisted of a lieutenant and three chief petty officers. Our Material Officer was Lieutenant Commander Hank Sanford who had been Chief Engineer in *OLIVER HAZARD PERRY (FFG-7)* and who had been a classmate of mine at Department Head School. Our Operations/Scheduling Officer was Lieutenant Bob Sweeney, another Naval Academy graduate and a shipmate of Hank's from *OLIVER HAZARD PERRY* as Ship Control Officer. The three of us became fast friends.

This tour in DESRON 8 would prove to be a great deal of fun and involved working with some terrific people and their wives which would result in lasting friendships. Much of the credit goes to Commodore Kalleres and Chief Staff Officer Berg, who had been shipmates years ago in *USS PREBLE (DLG-15)*. They both set a climate of cooperation, fun, and esprit de corps.

In April of 1982, Argentina invaded the Falkland Islands and the British, who claimed the islands and maintained a small contingent of military personnel, put together a task force to recapture the islands. What evolved over the next two months was modern warfare at sea which served as a valuable lesson for the United States Navy. The British prevailed in mid-June, but in the course of the fighting they lost six ships to Argentine 1,000 pound bombs and Exocet missiles. As a result of the British experience, the U.S. Navy accelerated the introduction of the Vulcan Phalanx CIWS and adopted improved damage control procedures. Not least of which was the wearing of "flash gear" in a combat situation to protect against burns. Decorative wood was removed from Navy ships, much like the stripping of ships for combat during World War II.

As I neared the end of my tour in DESRON 8, I began to look around for my next assignment. I was technically eligible for shore duty, although the DESRON 8 tour was, in practice, shore duty. Because career naval officers were expected to get an advanced degree, I investigated the possibility of attending postgraduate school to earn a Master's Degree. I knew that I was unlikely to receive orders to the Naval Postgraduate School in Monterey, California because at FSU I was in a non-technical major and had less than stellar grades. As a lieutenant commander I was also a little long in the tooth for PG School at Monterey.

I discovered a program in Political Science at the University of Florida in Gainesville, and talked to a helicopter pilot who was currently enrolled in the program. He was living in Jacksonville and making the hour and a half drive to Gainesville two or three times a week to attend classes. The Navy was paying his tuition and it was a full time assignment; he had no duties other than to earn his Master's Degree. I bought the study guide, took the Graduate Records Examination (GRE) and applied to Florida, the hated nemesis school of all self-respecting Florida State graduates. I did well on the GRE, went to Gainesville to interview with the head of the department, and by the summer of 1983 had been accepted into the program. The Navy had other ideas.

Instead I received orders to Commander, Cruiser-Destroyer Group 12, also in Mayport, as Flag Secretary. The good news was that we could stay in Mayport for a third consecutive tour and the Flag Sec job was a good one; a "looper" on the two-star admiral's personal staff. The Flag Sec was mainly an administrative position, but of course I would have watchstanding responsibilities when underway on the flagship. COMCRUDESGRU 12 was scheduled to deploy in the spring of 1984 to the Mediterranean aboard the aircraft carrier *USS SARATOGA (CV-60)*, also home ported in Mayport.

Returning to sea duty was fine with me although the University of Florida option would have been a nice alternative. Iris and I were happy to be staying in Jacksonville, the kids were involved in sports and cheerleading, had made good friends, and Iris was working as a picture framer at a small shop in Mandarin. I had bought a boat and Bernie and Sandy Hollenbeck from *SEMMES* days were our next door neighbors.

I reported aboard CRUDESGRU 12 on March 5, 1984, on the staff of Rear Admiral Joe Donnell. Admiral Donnell, a Surface Warfare Officer, was a big man, 6'7" tall and about 250 pounds. The Chief of Staff was Captain Dick Allsop, an S-3 pilot. Captain Allsop would be my most direct superior in the chain of command at the Group. In the 1980s Cruiser-Destroyer Group staffs were commanded by a surface warfare admiral with an aviator Chief of Staff. Carrier Group staffs were commanded by an aviator with a surface warfare designated Chief of Staff. The only other significant differences between these two virtually mirror-image staffs were that the Operations Officer at a CRUDESGRU was a surface officer and at a CARGRU an aviator. Both types of battle groups deployed aboard aircraft carriers. COMCRUDESGRU 12 was the next higher administrative commander in the chain of command for all the surface ships in Mayport after their respective DESRONs.

The rest of the staff was a mix of surface and aviation officers, an intelligence officer and one submarine officer. The Material Officer was Lieutenant Commander Dave Stone who, with his wife Faith, would become one of my very best friends in the Navy. Dave and I were to room together on *SARATOGA* for the deployment. There was a mix of assistants to the primary department heads as well as a fair number of Chief Petty Officers and Petty Officers; all told about 40 personnel. The Flag Lieutenant was Lieutenant Rick Payne, a graduate of Texas A&M ROTC. The Flag Sec, Flag Lieutenant, and Chief of Staff were the three "loopers" who wore the two-star aiguillettes of the admiral's personal staff.

The *SARATOGA* battle group departed Mayport the morning of April 2, 1984, for what was scheduled as a six-month deployment to the Mediterranean. We crossed the Atlantic and settled into the routine of running the battle group. In 1984, command and control systems were not what they are today. *SARATOGA* did not have a modern Tactical Flag Command Center with all the automatic feeds from all source intelligence, Naval Tactical Data System and Global Command and Control System inputs. Underway staff watches were stood in a bare room just adjacent to the ship's Combat Direction Center or CDC. In our "command" space we had a couple of secure radio circuits, a plotting table, and a SPA-25 radar repeater. We were almost blind, yet supposedly in charge of the battle group. Next door to this space was the carrier CDC where a much better operational and tactical picture was available.

The battle group ships sailed across the Atlantic in an old-fashioned sector screen formation which in those days was considered the best way to protect the high value unit, the aircraft carrier, from air, surface or submarine attack by those pesky Soviets. Each escort ship was assigned a sector, and lacking anything more important to do, the Chief of Staff would routinely stick his head in and raise hell if one of the ships was not in its assigned sector. This was very unusual for a naval aviator who would not normally care about such things. It was one reason the aviators on the staff were not big fans–they considered him an embarrassment to their tribe.

Other than keeping track on our SPA-25, keeping an accurate plot of all the ships was difficult in our flag operations room. The technique was to send one of our staff operations specialists into the ship CDC about every 15 minutes with a piece of maneuvering board paper to plot all of the ship positions. Returning, he would tape it to the bulkhead. The staff watch officers would all nervously await this dramatic moment, especially if Captain Allsop, the Ops Officer, Captain Killinger, or the admiral happened to be in the space. Woe be the Staff Watch Officer when that piece of mo-board paper went up with a ship plotted out of its sector and any of those three hanging around.

Halfway across the Atlantic, Admiral Donnell was flying around the formation visiting the ships when the SH-2 helicopter transporting him lost power while lifting off the deck of *USS TALBOT (FFG-4)* and went in the water. In addition to the crew and Admiral Donnell, Flag Lieutenant Rick Payne was on board. They all escaped from the sinking helicopter and were picked up by *TALBOT*. Admiral Donnell was back at work that afternoon as if nothing had happened, but Rick was a little shook up. He was the last one out of the helicopter as it sank and he described what it was like with Admiral Donnell's size 14 shoes kicking away above his head. I would get up close and personal with those size 14's myself in a couple of months.

We arrived in Naples on April 15th, and transferred from *SARATOGA* to the cruiser *USS BIDDLE (CG-34)*. This was necessitated by the 6th Fleet command organization. For years there had been a permanently assigned two-star admiral in the Mediterranean designated Commander, Task Force 60, or CTF-60. In 1984 it was Rear Admiral Jerry O. Tuttle. CTF-60 moved his flag from aircraft carrier to aircraft carrier as they came into and left the Mediterranean. Admiral Tuttle was senior to Admiral Donnell so our staff was kicked off *SARATOGA* so the CTF-60 staff could move aboard. We then crowded into *BIDDLE*, displacing many of her officers out of staterooms and into Chief's Berthing with many chiefs moving into enlisted berthing compartments in a classic example of shit rolling downhill. I'm sure they loved us.

We sailed on April 18th and pulled into Palma de Mallorca in the Spanish Balearic Islands on the 24th. Palma is a much desired liberty port in the Med and we made the most of it, setting up an "admin" in a hotel in town to use as liberty headquarters and stocking it with beer and booze. Liberty in Palma was fun, the admin was a great place from which to venture out into town and the local Navy League played great hosts and hostesses; especially the hostess part. I think there may have been some hanky-panky during those three days. Years later when Iris met me in Palma and saw the Navy League ladies in action she said I was never allowed to go to Palma without her.

We left Palma the morning of April 27th and proceeded to the eastern Mediterranean off the coast of Lebanon. The Lebanese civil war was ongoing and although we had pulled the Marines out after the Marine barracks bombing in October of 1983, the United States had a vested interest in the resolution of the conflict. Ships of the 6th Fleet were dispatched to the coast to support the government of Lebanon against the various militias and, if called upon, to provide naval gunfire support or air defense. Admiral Donnell was put in charge once we arrived on May 1st. In *BIDDLE* the staff watch was in CIC where we had all the command and control tools of a Navy cruiser as compared to the mushroom experience on *SARATOGA*.

Throughout the month of operations off Lebanon nothing significant happened, but that did not stop us from over-reacting to any suspicious activity. Of note was a high speed ferry that ran between the port of Larnaca on the island of Cyprus and the port of Tartus, Syria, just north of the Lebanese border. This hydrofoil ferry ran on a fairly predictable schedule, but every time a high speed surface contact was detected, especially as it left Tartus, the whole battle force would go to General Quarters until it was positively identified as the ferry. It became a running joke.

We left the eastern Med in early June and transited west through the Straits of Messina between Italy and Sicily and then the

Straits of Bonifacio between Corsica and Sardinia to arrive in Toulon, France on the 7th of June. We were to have a welcome ten-day port call in Toulon and some sporty liberty adventures. A significant number of 6th Fleet ships were in Toulon including *SARATOGA* with Admiral Tuttle embarked. Because Admiral Tuttle was present, he was the Senior Officer Present Afloat, or SOPA, and therefore Admiral Donnell did not have the normal number of ceremonial responsibilities.

One weekend day, Admiral Donnell wanted to take the barge, load it up with food and drink and along with the captain's gig and CO, Captain Tom Turpin, from *USS DALE (CG-19)*, take a group of the staff and ship officers on a trip to the island of Porquerolles about 14 miles from Toulon off the southern coast of France. Captain Turpin was a fellow graduate of Florida State, several years my senior. The Chief of Staff, me, and Dave Stone were among the participants.

We arrived off the western coast of the island in a small bay on a beautiful, sunny day. We swam and we drank and we ate and we drank and then we drank some more. There were windsurfers in the area and many of the young French girls were topless as they surfed by. About mid-afternoon, fully lubricated, we began to head back to Toulon. On the way we passed a tiny island and decided to stop and swim some more. The island was almost all rock and there were a number of caves into which we could swim. I was in a cave, dove down and saw light coming through an underwater tunnel from another section of the cave. I surfaced, took a gulp of air and swam into the tunnel. I popped up on the other side between Admiral Donnell and Captain Allsop who were treading water.

The admiral said, "Where did you come from?"

"There's a tunnel you can swim through and come out the other side."

"Come on, let's go!" and he dove down. I followed, and all the way through the tunnel I had those size 14 feet threatening to kick me in the face and drown me. We made it through and Admiral

Donnell was like a kid when we popped up on the other side. For years after, whenever I saw him, he would always ask me if I remembered that cave swim and then say how stupid we were; that we could have both drowned.

We got back on the two boats and began drinking some more and heading for Toulon. By now the enlisted boat crew had been relegated to passenger status and Turpin was driving his gig and Donnell was driving the barge. The two boats were barreling along at full throttle and a bottle of Jack Daniels was being handed back and forth between them. If we had a Romeo flag it would have been closed up on both boats. Looking to our right as we passed a point of land with a restaurant overlooking the water, we saw a small skiff with an outboard motor racing out to intercept us. Whoever was in the front was waving frantically so we slowed down. It was Captain Ed Killinger who had been at the restaurant, saw the two boats going by, and had commandeered the skiff which was being driven by a French fisherman. He had had a few drinks himself.

We loaded Killinger on board and headed towards Toulon harbor. Admiral Donnell, still at the helm of the barge, spotted *SARATOGA* at anchor outside the breakwater with the hated Jerry Tuttle on board and executed a sudden turn at high speed towards the quarterdeck with the accommodation ladder rigged. Ed Killinger was sitting on the bow of the barge with his legs straddling either side. Mumbling an obscenity, Donnell headed at high speed towards *SARATOGA*. We could see the people on the quarterdeck start to get nervous about this potential suicide attack. About 50 yards out Donnell began his turn, but gigs are not real maneuverable and it wasn't happening as fast as we all hoped. Killinger scrambled back so he wouldn't lose both legs at impact. We sped by the accommodation ladder, throwing up a big spray and headed into the harbor. Admiral Donnell took one hand off the wheel long enough to shoot *SARATOGA* the bird as we raced by.

Our next mission was to conduct Black Sea operations. This was serious business in 1984 with the Cold War in full swing. We would be sailing in the Soviet Union's back yard; much like if they had sent ships into the Gulf of Mexico. Sailing back through

Bonifacio and Messina, we went west of Crete and through the Aegean Sea in company with *USS TRIPPE (FF-1075)* who would accompany us into the Black Sea and to a port visit in Constanta, Romania. Sailing through the Dardanelles, the Sea of Marmara and the Bosporus Strait, we entered the Black Sea on June 24th.

The next day we tied up pierside in Constanta, Romania with *TRIPPE* moored outboard *BIDDLE.* In 1984 Romania was a Warsaw Pact, communist country, under the rule of dictator Nicolae Ceausescu. Vice Admiral Ed Martin, Commander 6th Fleet, would fly to Constanta to participate in the visit as would the U.S. Ambassador to Romania, David Funderburk, who would come from Bucharest.

We received a full round of briefings from the Embassy staff, including the resident CIA agent who informed us that it was likely that our hotel rooms would be bugged so we should be careful what we talked about off the ship. We were told that there was very little crime but we should travel in groups nonetheless. The Embassy had arranged a hotel with several rooms, including for Admiral Martin and Admiral Donnell, along with an admin room for the staff officers like we had in Palma. This same hotel would be the site for a formal dinner with the local Romanian military and political leaders. An open house aboard *BIDDLE* was planned for the townspeople on one of the days.

Visiting a communist country was a unique experience for all of us. We took liberty in town and did find some night life to enjoy. The day of the open house on *BIDDLE* the local authorities blatantly emptied a factory which was right up the road and made about 200 workers come down and tour the ship. It wasn't much of tour; nobody was allowed inside the skin of the ship. *BIDDLE* had rigged a brow on the port bow and a brow on the fantail and these people filed aboard at the bow, walked down the starboard side, and off back aft. They hardly looked at anything, asked no questions, and weren't allowed to take pictures. It was obviously a staged event with forced participation. The Constanta experience made us appreciate what we had in the United States, especially the young sailors.

On the 29th of June, *BIDDLE* and *TRIPPE* departed Constanta and ventured into the Black Sea for several days of routine operations, the main purpose of which was to demonstrate that these were international waters and to exercise our right of freedom of navigation. We were met just outside Romanian territorial waters by a Soviet *KRIVAK* class guided missile frigate who spent the next week shadowing our little task group.

On the 5th of July, our task group had the most significant encounter of the operation with the Soviet Union. We were sailing south of the Crimean Peninsula and the main Soviet Black Sea naval base at Sevastopol, when out of the west we picked up on radar and ESM a flight of Soviet BACKFIRE bombers. The Soviets were using the presence of the American ships as a training opportunity and conducting a simulated strike on our two ships. Coincidentally, their simulated strike provided an opportunity to test an experimental system installed in *BIDDLE*. *BIDDLE* was equipped with a system called Sunflyer which detected the characteristics of jet engines, recorded them, and entered them in a database. Theoretically it was like fingerprinting the engines such that if the same aircraft approached the ship at a later date, it could be identified by the unique signature put out by the engines. The idea was that in a hot war situation, an approaching aircraft could be engaged beyond visual range based on Sunflyer identification.

We went south through the Bosporus on July 6th and pulled into Naples on the 9th to disembark *BIDDLE* and go back aboard *SARATOGA*. The Navy had decided to disestablish the permanent CTF-60 position and turn CTF-60 responsibilities over to the rotating battle group commanders coming into the Med. Rear Admiral Tuttle would be the last permanent CTF-60 and Rear Admiral Donnell would be the first rotating CTF-60. What this meant to the CRUDESGRU 12 staff was that our deployment would be extended beyond its scheduled six months to just over seven months.

Our next operation was a freedom of navigation exercise in the Gulf of Sidra to challenge Qaddafi's claim to the entire gulf as Libyan waters. Since the U.S. shot down two Libyan SU-22 Fitter fighters in 1981, these operations were routinely conducted and given high visibility. This operation was no exception with Commander 6th Fleet, Vice Admiral Martin, flying to *SARATOGA* to observe the operation from CDC. Secretly everybody hoped the Libyans would do something stupid so that we could splash a couple more.

The concept was for two F-14's to fly a carefully scripted route below the "Line of Death" which had them approach the coast, turn west, parallel the coast, and then turn north to cross back north of the "Line." All of this would happen well outside Libyan territorial waters but well south of Qaddafi's claimed line. There were waypoints designated and the two F-14's were expected to hit each one exactly on a prescribed timeline. The Fighting Bedevilers of VF-74 were chosen to fly the mission.

Due to the heightened visibility resulting from Admiral Martin's visit, Admiral Donnell and Captain Allsop decided that only officers could perform the plotting which would be done on a greaseboard in CDC. I was dispatched to the radar room to supervise the radar operators, watch the video, plot the two fighters' positions, and relay via sound-powered phone to Dave Stone in CDC who would plot the tracks on the greaseboard which had a map of the Libyan coastline drawn to scale. Admirals Martin and Donnell, and Captains Killinger and Ready (Jack Ready, *SARATOGA*'s CO) and commanders too numerous to name would watch. What Dave and I were doing is normally done, and probably done better, by seamen just out of boot camp.

The aircraft launched and headed south across the "Line of Death." They reached the first waypoint on time and turned west to parallel the coast. They then began deviating from the script; little feints toward the coast, then back on the westerly track. They did this several times trying to bait the Libyans into coming up after them. Of course this threw the timing off for hitting all the waypoints on time which would have gotten the admirals all worked up in CDC and gotten Commander Kent Ewing, the airwing commander, in hot water.

Over the sound-powered phones I told Dave what was happening. He said, "Shit, when's the next waypoint?"

"20 seconds, they're nowhere near it."

"What should I do?"

"Gundeck it."

Precisely on time Dave made a grease pencil mark on the status board exactly on top of the waypoint.

Admirals and captains nodded approvingly.

This charade went on throughout the mission. The pilots tried unsuccessfully to bait the Libyans and Dave kept plotting them right on time and on position until they crossed north of the line.

Up in CDC Dave told me there were congratulatory back slaps and cigar lightings. We never ratted out the pilots and, of course, they never confessed to anybody in authority. And nothing happened; the Libyans never launched.

On the 30th of July, *SARATOGA* anchored off Benidorm, Spain; a beautiful coastal resort town just north of Alicante and south of Valencia. In July and August Benidorm is crawling with mostly British and German tourists on vacation and is a real liberty hotspot with great beaches, para-sailing, water skiing, and numerous bars, clubs and restaurants.

Iris and Faith Stone along with Judy Donnell and Rosemary Allsop were in town to meet the ship. We planned a driving tour of Europe to begin at the end of the Benidorm visit and Dave and I requested five days leave from Captain Allsop. To our surprise, he approved it without comment. We would miss the ship's transit from Benidorm to Toulon, France. We couldn't believe our good luck and attributed the Chief of Staff's magnanimous gesture to the fact that his wife was also visiting.

Iris, Faith, Dave and I rented a car and had a great travel adventure beginning on August 5th as *SARATOGA* put to sea. We drove up the Spanish coast through Barcelona and crossed into France for a night in Avignon, France. Avignon sits on the banks of the Rhone River and is a beautiful, well preserved, walled city which was the home of the Pope between 1309 and 1377 when six different Popes maintained residency there instead of in Rome. From Avignon we drove into Switzerland for one night in Geneva. The next day we visited Zermatt, Switzerland at the foot of the Matterhorn and then drove into France to stay in the beautiful ski resort town of St. Gervais. From St. Gervais we needed to head towards Toulon to rejoin the ship. Once in Toulon we rented a room at the lovely little La Corniche hotel near a small fishing harbor, and toured the south of France when not standing Staff Duty Officer on the ship. With the wives visiting, Admiral Donnell decided to recreate the Porquerolles barge trip although in a much tamer version. This time we took *SARATOGA*'s admiral's barge and loaded aboard food and drink along with wives and went to the same little bay where the fun began back in June.

August 1984 marked the 40th anniversary of the liberation of Paris during World War II and a special celebration was planned aboard *SARATOGA* to commemorate the event. The ship and the Marine Detachment put on a spectacular show. Unfortunately, the guest of honor, the widow of the Colonel who had led the French Forces of the Interior, Colonel Henri Rol-Tanguy, failed to arrive. They went ahead with the ceremony which had the Marine Silent Drill Team come down on an aircraft elevator as a huge American flag unfurled behind them. They marched to the center of the hangar bay and with perhaps 500 guests looking on, performed a flawless silent drill routine. They had no sooner finished than the ship's XO arrived from the quarterdeck with Madame Rol-Tanguy on his arm. She had arrived late at fleet landing. The Marines then executed a second, flawless, silent drill routine for the benefit of the widow. It was an inspirational performance.

We set sail for Tunis, Tunisia on August 20th after saying goodbye to the wives. *SARATOGA* anchored offshore at Tunis for three days but I never left the ship. I was so far behind on paperwork after our little trip from Benidorm to Toulon via the

Swiss and French Alps that I spent the entire time on board catching up. Our next stop was to be in Naples to transfer the flag from *SARATOGA* to *USS AMERICA (CV-66)*. Because CRUDESGRU 12 was now the rotating Commander Task Force 60, we would be extended, *AMERICA* would take over Mediterranean duties and *SARATOGA* would head home to Mayport without us. We left Tunis and arrived in Naples on the 6th of September where we disembarked *SARATOGA* and embarked in *AMERICA*. *AMERICA* was commanded by Captain Leighton W. "Snuffy" Smith, Jr., who would go on to four-star rank.

In an unusual piece of scheduling, much of it having to do with conserving fuel, we left Naples on the 11th, sailed through the Straits of Bonifacio and anchored at Monaco on the 13th for a ten-day port visit. Along with *AMERICA* were three escort ships who also anchored offshore. Admiral Donnell would spend his nights ashore with a heavy official function schedule so it was decided that in addition to the Staff Duty Officer aboard the carrier, we would set up an ashore Staff Duty Officer in a hotel on the beach. This became a highly desirable duty day. Lounge around the room, which had a balcony, and was fully stocked, ready to respond to some crisis ashore, such as a problem with the official car.

One Sunday morning however, I was the Staff Duty Officer on the carrier and someone reported an oil slick which was believed to be coming from one of the U.S. Navy ships at anchor. This was a major crisis due to the bad publicity which would ensue if the U.S. Navy trashed the coastline of Monaco. Captain Allsop went on high alert and directed me to have Dave Stone, our Material Officer, go up in a helicopter and verify the report. He was also to identify the source of the spill. In Captain Allsop's mind, the Staff Material Officer was most qualified to identify an oil slick in the bay. Dave and I were rooming together so I went to the stateroom and rousted him out of the rack where he was completely under the covers with a hooded sweatshirt pulled over his head to keep out noise and light, it being 9 o'clock in the morning. I described his mission.

"Get out of here, you're shitting me."

"No, really, they've got a helo getting ready to launch, COS wants you up there."

Dave was doubting me because earlier I had played a trick on him that ended up with him being designated the Staff Physical Fitness Coordinator. He thought this was another bogus deal.

He got up, got dressed and went to the flight deck and boarded an SH-3 Sea King helicopter which then launched and went looking for oil. When he got back, he reported no oil sheen on the surface and then told me that they had made a quick pass around the anchored ships and then spent the next hour flying low over the swimming pools of Monaco looking for hot babes.

The Physical Fitness Coordinator caper occurred on *SARATOGA*. The Navy had introduced a new Navy-wide physical fitness program which required every command to designate an officer to serve as collateral duty Physical Fitness Coordinator and manage the program for the command. The NAVADMIN message came to me as Flag Secretary and I made a copy and wrote on it in red ink, used exclusively by the Chief of Staff, "*Dave, I'd like you to run this for the staff, COS.*"

I tossed it in Dave's inbox and figured his first move would be to get mad and then come show it to me to complain. I'd string him along for a while and then tell him the truth. Dave didn't do that; instead he grabbed the message and stormed off to the Chief of Staff's stateroom, knocked on the door and said to the COS, "Sir, do you really want me to do this?"

Captain Allsop looked at the message, thought he must have written the note, and said yes. Then he told Dave he didn't want some "real jock" running the program because he would probably overdo it. Dave was a good athlete who had been recruited to play basketball at the Naval Academy after a stellar high school career in Illinois. This really pissed him off and he stormed out.

Next stop was my desk and he was all fired up. "The goddam COS gave me Physical Fitness Coordinator. I'm busy as hell; why doesn't he give it to one of the fucking aviators who don't do shit around here?"

I said, "What happened?"

He told me and I said, "Jeez, COS didn't write that note, I did. I figured you'd see me before COS."

"Goddam, the stupid son of a bitch doesn't even know he didn't write the fucking note!"

He was madder at COS than he was at me. This prank became a running joke between the two of us and our wives.

On September 20, 1984, a truck bomb exploded outside the U.S. Embassy Annex in Beirut, Lebanon, killing 24, including two U.S. servicemen. Lebanese Hezbollah was blamed for the attack and at high levels discussions began as to how the United States should respond. Admiral Donnell was advised via Admiral Martin that the National Command Authority was debating the possibility of a retaliatory strike against Hezbollah training camps in the Bekaa Valley of Lebanon. We began planning for a sprint to the Eastern Med to launch the strikes if tasked. Many lessons had been learned from the shootdown of an A-6 Intruder in 1983 and there was respect for the capabilities of the Syrian air defenses, all of which had been provided by the Soviet Union. *USS JOHN F. KENNEDY (CV-67)* was also entering the Mediterranean to relieve *AMERICA,* bringing the next rotational CTF-60 and there was some angst that because we were soon heading home, we'd miss the action. In the end, the United States did not retaliate for the Embassy attack.

After a turnover in Augusta Bay, Sicily with *JOHN F. KENNEDY* and Carrier Group 6, we headed west on the 27th of October to begin our transit home. We had a one-night stay in Rota, Spain and then headed across the Atlantic for Bermuda. *AMERICA* was scheduled for an inspection by the Board of Inspection and Survey, the INSURV, who would embark *AMERICA* in Bermuda. The INSURV team for an aircraft carrier was so large that the CRUDESGRU 12 staff would have to leave *AMERICA* in Bermuda and fly back to Mayport aboard Navy C-9 aircraft.

We arrived in Bermuda on the 10th of November and helicoptered all the staff and our packed up cruise boxes off the ship to make room for the INSURV team. In what turned out to be a welcome break, Admiral Donnell decided we would relax in Bermuda and leave the palletized cruise boxes on the tarmac at the airfield. Due to a lack of available aircraft, our C-9 ride home was not scheduled until November 12th. It was a great homecoming in time for the Thanksgiving and Christmas holidays, and although I had seen Iris last in Toulon in August, the ensuing three months had been long and hard. Overall we had been out of homeport for over seven months during which I had not seen Chris or Amy, now 11 and 8 respectively. It was great to be home for a while.

On the 17th of March 1985, the nuclear powered guided missile cruiser *USS SOUTH CAROLINA (CGN-37)* entered Mayport to embark the Group 12 staff for Exercise READEX 1-85, a major fleet exercise in the Puerto Rican operating areas. For this exercise we would be simulating operations in the Norwegian Sea as part of a new strategy coming into vogue in the U.S. Navy; operating aircraft carriers in the Norwegian fjord of Vestfjord. The concept was to take the fight to the doorstep of the Soviet Union and to use the mountainous terrain around the fjord to deny the Soviets a clear picture of the disposition of our forces. The Norwegians would provide early warning of approaching Soviet air or naval forces and our carrier-based aircraft were within range to strike targets inside the Soviet Union. The geography of the Norwegian Sea, the Barents Sea, Norway and Vestfjord was simulated in the open waters of the Atlantic and Caribbean. My brother Steve was underway with his A-7 squadron, VA-82, aboard *USS NIMITZ (CVN-68)* and on the 23rd of March I flew over to *NIMITZ* to visit Lieutenant (junior grade) Sullivan.

The summer of 1985 saw Rear Admiral Donnell complete his tour as Commander, Cruiser-Destroyer Group 12 to be replaced by Rear Admiral Hank Mauz. On the 18th of August the staff flew to Norfolk and embarked *USS TICONDEROGA (CG-47)* for Exercise Ocean Venture 85. *TICONDEROGA* was the first Aegis class cruiser and the hottest surface combatant in the U.S. Navy. On the day we sailed, August 27th, she fired her 100th missile since commissioning in January 1983. 100 missile firings in the 30-year life of a Navy ship is more likely the norm. Because she was the first of her class and the first ship to take the Aegis combat system to sea, *TICONDEROGA* had fired an extraordinary number of exercise and test missiles in her two years of commissioned service.

Ocean Safari was a major fleet exercise to put into practice operations in the Vjestfjord that we had simulated earlier in the year in the Caribbean. Commander, Second Fleet, Vice Admiral Hank Mustin, ran the exercise from the aircraft carrier *DWIGHT D. EISENHOWER (CVN-69)*. Admiral Mauz, in *TICONDEROGA*, would serve as Anti-Air Warfare Commander, or AAWC.

On the way to Vjestfjord as we transited the North Sea and the Norwegian Sea we encountered some of the worst weather I have experienced. We were literally walking on the bulkheads as *TICONDEROGA* rolled heavily in 25–30 foot seas. On two or three occasions one or the other of her screws came out of the water as she crested a wave and the main engine would shut down as the over-speed trip engaged.

We crossed the Arctic Circle on the 15th of September and entered Vjestfjord on the 17th to begin testing the theory of this new maritime strategy. The Soviets did not disappoint us as they probed outside Norwegian territorial sea and air space to learn as much as they could about the U.S. tactics. Soviet Naval Air was always detected and intercepted far out, generally over 200 miles from the carrier, and never approached without a U.S. fighter escort.

When the exercise was over we transited south through the English Channel and tied up in Portsmouth, England where, on the 26th of September we disembarked *TICONDEROGA* and took busses and trucks up to RAF Mildenhall to catch, once again, a couple of C-9's for the flight home to Mayport. I had orders to become Executive Officer in *USS AUBREY FITCH (FFG-34)*, my fourth consecutive tour in Mayport. I detached from Group 12 on the 22nd of October and on the 28th arrived in Newport, Rhode Island for the Prospective Executive Officer (PXO) course. This was to be followed by a navigation course following the Christmas holidays. In 1985 it had been mandated in the Atlantic Fleet that surface ship Executive Officers would also have duties as navigator in response to a series of navigation incidents attributed to very junior and inexperienced officers being assigned the job. After finishing the navigation course, I was scheduled to report aboard *AUBREY FITCH* on January 20th.

CHAPTER 9

Challenger

I reported aboard the guided missile frigate *USS AUBREY FITCH (FFG 34)* as XO on January 20, 1986. We were underway the next day for AUTEC, the Navy's undersea test and evaluation range near Andros Island in the Bahamas, for ASW training. My new CO was Commander John Langknecht. Once underway from Mayport, I finished relieving as XO and Navigator. I had a junior officer Assistant Navigator to take care of all the grunt work, but I really enjoyed the navigation and route planning as it kept me focused on the ship's operations and not bogged down with the myriad administrative duties of an XO. *AUBREY FITCH* was a very squared away and clean ship. John Langknecht and I became a good team. I never subscribed to the theory that the XO had to play bad cop so the CO could play good cop. Captain Langknecht and I quickly established a good rapport while also maintaining high standards. John was a by the book perfectionist, but he did it in a calm and positive manner that elicited loyalty from the crew. He taught me a lot about being a commanding officer.

We conducted five days of ASW on the range at AUTEC, firing exercise torpedoes at U.S. attack submarines. The torpedoes were configured with a turn-away feature that prevented an accurate shot from hitting the submarine. The range operators would evaluate the submarine's attacks on us and ours on them—the turn-away feature worked. The training was dual purpose; good for both the ship and the submarine force, which was training prospective commanding officers. When AUTEC operations were complete, on the evening of January 27th, we turned north for Mayport on what should have been about a 24-hour transit. The space shuttle *Challenger* was scheduled to launch around 11:35 AM on the 28th and a closure area had been declared to keep ships and aircraft out of the way. We were aware of the launch and planned our track north accordingly.

On the morning of the 28th, *AUBREY FITCH* was about 50 miles out to sea, more or less due east of Cape Canaveral. We were in the Gulf Stream where the ocean and weather conditions, especially in winter, are often more confused than when closer to shore or further out in the Atlantic. That morning we experienced a low overcast and choppy seas while Cape Canaveral was enjoying a bright blue, clear, but cold day.

Alerted to the launch timing, the bridge watch team notified Captain Langknecht, who came to the bridge to watch. Seeing the low overcast and thinking there would be nothing to see, he went below to the wardroom for lunch. The bridge watch team, however, did see the exhaust flame from the shuttle launch and watched it ascend uneventfully until it disappeared behind the low cloud cover. It was 11:38 AM. They dutifully called the Captain in the wardroom, reported the launch, and made a log entry. I was in my stateroom, also getting ready for lunch, having just finished my daily messing and berthing inspection. The bridge team and lookouts did not see the explosion or any indications of debris falling.

In CIC, the watch team heard the bridge report the launch and checked the SPS-49 air search radar. They picked up the track of the shuttle and watched it on the scope as it ascended. The SPS-49 is a two-dimensional radar capable of reporting bearing and range, but not altitude.

Seventy-three seconds into flight, *Challenger* began to break up as the result of a failed joint O-ring on the right-hand solid rocket booster. That booster pulled away from the aft strut attaching it to the external tank. The aft dome of the liquid hydrogen tank failed, producing a propulsive force that pushed the liquid hydrogen tank into the liquid oxygen tank in the forward part of the external reservoir. At the same time, the right-hand solid rocket booster rotated about the forward attachment strut and struck the inter-tank structure.

The break-up of the shuttle began at 48,000 feet, although none of this was evident on radar aboard *AUBREY FITCH*. The shuttle did not actually explode, rather it rapidly fragmented under the tremendous aerodynamic forces at play. When the external tank disintegrated, the fuel and oxidizer were released causing the appearance of a massive fireball.

None of this was visible aboard ship due to the cloud layer. CIC continued to track a target which then separated into two distinct targets. According to NASA, the forward momentum and trajectory carried the crew compartment to an altitude of 65,000 feet before it began to descend. In CIC, the watch officer ordered that a plot be maintained of the descending targets which he assumed to be the two solid rocket boosters which are detached to fall into the ocean during a routine launch once they have done their job. He reasoned that by entering a fix in the ship's NTDS system where he had tracked the two solid rocket boosters into the water, we would be ready to respond to any inquiries about the potential hazard to navigation posed by the two boosters which are designed to float if they survive the fall.

Thus, we thought, ended the shuttle adventure.

About 10 minutes later, Atlantic Fleet Headquarters broadcast a verbal call for position reports over the HICOM circuit to ships which, based on their Movement Reports (MOVREPS) were deemed to be closest to Cape Canaveral. They did not call *AUBREY FITCH* because we were four hours ahead of our MOVREP track, which was permitted under the rules. Hearing this, Operations Officer Lieutenant Tom McGuire asked Captain Langknecht if we should report our actual position. He said yes, and once done, Atlantic Fleet Headquarters realized that *AUBREY FITCH* was the closest ship.

Five minutes later a Radioman from Radio Central rushed to CIC with a FLASH message from CINCLANTFLT to *AUBREY*

FITCH (a FLASH message is the highest precedence and requires expedited handling):

```
FM: CINCLANTFLT NORFOLK VA

TO: USS AUBREY FITCH

PROCEED  IMMEDIATELY  AT  BEST  SPEED
TO  LAT  28.25'N/LONG  079.59'W  FOR
SAR.
```

By now the Captain and I were on the bridge. SAR meant "search and rescue" so we knew something had happened, but not what. We brought the second gas turbine engine online, I plotted the position on the chart and we headed toward it at 30 knots. About then, the CIC Watch Officer came to the bridge and told John Langknecht about the targets he had tracked into the water via the SPS-49 radar. We immediately sent another FLASH message to CINCLANTFLT reporting the two positions we had plotted and which we initially thought were the solid rocket boosters.

In less than five minutes we were directed to proceed to the nearest of our two positions. On the bridge, the Captain and I speculated as to the nature of the SAR. Nothing we had received suggested any problem with the space shuttle. In 1986, Navy ships did not have the kind of EHF satellite receivers and other equipment to receive satellite television programs or exchange emails that exist on today's ships. We were too far from the coast to pick up any regular television signals, although we had an antenna for use when the ship was in port. We thought that perhaps a small plane had gone down, maybe a private pilot trying to watch the shuttle launch, or perhaps a military aircraft assigned to shoo private aircraft away from the closure area. We were completely in the dark.

After a 30-minute top speed run, we entered an area which smelled of aviation fuel and had a light sheen of fuel on the surface. The ship was fully rigged for SAR operations, the rigid-hulled inflatable boat (RHIB) crew and the motor whaleboat crew were manned and ready, rescue swimmers were on station, and everyone not doing something else was topside scanning the water for whatever and whoever we were sent to save. Since the message traffic between *AUBREY FITCH* and LANTFLT, we had seen further message traffic directing every ship underway within 200 miles of Cape Canaveral to join the search. But we still didn't know what we were searching for. We thought it was an aircraft, probably military given the interest.

As we proceeded slowly through the fuel slick, we began to see small pieces of foam and small sections of what looked like insulation coated with what appeared to be heat-resistant aluminum; like a firefighting ensemble. Seeing nothing else significant in the area, we put the RHIB and motor whaleboat in the water and had the boat crews pick up some of the debris so we could attempt to identify it. Throughout we sent regular reports back to CINCLANTFLT. Whatever we had found looked like it came off an airplane; perhaps from around some electronic equipment bays, or cargo area, or even from the cockpit area.

About the time we recovered the boats to continue our search, we received another message from CINCLANTFLT indicating our SAR was for the space shuttle *Challenger*. This message provided no further details so we did not know there had been an explosion but we now knew we were trying to save astronauts. At about this time we were informed that the Coast Guard had been designated SAR Commander and all the Navy ships were in support.

Proceeding closer to shore, but still 30 miles or so at sea and out of sight of land, we came to an area with hundreds of the heat shield tiles and began picking them up in the boats. Some we could scoop out of the water with a boat hook from the deck of the ship. As the day progressed, we began to pick up more and larger pieces of debris, including a main landing gear wheel assembly with the tires still intact, its strut, all the hydraulics, and the landing gear door. We also recovered some odd spheres about three feet in diameter with nozzles protruding at various points. Not having a helicopter embarked, we began staging everything on the flight deck and in the helicopter hangar. The largest piece we recovered was a part of one of the booster tanks, about 8 feet by 5 feet.

Eventually, an Air Force C-130 arrived in the area and began vectoring our RHIB to areas of concentrated debris. All communications were by bridge-to-bridge radio and it became amusing when our coxswain in the RHIB began communicating with the Air Force pilots and addressing them as "Air Force One," not knowing what else to call them.

Throughout the day, we continued recovering debris without fully appreciating the magnitude of what had happened to *Challenger*. The crew performed magnificently, finding ingenious ways to recover debris, including large sections, and hoist them aboard ship. We avoided putting the divers in the water as we saw lots of sharks, including a school of about 200 relatively small, 3-5 foot, Blacktips. We did use the swimmers, when necessary, to tie off a large piece of debris for hoisting aboard using the swimmer/man overboard davits. Boatswain Mate First Class Teddy Skalecki was the leading Petty Officer under Boatswain Mate Senior Chief Johnny Ray Hatcher and they did an excellent job. Skalecki had been in my Weapons Department aboard *TATTNALL* and it had been him and me who had picked up the pieces after the A-7 and F-4 midair collision near Diego Garcia.

As darkness set in, search operations were suspended. We had been steadily closing the coast while picking up debris and decided, when within a few miles of Cape Canaveral, to anchor for the night to let everybody get a good night's sleep for what would be a busy and full following day. As we approached the coast, our TV antenna began to pick up the signal from the beach. It was not until then that we saw the film of what had happened to *Challenger*.

It is possible that the astronauts survived the break-up of *Challenger* and were alive as the crew compartment continued on its trajectory to 65,000 feet and then fell into the ocean at over 200 MPH. During vehicle break-up, the crew cabin remained intact and began to tumble. NASA estimates that the initial g-forces were as high as 12 to 20 times the strength of gravity very briefly, but within two seconds dropped to 4 g's and within 10 seconds the cabin was in free fall. These effects were considered unlikely to have been fatal. At least some of the astronauts were likely alive and briefly conscious after the break-up because three of the four Personal Egress Air Packs on the flight deck were found to have been activated. Investigators found the remaining oxygen supply roughly consistent with the expected consumption of the 2 minute, 45-second free fall to the ocean. The 200 MPH impact with the ocean caused an instant deceleration of roughly 200 g's which far exceeded the ability of the crew cabin or a human being to survive. The prospect of finding survivors was improbable.

On the second day of the search, we continued recovery operations within 20–25 miles of the coast. By this time the Coast Guard had dispatched a High Endurance Cutter, *USCG DALLAS (WHEC-716)* as On-Scene Commander and the organization of the search became much more orderly. Calculating the effects of the Gulf Stream the vector of the entire search grid gradually moved north, eventually as much as 400 miles, before it ended.

Around 3:00 PM, we were ordered to enter Port Canaveral, tie up at a pier to transfer recovered debris ashore and then move to a refueling dock before resuming the search the next day. As soon as we tied up and put the brow across to the pier, a team of NASA specialists, including one shuttle astronaut came aboard and began examining our collected debris. We were the first ship to enter Port Canaveral to offload, so they were very interested in what we had collected.

AUBREY FITCH continued the search until we returned to Mayport on the 3rd of February. We returned once more to Port Canaveral to offload recovered shuttle pieces on January 31st. As the search progressed, the amount recovered became less and our search area continued to move north with the Gulf Stream. By the last night, we were practically due east of Mayport. The at sea surface search was terminated on February 7th, although an underwater search continued for several months. Shuttle pieces continued to wash up on beaches as far north as the Outer Banks of North Carolina and as recently as 1996 at Cocoa Beach, Florida. Fifty-five percent of the shuttle body, 5% of the crew compartment, and 65% of the satellite cargo is still missing.

The crew cabin was eventually located on the ocean floor and the astronaut's remains collected. The identifiable remains of Dick Scobee and Michael Smith were buried at Arlington National Cemetery and the remains of Lieutenant Colonel Ellison Onizuka were buried at the Punchbowl National Cemetery in Hawaii. The unidentifiable remains were buried at the Space Shuttle *Challenger* Memorial in Arlington.

AUBREY FITCH was awarded the Coast Guard Unit Citation with operational distinguishing device by the Coast Guard and each crewmember received a certificate commemorating our part in the search from NASA.

CHAPTER 10
Back to the Persian Gulf

With the *Challenger* disaster serving as a "come as you are" introduction to *AUBREY FITCH* and my duties as XO and Navigator, I settled into my routine aboard ship. Commander John Langknecht was a positive leader, but going through a divorce, which left Iris as the "senior wife." She settled right into the role and I know John appreciated her willingness to take on the unofficial but important responsibilities that normally fall to the wife of a Navy ship commanding officer.

AUBREY FITCH was an *OLIVER HAZARD PERRY* class guided missile frigate and part of Destroyer Squadron 8, where I had been Combat Systems Officer, so I was very familiar with the ship class. *PERRY* class frigates had twin LM2500 gas turbine engines and a single screw; my first shiphandling exposure to both, having previously served on twin screw, steam powered ships. The *PERRY* class frigates also had electric motor driven Auxiliary Power Units, or APU's, which were lowered beneath the hull of the ship at slow speeds and were trainable 360 degrees. The APU's greatly assisted maneuverability around the pier, serving as a built-in tug. *AUBREY FITCH* also had a helicopter hangar and deck for the SH-2 Seasprite helicopter. I had not served on a ship which could support an embarked helo since *NEWPORT NEWS*.

The schedule which faced *AUBREY FITCH* in 1986 was a major fleet exercise, an INSURV inspection, and the normal series of work-up training required in advance of a regular deployment to the Persian Gulf which was scheduled for June. Much as both *SEMMES* and *TATTNALL* had done, *AUBREY FITCH* was scheduled to deploy to the Persian Gulf as a unit of the Middle East Force, not as part of an aircraft carrier battle group. The Iran-Iraq war was still underway and both nations had begun targeting each other's shipping in the Gulf; the so called Tanker War. This development put all merchant ships at risk as well as any U.S. Navy ships operating in the vicinity.

We were underway the 11th of February for Exercise FLEETEX 1-86 in the Atlantic and Caribbean operating areas. Once again, the exercise scenario tested the Maritime Strategy with simulated land and sea areas to mirror the Vjestfjord in Norway. We returned to Mayport on the 28th of February and were underway again with DESRON 8 staff embarked on the 11th of March to dry run our upcoming INSURV Underway Material Inspection (UMI). A week later we had the INSURV inspection and the ship passed with flying colors. *AUBREY FITCH* was a particularly clean ship. For my part, I was meticulous about conducting the XO's Inspection of Messing and Berthing, also known as "heads and beds," every day, both underway and inport. Often, when the word was passed, normally at 10:00 AM, I was busy doing something else. Groaning at the interruption, I stopped whatever I was doing, but then got into it and actually enjoyed the inspection. I inspected all the berthing compartments and heads as well as passageways, the galley and messdecks, and the cooks and messcooks. It was a great way to get to know the crew and the ship and it sent the right message to the crew doing the cleaning that it was important.

One day, I had one of those strange experiences where I varied my routine and it had significant consequences. We were in port, I had finished the messing and berthing inspection, and for no particular reason decided to walk forward on the second deck and look around. I came to an access trunk that opened to the main deck above on the forecastle and decided to open the watertight hatch and take a look inside. When I did, there, strung through the scuttle wheel leading to the main deck, was a hangman's noose tied off to the ladder rungs on the trunk bulkhead. It was made of 3" manila line and was perfectly tied.

I took it down and carried it to the Captain's cabin to show John Langknecht. He called down to the Chief's Mess and had our

Command Master Chief, Fire Controlman Senior Chief Charles Jarvis, come up for a talk. We sent Senior Chief Jarvis off to see what he could find out and about an hour later he came back to report that one of the Operations Specialists had been acting strangely enough to attract the attention of his shipmates. When he was confronted, he broke down and admitted that he had rigged the noose and was considering suicide. We sent him to the hospital for evaluation and he was lost to the ship. I often wondered what it was that made me go look in that access trunk on that particular morning, and what if I hadn't. Did it perhaps save that sailor's life? I hope so.

We were underway several more times in April and May, conducting preparations for our June 4th deployment. We conducted work-ups with the helicopter detachment from HSL-34 who would make the deployment and got to know the four pilots and the 20 enlisted who would make up the detachment. Lieutenant Commander Ian Fetterman was the Detachment Officer in Charge, or Det OIC, and he would room with me in the XO's stateroom. They were a good group and would prove to be a valuable addition to the team.

On the 16th of May, we held a Tiger Cruise and permitted male family members to ride the ship overnight. We pulled into Mayport the morning of the 17th and loaded up all types of family members for a family day cruise, getting back underway and returning that afternoon. My Mom and Dad made the trip along with my brother Paul, and Iris, Chris and Amy. Chris was now 14 and Amy 11. My brother Steve had moved from VA-82 and the A-7 Corsair to VFA-106 and the newest, hottest jet in the United States Navy, the F/A-18 Hornet. Through Steve I had arranged for two F/A-18's from VFA-106, the training squadron at Naval Air Station Cecil Field, to put on a little airshow. They did a great job with some aerial maneuvers, including dropping inert ordnance using our wake as the target. Of course my Dad, the ultimate NAVAL AVIATOR, was most enthralled with the air show.

Finally, on the 4th of June, we set sail for the Persian Gulf, rendezvousing at sea with the *SPRUANCE* class destroyer *USS*

NICHOLSON (DD-982), my old ship *USS SEMMES (DDG-18)*, and *USS TALBOT (FFG-4)*, who would accompany us to the Gulf.

Our Atlantic crossing was uneventful in good weather. We passed through the Strait of Gibraltar on June 14th and entered the Mediterranean Sea. Our first stop was in Port Mahon, on the island of Menorca, the smaller of the two main Spanish Balearic Islands, the other being Palma de Mallorca. Menorca takes its name from being smaller than Mallorca which takes its name from being larger than Menorca—a chicken and egg kind of deal.

Menorca featured a beautiful natural harbor cutting into the island on the eastern side via a narrow channel. We left Port Mahon on the 19th arriving in Port Said, Egypt on the 23rd for our Suez Canal transit. *AUBREY FITCH* was permitted into the inner harbor of the city where we moored to a buoy to await the midnight transit of the canal. Our transit was uneventful save for the usual thrashing about as the Egyptians got the convoy moving. We had a particularly aggressive pilot for the longest leg down to the Great Bitter Lake for our anchorage to let the northbound convoy pass. As we entered the Great Bitter Lake, he wanted to race to the southern end of the lake and drop anchor so that he could have lunch (on us) and take a nap. As navigator, I had marked an area of shallow water on the chart to make sure we went around it, but the pilot insisted it would be no problem for us to pass directly over in order to get to our anchorage location more quickly. I showed it to him on the chart and said we'd go around.

"No, no," he exclaimed, "I dredged it myself!"

I glanced over at John Langknecht, he shook his head, and we went around it, much to the disappointment of our pilot.

Exiting the canal on the 24th, we sailed straight through the Red Sea, the Bab al Mandeb, and around the Arabian Peninsula for a refueling stop in a place called Mina-al-Raysut, on the Arabian Sea coast of Oman. After transiting the Strait of Hormuz we pulled into Bahrain, anchoring at Sitrah anchorage, on the 8th of July to refuel, resupply, and receive all the incoming briefings from the

Middle East Force staff. The Iran-Iraq war was in its sixth year and the Iranians and Iraqis had been attacking each other's commercial shipping in the Gulf. It was not uncommon for tankers flying the flags of neutral nations to be attacked because the idea was to ruin each other's economies and those ships might very well be carrying Iraqi or Iranian oil to market. Most of the oil moving through the Gulf came from Saudi Arabia, but neither Iran nor Iraq seemed particular about who they hit. Because of this, the U.S. Navy was escorting U.S. flagged shipping operating in the Persian Gulf. An escort ship was responsible for the protection of its customer from air or surface attack. It was not uncommon for the Iranian Revolutionary Guard, in Boston Whaler small boats, to attack a large tanker with a shoulder fired RPG. The Iraqi's, on the other hand, preferred air attack using French-made Exocet missiles launched from their French-made Mirage jets. The Exocet is a fire and forget missile that homes on the first good radar return the seeker head detects. The Iranian's also occasionally used their American-made F-4 Phantom's, with American-made Maverick missiles. The Maverick missile was optically guided and preferred a sharp contrast to improve its homing ability. This was about the time the U.S. Navy began graying out its hull numbers so the white numbers wouldn't make such an inviting target for a Maverick. On the other hand, the radar dome on the CIWS was a bright white, and if the Maverick homed on that, it would be flying directly at our best defense against an incoming missile.

Over the next six weeks, *AUBREY FITCH* conducted five escort operations for U.S. flagged shipping passing in and out of the Persian Gulf while escorting ships to the safety of the Gulf of Oman, outside the Gulf, or to the vicinity of their destinations inside the Gulf. With the exception of a maintenance period in Bahrain, we had no liberty. We refueled either from an oiler in the Gulf, including British and French oilers, or during brief stops for fuel in a variety of locations in and outside the Gulf.

On the 6th of August, we escorted another ship through the Strait of Hormuz and then continued east through the North Arabian Sea for a scheduled port visit in Karachi, Pakistan. We entered the channel into the Port of Karachi in a driving rainstorm, on the 9th of August, negotiating a winding channel flanked by shallow sand bars, and tied up at a pier in the port. The city of Karachi, the largest in Pakistan, is today a sprawling metropolis of approximately 20 million, one of the world's largest cities in terms of population. It is also dreadfully poor and depressing. The poverty we saw in Karachi was appalling, with people literally living in ditches alongside the road with tin, plywood, or cardboard lean-tos as their only shelter. The streets were dirty and crowded, with open sewage in the gutters. Until I visited Afghanistan some 20 years later, Karachi was the most dismal place I had ever seen.

Having been warned not to drink the water, we made plans to keep one of our fresh water tanks on the ship topped off as we entered port. The harbor was too shallow and too dirty for us to operate the ship's fresh water evaporators which turn sea water into fresh water. We did take water from the pier, but we isolated the two tanks we topped off, and only used the one tank we had filled at sea. It was a good thing. The ship's Corpsman, Hospital Corpsman Chief James "Doc" Smith, took a water sample from the riser on the pier and put it in a petri dish. A day later it looked like a science experiment gone bad. A disgusting, ugly, growth of bacteria was literally overflowing the petri dish. For the four days in Karachi, we put the ship on water hours and carefully husbanded the one good tank of fresh water we had.

Pakistan was known for its inlaid wood and I bought some gifts out in town. The country is also known for the ready availability of drugs, and one of our sailors was tempted and caught with a brick of hashish once we left port. Our investigation widened, and ultimately a dozen sailors were implicated in the purchase and use of the hash. This was a low point in my tour and in John Langknecht's. We held a group Captain's Mast at sea and processed out a dozen sailors, including an air crewman from the helicopter detachment, for violating the Navy's zero tolerance drug policy. It was a sad day.

August to October saw us continue the routine of escorting U.S. flagged ships through the Gulf and the Strait of Hormuz. In all, we were through Hormuz nine more times over this period, and in and out of Bahrain and other ports to refuel and resupply. Although it sounds routine, there was plenty of excitement and things were never boring, especially in the southern Persian Gulf which we nicknamed "Wally World" after the amusement park in the Chevy Chase movie *Vacation*. We started referring to that part of the Gulf as Wally World in our nightly situation reports and it caught on with the Middle East Force staff. The shipping traffic was denser in Wally World as ships entered the narrower waters in the approaches to the Strait of Hormuz. The Iranians had declared an exclusion zone as part of the war with Iraq and had announced that shipping inside the exclusion zone was subject to attack. The exclusion zone squeezed down the available sea room for ship navigation even further than the natural geography of the approaches to the strait.

One night, our LAMPS helicopter was airborne in the southern Gulf with Lieutenant Jeff Berger flying pilot-in command and Lieutenant Jim Stahlman as co-pilot. An Iranian frigate was in the area and began challenging our helicopter over the bridge-to-bridge radio. Jeff responded that he was an American aircraft conducting routine operations in international airspace; all of which was true. But the Iranians persisted in warning him away. They had picked up this practice from our own U.S. Navy and were using it against us.

John Langknecht and I were in CIC listening to the exchange and considering whether or not to jump in to the conversation and let the Iranians know we were around and to leave our helicopter alone. Unfortunately, the pilots had switched off the control frequency and Guard channel to talk to the Iranians so we were unable to talk secure to them, give them advice, or vector them back to *AUBREY FITCH*. Ultimately, we decided not to come up on bridge-to-bridge to tell the Iranians to lay off because we thought the aircrew was handling the situation. Once the helicopter had recovered on deck, Captain Langknecht had the two pilots in his stateroom for an ass-chewing for breaking voice contact with the ship. Ian spoke to me and was a little angry that we hadn't jumped in and given the crew some radio support. I explained our thinking, but he was right, we probably should have piped up.

In September, we were outside the Gulf in the Gulf of Oman for a scheduled brief stop for fuel off the coast of Fujairah, United Arab Emirates, when we received an intelligence report from MIDEASTFOR indicating that the Iranians might conduct an attack on shipping outside the Gulf using F-4 Phantoms out of Cha Bahar, their base on the southern coast, east of Hormuz. The Fujairah anchorage was full of merchant ships and reasonably close to Cha Bahar. Our guidance was to defend shipping if possible, but we had to be sure an attack was in progress. We couldn't just shoot down an F-4 flying in the area. We made sure our TAO and missile system were ready for action and then John pulled me into the chart room to think through what action we might take. It was a given that if we were present for an attack on the anchorage, and had a chance to shoot down the attacker we would do it. The question John wanted to discuss was, what if an F-4 gets off a missile and is exiting the area and we have a shot? He wanted both of us to talk this through. My advice was that even if he's headed back to Cha Bahar and we have a shot we should take it; that was his thinking too, and he agreed. Nothing happened that day, but it had given us a rules of engagement problem to think through.

Finally, on October 27th, we transited the Strait of Hormuz for the final time and went to Fujairah for the last time to refuel. Altogether we had transited Hormuz 16 times in the previous four months. The next event on our schedule was to visit Aqaba, Jordan to serve as host platform for a visit by Rear Admiral Harold J. Bernsen, Commander Middle East Force, for an official visit. We would host a cocktail reception at sunset on the flight deck the second night in.

We sailed north through the Red Sea and transited the Strait of Tiran on the 8th of November. The Strait of Tiran is a narrow waterway that connects the Gulf of Aqaba to the Red Sea. It was an interesting transit, with many half sunken hulks littering both sides of the strait, left over from the 1973 Yom Kippur War. There are treacherous reefs on both sides of the channel which is only about a quarter of a mile wide, but also beautiful, clear water which provides some of the world's best scuba diving. As you sail north up the Gulf of Aqaba, the Sinai Peninsula of Egypt is to port and the deserts of Saudi Arabia to starboard.

Aqaba port did not have a place for us to go pierside, so we anchored in the harbor on November 9th and began preparations for the big reception the following night. At anchor in the harbor you can see four countries with the naked eye. Moving clockwise is Egypt, Israel and the town of Eilat, bordered by Jordan and Aqaba, and then Saudi Arabia. Although the distance between Aqaba and Eilat is only three miles, the border is closed. To get to Eilat you'd have to fly out of Jordan to a third country, and then fly into Israel. And if you then had an Israeli stamp in your passport, you would be denied entry into any Arab country, including back into Jordan.

The night of the 10th, we donned our choker white uniforms and hosted a very successful sunset reception with Admiral Bernsen and the senior military officers of the region from Jordan. When the dignitaries and visitors left by boat, the real party started. We had leftover beer, wine, and food so Captain Langknecht invited all members of the crew who had played a part in the reception back to the flight deck to polish off the leftovers. We had the color guard, the waiters, the cooks, the sideboys, and everyone not on watch, back on the flight deck. Somebody cranked up a boom box, the Captain thanked everybody for a great job and we took care of the rest of the food and drink. This was not exactly in accordance with Navy Regulations, but it was great for morale.

On the 12th of November, we set sail south down the Gulf of Aqaba, through the Strait of Tiran, and around the Sinai Peninsula to enter the Gulf of Suez for our northbound Suez Canal transit. Transiting the canal on the 15th of November, we entered the Mediterranean that night and headed across to Gibraltar where we would have our one port visit outside the Middle East on the way home. Mooring inside the quay wall in Gibraltar on the 21st of November we looked forward to a two-night stay in a port outside the Middle East. Gibraltar is a British Overseas Territory which sits at the southern tip of the Iberian Peninsula at the entrance to the

Mediterranean Sea at Point Europa, dominated by the iconic Rock of Gibraltar. It is tiny, only 2.6 square miles, and is bordered by Andalusian Spain, which disputes the British claim to the territory. The area was conquered by an Anglo-Dutch force in 1704 during the War of the Spanish Succession, and granted to Great Britain in perpetuity under the Treaty of Utrecht in 1713. The Spanish have never gotten over this British indignity and when we were there in 1986, the border with Spain had only been fully opened the year before.

The first day in, the Captain and I made the obligatory trip up the rock to see the sights, feed the baboons, and do some shopping in the quaint little town of Gibraltar. The second night in, Ian and I went out and did the town, hitting a few British pubs and having a nice time. With our underway for the Atlantic crossing scheduled for the morning, we were back on the ship and in the sack before midnight.

That is until the CDO, Lieutenant Jerry Luegers, knocked on my door at 1:00 AM.

"XO, we've got a problem, a bunch of our guys are in jail in town."

"What happened?" A bunch sounded like a fight or something. A rumble with the Brits maybe?

"Something about a theft."

Groaning, Ian and I rolled out of our racks, put on our uniforms, and hopped into the duty vehicle and went to the police station. When we got there, I identified myself and asked for the details. I was told that a group of *AUBREY FITCH* sailors had been hauled in out of a dance club because a girl claimed one of them had ripped a gold necklace off her neck out on the dance floor. She couldn't identify the culprit, but said whoever did it was black.

I asked if I could see them and they let me in to a room where a dozen *AUBREY FITCH* sailors, all black, were gathered.

"XO, this is bullshit, we didn't do nothing. They just threw us all in here for no reason."

I realized what the police had done. When the girl filed her complaint with the manager, he called the cops. When they arrived and questioned her, she said a black guy had ripped the necklace off of her neck. Since she couldn't identify the individual, they rounded up every black male in the place, all of whom were from *AUBREY FITCH*.

I went back outside and asked the police what would happen if I got the necklace back. They said they'd let them go as long as they all went back to the ship.

Back in the room I said, "OK, here's the deal, you're all in here because you're black." I was deliberately blunt.

Groans of complaint, "Man that is fucked up."

"Hey, we're not in the United States. A girl claims a black guy stole her necklace. She can't identify who did it so the cops picked up every black guy in the place. Now here's the deal; I don't give a shit who did it. I don't want to know. But if you guys want to get out of here, somebody better come up with the necklace. I'm going to leave the room for a minute and when I come back I want to see the necklace on that chair over there."

And I left the room. When I came back, the necklace was on the chair and our guys were standing there looking sheepish. I turned the necklace over to the police and they let everyone go. I had all their names, and said, "Everyone back to the ship, anyone not back in the next half hour is on report." It was about 3:30 AM when my head hit the pillow and I was up again at 6:00 to make preparations for the underway sea detail. All the jailbirds had come straight back to the ship. I never found out who took the necklace and I didn't pursue it. In the morning I told John Langknecht what had happened. I didn't want him to think the reason I looked so bad was that I had been out steaming all night. Naturally, my roomie, the helicopter pilot, slept in that morning.

As we crossed the Atlantic we drilled and buffed up the engineering spaces in preparation for a scheduled "OUTCHOP" Operational Propulsion Plant Examination, or OPPE. The plan was for the OPPE team to fly to Bermuda, helo out to the ship, and conduct the inspection between Bermuda and Mayport. An OPPE is a notoriously difficult inspection, and having to do one in the final days of a six-month deployment was common practice in the Atlantic Fleet.

After a brief stop for fuel in the Azores at Ponta Delgada, we arrived off the south coast of Bermuda on the morning of the 1st of December and embarked the OPPE team via our helicopter. They began with a briefing in the wardroom and then launched into the material portion of the inspection. Our engineering spaces were in good shape and especially clean and we felt confident that this part of the inspection would go well. The concern was the drills. We had to demonstrate three different watch teams and two of them had to pass for us to pass the inspection. As we sailed west the inspection continued and, although we weren't tearing it up on the engineering drills and fire party performance, we were achieving satisfactory results. The night before pulling into Mayport, December 3rd, we were running drills when a circuit board failed in the Free Standing Electronic Enclosure, or FSEE. This was enough of a problem that the OPPE team declared that we would not be able to complete the inspection until it was repaired. We did not have a spare circuit board in the spare parts allowance.

We sprang into action to mobilize DESRON 8 for support despite it already being 9 o'clock at night. They came through by going to one of the other FFG's in port and cannibalizing the board. We launched Ian Fetterman in the helicopter around 1:00 AM and he flew into Mayport, picked up the part and flew back to the ship. The Gas Turbine Electricians installed the part, powered up the FSEE, and fried the new board. That was it, we were out of Schlitz. I got to bed about 4:00 AM as did the Captain and most of the crew.

As we pulled into Mayport the next morning about 10:00 for what should have been a joyous reunion with our families, we were tired and hangdog. It was no way to end an otherwise very successful deployment. We now faced the normal 30-day post-deployment stand-down period and the Christmas holidays with the prospect of having to complete the OPPE after the holidays. The trick would be to keep our edge during the layoff. To his great credit, John Langknecht did not change a thing over Christmas. We enjoyed the break just as we would if the OPPE were successfully behind us. Our January 3rd OPPE follow-up inspection was conducted in port with only one watch team being drilled. John Langknecht's decision to allow the crew to enjoy their post-deployment leave and holiday time had been vindicated.

CHAPTER 11

East Coast Sailors

1987 would prove to be a busy year for *AUBREY FITCH* with an active underway schedule, a late May change of command, and a Northern Europe–Baltic Sea deployment in the fall. Because John Langknecht would be relieved at the end of May, my normal 18-month tour as XO would be extended to preclude the CO and XO changing over in close proximity.

After a short trip to Charleston to take on exercise MK-46 torpedoes at the Naval Weapons Station, *AUBREY FITCH* was underway on February 10th for a week of escort operations in support of *USS SARATOGA (CV-60)* which we finished up with a port visit to Charlotte Amalie, St. Thomas, in the U.S. Virgin Islands. When I went ashore in St. Thomas, Iris was there to meet me and spend the next three days with me on the island. She had arranged for her parents to once again stay with Chris and Amy, who were now 15 and 12, and almost old enough to stay home alone. Actually, almost *too old* to stay home alone; it's a small window.

We left St. Thomas on the 22nd, returned to Mayport on the 25th, and were back underway for Andros Island in the Bahamas on the AUTEC underwater range on March 2nd. We spent three days in the very deep waters of the Tongue of the Ocean conducting ASW operations against *LOS ANGELES* class attack submarines doing their Prospective Commanding Officer (PCO) training. Following the AUTEC operations we made another port visit, this time to Freeport in the Bahamas. Another nice break and another rendezvous with Iris. We left Freeport on the 9th of March, refueled in Roosevelt Roads, Puerto Rico on the 11th, and arrived in Port Everglades, Florida for another port visit on the 17th of March.

The Fort Lauderdale Chapter of the Navy League is famous for rolling out the red carpet for visiting Navy ships and our visit was no different. For reasons of logistics, Iris could not make the trip to Fort Lauderdale, so John Langknecht and I were left to our own devices. Ever the conscientious steward of the taxpayer dollar, John rented a convertible Mustang at his own expense so that we could go on liberty and not worry about misusing the official vehicle that the ship paid for out of its Navy budget.

Leaving Port Everglades on March 20th and arriving in Mayport on the 21st, we were underway again a week later for an interesting series of east coast visits. Our first stop was in Charleston, South Carolina where we were in and out the same day after loading an SPS-48D, air search radar and pedestal on the flight deck. The radar was for *USS MAHAN (DDG-42)* which was in the shipyard in Norfolk undergoing overhaul. The radar had been refurbished in Charleston and *AUBREY FITCH* was the means to deliver it. The SPS-48D radar and pedestal are too large to truck up I-95 to Norfolk, unable to clear the highway overpasses along the route.

Underway again on March 30th, we headed further north to Newport, Rhode Island where *AUBREY FITCH* would serve as School Ship for the Surface Warfare Officer's School (SWOS). The Commanding Officer of SWOS was my old CO in *TATTNALL*, Captain Paul Tobin. The School Ship was there to give students a real ship to train on, and ships that were selected were generally nominated for the job because they were squared away. It was an honor to be selected. SWOS did not want brand new ensign students going aboard a ship that was dirty, in disrepair, and not well run.

Leaving Newport on April 6th, we headed south to visit Wilmington, North Carolina for the Azalea Festival. Each year the U.S. Navy sent a ship to Wilmington as part of the Azalea Festival and we were chosen for the 1987 edition. Wilmington is located about 20 miles up the Cape Fear River and is a tricky sea detail. The river entrance is surrounded by sand bars and features a sharp left and then a sharp right turn before winding its way upriver to the city of Wilmington. In the downtown area where we were to tie up the ship, the river is quite narrow. The plan was to go past our berth to the U.S. Route 17 Bridge, turn the ship around with the assistance of a tug, and tie up port side to, facing downstream. The river looked like it was barely big enough for the ship to turn around. We made it, the bow swinging by the town square and the stern swinging by the battleship *NORTH CAROLINA (BB-55)* which was permanently moored in Wilmington as a museum and tourist attraction.

We spent five days in Wilmington participating in the Azalea Festival events. John Langknecht was given a seat of honor in the reviewing stand for the parade and I gave a tour of the ship to the actor Lorenzo Lamas whose girlfriend was the Azalea Queen. He acted interested, but I don't think he really was. I later told Iris that he was the best looking guy I'd ever seen. His girlfriend was pretty nice looking too. Lorenzo Lamas had attended a military prep school, Admiral Farragut Academy, during his high school years and had been the roommate of an officer I would meet later in my career, Rear Admiral Mark "Buz" Buzby.

On the 18th of May, we heard about *USS STARK (FFG-31)* being hit in the Persian Gulf the night before with two Exocet missiles fired from an Iraqi Mirage F-1. *STARK* was a Mayport based ship and a squadron-mate in DESRON 8. *STARK* had been conducting the same operations as *AUBREY FITCH* had the year before. In *STARK's* case she had recently left Bahrain and was operating north of the island nation, but outside the declared exclusion zone. Iraq claimed that the pilot mistook *STARK* for an Iranian tanker inside the exclusion zone and therefore felt she was fair game. The attack took place at night and the missiles were fired from 22 and 15 miles respectively; the pilot had no visual confirmation of his assumption, merely firing his missiles at a blip on his radar. This was standard practice for the Iraqi Air Force.

STARK on the other hand, was first warned about the aircraft by the AWACS aircraft on patrol over Saudi Arabia with a mixed American and Saudi crew when it was 200 miles away and headed south over the Gulf. *STARK* then acquired the aircraft on her own SPS-49 air search radar. This was a common occurrence in these waters and the ship was not alarmed; they, as had we the year before, had seen this many times in the past. As the Mirage continued to close, the ship issued the standard warnings identifying herself as a U.S. warship and requesting identification. They received no response from the pilot.

The ship's electronic warfare operator then detected the F-1 Cyrano-IV fire control radar lock-on with the SLQ-32 ESM gear, but the ship's watch officers still did not realize they were under attack. The Exocet is a sea skimming, subsonic missile that comes in about 10 feet off the water and is difficult to detect. *STARK* did not realize she was under attack until the port lookout spotted the flame from the first missile. By then it was too late to react. The ship was not in a condition of readiness to fight off a surprise attack. The Vulcan Phalanx CIWS was, for safety reasons, not in the enabled mode which would have allowed it to autonomously detect and engage the missiles with 2,000 rounds per minute 30-millimeter depleted uranium bullets. Because the CIWS is an autonomous system, ships only activate it in known high threat situations. The system has no way of discriminating between enemy and friendly air tracks and will automatically engage anything flying towards the ship which meets the pre-set parameters. Both missiles hit and ultimately 37 American sailors were killed. *STARK* managed to fight the fires over almost a 24-hour period and limp into Bahrain late on the 18th of May.

Captain Glen Brindel was relieved of duty and retired for not defending his ship. The loss of life and damage to the ship was tragic, but equally troubling to me were the overall circumstances. The ship was in a difficult geo-political situation, operating in close proximity to two combatant nations fighting a war which did not involve the United States and under somewhat murky rules of engagement. They had been de-sensitized to the danger by the routine occurrence of Iraqi nighttime raids on Iranian shipping and by the political decision made at higher levels of the U.S. government to not designate Iraqi aircraft with hostile symbology in the tactical data system. Of the two nations at war, the United

States was more sympathetic to Iraq than to Iran; an ongoing reflection of the Iran hostage crisis during the Carter administration and the radical Islamic hostility of Iran.

Somewhat downplayed in the ensuing investigation was the fact that *STARK* faced an OUTCHOP OPPE, just as we had in *AUBREY FITCH*. At the time of the attack she was not engaged in escort operations and was focused on conducting engineering drills in preparation for the OPPE inspection. As we have seen throughout our Navy's history, an incident like *STARK* brought on a flurry of new guidance and a heightened awareness of the right of self-defense. *STARK* of course, always had the right to defend herself, she just didn't realize she was under attack until it was too late. The *STARK* incident no doubt contributed to *USS VINCENNES (CG-49)* accidently shooting down an Iranian airliner the following year. Likewise, years later, the small boat attack on *USS COLE (DDG-69)* later resulted in Navy ships taking innocent fishing vessels under fire that approached too close and did not respond to warnings.

On the morning of Friday, May 22nd, 1987, John Langknecht was relieved as CO of *AUBREY FITCH* by Commander Gary Storm. I would miss John Langknecht very much. He was a great CO and a good friend. He taught me a lot about being a CO myself and in later years I would channel him when faced with a tough situation.

The week prior to the change of command there had been a pre-sail conference in Charleston for an upcoming exercise in the Gulf of Mexico that was being run by Rear Admiral Grant Sharp, Commander, Cruiser-Destroyer Group 2. Each ship was expected to send its CO to the conference and be prepared to brief the admiral on how they would be prepared to deal with a provocation from Cuba as we transited the Florida Straits. John Langknecht would not attend because he would be gone by then. Gary Storm would not attend because he wasn't yet the Captain. Consequently, I went and briefed Admiral Sharp on how *AUBREY FITCH* would be ready to fight off the Cubans in the Florida Straits. Not like I didn't have enough to do without spending Tuesday and Wednesday in Charleston with a change of command on Friday.

We were in and out of Mayport several times in June for routine operations before leaving on the 7th of July for FLEETEX 3-87 in the Virginia Capes Operating Areas and the Gulf of Mexico. *USS IOWA (BB-61)* was one of the ships in the exercise and the reason for operating in the Gulf of Mexico was to allow *IOWA* to fire Tomahawk missiles into the range at Eglin Air Force Base, Florida in the panhandle. When brought back into commission in the 1980s, the four *IOWA* class battleships had been outfitted with the Mk-143 Tomahawk Armored Box Launchers which gave them eight missiles in canisters and an additional 24 missiles in the associated magazines.

We returned to Mayport on July 22nd, having managed to transit the Florida Straits in both directions without being attacked by the Cubans. Exercise OCEAN SAFARI 87 was next on the schedule, once again practicing the Maritime Strategy north of the Arctic Circle in Vjestfjord, Norway. I would be relieved as XO during the exercise. Following OCEAN SAFARI, *AUBREY FITCH* was scheduled to continue on in Baltic Sea Operations, or BALTOPS. I would be headed for duty in the Pentagon before BALTOPS began.

During the summer of 1987, I was in negotiations with my detailer about my next set of orders. I was due for shore duty and the conventional wisdom was that I should probably take an assignment on the Navy staff in the Pentagon in order to gain that experience while still relatively junior. I had screened for promotion to commander, although I was still wearing the uniform of a lieutenant commander. More importantly, I had also completed all the requirements for command of a surface ship, including the oral board administered by a group of three serving commanding officers, and been screened for command by the selection board convened by BuPers.

When I called my detailer to find out what was in the works, he advised that he was going to send me to some place called OP-945 in the Pentagon. "What's OP-945?" I asked.

"Something to do with computers." Hmm, that didn't sound like a good fit. I was a computer illiterate, except for what I knew about fire control computers. The *PERRY* class frigates, like *AUBREY FITCH*, had a rudimentary administrative computer system on board called SNAP II. The XO's stateroom on these ships had a SNAP II terminal installed and I had mine removed on *AUBREY FITCH* and relocated to the Ship's Office where the crew could use it; I sure wasn't. I found the telephone number for OP-945, and called to find out what they did. A civilian answered the phone and told me they did "non-tactical ADP (Automatic Data Processing) policy." This was sounding even worse. I called my detailer back again and said, "I don't want to go there, I don't know anything about computers, send me to OP-03 (Surface Warfare) or something like that."

"Nope, it's coded 1000, which means anybody can do it; we need to fill it, and you're it. Goodbye."

At the same time, my former CO in *TATTNALL*, Captain Paul Tobin, was still CO of the Surface Warfare Officer's School in Newport, Rhode Island. I consulted with him as a mentor and he suggested I come to Newport and be on his staff. I politely declined, explaining that I thought I needed the Pentagon experience at that point in my career. He was disappointed, but said he understood and didn't try to twist my arm or get my orders changed himself.

AUBREY FITCH sailed out of Mayport on the 28th of August for Ocean Safari 87. We crossed the Arctic Circle on the 13th of September and the "George" ensign, Ensign John Kirby, decked out in a jockstrap, boondockers and kapok lifejacket, went forward and painted the bullnose blue as is tradition. The bullnose is the forward-most line handling chock on the pointy end of the bow of a Navy ship. We ran John through all the routine pranks for this evolution including making him stand watch on the fo'csle in that same outfit to keep an eye out for the Arctic Circle and report his sighting to the bridge when he spotted it. John was one of the best junior officers in the wardroom and a good sport. He later converted to Public Affairs, spent several years with the Blue Angels, and ended up being the spokesman for Admiral Mike

Mullen when Mullen was both CNO and Chairman of the Joint Chiefs. When Admiral Mullen retired in 2011, then Captain John Kirby shifted over to be a spokesman for Secretary of Defense Leon Panetta. In 2012 he was selected for promotion to rear admiral and would become the Navy's chief spokesman, the Chief of Information, or CHINFO. Finally, he became the OSD spokesman for Secretary of Defense John Hagel. After his retirement he became the chief spokesman for the Department of State.

We operated inside Vjestfjord for four days, screening the carrier against simulated Soviet submarines and missile patrol boats being played by the Norwegians, and my relief, Lieutenant Commander Larry Watson, flew out to the ship to begin turnover. Larry would relieve me in Fredrikstad, Norway where I would leave the ship.

Fredrikstad, Norway lies just outside the Oslo Fjord and up its own very small and narrow fjord to the east. I left *AUBREY FITCH* that afternoon, September 21st, and took the train to Oslo to spend the night before catching a flight the next day to Washington. The train ride north along the Oslo Fjord was beautiful. I had enjoyed a good 21 month tour as XO, was headed for a couple of years of shore duty, was on the list for promotion to commander, and had screened for command. Thinking back on my uncertainty as to remaining in the Navy when I was on recruiting duty in Atlanta, I felt gratified that I had stayed in, even if it was more out of inertia than as part of a grand plan.

When I later received my copy of the cruisebook from the Ocean Safari 87, North Atlantic and Baltic Sea cruise, a very nice dedication had been written on the inside cover. It read:

Dedication

This book is dedicated to CDR Bill Sullivan, whose tireless devotion to the combat readiness of AUBREY FITCH was surpassed only by his commitment to the welfare of her crew. To him, no task was too great to accomplish; no problem too small to warrant his personal attention. If we are, indeed, a ship of professionals, we owe that attribute in no small part to his leadership and guidance as Executive Officer. Fair winds and following seas to you CDR Sullivan. Remember us fondly.

THE AUBREY FITCH CREW

I felt pretty good about that, especially since I hadn't been there when the cruisebook was put together. Beginning his PAO career early, John Kirby had been its editor.

CHAPTER 12

Assignment Pentagon

I reported to the OP-945 staff in the Pentagon on October 26, 1987. We had a small office on the 5th floor, C ring; miles from anything important. My immediate office, save for civilian Paula Davis, was a weird collection of individuals involved in writing computer policy for the U.S. Navy. OP-945 had a Secretary of the Navy title as well; DONIRM, which stood for Department of the Navy Information Resources Management. It was an odd bunch and I really felt out of place.

I was sent to a couple of local area training courses to learn something about computer security and then I was put in charge of updating the Navy's computer security policy. It felt like nothing ever got done in our office. We were like hamsters spinning the wheel. The upside was that I could take a long lunch break and go to the Pentagon Officer's Athletic Club, the old POAC, and work out and run every day. My running program really took off during my tour in OP-945. However, the positive aspects notwithstanding, I really didn't enjoy my work. Among other things, I was the subspecialty coordinator for the Navy computer systems subspecialty. When a naval officer earned an advanced degree at the Naval Postgraduate School (NPGS), he or she was awarded a subspecialty code indicating that particular skill set. The idea was that since the Navy paid for a master's degree in a specific academic discipline, the officer owed the Navy back an assignment that put those skills to work for the Navy. A degree from NPGS automatically conferred that subspecialty on the officer. A degree from another institution of higher learning had to be assessed as to whether it met the Navy criteria for subspecialty designation. This assignment made me the one who reviewed transcripts from schools other than NPGS and wielded the power to say yea or nay to subspecialty designation. Nobody above me reviewed my decisions. I didn't know how to turn on my desktop computer when I reported to OP-945. I was the guy who had the SNAP II terminal taken out of my stateroom on *AUBREY FITCH*. Needless to say, if somebody walked by the computer lab at a non-Navy postgraduate school, I conferred on them the subspecialty blessing.

I stayed in touch with Captain Paul Tobin and told him about my unhappiness. To his credit, he didn't say I told you so for not joining him in Newport. I told him that I would give it a year and then try move to another position on the Navy staff. One day in 1988 my phone rang and it was Captain Tobin who had been selected for promotion to rear admiral. He said, "Are you still trying to get out of that job you're in?"

"Well, I haven't tried too hard because I enrolled in night school at Georgetown and this job gives me the time to do it."

"Well good, don't try any more, I'm coming down to be your new boss."

Paul Tobin was a computer whiz and a good fit for the OP-945 job. It worked out after all, instead of me going to Paul Tobin, he would be coming to me.

The Georgetown enrollment I credit to Iris. I had heard about a program called National Security Studies offered by Georgetown University and told Iris about it. Getting an advanced degree was one of the tickets a naval officer was supposed to punch and I did not have one. I had been promoted to commander on January 1, 1988, so I was past the window when the Navy was likely to send me at Navy expense. The National Security Studies program was tailored to the military, and during the Fall, Winter and Spring Semesters, the classes were taught in the Pentagon beginning at 6:00 PM. It was very convenient. During the summer they were held on campus at Georgetown.

1988 was a busy year for the United States Navy in the Persian Gulf, but I was watching from the sidelines in the Pentagon. On April 14th, the *PERRY* class guided missile frigate *USS SAMUEL*

B. ROBERTS (FFG-58) hit an Iranian mine in the Persian Gulf and nearly sank. Only the heroic efforts of the crew saved the ship. *ROBERTS*, assigned to the Earnest Will mission escorting re-flagged Kuwaiti tankers through the Gulf, was enroute to a refueling rendezvous when she hit the Iranian M-08 naval mine. The mine blew a 15-foot hole in the hull, flooded the engine room, knocked the two gas turbine engines from their mounts and broke the keel of the ship. When U.S. divers later recovered several unexploded mines in the same area, they found that their serial numbers matched the sequence on mines seized the previous September aboard an Iranian mine layer, the *IRAN AJR*. On April 18th, U.S. forces retaliated in Operation Praying Mantis, a one-day campaign that was the largest American surface engagement since World War II. U.S. ships, aircraft, and troops destroyed two Iranian oil platforms used to control Iranian forces in the Persian Gulf, sank one Iranian frigate, damaged another, and sent at least three armed, high speed boats to the bottom.

All of this was very exciting for we armchair quarterbacks in the Pentagon. Things were to get even more interesting for Monday morning quarterbacking on July 3rd when the Aegis guided missile cruiser *USS VINCENNES (CG-49)* shot down an Iranian airliner on a flight between Bandar Abbas, Iran and Dubai, United Arab Emirates. *VINCENNES* was operating in the southern Persian Gulf, west of the Strait of Hormuz when she became engaged in a surface battle with Iranian armed small boats. During the engagement, Iran Air flight 655 took off from Bandar Abbas, a dual military and civil airfield, on its regularly scheduled flight to Dubai. Apparently *VINCENNES* had detected an IFF transmission from an Iranian F-14 on the ground at Bandar Abbas and when Iran Air 655 left the ground, the CIC operators and TAO assumed it was the F-14. Despite the fact that the airliner was climbing and on a known commercial air route, the TAO reported to the captain that it was descending and not responding to warning calls over the International Air Distress frequency. As the airliner closed the ship, the CO, Captain Will Rogers III, ordered it engaged with Standard SM-2 surface to air missiles. All 290 passengers perished in the shootdown. Opinions were all over the map after the incident.

Captain Rogers had earned a reputation for over-aggressiveness, so those critical of his actions blamed him for being trigger happy. Those who defended his actions cited the fact that he was already engaged in a firefight with Iranian forces, that he was misinformed by the TAO about the identity and flight profile of the aircraft, and that in the wake of the *STARK* incident, no CO was going to wait to be fired on before engaging a potentially hostile target. I was in the latter camp and believe that had I been in the same circumstances as Captain Rogers and fed the same information, I would have given the same order.

As we moved into 1989, I began negotiations with my detailer, Captain Dallas Bethea, on which ship I would get to command. The Navy "dream sheet" has three basic categories which must be prioritized: ship type, billet, and location, or home port. Billet was a given, I would be a ship captain next. For ship type I listed, *OLIVER HAZARD PERRY* class frigate, *SPRUANCE* class destroyer, and *KIDD* class destroyer. All were Commander-level commands and they were the newest available. Although I had served on two *ADAMS* class destroyers and loved them, they were getting old, had less advanced combat systems, and high maintenance 1200 psi steam propulsion plants. All the ships I listed had gas turbine engines like *AUBREY FITCH*. For location, I listed the same three I always had: Mayport, Florida; San Diego, California; and Pearl Harbor, Hawaii – warm weather being the common denominator. When I talked to Dallas he said, "You look like an FFG guy to me."

When the slate came out from PERS-41, the Surface Warfare detailing shop, I was slated to *USS SAMPSON (DDG-10)*. I was disappointed to be going to an older ship. *SAMPSON* was even older than *SEMMES* and *TATTNALL*, my first two DDGs, having been commissioned in 1961. On the plus side, *SAMPSON* was homeported in Mayport, my first choice. I dug into *SAMPSON*'s schedule and found out that she was on the list for decommissioning in mid-1991; about a year after I would take command. Further, she was not scheduled to deploy before decommissioning. Making a deployment as a commanding officer is important. Not only is it the most personally rewarding part of command—to deploy your ship in support of real world operations and national priorities—it becomes important in the eyes of selection boards when it comes time to decide who gets promoted and who gets selected for a second "major" command. *SAMPSON*'s main operational assignment before decommissioning would be to escort the aircraft carrier *USS ABRAHAM LINCOLN (CVN-72)* around South America as she made a homeport shift from Norfolk to her new homeport of San Diego. That trip might be interesting and fun, but was nothing compared to an operational deployment. I was disappointed. *SAMPSON* had been in the *USS SARATOGA (CV-60)* Battle Group and scheduled to deploy to the Mediterranean in August of 1990, but the Navy had decided to scale back the number of *ADAMS* class DDGs in the battle groups because they were getting old, were scheduled for decommissioning, and difficult to maintain. There were two of the *ADAMS* class ships in the *SARATOGA* group, *SAMPSON* and *USS CONYINGHAM (DDG-17)*. The *SARATOGA* Battle Group was under the command of Rear Admiral Nick Gee, Commander Cruiser-Destroyer Group 8, in Norfolk. *CONYINGHAM* was a Norfolk ship and *SAMPSON* was a Mayport ship. When told to drop one of the two from the group, Admiral Gee chose *SAMPSON*.

I complained about my orders to Rear Admiral Tobin and he asked me what I had put down for the first choice.

"Mayport."

"Well, you got your first choice; what you should have done is put down ship type anywhere."

He was right. He was also against me going back to Mayport. I had spent seven years there already, including my time with him on *TATTNALL*. He warned me against getting a reputation for running to the comfort zone of what was already known and not being willing to take on new and different challenges.

Finishing my tour in the Pentagon I made the drive to Newport and on the 5th of February 1990 checked in to begin the

Senior Officer Ship Material Course (SOSMRC) which was the first step in the pre-command training pipeline. Iris, Chris and Amy stayed behind in northern Virginia so that Amy could finish her high school freshman year and Chris could graduate high school before starting Florida State in the fall. We would move to Jacksonville over the summer and planned to rent our house in Virginia on the assumption that I would be coming back to the Pentagon when my command tour was complete. SOSMRC was a course that arose out of the realization that Navy surface warfare officers often reported to their first commands with widely varying levels of understanding of their engineering plants (especially if they were like me who had never served in the engineering department) and similarly uneven knowledge of how to properly assess the material condition of their ships.

I met my fellow pre-command officers (PCOs) and we were a cocky bunch; after all, we were going to command United States Navy warships. This was pretty heady stuff given the accountability and responsibility that the Navy gives to its ship commanding officers. There is a passage attributed to the author Joseph Conrad, often re-printed in Navy change of command programs, which captures this responsibility perfectly:

"Only a seaman realizes to what extent an entire ship reflects the personality and ability of one individual, her commanding officer. To a landsman this is not understandable and at times it is even difficult for us to comprehend, but it is so!

"A ship at sea is a distinct world in herself and in consideration of the protracted and distant operations of fleet units, the Navy must place great power, responsibility, and trust in the hands of those chosen for command.

"In each ship there is one man who, in the hour of emergency or peril at sea, can turn to no other man. There is one alone who is ultimately responsible for the safe navigation, engineering performance, accurate gunfire and morale of the ship. He is the Commanding Officer. He is the ship.

"This is the most difficult and demanding assignment in the Navy. There is not an instant during his tour as commanding officer that he can escape the grasp of command responsibility. His privileges in view of his obligations are almost ludicrously small; nevertheless, command is the spur which has given the Navy its great leaders.

"It is duty which most richly deserves the highest, time-honored title of the seagoing world... CAPTAIN."

This sense of responsibility and accountability was a major theme throughout the PCO course. It is not as though we didn't understand it intellectually, after all, each of us had served several tours at sea and been commissioned officers on average about 18 years. Joseph Conrad wrote those words long before today's modern communications systems, satellite radios and other capabilities that, today, tie a ship to higher authority ashore in a way that only science fiction writers imagined in the early twentieth century. Nevertheless, classroom discussions notwithstanding, it was not until a brand new ship captain for the first time set the sea detail in his first ship command, ordered the lines cast off the pier, and moved his ship from the harbor to the open sea that the enormity of his personal responsibility hit home.

On the 8th of May, my life changed in ways I will never fully know. Unfortunately, it was due to a tragedy which struck *USS CONYINGHAM*. While underway conducting work-up training for her deployment to the Mediterranean with the *SARATOGA* Battle Group, she experienced a major conflagration in the forward fireroom. A valve on a main fuel pump failed catastrophically, spraying fuel oil under pressure into the fireroom. Immediately sparking to fire, the fuel continued to spray, feeding the fire which eventually burned into the superstructure and isolated the ship fore and aft. In the course of the firefighting effort, the ship's Operations Officer was killed and 18 sailors injured; some severely. The ship was so badly damaged that the decision was made to decommission and scrap her.

As a result, *SAMPSON* was now back in the *SARATOGA* Battle Group and scheduled to deploy shortly after I took command. I was naturally happy for that, but not for the way it came about. I will never know if *SAMPSON* would have been sent to Desert Shield and Desert Storm if *CONYINGHAM* had sailed as scheduled with the *SARATOGA* group. I have no way of knowing how my career might have turned out differently had *CONYINGHAM* not had the fire. Instead of escorting *ABRAHAM LINCOLN* around South America and then beginning preparations for decommissioning, I would be sailing with the carrier battle group on what would turn out to be an eight-month deployment in support of operations Desert Shield and Desert Storm. Of course, in May of 1990 nobody knew that in August of that year Iraq would invade Kuwait and that the United States would go to war to right that wrong.

Next on the schedule was the PCO course itself, also in Newport. The PCO course was 6 weeks long and designed to get officers ready to command a ship in all of the other warfare areas besides engineering, including tactics, navigation, leadership, and to otherwise prepare for the awesome responsibility about to be assumed. It afforded the opportunity to think about our command philosophy and emphasized the necessity to be ready to fight the ship in wartime. The course was taught by more senior officers, all of whom had already commanded a ship at the rank of commander or above. Probably the most valuable aspect of the course was the wisdom imparted by these officers in discussing situations and scenarios which we were all likely to confront at one time or another.

The "command philosophy" angle was played up pretty big and one of the things we were encouraged to do was draft up a written command philosophy laying out our beliefs and standards for the ship we were to command. This would be turned into a ship's instruction once you took command and all officers and chiefs would be expected to read it and know what you believed in. I did it but never published it on *SAMPSON*; it made me uncomfortable. First of all, it reeked of self-importance. Secondly, I believed that the way the captain sets the command climate and establishes his standards is how he acts, not what he writes down on a piece of paper. I hearkened back to the old adage that your crew would read 25% of what you wrote and listen to 50% of what you said, but watch 100% of what you did.

The remainder of the pre-command training pipeline included two weeks at the Tactical Training Group, Atlantic in Dam Neck, Virginia where we were brought up to speed on all the latest tactics and procedures for battle group operations. My time at CRUDESGRU 12 stood me in good stead for this training. That was followed by a one-week Harpoon Surface to Surface missile course, also at Dam Neck. Much attention was placed on the employment of the Harpoon missile when after action analysis of engagements with the Libyans in the Gulf of Sidra revealed that the U.S. Navy had not covered itself in glory in employing the Harpoon.

My last stop before reporting to *SAMPSON* in Mayport was at Commander, Naval Surfaces Forces, Atlantic (SURFLANT) in Norfolk for two days of briefings on how important it was to pay attention to all the various SURFLANT rules and regulations. SURFLANT was commanded by my former boss at CRUDESGRU 12, Joe Donnell, now a three-star vice admiral. When it was time on the schedule to have a meeting with Admiral Donnell, all he wanted to talk about was our first barge trip to the Porquerolles and our swim through the underwater cave.

"Man that was dumb, we coulda both drowned!"

PART III

Desert Shield / Desert Storm

CHAPTER 13

First Command

On Friday, July 27th 1990, I awoke early in our rented house in Jacksonville, Florida and drove to Mayport Naval Station, arriving before sunrise to board *USS SAMPSON (DDG-10)* as her prospective commanding officer. *SAMPSON* was due to get underway at 7:00 that morning for a one-day sea trial before deploying on August 7th for the Mediterranean. This was to be my one underway opportunity as PCO before relieving Commander Al Myers the following Friday, August 3rd.

I was met on the quarterdeck by the acting XO, and CDO, Weapons Officer Lieutenant Commander Tony Nardella. The XO, Lieutenant Commander Dave Birdwell, was on pre-deployment leave until mid-week. Tony walked me up to the CO's cabin where I met Al Myers for the first time. Al was a gracious host. Throughout the week of turnover, he could not have been nicer and more supportive. *SAMPSON* enjoyed an excellent reputation on the Mayport waterfront under Al's leadership.

Over the next week I got to know my crew and my wardroom and I was impressed with what I saw. The XO, Lieutenant Commander Dave Birdwell, had worked for my buddy Dave Stone when Dave was XO in *USS RICHMOND K. TURNER (CG-20)* and Birdwell was Combat Systems Officer. Nothing is more important than a good relationship between the CO and the XO of a Navy ship in setting the command climate and operating the ship. Dave Birdwell went out of his way in accommodating me, almost to the point of obsequiousness. This was initially somewhat satisfying, but over time it began to grate on me as I learned more about his style when dealing with subordinates.

We were out in the morning and back in in the afternoon for the one-day sea trial and my opportunity to see the ship in action under Al Myers' command. I was quite comfortable with the *ADAMS* class DDG having served in *SEMMES* and *TATTNALL*. The next week, leading up to the Friday change of command ceremony was routine until Thursday. I was briefed by all the Department Heads, toured the ship, met with Division Officers and Chief Petty Officers, and signed for all accountable items.

The *ADAMS* class DDGs were pure destroyer. Bristling with weapons and featuring the sleek lines of a true "greyhound of the sea," they were good looking warships and in their heyday the most desirable destroyer ship command. 29 were built between 1958 and 1967, with three going to the Australian Navy and three to the German Navy. By 1990 however, the *ADAMS* class was nearing the end of service life and, without the modern defenses and tactical data systems of the *SPRUANCE* class destroyers and *TICONDEROGA* class Aegis cruisers, they were considered ill-equipped to survive modern warfare at sea. That is why *SAMPSON* was scheduled to decommission in 1991 and why the *SARATOGA* Battle Group had initially dropped *SAMPSON* out of the deployment in favor of *CONYINGHAM*. Nevertheless, with two five-inch gun mounts, the MK-11 guided missile launching system, SM-1 surface to air missiles, MK-32 anti-submarine torpedo tubes and the ASROC launching system, *SAMPSON* was an impressive ship. 437 feet in length and displacing 4,500 tons when fully loaded, her four 1,200 psi boilers and 70,000 horsepower twin screw turbines were capable of moving her through the water at 32 knots.

On Thursday, August 2, 1990, Iraq invaded Kuwait. There had been advance warning of an Iraqi buildup of forces near the Kuwait border, but the United States believed Iraq was merely trying to pressure Kuwait to forgive some debt that had been built up during the Iran-Iraq War. Iraq had also accused Kuwait of stealing Iraqi petroleum through slant drilling. Iraq was unable to pay back more than $80 billion, $14 billion of which was owed to Kuwait, that had been borrowed to finance the Iran-Iraq War. Iraq further accused Kuwait of over-production of oil which kept revenues down for Iraq. There was also a longstanding belief in Iraq that Kuwait was a natural part of Iraq carved off as a result of British imperialism. After signing the Anglo-Ottoman Convention of 1913, the United Kingdom split Kuwait from the Ottoman territories into a separate sheikhdom.

On August 2nd at 2:00 AM local time, Iraq launched an invasion of Kuwait with four elite Iraqi Republican Guard divisions and Army Special Forces units equivalent to a fifth division. Within two days of intense combat, most of the Kuwaiti armed forces were either overrun or escaped to neighboring Saudi Arabia and Bahrain. The state of Kuwait was annexed, and Saddam Hussein announced that it was now the 19th Province of Iraq.

I took command of *SAMPSON* the next day, Friday August 3rd with the events in Kuwait lending an air of uncertainty to what the future held in store for *SAMPSON* and the *SARATOGA* Battle Group. Captain John Mitchell, Commodore of Destroyer Squadron 12, my new boss, was the guest speaker for the ceremony and made note of the fact that *SAMPSON* would sail off on a six-month Mediterranean deployment in a mere four days with her new captain amid much uncertainty and a developing crisis in the Middle East. I had known and liked John Mitchell during my DESRON 8 days when he was CO of *USS FAHRION (FFG-22)*. I suspect that when my orders were seen to almost exactly coincide with the ship's departure on deployment, eyebrows were raised and questions asked as to whether this was a smart thing to do. My guess is that John Mitchell went to bat for me, knowing me from those days when he commanded *FAHRION*.

It was a great day, although my father was convinced that I had been given command of this old ship because I was not a Naval Academy graduate. He was proud, but he still believed the "ring knockers" ran the Navy and they would do whatever it took to hold down some OCS upstart. He later told Iris to not be surprised if I was never promoted to captain for the same reason.

We used the occasion for a big family reunion that weekend and had everybody down to the ship on Saturday to be toured around and take pictures. In the meantime, the United States was beginning to figure out how to deal with the Iraqi invasion of Kuwait. President George H. W. Bush was famously quoted stating that "this will not stand." What that meant for *SAMPSON* we did not yet know, but speculation was that our Mediterranean deployment might become a wartime deployment to the Middle East. On the 3rd of August, the United Nations Security Council passed Resolution 660 condemning the Iraqi invasion of Kuwait and demanding that Iraq unconditionally withdraws all forces.

Once entering the Med, *SAMPSON* was scheduled to detach from the *SARATOGA* Battle Group and represent the United States in something called the NATO On-Call Force Mediterranean (NAVOCFORMED). NAVOCFORMED was a periodically assembled gathering of NATO naval assets which would exercise and operate together in the Mediterranean Sea for a period of six months per year. In 1990 that group would include ships from the U.S., Great Britain, Germany, Italy, Spain, Portugal, Greece, and Turkey under the command of a Greek commodore. We were looking forward to this experience and had loaded the ship with a good supply of American beer and California wines which we knew would be put to good use during port visits when it was our turn to host a reception.

On Monday August 6th, the day before sailing, we made all the final preparations for a six-month deployment that would begin the next morning with a 10:00 AM sortie from Mayport. At the navigation brief, I declined to take a harbor pilot for the underway, asking only that we have one tug assigned to make up to the bow and help pull us away from the pier. This raised a few eyebrows, but I had served on two ships in Mayport, which featured a simple sea detail, and had served in two *ADAMS* class DDGs, so was comfortable that I didn't need any help.

I slept restlessly the night of the 6th, both because I was about to take a destroyer to sea for the first time as her captain, and because I would once again be leaving the family for six months. Chris had graduated from high school in Virginia the previous June and would be heading off to Florida State to begin his freshman year later that month. Amy would be entering the tenth grade at

Englewood High School in Jacksonville. These departures were always bittersweet; the knowledge that we would be apart for half a year was difficult for both me and Iris, but I had the parallel excitement of setting sea detail and heading off on a whole new series of adventures. I believe that, knowing I was thus conflicted, Iris was also anxious for the cruise to begin; just to get it started and bring the day of return that much closer. The final couple of weeks were always stressful, with me being distracted by the preparations and the pull of the ship, and both of us feeling the stress of taking care of all the little details of preparing for a six-month separation.

I was up early on August 7th and out the door in my summer white uniform to go to the ship. Iris, Chris, and Amy would follow later to be on the pier with the other families to watch us leave. It was to be a big underway in Mayport. In addition to *SAMPSON*, the carrier *SARATOGA*, the Aegis cruiser *USS PHILIPPINE SEA (CG-58)*, the destroyer *USS SPRUANCE (DD-963)*, and the frigate *USS ELMER MONTGOMERY (FF-1082)* would sortie that morning. We would rendezvous at sea with the Norfolk-based cruiser *USS BIDDLE (CG-34)*, Charleston-based frigate *USS THOMAS C. HART (FF-1092)* and the combat support ship *USS DETROIT (AOE-4)* from Earle, New Jersey. To add to the excitement were the rumors swirling that because of the Iraq invasion our mission could be drastically altered—we might be going to war.

As I got out of the car on the pier, there was already a gathering of families saying goodbye to their sailors. The quarterdeck rang four bells and announced "*SAMPSON*, Arriving." One of the wives walked up to me as I crossed the pier and said, "Bring them home safely Captain." It was a sobering moment.

I was met on the quarterdeck by Chief Engineer and CDO from last night, Lieutenant Terry Culton. It made sense, we had lit the plant off the day prior and Terry probably figured he should spend the night on the ship, so he might as well stand CDO too. He probably swapped with one of the other department heads to give him one last night at home with his family.

"How we doing, CHENG?"

"Ready to go, Captain, 1B and 2A boilers on the line; we're on ship's power; only taking water, sewage and phone lines from the pier. Having a little trouble with the ABC in the Forward Fireroom." ABC was Automatic Boiler Controls.

"Anything to worry about?"

"No sir, we might make a little smoke before we get it under control when we change steam demand."

"How about comms?" The first day underway for a battle group always featured communications problems.

"All up and checked out. Ops was in early this morning."

"No changes to the underway plan?"

"No sir."

The XO came to the quarterdeck and we went to my cabin and talked about what had to be done that morning before sailing, when we'd ask the family members to leave the ship, and so forth.

Iris, Chris and Amy showed up around 8:30 and we joined other wives and children in the wardroom. We took a picture in front of the portrait of old Rear Admiral William T. Sampson, a hero of the Spanish-American War.

I received the muster report; one unauthorized absentee, a seaman from 1st Division.

At 9:30 the word was passed, "Now station the special sea and anchor detail, all hands man your sea and anchor detail stations. The ship expects to get underway at 1000. The uniform for sea and anchor detail is summer white. All guests are requested to depart the ship."

I gave Iris and Amy big kisses and hugs and shook Chris's hand. We still joke that Sullivan men don't hug. Iris told me to "do good." They went to the pier and I went to the bridge.

At 10:00, with one tug made up to the bow to help us move away from the pier, we took in all lines and got underway. As soon as I put a twist on the ship to kick the stern out, a huge cloud of black smoke poured out of the forward stack. It went on for almost 30 seconds and looked like Mount Krakatoa erupting. The damn automatic boiler controls. What a dramatic way to begin. I was sure Admiral Gee was over on the Flag Bridge in SARATOGA and watching his flotilla get underway. He was probably standing next to Captain Jim Hinkle, Commodore of Destroyer Squadron 24, who would be my operational boss for the deployment.

The engineers balanced the fuel- air mixture manually and the smoke cleared. Still, the big black cloud drifted lazily over Naval Air Station Mayport on the incoming sea breeze. Forward fireroom ABC would be a problem for some time, but I had a bigger engineering problem on the horizon.

We negotiated the channel and made our way to the open sea, securing sea detail and changing into working uniform to begin the Atlantic transit. SARATOGA had to wait for the tides a little later that morning before she got underway. Once she reached the open sea, COMDESRON 24 ordered a sector screen around the carrier and put SAMPSON on the port bow of the carrier. A sector screen was a cold war, fight the Soviets, formation intended to provide defense-in-depth for the carrier, or high-value unit, against air, surface or sub-surface attack.

We raced into our assigned sector at 25 knots and just as we were about to report "Alpha Station," indicating we were on station, there was a loud bang and the ship began to lose speed. Quickly on the 21MC or "bitch box," came the report from Terry Culton in Main Control, "Lost fires in 1B boiler, cross-connecting the plant."

"What happened?"

"Don't know yet. Sounded like an explosion in the forward fireroom."

The engineers rapidly cross connected the plant, running both shafts off 2A boiler in the after fireroom. They began lighting fires in 1A boiler and, although we could no longer make 25 knots on one boiler, we were in our sector with enough speed available to patrol. Shortly thereafter Terry came to the bridge.

"We blew out the outer air casing in 1B boiler." The air casing feeds air under pressure to the boiler and is fed by the ship's forced draft blowers which run off 1200-pound steam. Because the boiler is pressurized to 1275 psi, the air must be pressurized to enter the system. Terry told me that the same boiler air casing had blown out three months earlier and been repaired by the destroyer tender in Mayport, *USS YOSEMITE (AD-19)*. The welds must not have been strong enough. Fortunately, the section that blew out was on the back of the boiler, forward, with only a catwalk between the boiler and the forward bulkhead of the fireroom. Nobody had been in the way and nobody was hurt. The noise scared the hell out of everyone.

I picked up the red phone and reported the casualty to Commodore Hinkle. A few minutes later Admiral Gee came on the circuit. My mind was racing; would I have to turn around and go back to Mayport for repairs? How humiliating after the glorious sailing of the battle group only two hours earlier. We still had three boilers and that was enough, but what about fixing 1B? It sounded like a depot level job.

"Bill, what do you think?" asked Admiral Gee.

"Sir, we're fine now, we can keep going, but I'm going to need some help fixing the air casing." I told him it had blown out three months earlier and been repaired.

"OK, we'll work it from here. Keep me posted. Over."

"Aye, aye, sir. Out."

As we continued our transit of the Atlantic, the United States continued to fashion a response to the Iraqi invasion. On August 7th, the day we departed Mayport, President Bush authorized the deployment of U.S. ground forces to Saudi Arabia to protect against a further incursion by Iraq into the Saudi oil fields. We learned that this response, including the dispatch of Air Force F-15's from Langley Air Force Base in Virginia, was called Operation Desert Shield. An arms embargo was declared on weapons and military equipment destined for Iraq and even the Russians and Chinese joined in. All major world powers and most of the Arab world condemned the invasion.

The *USS DWIGHT D. EISENHOWER (CVN-69)* Battle Group who had been about to depart the Mediterranean and be replaced by our *SARATOGA* group, was sent through the Suez Canal to the Red Sea to enforce the embargo from that direction. Goods intended for Iraq entered over land after being offloaded in Aqaba, Jordan. Ships were similarly ordered to the Persian Gulf to blockade the only sea approach to Iraq.

On Friday the 10th of August, it was decided that *SARATOGA*, with COMCRUDESGRU 8 embarked and accompanied by *PHILIPPINE SEA*, would sprint ahead of the rest of the group, make a high speed transit of the Med, and pass through the Suez Canal to replace *EISENHOWER. EISENHOWER*, at the end of a six-month deployment, would return to Norfolk.

Earlier that day we had set EMCON A (alpha) in the battle group, meaning that no radars and no radio transmissions were authorized except in a dire emergency. All communications would be by satellite message traffic or, locally, via flashing light or flaghoist. I questioned the need for this. This was what we would do to avoid detection by the Soviets with their ELINT reconnaissance satellites. The Iraqis had no such capability and the Russians were supposed to be on our side. Wouldn't it be better if Saddam Hussein knew that forces were massing against him? He might lose his nerve and leave Kuwait. Everything happening was all over the news anyway.

The decision to begin the *SARATOGA/PHILIPPINE SEA* sprint was made that night and we received a FLASH message so informing the battle group. We were still in our screen sector on the port bow and forward of *SARATOGA* when they began the sprint around midnight on the 10th. I was in my rack asleep when the OOD, a lieutenant, called me.

"Sir, we're getting flashing light from *SARATOGA* and she appears to have sped up." No radars, no bridge-to-bridge radio, it was all guesswork.

"OK, where is she now?"

"Just off the starboard quarter. I'm going to ease over to the far right of our sector and let her go by."

"OK, let me know when she's past us."

I hung up the phone and started to go back to sleep when suddenly, what he had just told me popped clearly into my head. He was proposing to cut across the carrier's bow and let her pass up our port side. I hopped out of bed, pulled on my trousers and shoes and raced to the bridge. Everyone was out on the starboard bridge wing and I joined them. Looming huge, almost directly astern but still slightly to starboard, and flashing her signal lamps furiously was *SARATOGA* with a full head of steam up. Her range was difficult to judge at night but she was pretty close.

"Left full rudder, all ahead flank!" I shouted. I now had the conn by Navy Regulations. We turned 90 degrees and *SARATOGA* whipped by astern of us, still flashing away on the signal lamps. Our signalmen were responding and shouting down from the signal bridge as they broke the signal.

Loosely translated, *SARA* was saying, "Get the hell out of the way, coming through!"

After we'd returned to base course and assumed our station on the new Guide, *DETROIT*, I spoke to the OOD.

"What were you thinking cutting across *SARA*'s bow?"

"Sir, I didn't want to get out of our sector or fall behind."

That night I lost confidence in this particular officer on the bridge and watched him carefully when he was the OOD; but I did not disqualify him and I never hurt him in a fitness report. I never made him an inport CDO despite him being one of the more senior junior officers in the ship. When I was turning over with Al Myers, Al told me this officer was one of his better OODs. Years later I ran into the same officer who had left the Navy but stayed in the reserves and had made commander. He was, by coincidence, part of my own reserve detachment when I was stationed in Korea as Commander of U.S. Naval Forces. He asked me why I'd never let him become a CDO. I told him that night caused me to lose confidence in him and that a later incident only added to my doubts.

Weeks after the incident I received a handwritten letter from the Navigator in *SARATOGA* apologizing for almost running us down and explaining how the EMCON condition limited his options to communicate. I wrote him back and told him the foul-up was ours and not to worry.

As we continued across the Atlantic, we received word that in order to enforce the arms embargo on Iraq, naval forces would begin conducting Maritime Interception Operations (MIO) in the Red Sea and Persian Gulf in order to board, search and clear or not clear ships heading either into Aqaba, Jordan or Iraq or Kuwait in the Persian Gulf. We were told to dust-off our Visit, Board and Search Bills and be ready. For decades every Navy ship had a Visit, Board and Search Bill or a Salvage Bill which laid out the procedures and personnel assignments to do these missions. In practice, these generally existed on paper and were not routinely exercised. Although the Navy, with Coast Guard law enforcement detachments, had been doing counter-drug board and searches for several years and had performed a similar mission during the Vietnam War in Operation Market Time, these were not routine operations. I was initially skeptical based on my own experience, but it quickly became evident that this was not a drill; we needed to get ready. All the while, our exact fate remained unknown although it was becoming more and more apparent that we would likely end up in the Middle East after merely passing through the Mediterranean.

We pulled together two boarding teams with Operations Officer Lieutenant Commander Jim Carr leading one and Weapons Officer Lieutenant Commander Tony Nardella the other. We had no shortage of volunteers from the crew to fill out the teams so we picked the most physically fit and imposing from among those we could spare off the ship and began rehearsing our procedures. We were in receipt of numerous guidance messages about the composition of the teams, how they were to be armed, what to look for in searching a ship and reviewing its manifest, and what to say on the radio when hauling them over for inspection. The rules of engagement, or ROE, were carefully laid out.

We were poorly equipped for the mission. Using the motor whaleboat as the boarding vessel, our teams would be wearing bulky kapok life jackets and heavy WWII era steel helmets while they climbed the sometimes very steep and tall sides of merchant ships. We didn't have flak jackets or more suitable headgear and we didn't have weapons, other than the .45 pistol, that would be easy to use in the cramped quarters below decks on a ship–we had M-14 rifles which were large and heavy. Because there was concern about the vulnerability of the first man to stick his head over the railing, we would have helicopter support to surveil the decks for any ambushes and procedures which called for the merchant masters to tell us the number of crewmembers on board and muster them in a visible place on the main deck, away from the ladder, with only those absolutely necessary allowed to remain on the bridge and in the engine room.

We transited Gibraltar on the 16th of August and sailed straight through the Med towards Port Said, Egypt for the canal transit. Ironically, we caught back up with *SARATOGA* and *PHILIPPINE SEA* who, after the sprint across the Atlantic had been held up in the Med.

Meanwhile, in the forward fireroom, repairs were underway on 1B boiler air casing. The 6ᵗʰ Fleet staff, at the behest of CRUDESGRU 8, had sent a couple of boiler technicians from the tender and some appropriate metal stock out to the ship as we went by Naples. Our own Hull Technician Second Class James Taylor from Repair Division had been working with them and welding a new section of outer air casing to the boiler. I later awarded Petty Officer Taylor a Navy Achievement Medal for his outstanding work as the welder who fixed 1B boiler. We never had any more trouble with that air casing. We also got some help from *USS BIDDLE (CG-34)* in the person of Boiler Tender Third Class Paul Lloyd, an Automatic Boiler Controls Technician. Petty Officer Lloyd solved our ABC problems and liked it on *SAMPSON* so much he asked if he could stay.

On the 21ˢᵗ of August, *SARATOGA, PHILIPPINE SEA, BIDDLE* and *DETROIT* again moved ahead of the rest of us in order to transit the Suez Canal one day before we would. *SPRUANCE* had been dropped off in the central Mediterranean and she took up *SAMPSON*'s spot in the NATO NAVOCFORMED task force. *SPRUANCE* had been upgraded with the MK-41 Vertical Launch system and carried a full load of Tomahawk cruise missiles. If necessary she could launch these into targets in Iraq from the eastern Med, overflying either friendly Turkey or not so friendly Syria.

SAMPSON remained in company with the frigates *ELMER MONTGOMERY* and *THOMAS C. HART* and was to be the third ship of the Suez Canal convoy south behind the two frigates on August 23ʳᵈ, me being the junior of the three CO's. This was to be my fourth time through the canal, but my first in command. Little did I know that a challenge lay ahead which would test my abilities and draw heavily on that prior experience.

CHAPTER 14

Déjà Vu in the Suez Canal

T he evening before the transit was typical of all such evolutions, as I have previously described, and I was unable to get any sleep before the transit was to begin. At about 11:00 PM I was on the bridge reviewing the charts and trying to get my situational awareness and night vision up to par for our movement into the canal. As I stood outside on the port bridge wing looking out at the lights of Port Said, my hand came in contact with the bridge bulkhead. It was soaking wet with condensation. Being a warm, humid night in the Middle East, I was not surprised, but I immediately thought back to my experience in *SEMMES*. In a rare moment of prescience, I thought to myself, "We could have fog tonight in the canal."

Earlier that evening in the Wardroom, we had conducted our navigation brief for the canal transit. I had briefly talked to the officers, chiefs and petty officers present about my *SEMMES* experience in the canal and had made it clear that I took the requirement to have a boat ready to go very seriously. I also described how we had shackled lines together and run them across the canal and warned that we needed to be prepared to do the same if necessary. How right I was to be.

We set sea detail around 11:45 as things were beginning to happen on the bridge-to-bridge radio and I wanted to be ready to move when it was our turn. This time we would have the advantage of following *MONTGOMERY* and *HART* so would have some warning before it was time to weigh anchor.

About 20 minutes before weighing anchor, Chief Engineer Terry Culton, called me on the bitch box from Main Control to report that while warming up main engines, the valve stem on the port engine astern throttle valve had snapped in two. The good news was that it had snapped with the valve in the closed position. The bad news was that without a repair, we would be unable to back the port engine. We had a spare valve stem in the supply storeroom, but no time to repair it before getting underway. I asked Terry if the valve was fully closed and he said it was. "And we can operate the port engine ahead?" I asked. "Yes sir," said Terry, "we just won't be able to back the port engine."

This was "command decision" time. We *could* delay going through the canal. Maybe we could bring up the rear after repairs, otherwise it meant a 24-hour delay in transiting the canal. We *were* in a hurry after all, responding with a show of force to the Iraqi invasion of Kuwait. Would one little DDG make a difference to Saddam Hussein? Doubtful, but that wasn't the point.

I went through the upcoming canal transit in my mind. All things being equal, I should only have to back down once, when we dropped the anchor and set it in the Great Bitter Lake. I could do that on one engine, no sweat. It wasn't even a precision anchoring–just find an open spot and drop the hook. What if the ship in front of us in the canal had an emergency and we had to stop in a hurry? It would take a bigger bell on the starboard engine and the ship wouldn't back straight, but we could stop her. I decided to get underway as scheduled.

We got underway without incident, transited through the city of Port Said with Pilot #1, and traded him for Pilot #2 for the trip down to Ismailia. Suez Canal pilots are an interesting group and this one was no different. He reminded me of the *Dallas* fan we had in *AUBREY FITCH*; loud, blustery, and full of self-importance. All was normal as we entered the long 180 degrees' true leg which leads to Ismailia. At about 2:00 AM the fog started to rapidly set in. Gradually, *T.C. HART* began to fade from view. I began to get that sinking feeling in my stomach that things were about to get dicey–I had seen this before, 14 years earlier. Then it hadn't been my ship. That makes a difference.

I began to gain an appreciation for what Fred Williamson had gone through in *SEMMES*. I had to communicate concerns and desires to my Egyptian pilot who was the only one who could talk reliably to the ships behind us, including 300,000 tons of supertanker a half mile back. I called Commander Bob Higgins, the CO of *ELMER MONTGOMERY*, and asked him about his visibility. He said it was fine. Maybe we would punch through this in a few minutes.

About then, *T.C. HART*'s stern light disappeared from view completely and the sides of the canal began to get hard to see. With a knot in my stomach and a premonition of trouble ahead I told conning officer Warrant Officer Dave Stoudt to slow to five knots and looked at the pilot. He nodded and immediately called somebody, presumably his fellow pilot on the supertanker, and said something in Arabic.

As we slowed, the fog closed in completely. I could not see the sides of the canal and could barely see the bullnose a mere 125 feet ahead. *SAMPSON* was equipped with the standard SPS-10 surface search radar which was fine for the open ocean but not much good for close in navigation in a confined area like the canal. We also had a Marconi commercial short range navigation radar, the LN-66, with a repeater on the bridge which could be tuned to provide a reliable, close-quarters radar picture. The pilot and I, unable to see anything out the windows immediately turned our attention to the LN-66. The last time I could see, we seemed to be in the middle of the channel so I told Dave Stoudt to steer 180 until I told him otherwise. "XO," I said, "tell the fo'csle to stand by the starboard anchor." "Dave," I said to Warrant Officer Stoudt, "indicate 999." "999" is indicated on the engine order telegraph to tell the engine room we wanted "maneuvering combinations," a simplified way to order speed changes in five knot increments for rapid engine order changes while maneuvering.

For what seemed like a full nautical mile, the pilot and I peered at the LN-66, making minute, one degree, course changes when the radar picture made it look like we were drifting to one side of the canal or the other. Just as in 1976, we had a two knot following current, which at five knots rung up, made the ship respond sluggishly to rudder orders.

I had a sinking feeling that we were going to have to stop or risk running into the side of the canal. I also knew what would happen if we got too close to the sides with a following current. If we anchored, we would have to try to do it in the middle of the channel and use the engines to keep the ship upstream against the anchor. Sure would be nice to have a backing capability on the port shaft if it came to that. No one else on the bridge said a word except to acknowledge orders.

Navigating by the LN-66 was getting sloppier and sloppier. It had been so long since I had seen the sides of the canal that I had no confidence in our position relative to the canal banks. The last two lights I had seen had been close aboard to port. The pilot didn't seem at all confident in what we were doing and was perfectly content to let me give all the course correction orders—a sure sign that he felt lost too.

Finally, we passed close aboard another of the lighted posts on the port side. This after we had been steering 183 for several nervous minutes. That did it for me. We needed to stop the ship before something bad happened. I sensed we were getting closer and closer to the port side of the canal and if I waited too long to drop the hook, it would be too late; we'd get pushed into the side by the current and it would be *SEMMES* all over again.

I told Dave Stoudt to ring up All Stop and told the fo'csle again to stand by the anchor. I went to the starboard bridge wing and decided I couldn't wait any longer and gave the order to back down the starboard engine and let go the starboard anchor. The ship was still moving ahead at about two knots, but I didn't care. To his credit, the pilot immediately began shouting into the bridge-to-bridge radio to warn the ships behind us.

Backing only the starboard engine will tend to drive the stern to port which was exactly the wrong direction, but without that port astern throttle valve, I had no choice. Somehow, with full right rudder, backing one-third on the starboard engine and the effect of the anchor dragging along the bottom forward, the ship stayed fairly straight in the channel. As it worked out, the following current caught the ship on the port quarter and pushed the stern to starboard. This was extremely fortunate because we were able to twist the ship to starboard by going ahead on the port engine and back on the starboard. I thought if we could keep this up, using more power backing than ahead and working against the anchor, we might be able to keep the ship in the middle of the canal.

This was no time to be relaying my thoughts to Dave Stoudt so I took the conn myself. For the next two hours we jockeyed the engines and rudders and either heaved around or payed out anchor chain in a desperate battle to keep the ship in the channel. The southerly current was alternately our friend and our enemy. At one point, we were across the canal at a 60-degree angle, but managed to get back straight and headed fair.

By 4:30, the fog was beginning to lift and the sky was lightening and we began to see exactly where we were in relation to the canal banks. Looking aft, I could see the supertanker and the several ships astern of him leaning against the east bank of the canal. Looking ahead I saw nothing but empty channel. *MONTGOMERY* and *T.C. HART* must have been just ahead of the fog. I briefly kicked myself, wondering if I had just pressed on a little further, would we have broken out of the fog and now be steaming happily towards the Great Bitter Lake? No way of knowing so I didn't dwell on it. CIC had been keeping *MONTGOMERY*, the senior ship, aware of our status.

While we had been maneuvering violently to stay in the channel, I had told the XO to get the mooring lines on deck and shackled together and to ready the motor whaleboat and boat crew to use them as we had done in *SEMMES*. We were still too close to the canal bank to port and I was afraid we would lose control of the ship while bringing up the anchor. Weapons Officer Tony Nardella had come to the bridge and been briefed on my intentions while we were maneuvering and he understood the plan.

We lowered the Motor Whaleboat with the Auxiliaries Officer, Ensign Marvin Foster, as the boat officer. This was less than three weeks after the Iraqi invasion of Kuwait and while President Bush was still building a coalition for what would become Operation Desert Storm. The threat of a terrorist attack in the Suez Canal was taken very seriously and the Egyptians had agreed to provide extra security. A ship sunk in the canal would have created a major problem for the force buildup for Desert Shield. So would a DDG stuck sideways in the canal for that matter. We sent Marvin and the whale boat crew towing a shackled mooring line over to the west bank of the canal, not knowing how the Egyptian soldiers might react. Unlike that night on *SEMMES*, this time there were soldiers there and they proved more than eager to help heave the lines onto the bollards once Marvin had communicated our plans through a combination of sign language and Indian-talk.

Our situation was considerably different than it had been on *SEMMES*. We had never touched the banks and were not stuck in the mud. Once we got the lines to bollards fore and aft and warped the ship to the middle of the channel, she sat there nicely with just an occasional backing bell on the starboard engine to offset the effects of the current. The anchor chain was tending across the stem of the ship to port. This helped stabilize the ship with tension on the forward line to starboard, like a hammerlock moor.

For the first time in four hours I relaxed a little while the XO, department heads, and I talked through our procedures to slip the moor and get underway. The pilot was anxious to get going and by 5:00 the sun was coming up and the fog was almost entirely gone. We put a group of four seamen ashore at each bollard, dragged the anchor under the stem of the ship and up to the hawsepipe, secured it, disengaged the wildcat, and then slipped both lines together while moving slowly forward. The ship smoothly moved forward while we hauled in the mooring lines fore and aft and then recovered the motor whaleboat and the linehandlers. Marvin Foster had a story to tell as did all the linehandlers who had set foot on the banks of the Suez Canal.

When the pilot left the ship in Ismailia, I shook his hand and had the Supply Officer bring up an extra carton of Marlboro's to show my appreciation for his assistance. He had hung tough while we were scrambling about trying to keep the ship off the bank and had kept us from getting run down by a supertanker in the process. I have no idea what he told pilot #3 when he came aboard; either to watch out for us because we were dangerous, or perhaps that we were actually fairly resourceful.

At about noon we anchored in the Great Bitter Lake and I went to my cabin for the first time in 14 hours. As I paused, out of sight of my crew for the first time since the crisis had begun, my knees began shaking uncontrollably and an overwhelming sense of emotional relief came over me. I felt a tear run down my cheek. I had been in command only 20 days and had almost run my ship aground in the Suez Canal at the height of a major U.S. military response to an international crisis. Having been First Lieutenant in *SEMMES* in 1976 had been a saving grace. Because of that experience, I had known what to expect and what could be done to overcome it.

After the northbound convoy passed us in the Great Bitter Lake we were underway south again to exit the canal at Port Suez and complete the all night transit of the Gulf Suez. Once entering the Red Sea, we would begin Maritime Intercept Operations on the Aqaba Gate Guard station in support of the UN sanctions against Iraq.

CHAPTER 15

Stop, Board, and Search

*S*ARATOGA took up station about 100 miles south of our Gate Guard stations and began conducting flight operations. The Gate Guard ships, all cruisers, destroyers and frigates, were arrayed across the northern end of the Red Sea with orders to stop, board, and search any ship intending to enter or exiting the Gulf of Aqaba. Those exiting were to be searched for contraband from Iraq or Kuwait. A shotgun escort was assigned to *SARATOGA*, normally *PHILIPPINE SEA* or *BIDDLE*, but occasionally *SAMPSON* when it was our turn to go south, rendezvous with *SARA* and take on fuel—about every third or fourth day. *T.C. HART* and *MONTGOMERY* were not guided missile ships so not suitable for shotgun duty. We didn't really think the Iraqis would be able to fly a mission down through western Saudi Arabia and do any damage to the Red Sea ships, but leaving the carrier unescorted was not an option. *DETROIT* had continued on to be the gas station in the Persian Gulf so *SARATOGA* was our only source of fuel.

Our first business came on the evening of August 25th when the small container ship *M/V ZORBA EXPRESS* was detected heading our way. We were the closest ship and it fell to *SAMPSON* to conduct the very first Red Sea boarding as part of Desert Shield Maritime Interception Operations. Because it was just turning dark as we came alongside *ZORBA EXPRESS* and ordered her to stop after determining that she was headed for Aqaba, Commodore Hinkle, as MIO Commander, made the decision that we would hold her all night and board her first thing in the morning.

What a night that turned out to be. You would have thought it was June 5, 1944 off Normandy—except they probably didn't talk as much as we did. Everybody was on edge because it was the first one. I was up most of the night on the radio with Jim Hinkle, and he in turn was talking to Admiral Gee, who was, in turn, talking to Commander 7th Fleet, my old Group 12 boss Vice Admiral Hank Mauz, and on up the chain. It was 7th Fleet because in 1990, there was no 5th Fleet and Commander Middle East Force was only a two-star. Under the arrangement in 1990, 7th Fleet had wartime responsibility for the Central Command as well as the Pacific.

Meanwhile, the master in *ZORBA EXPRESS* was totally cooperative and sat there all night patiently waiting to be boarded. The next morning, our boarding team, led by Jim Carr, motored over to *ZORBA EXPRESS* in the motor whaleboat and conducted an uneventful board and search. Jim radioed that his manifest was in order, there was no prohibited cargo found, and recommended we let her go. I passed this up the chain and eventually received the all clear. Jim Hinkle asked that we write up a detailed lessons learned message and send it to him which we did. This lessons learned message was then disseminated throughout the fleet. One of the key recommendations was that we were rank amateurs when it came to reading, and understanding, a cargo manifest. We recommended assigning a Coast Guard officer or senior petty officer, experienced in these matters, to the Gate Guard ships. This was later done and we ended up with an ensign and two petty officers.

SAMPSON conducted the first three boardings in the Red Sea as we did two more on the 28th. The first, on another container ship, the *M/V KOTA WIRAMA*, registered in Sri Lanka, we turned away because we found cargo on board which was consigned to Iraq. That became newsworthy. It was the first time since the UN sanctions had been put in place that a ship was turned away. Later that day we boarded and searched the *M/V CONNY*, a tanker registered in Liberia and cleared her into Aqaba. Several days later on September 3rd, Admiral Gee helo'd over to *SAMPSON* and presented me with the CRUDESGRU 8 "Eight Ball Award," a number eight pool ball mounted on a plaque for being the first ship in the group to conduct a board and search during Operation Desert Shield.

Over the next three weeks we continued board and search operations alternated with trips south to take on fuel and ride shotgun for *SARATOGA*. Virtually all of the ships we stopped and boarded were fully cooperative and we didn't have any trouble to speak of. The German master of the German flagged *RED SEA ENERGY*, a container ship, gave me an argument over the bridge-to-bridge radio on September 8th, challenging our right to stop him, but that was about it. Nonetheless, if we were boarding a ship and didn't have a helicopter available to verify the crew was behaving while the motor whale boat approached, we'd have an F-14 flying CAP (combat air patrol) overhead. They would make a low pass over the ship to be boarded just to let them know they were there. The XO of VF-74 later mailed me a nice 8x10 black and white photo they shot while we were alongside a ship doing a boarding.

These operations were big news back home and one night we made the ABC Evening News with Peter Jennings. We had been doing a boarding and noticed a commercial helicopter flying in the area. They were filming with a news crew and listening in on bridge-to-bridge radio as we challenged a ship and made them stop. My voice was distinctly heard reading the obligatory standard demand and they had footage of *SAMPSON* taken from the helicopter. Iris recorded this at home and I saw it later when we returned. She then mistakenly taped over it with an episode of *The Thorn Birds*.

Other than a merchant ship that was set up to ambush a boarding party, the biggest concern, although unlikely, was that Iraq would try a sneak attack on the force with Mirage jets and Exocet missiles like those that had struck *STARK* three years earlier. It would have required evading the rapidly building U.S. Air Force in Saudi Arabia as well as our own carrier-based Combat Air Patrol; but it had to be considered.

We received a message from the Surface Warfare Development Group (SWDG) in Norfolk advising each class of ship on its best defense against the Exocet. For most of us, except the Aegis cruisers, firing chaff was considered the best thing to do. The *SPRUANCE* class destroyers, *PERRY* class frigates and Aegis cruisers had the Close-in-Weapons System, or CIWS, a 2,000 round per minute, 30 caliber Gatling gun, but *SAMPSON* did not.

When it came to the *ADAMS* class DDG, SWDG advised that we should not even try to shoot down an Exocet with our TARTAR Standard Missile System. The reason given was that when the SPG-51 Missile Fire Control Radars were slewed to the target, the ship's radar cross-section, on which the Exocet seeker homes, would grow about ten times bigger, making us an even more inviting target, and negating whatever benefits the chaff might have provided.

I decided on two approaches to deal with this threat. We would load out the 5-inch gun mounts with a mix, every other round, of Variable Time (VT) and Radio Frequency (RF) ammunition. The idea was to lay a barrage of 5" down the bearing with the gun mount at a pre-determined elevation to set off the RF, detecting the water's surface, at about 2,000 yards. We'd set the VT rounds with the fuse-setter for the 2,000-yard range, and hope we could create a wall of flak about a mile from the ship that the Exocet would have to fly through. Both rounds would detonate above the surface of the water and by mixing the ammo I hoped we'd have a better chance of an air burst. Fuse setters sometimes malfunctioned, particularly in rapid fire mode. I realized this was a long shot at best, so the primary plan was to turn the ship away from the incoming missile, fire chaff, and evacuate after steering and Repair 3 up to the safety of amidships, setting material condition Zebra (securing all the watertight doors and hatches) as the crew vacated the after spaces. We'd take a missile hit aft unless the chaff worked, but maybe nobody would get killed and we'd go back and fight the fire and flooding. The Exocet flies about 10 feet above the water so it would likely hit the transom or perhaps the MK-11 guided missile launcher magazine. I was serious about this plan and had the crew practice it at general quarters.

I put Tony Nardella and Gunnery Officer Lieutenant (junior grade) Corey Keehn to work punching the pubs to figure out what our gun barrel elevation should be to set off the RF rounds at about 2,000 yards when the RF signal detected the ocean's surface. We then decided to experiment to refine the calculations. The idea was that at the first indication of a missile inbound, me or the TAO, acting on his own authority to defend the ship, would order barrage fire and the fire controlmen would initiate this pre-determined elevation order and start shooting rapid fire with both mounts. We would also fire chaff. The flaw in this plan was that something like a broadside would allow us to fire both mounts, but also make us a more inviting target for the missile. More likely we would just turn and run, firing directly aft from Mount 52 only. Even this plan had its flaws as Mount 52 sat forward of the missile launcher. The gun cut-outs would not allow the gun to fire into the missile launcher which would be in the way at the gun barrel elevation required to achieve the 2,000-yard air bursts. Turning the ship enough to open up Mount 52 would also increase our radar cross-section, somewhat negating the effects of the chaff. Nonetheless, we went ahead with the experiment because this gave us some tactical problems to solve despite the fact that the likelihood of Exocet attack from Iraq in the northern Red Sea was virtually nil.

We loaded Mount 51 with RF ammunition and trained it out to starboard. "Batteries released, one round, Mount 51," I said. **BLAM!-BLAM!** I think that round exploded about 500 feet from the ship. The shock wave washed over me and Tony Nardella on the bridge wing almost knocking us over. Fortunately, all the shrapnel was moving away from the ship. A little too close. We raised the elevation a hair, recorded the setting and tried it again. This time Tony and I stood inside the pilot house with the door shut and all topside personnel went inside the ship or to the port side. Round two seemed to work better, going off at about 2,000 yards, so we had our setting and I made a change to the Battle Orders to make this doctrine if the conditions were right. Our first choice, in the unlikely event we came under attack, was the turn, run, fire chaff, and evacuate the after end of the ship plan.

One of the rules of engagement authorized us to fire warning shots with an uncooperative ship and to fire disabling shots if necessary. The preferred technique however was to fly Navy SEALS over from *SARATOGA* on an SH-3 helicopter and have them fast-rope down and take the ship by force.

I thought it would be a good idea to figure out how we would disable a ship with our 5-inch gun without doing more damage than intended. After the 5-inch, the next biggest weapon we had was the 50 caliber machine guns; nothing in between. We discussed it in the wardroom and decided we could come up just outside the other ship's wake and with Mount 51 in local control, depress the gun barrel and let the mount captain manually fire a round into the rudder or screw area from about 100 yards away. We could even use BLP (blind loaded projectile), which is a training round with no explosive. A 70-pound projectile screaming into the rudder or screw of a merchant ship at close range would probably do enough damage without an explosion. If nothing else, it would convince the master that we were crazy and he ought to stop his ship.

To test this procedure, we threw an empty oil drum in the water and maneuvered the ship to the right position and gave Mount 51 the go ahead to see how close they could come with an inert round. When they fired, something didn't sound right and the round weakly went into the water, not with the kind of velocity you would expect. I looked over the port bridge wing at Mount 51 and big clouds of black smoke were pouring out of the doors on both sides of the mount. We sounded General Quarters for a fire in Mount 51 and the ship's damage control team rapidly responded. I was worried for the safety of the mount captain, GMG2 Donald Johnson, and his pointer, GMG3 Ricky Blaskowitz. We couldn't have had an in-bore explosion, I had seen the round hit the water, so what had happened?

It turned out that all that was burning was the lagging, rubberized insulation, inside the mount and both Johnson and Blaskowitz had immediately bailed out the port and starboard doors and run for cover. They were not hurt and the fire party quickly extinguished the fire. Other than the cause, the only damage was the burned insulation. We investigated and determined that the firing pin, which is threaded into the breech block and provides the electrical charge which ignites the powder, had slowly backed out each time the mount had been fired. When we fired this round, the force blasted the firing pin out the back of the breech block and flames ignited the lagging. Somehow *SAMPSON* had missed a change to the required Preventive Maintenance System (PMS) for the 5-inch/54 MK 42 Gun Mount that required tightening the firing pin as part of the pre-fire checks. Upon further investigation I learned that the breech blocks had been recently modified so that the firing pin screwed in from the back, not the inside, necessitating this PMS change. Had the old configuration of screwing it in from the front of the breech block remained, it would have been impossible for the pin to slowly unscrew itself. We CASREP'd (casualty reported) Mount 51 until we could repair the damage and I submitted all the appropriate paperwork putting us on report for our own negligence. This incident cost *SAMPSON* the DESRON 12 Battle Efficiency Award; we would have won it hands down otherwise.

On the 6th of September, we were given an unusual task which symbolized the unique nature of the coalition that President Bush had built to confront Saddam Hussein. *SAMPSON* was instructed to loiter at the southern end of the Gulf of Suez that afternoon and intercept a passenger ship full of Syrian soldiers and escort her about 350 miles south to the port of Yanbu, Saudi Arabia. The Syrians, neighbors of Iraq, known sponsors of terrorism, occupiers of Lebanon, and the ones who shot down our A-6 seven years earlier, had joined the coalition against Iraq.

By the 11th of September, we had boarded and searched 11 vessels since arriving in the Red Sea and it was obvious it was taking a toll on Jim Carr and Tony Nardella. They were department heads and busy enough without spending up to eight hours searching a container ship. Moreover, we had begun doing nighttime boardings which often lasted into the wee hours of the morning. We tapped three of our more talented junior officers to take on the team leader role. Lieutenant Eric Alfaro, the CIC Officer, Lieutenant Don Ebner, the Main Propulsion Assistant (MPA), and Lieutenant John Steinberger, the Navigator, became our three team leaders.

One night we were in our patrol area and the OOD called me in my cabin and said that the *BIDDLE* boarding team was conducting a boarding of a container ship and reporting back to *BIDDLE* that the ship's master was uncooperative. We were monitoring the radio transmissions.

"Where's *BIDDLE*?" I asked.

"Sir, she's about three miles away from the boarding, just sitting there."

I made it standard practice to put *SAMPSON* right next to the ship we were boarding so that the boarding team had a short trip in the motor whaleboat and so that we could easily rotate people if we had to, or send over sandwiches and water, but mainly so that the ship being boarded knew we had the boarding team's back.

"How far are we?" I asked.

"About 10,000 yards." Five miles.

"OK, let's head over there, I'll be right up."

It was around 10:00 PM and we weren't doing anything else, so I thought we'd go give the *BIDDLE* boarding team a little moral support. We pulled *SAMPSON* up alongside the ship and told the boarding team leader we would be there if he needed anything. I looked over at the lights of *BIDDLE* about three miles away and wondered about their lack of concern. By 1 o'clock in the morning I was regretting my decision because I wanted to hit the rack, but in the meantime, the master of the ship had stopped bellyaching and we had sent over some sandwiches and water for *BIDDLE*'s team. I think they really appreciated the support.

On the 11th of September, Commodore Hinkle flew over to *SAMPSON* for a visit and lunch. He told me that it looked like this operation was going to go on for a long time and, as things stood, there was no port for the Navy ships to visit for a break. The *USS AMERICA (CV-66)* Battle Group had joined the *SARATOGA* group in the northern Red Sea so there were plenty of ships to cover the approaches to the Gulf of Aqaba. After conferring with Commander,

Middle East Force, Admiral Gee's staff had determined that the port of Hurghada, Egypt might be a suitable R & R stop for the U.S. Navy. *SAMPSON* was chosen for an exploratory visit with tasking to write a detailed report on its suitability for future port visits.

Hurghada sits on the western side of the Red Sea, just south of where the Gulf of Suez empties into the northern Red Sea. It has a commercial airport which made it suitable for personnel transfers and parts delivery and several resort hotels which supported the local diving industry, which was the main attraction. It had to be approached from the north, skirting some barrier islands, and then accessible through a narrow channel between the Egyptian mainland and the barrier islands and coral reefs. The area was covered with coral reefs which were what made the diving so attractive.

Jim Hinkle said there was one problem; the U.S. Navy had no charts for Hurghada. He had brought with him an old British Admiralty chart from the 1930s that had been provided by COMIDEASTFOR. Years earlier the COMIDEASTFOR flagship had visited Safaga, about 30 miles further south on the Egyptian coast, and had received this chart from the Egyptians.

"You're scheduled in there on the 15th for a three-day visit. This is no vacation. You need to write a comprehensive report and advise as to whether other ships should go there."

I looked at the chart which was almost like a cartoon, not nearly as detailed as a U.S. Navy chart. It did show some navigation aids on shore and the water depths; at least what they were in 1935. The harbor area itself was decent sized, with a small pier which was not large enough to handle a destroyer. The harbor was aligned on a more or less north-south axis and dead-ended at the southern end in reefs and the Egyptian mainland. To the seaward eastern side was a large coral reef. There was one way in and one way out.

"Got it." I said and took the chart from him.

We left the Gate Guard operating area the evening of September 14th and headed east to make our approach to Hurghada the following morning. Our last boarding had been the day prior, of the bulk cargo carrier *M/V MARITIME FRIENDSHIP*, registered in Panama, which we had allowed to proceed to Aqaba. That ship marked our 13th boarding since arriving in the Red Sea on August 24th. Among those we had boarded, the first, the *ZORBA EXPRESS*, we had boarded two additional times. We and *ZORBA EXPRESS* were beginning to establish a relationship! The *M/V KOTA WIRAMA* remained the only ship to have been turned away. When we dropped the hook in Hurghada on the 15th, it would mark 40 straight days at sea. The chance to touch dry land, even in Egypt, was welcome.

That night we held the navigation brief in the wardroom for the Hurghada sea detail and I emphasized the importance of making note of every detail as we entered the harbor and while we were inport for the report we were to submit. Of particular importance was the navigation and sea detail as, once we left Hurghada, I owed Commodore Hinkle back the British Admiralty chart, with annotations, which would then be copied and distributed to all the ships. Operations Officer Jim Carr was put in overall charge of drafting the report and soliciting input from the rest of the officers and crew. Everybody had a role to play from navigation to the Supply Officer who would have significant input on husbanding costs, the quality of fresh fruits and vegetables, garbage, and other services available.

Also during Commodore Hinkle's visit we learned that the *SARATOGA* group would be leaving the Red Sea on the 20th of September and going to the Mediterranean for some liberty call. With negotiations with Iraq ongoing, it was obvious that we were still months away from going to war and the *AMERICA* group could hold down the fort in the Red Sea for a few weeks. Upon entering the Mediterranean, *SAMPSON* was scheduled to relieve *SPRUANCE* in the NATO NAVOCFORMED task group.

At the navigation brief we poured over the British Admiralty chart and picked out what looked like reasonable navigation aids for the transit between the reefs. The chart was so old, likely nothing would look the same once we got close to land. We did see that there was supposed to be a navigation range on a hillside south of the harbor which would be helpful. We also took note of two coral pinnacles about 100 feet apart, which were charted in the middle of the channel as the bay was entered, marked as being 30 feet below the surface at mean low water (low tide). *SAMPSON* drew 25 feet and had a 47-foot beam so, theoretically, if we were off a little as we passed between them we'd clear safely. Nevertheless, I said we would try to shoot between them if we could. There was no information as to how busy this port was and how much commercial or fishing traffic we might encounter. We had also been informed by COMDESRON 24 that an Egyptian officer from one of their minesweepers would meet us in the approaches to the harbor to serve as the local knowledge expert, much like a harbor pilot.

The next morning, after we had crossed the mouth of the Gulf of Suez north of the barrier islands, we found ourselves in gale force winds and 10 foot seas. This was a natural phenomenon we had not anticipated but learned was quite common. The Gulf of Suez acts like a funnel and winds out of the north dump into the Red Sea with some velocity. Just a few miles east, in the lee of the Sinai Peninsula, it could be perfectly calm while this gale blew at the mouth of the Gulf of Suez.

We rounded the barrier islands and headed south between the reefs for Hurghada harbor. No sign of our guide. Even as we moved south between the reefs it was very rough and windy. It would have been difficult to get him safely aboard anyway. Finally, we spotted something that looked like a shrimp boat or fishing boat headed straight out towards us which, although unusual, could have been carrying our Egyptian "pilot." We tried raising him on bridge-to-bridge channel 13 and 16, but received no answer. He pulled along our port side on a reciprocal course, bouncing around in the seas, and a guy in a navy-looking uniform stepped out of the pilot house, gave us a big wave, and pointed south. We already had that much figured out. The boat then made a sweeping turn and sped up to get in front of us, surfing along in the following seas. There were still no radio communications. "OK, let's follow him." I said.

We spotted a few of the navigation aids on the beach and made note of them, but as we approached the mouth of the harbor which widened out to port and where we should have been able to see the range on the hillside, we couldn't find it. I took a close look at the chart as we approached the two coral pinnacles and we made our best guess as to what course would take us between them. We guessed right as I was to learn later.

Once into the section where the harbor opened up to the east, I decided we should move over in that direction and get out of the main ship channel so we wouldn't be in the way of shipping coming and going, although I saw no other large ships at anchor; just the two Egyptian minesweepers at the little pier.

We moved well to the east and dropped the anchor. The wind quickly swung us around so we were pointed northwest. Fire Controlman Chief Mark Wells, in charge on the fantail, radioed on his walkie-talkie that he could see the bottom. I didn't like the sound of that so we picked up the anchor and moved a little further from the reef and dropped it again. Chief Wells called back and said he could still see the bottom and it looked pretty close. A second time we picked up the anchor and moved more to the middle of the harbor and dropped it a third time. Chief Wells gave the all clear from back aft.

As we were securing from sea detail and fixing our position, we finally saw the two range markers on the hillside to the south. They were painted white and brown! They blended right in to the desert hillside behind them. The standard navigation range is a bright international orange with a broad white vertical stripe down the middle. Good grief. Shortly thereafter, our Egyptian "pilot," a Navy lieutenant, came into the pilot house. He was to be my escort to go pay a call on the senior Egyptian Navy officer who was also in charge of the minesweepers.

I took the gig to the little pier, accompanied by Lieutenant Said, and was escorted into the office of Commodore Muhammed Said, Commander, Naval Base Safaga. He was a pleasant fellow and we exchanged token gifts. I explained the purpose of my visit and told him that if things worked out, many U.S. Navy ships would be visiting Hurghada in the coming months. I requested permission to put my motor whaleboat in the water and take soundings around the harbor to chart the water depths. He agreed.

He then relayed that they were watching us anchor and were very concerned because I was so close to the reef. I explained that I wanted to anchor clear of the main ship channel. He said, "No ships come in here, only fishing boats, tour boats, and dive boats." I had brought the chart with me and showed him the pinnacles and asked about them; he, the commander with him, and the lieutenant, acted like they knew nothing about them. On his coffee table was another harbor chart that looked newer than mine but all the writing was in Arabic so I couldn't be sure. The two pinnacles did not even show on this chart. Maybe they'd been blasted away in the past 60 years. I asked if I could have it and he gave it to me.

I then met with an Air Force colonel, the U.S. Defense Air Attaché from the Embassy in Cairo, who took me on a driving tour of Hurghada. He told me the Egyptians were thrilled that the U.S. Navy was thinking of making regular port visits to Hurghada. Dollar signs were dancing in their eyes. He explained that the beaches were good, there were some decent resort hotels frequented by German and British tourists there for the diving, and that the Egyptians had set up a special beach for the *SAMPSON* crew to use on liberty. He explained that because of the tensions over Iraq, there was a curfew for Americans and everyone would have to be back aboard ship by midnight. That was fine with me; nothing good ever happens after midnight when sailors are on liberty anyway. He warned that the water was not safe to drink and to be careful what we ate. He said there were two beers here, both named Stella (not Stella Artois), but one was the export version and was better but more expensive. Both were safe to drink.

When I returned to the ship I sat down in the wardroom and went over all the things we needed to do with the XO and Department Heads and discussed the liberty policy. We would be chartering a launch to take the crew to and from shore. I then got on the 1MC and told the crew we would soon be putting down liberty call and what the rules were. I really emphasized the importance of this being a successful, no incident, port visit because the rest of the fleet out in the Red Sea was counting on us to open the door for them to visit Hurghada.

The Egyptians had set up the special beach for us to use behind the Sonesta Hotel, complete with the local rug and brass pot merchants to sell us junk and a big sign that said, in English:

Sonesta Hotels Egypt

Welcome U.S. Marines

Jim Carr had discovered a tourist submarine, The Yellow Submarine, and bought a ticket. He got a good look at the underside of the ship, but more importantly, he saw the two pinnacles we had avoided. When he next saw me he said they looked like they were only about 10 feet below the surface. It was a good thing we had managed to pass between them on the way in. I told Jim to go find them again in the motor whaleboat and mark them with some plastic floating buoys so we'd know where they were when it was time to leave. Jim did so that afternoon and damn if they weren't sitting out there about 200 yards in front of the ship as we sat at anchor. The winds had died by the next day, but the ship was still sitting facing to the northwest. When Jim sounded them, he found they were only 15 feet beneath the surface. Had we not managed to get between them we might have torn the bottom out of the ship.

The last night in port I had to attend a dinner onboard one of the minesweepers hosted by Commodore Said. I ate all sorts of weird food, drank no water, but did drink the tea. There were no alcoholic beverages served, of course. The next morning, I had to sprint to the head. Probably shouldn't have eaten all that strange food or even drunk the tea. I summoned our Chief Corpsman and he started me on the Imodium so I could function. It was touch and go all the way through the Suez Canal three days later.

On Tuesday, September 18, we set sea detail, did some fancy twisting and turning to pass between Jim Carr's pinnacle buoys, and made our way out to Gate Guard station to resume our duties.

We had no customers on the 19th and so headed independently north up the Gulf of Suez on the 20th to rejoin *SARATOGA* and *PHILIPPINE SEA* at Port Suez for the northbound canal transit.

While at anchorage at Port Suez the night of the 20th, we hand delivered our Hurghada Port Visit Report to Commodore Hinkle on the carrier along with the British Admiralty chart and the Egyptian chart given to me by Commodore Said. Among other recommendations, I recommended against proceeding as deeply into the harbor as we had because of the danger of the two pinnacles and the better water to the north. Our report became the bible for U.S. Navy ships visiting Hurghada; and no one ever penetrated as deeply into the harbor as had *SAMPSON*.

Keeping my Imodium supply close at hand, we transited the Suez Canal northbound on September 21st and entered the Mediterranean Sea with orders to join the Naval On-Call Force Mediterranean (NAVOCFORMED) to replace *USS SPRUANCE (DD-963)*.

CHAPTER 16

NATO Ops

*S*AMPSON's join-up with NAVOCFORMED was executed in a round-about way via naval gunfire support training on the southern tip of Sardinia near Cagliari and a brief stop in Augusta Bay, Sicily to load a deception van for an upcoming NATO exercise. The deception van emitted signals mimicking a U.S. aircraft carrier in order to deceive the exercise enemy forces in exercise Display Determination. *SPRUANCE* was across the pier so I walked over and talked to her CO, Commander Chris Weaver, about NAVOCFORMED. Chris said he had been enjoying the operations, the Greek commodore in charge was a good guy, and it had been good training for the crew, particularly formation steaming and seamanship evolutions. "Brush up on your NATO procedures," he said, "they're different."

We sailed that evening after dark and headed out to the Ionian Sea for the exercise. We rendezvoused with the NAVOCFORMED group on October 3rd and commenced a series of routine naval exercises before heading north towards the Adriatic Sea via the Strait of Otranto between the heel of the boot of Italy and the coast of Albania. We would conduct our first port visit as a group in Bari, Italy. The Greek Commodore visited *SAMPSON* for lunch one day and I found him to be a very friendly and engaging. His flagship was an old U.S. built *GEARING* class destroyer which the U.S. had transferred to Greece years ago when it became obsolete by our standards. When they needed to crank up the speed they had to fire up the superheater for the boilers on line and great clouds of thick black smoke would pour out of the stacks. In Bari, the Spanish were scheduled to host the inport reception on October 13th, which was the U.S. Navy's 215th birthday. I requested to be allowed to host instead. He agreed and the CO of the Spanish frigate

SNS EXTREMADURA (F-75), another U.S. built *KNOX* class, graciously agreed to step aside.

We pulled into Bari on the 11th of October and squeezed all eight ships into the tiny, nook and cranny harbor protected by a stone sea wall on the western side of the Adriatic Sea. All of the CO's went en masse to pay a call on the mayor and bring him ship's plaques. The mayor gave each of us a necktie. I was meeting my compatriots for the first time and they were all friendly and very welcoming. The Spanish frigate tied up outboard *SAMPSON* and, because he was undergoing generator repairs, we provided all his electrical power for three days. He was very grateful and I think our support helped smooth things over after my request to usurp his turn as the host reception ship.

Our reception on the 13th was a big success and we put a major dent in the supply of American beer and California wines we had stocked up before Iraq invaded Kuwait. When it was my turn to speak and propose a toast I poked some good natured fun at my British colleague, crediting British oppression in the 18th Century with inspiring us to build a Navy. I allowed as how we had modeled our Navy after theirs and implied that it must have been a little unnerving for big brother navy to watch little brother navy get so big.

We were underway on the 15th and assembled at sea as we headed south and formed up for a Form Photo to get a picture of all the ships in a tight formation taken from one of the helicopters. One of the problems we were having in the engineering plant was weeping fuel oil lines in the bilges where they fed fuel oil from the fuel tanks to the fuel pumps which pressurized the fuel and sent it into the boiler fireboxes. The lines were so old and worn out that fuel oil was literally leaking through the skin of the piping. This was potentially very dangerous and could result in a main space fire, possibly as damaging as what had happened in *CONYINGHAM*. Terry Culton had been trying to stay on top of this with band-aid fixes but we clearly needed some depot level repairs. I had reported this up the chain and CASREP'd the system even though it was still operational.

I received a message from 6th Fleet directing me to detach from NAVOCFORMED on the 22nd of October and proceed to Alexandria, Egypt to go alongside the destroyer tender *USS YELLOWSTONE (AD-41)* for some repair work, including on the fuel lines. *SPRUANCE* would once again replace *SAMPSON* in NAVOCFORMED.

I had been warned that in typical Egyptian fashion, Alexandria was a disorganized harbor with unpredictable harbor pilots, ships anchoring randomly, including in the channel, and unreliable charts. Sounded like fun. We made the approach to Alexandria on the Mediterranean north coast of Egypt about 120 miles west of Port Said. The Alexandria harbor is a natural hook-shaped harbor running west to east, augmented by a 3,000-yard-long seawall that provides additional protection. The harbor entrance is fairly narrow but then opens up with plenty of room inside the seawall and the natural spit of land from which it extends. The harbor itself is about 2 ½ miles long and our berth alongside *YELLOWSTONE* was all the way at the eastern end of the harbor. We picked up an Egyptian pilot at the sea buoy and made our way through the breakwater and headed towards *YELLOWSTONE* along the axis of the harbor. About a mile inside the pilot told me we had to stop due to some ship movements up ahead. When I asked how long he replied that he didn't know so I decided to anchor and wait our turn. When I asked him where to go to anchor he said we could drop it right where we were, in the middle of the channel. I would be contributing to the general chaos of Alexandria harbor, but we went ahead and anchored. When it was time to move, the anchor was snagged on a cable on the bottom. After bouncing the anchor a couple of times, the cable came free and we were able to move. The pilot had been no help and had no idea what kind of cable we had snagged.

We made our way to *YELLOWSTONE* who was tucked in a corner at the far end of the harbor and backed in along her port side, starboard side to. *YELLOWSTONE* was huge next to us, 642 feet and 20,200 tons to our 437 feet and 4,500 tons. I exchanged pleasantries on bridge-to-bridge with the captain who told me where to position the ship so that he could make the best use of his cranes. We were to stay in Alexandria alongside *YELLOWSTONE* for nine days. I went aboard when the brow was over and talked to Captain Robert Pratt, the CO. He told me that he was not allowing liberty in town because it was too dangerous. As he was the senior U.S. Navy officer present, known as SOPA, or Senior Officer Present Afloat, I would follow his rules. To give the crew a break he had instituted "Beer on the Pier" and offered for the *SAMPSON* crew to participate. Every evening beginning at 6:00 the ship's cooks fired up the grills and brought out the iced down Budweiser and the crew who were off duty were allowed to purchase two beer tickets each and eat all the hot dogs, hamburgers and grilled chicken they wanted. Beer tickets were 50 cents each. Everybody had to stay within a certain area on the pier. This became hugely popular with my crew as well as the *YELLOWSTONE* crew and we enjoyed many an evening of beer and burgers on the pier.

I had been assigned a car with an Egyptian driver, but was not making much use of him until I decided that the XO and I would take a day trip to Cairo and see the pyramids. Cairo was a little over a 100 miles south- southeast of Alexandria; about a two-hour drive through the desert. I met our driver, Muhammad Ali Muhammad, a cheerful Egyptian who associated his name more with the boxer Muhammad Ali than with the Muslim Prophet and informed Dave Birdwell and me that he "looked like Tony Curtis." He actually did.

We made the drive to Cairo, a teaming city of 7 million people, and first visited the national museum, the Museum of Egyptian Antiquities, at Muhammad's insistence. We were glad we did. All of the relics of King Tutankhamun the famous 14th Century Pharaoh were on display. We then went to the pyramids and spent the afternoon at Giza seeing the great pyramids and being harassed by all the Arabs who wanted us to ride camels and buy souvenirs. Muhammad Ali proved fairly efficient at shooing them away. He made a great guide as well as driver and went everywhere with Dave and me.

About 4 o'clock we were ready to head back to Alexandria, but Muhammad Ali wanted to visit some friends on the way out of town. Since he had been such a good escort all day we agreed. We began to regret our decision when he headed away from the center of town and into the poorer neighborhoods of Cairo. Well, what did we expect, that his friends would own condos on the Nile? Consequently, courtesy of Muhammad Ali Muhammad, we got to see what real Egyptians lived like. We stopped at a little mud house in a neighborhood of mud houses all jammed together. Dave and I sat nearby while Muhammad Ali had tea with about four men friends. They were as pleasant as could be. There were no women anywhere in sight, but there were dozens of dirty little Egyptian boys playing soccer in the streets. When we got back to the ship that evening I gave Muhammad Ali a tip and thanked him. Dave and I then discussed what a risk we had taken. Once we were in those back alleys, we were completely at the mercy of Muhammad Ali and his friends.

We left Alexandria on October 31st having had a great availability alongside *YELLOWSTONE*. Her sailors had accomplished a number of repairs that were beyond the ability of my crew to complete, such as rewinding electric motors and doing some high pressure welding. The fuel oil lines had been hard patched in the areas we knew they were weeping, but Terry had no confidence that it wouldn't happen again in different spots. *YELLOWSTONE* had female sailors in her crew and I think I saw a few teary eyes as we set sea detail, singled up the lines and took in the brow. A few romances had begun during Beer on the Pier.

My excitement with the Alexandria harbor pilots was not over however. Our pilot came aboard and while we had all the lines singled up, a big container ship backed into a slip perpendicular to ours and disappeared behind *YELLOWSTONE*'s bow. I said to the pilot, "Are we clear to go?" He babbled something in Arabic into his radio and told me yes. We were starboard side to, facing in the direction we wanted to go, so we took in the lines, put on right full rudder and went ahead two-thirds on the starboard engine. We moved smoothly away from *YELLOWSTONE*'s side and began moving forward. It was a nice maneuver. And then the container ship's bow reappeared pulling forward out of the slip he had backed into, about 200 yards in front of us.

I stopped engines but continued drifting forward and turned angrily to the pilot and said, "I thought you said it was clear!" He just shrugged his shoulders and babbled some more into the radio.

The container ship stopped, dropped his anchor, and began backing again into the slip from which he had come. Now we had a taut anchor chain angling up to his hawsepipe and blocking our path as he backed away. We continued forward until my stern was clear of YELLOWSTONE's bow and then we did a hard left followed by a hard right to snake around the anchor chain. The pilot never said a word and I had not asked for tugs so had none available to help. As we passed the bow of the container ship I waited for a crunch or a shudder as our starboard screw snagged on his anchor chain, but we cleared it. Once out of the harbor and back to sea we headed east to Port Said to head back to the Red Sea for more MIO.

SAMPSON uneventfully transited the Suez Canal and the Gulf of Suez on the 1st of November and took up the assigned Gate Guard station on the 2nd. We were in business almost immediately, boarding and searching the Cyprus registered M/V ESPRIT, a bulk cargo carrier outbound from Aqaba enroute to Jeddah. Over the next week we continued Gate Guard operations, routinely boarding three more ships uneventfully until the night of the 8th of November. Around 10:00 PM that night we stopped a large container ship outbound from Aqaba shortly after it had passed through the Strait of Tiran. The ship was the M/V NPC NIPPON registered in Antigua and enroute Singapore. Lieutenant Eric Alfaro was the boarding team leader and when he had climbed aboard he called me on the walkie-talkie from the main deck and told me everybody in the Japanese crew was drunk.

"Everybody? Who's driving the ship?" The Strait of Tiran is about a half mile wide at the mouth between the reefs and it was nighttime.

"Everybody. They told me the master is passed out in his bunk."

"Real drunk?"

"Yessir, they can hardly talk or stand up."

"Are you OK with going ahead with this?"

Eric hesitated a few seconds and said, "A couple of these guys are acting strange and looking like they might want to pick a fight."

"OK, ask them to back away to give you some room and bring the team back to the ship."

When Eric returned aboard, I called whoever was on the bridge that I had hailed to stop the ship, and who didn't sound drunk, and told them to be on their way but be careful. Then I got the story that Eric had been able to piece together while onboard. While in Aqaba, the ship's cook had died. They stuck him in the freezer, and when they left port they broke out the sake and held a wake. I filed a report including the circumstances and explained why we hadn't conducted the search.

The area near the Strait of Tiran features many reefs and very clear water which makes it a popular place for scuba divers. One day I was in my chair on the starboard bridge wing when I saw two things that looked like small killer whales, Orcas, swim by the ship. I was flabbergasted, I knew the Red Sea was full of sharks, but killer whales? I thought they liked cold water. These creatures had the black and white markings and sure looked like killer whales, only smaller, about the size of a dolphin.

Several days later one of the local dive boats was in the area so I called him up on bridge-to-bridge and asked about my killer whales. A British accent answered and said that what I had seen was a False Killer Whale, a type of dolphin found in warm waters that have similar markings to an Orca. He even knew the scientific name, which made sense when I asked him to spell it: *psuedorca crassidens*. Learn something new every day.

On the 11th of November, *SAMPSON* was assigned to conduct a first-ever ASROC firing in the Red Sea. ASROC stands for anti-submarine rocket. As the name implies, it is a weapon for killing submarines. The rocket delivers a MK-46 ASW torpedo up to 12 miles from the ship, providing a greater standoff distance from the submarine. At a pre-set distance the torpedo separates from the rocket, a parachute deploys and the torpedo enters the water, releases the parachute, the salt water activates the torpedo motor, and off it goes to begin its search for the submarine.

We needed this exercise for our battle efficiency qualifications and with the help of Commodore John Mitchell of DESRON 12 in Mayport and Commodore Jim Hinkle of DESRON 24 in the Red Sea, we gained permission. I had embarked a lieutenant from *YELLOWSTONE* in Alexandria who wanted to see some action and we used him as our exercise observer for every exercise that required an outside observer. I had promised Captain Pratt that I'd return him when we next went alongside *YELLOWSTONE* which was scheduled over Christmas in Izmir, Turkey.

With no enemy sub to shoot, we deployed a "mini-mobile target," or MMT. The MMT has a battery powered motor and emits a signal which can be detected on surface ship sonar systems. We launched the MMT, opened the distance, and acquired it on sonar. When the firing solution was right, we launched the ASROC with a loud WHOOSH and off it went.

In early December, we were visited by Molly Moore, military affairs writer for the *Washington Post,* for a two day stay to write a story on Maritime Interception Operations. She interviewed the crew, watched us conduct a couple of boardings, and published a two-page story which prominently featured *SAMPSON.* I had some less than stellar quotes attributed to me including describing the crew of the *NPC NIPPON* as "drunk as skunks."

On the 13th of December, we stopped a large container ship departing Aqaba and heading for Sudan, the *M/V DONGOLA,* registered in Cyprus. By this time our crew had been augmented with an Arabic linguist, as had all the other ships. When our boarding team, led by Lieutenant Don Ebner, boarded, they found a great number of vehicles, including trucks and vans, but also high-end Mercedes Benz and other sedans. Don was suspicious but didn't know what to make of it. They all had what appeared to be freshly painted license plates in Arabic.

We sent over the young petty officer linguist to translate. Don reported back that the license plates all identified the cars as being from the 19th province of Iraq; what Saddam Hussein had declared Kuwait to be right after the invasion and occupation. We reported this and were directed to require the ship to return to Aqaba and offload the vehicles. Sudan, along with Yemen and the Palestinians were the only entities which had supported the Iraqi invasion of Kuwait. This event also made the national news and was the most significant find during Desert Shield.

Throughout Desert Shield and Desert Storm, we received countless letters from school children and care packages from Americans at home with all kinds of goodies to hand out to the crew. I received all the letters first so I could write thank you letters to the teachers or to whatever organization had sent the gifts. We would then randomly distribute them to the crew. Sometimes, these packages were addressed to "Commanding Officer, *USS SAMPSON*," but most of the time they were sent to "Any Ship, Operation Desert Shield." These letters and packages were great for morale, but made life tough on the military postal system.

One day a stack of letters came in from a Tampa, Florida second grade class addressed to me by name. I could see from the top letter that this was Lorraine Skelton's class. Lorraine was the wife of my fraternity brother and freshman year dorm roommate, Bruce Skelton. Bruce and Lorraine and Iris and I were great friends and they had come to Mayport in August for my change of command ceremony.

I started reading the letters which were written in pencil on that elementary school lined writing paper with the thinner, mid-level line to denote where lower case letters should top out and the thicker lines where capital letters fit. They were all addressed to me personally and were really cute. About halfway through the stack I came to a letter that looked like all the rest and started out the same but quickly turned obscene with questions about sexual relations with camels and Arab women. I was shocked. And then I looked down and saw that it was signed by Bruce.

SAMPSON had one more visit to Hurghada, Egypt from the 3rd to the 6th of December which was uneventful. Like everybody else after our first visit, we anchored outside the main harbor and north of the coral pinnacles. By now the Egyptians had figured out what a bonanza they had with the U.S. Navy as a customer and everything was more expensive than it had been on our first visit, from husbanding services to Stella beer.

On the 14th of December, we boarded our last, and 33rd overall, ship before heading north through the Gulf of Suez to once again transit the Suez Canal and enter the Mediterranean. This time we were scheduled for another maintenance availability with *YELLOWSTONE* in Izmir, Turkey where we would be inport for two weeks over Christmas and New Years.

CHAPTER 17

The Mediterranean and Beyond

O n the 19th of December, we arrived in the harbor of Izmir, Turkey, having navigated our way west of the island of Karpathou, home to Rhodes, and up through the Aegean Sea between Greece and Turkey and into Izmir Bay, a very well-protected 10 mile long bay running east to west. *YELLOWSTONE* would again be our home, anchored a short boat ride from the pier and Fleet Landing adjacent to downtown Izmir. Izmir is Turkey's third largest city, a bustling, cosmopolitan city of around 4 million.

The night before, we held the navigation brief in the wardroom and discussed the fact that the Izmir port pilots were on strike and no tugs or pilots would be available. I was comfortable making the approach on *YELLOWSTONE* unassisted. In a message, Captain Pratt said he wanted me all the way forward, bow to bow starboard side to. A small barge would be between the ships to fend us off.

As *YELLOWSTONE* came into sight, I saw that in addition to the aforementioned barge, there was a larger barge further aft which, by radio, we were informed was a garbage barge. I was using *YELLOWSTONE*'s lieutenant to talk to his counterparts on the tender because of his familiarity with the ship and the people. It also appeared that *YELLOWSTONE* was swinging at anchor slowly to port. I decided I would make the approach a little wider, coming from astern to allow for the swing and to get by the garbage barge. If she swung too far we could abort the landing, come around, and try again when she settled out.

We came in wide and then had to adjust once past the garbage barge in order to close the distance to get lines over. We ended up cocked bow in as we arrived more or less in position.

YELLOWSTONE swung some more to port and suddenly my starboard bridge wing was only about 12 inches from the big, flat sides of the tender. I actually had my hand out on the side of YELLOWSTONE trying to hold us off. Nobody is that strong. Above my head was a three-inch diameter steel bar to which the High-Frequency Fan Antennas running from the yardarms on the forward mast were attached. The end of this bar made contact with YELLOWSTONE's side and began to bow directly over my head. Paint chips were flying off under the stress.

I was gradually getting the ship aligned parallel to YELLOWSTONE and so far, no real damage had been done. The distance between my bridge wing and YELLOWSTONE's side began to widen as we straightened out and the fan antenna bar lost contact and returned to its normal shape. Captain Pratt was watching from the port bridge wing about 30 feet above me. As we settled in parallel, a new problem became apparent. YELLOWSTONE's life raft canisters hung off the outside of the hull at deck edge level and one of them was lining up perfectly with my starboard side SLQ-32 Electronic Warfare System antenna one level above the bridge. The SLQ-32 antenna is a box-like structure on struts which receives electronic emissions for analysis against a library of known emitters. Electronic Warfare Technician Third Class Chris Dalldorf, responsible for the SLQ-32, ran towards the impending contact as if he wanted to do something to save his antenna. Both Captain Pratt and I yelled at him to get out of there. He came close to getting squashed. The active transmission antenna fiberglass cover shattered and the life raft canister popped open, although nothing fell out.

Once we were tied up, I had Jim Carr and Electronic Material Officer Dave Stout assess the damage. Our starboard SLQ-32 was out of commission, the active antenna damaged and the receive antenna probably requiring a re-alignment. I reported all this up the chain via secure satellite and ended up speaking to Admiral Gee. He said, "We're going to have to conduct an investigation, I'll get back to you." We would also need a new active antenna and some technical expertise to re-align and re-certify the system.

The cruiser *PHILIPPINE SEA* was in Izmir, and Captain Pat Callahan, her skipper, was assigned to do the Judge Advocate General's investigation of my "incident." A couple of days later I went over to *PHILIPPINE SEA* and had a meeting with Captain Callahan. I handed him my written statement describing everything that had happened. Pat said, "Hey, this is all part of doing business, don't worry about it." He submitted his report, exonerating me of any negligence, and that was the end of it. By the time we left Izmir on January 4, 1991, my SLQ-32 was back up and fully operational, the repairs having been made with the help of two technicians sent to Izmir by the 6th Fleet staff.

Christmas in Izmir was a subdued affair. Of course Turkey is a 90% Muslim country, but there were a surprising number of Christmas-themed decorations around town. I called Iris and the kids and realized that I had really been lucky; in 18 years in the Navy, this was my first Christmas spent away from home. It began with that December 24th homecoming in 1972 aboard *NEWPORT NEWS*.

When we left Izmir on January 4th, *SAMPSON* was still assigned to NAVOCFORMED, but the group had split apart and the ships were not operating together as a task force. Instead, each country had decided to use the ships to patrol the Mediterranean to be on the lookout for trouble from the Iraqis and any sympathetic terrorist group that might want to make mischief. It was a hollow assignment and all of the European nations had their ships return to the vicinity of home waters to carry out this mission. Being impractical for the American ship, we were given a patrol area in the eastern Med protecting shipping in the approaches to the Suez Canal. Our resupply and refueling port, when we couldn't rendezvous with an oiler, was to be Antalya, Turkey on the southern coast about 400 miles north of Port Said, Egypt and the Suez Canal.

We made our first stop in Antalya on January 10th. The little harbor we were assigned would become very familiar over the next six weeks. The harbor was small, but extremely well sheltered and sat about 6 miles west of the quaint seaport town of Antalya. Today Antalya is a large resort town of about one million with large hotels, golf courses and beautiful beaches. In 1991 it had not been discovered and was fairly quiet. It did have a casino and a pretty little downtown harbor. Commander 6th Fleet had directed a curfew which mandated liberty expire at midnight. Taking a page from *YELLOWSTONE* in Alexandria, we set up the pier area as our recreation area and served beer on the pier and held cookouts. There was a nearby field with volleyball nets and enough room for softball or touch football. The port was primarily a fishing and small freighter port and over the four visits, totaling 15 days in port, we made friends with many of the locals.

Leaving Antalya on the 14th of January, we joined up with a German oiler, *FGS RHON (A-1442)* and a Turkish *GEARING* FRAM I class destroyer, *TCG SAVASTEPE (D-348)*, to patrol our area. I was designated the commander of this little task force by the Greek commander of NAVOCFORMED. We would be underway for two weeks, including on the 17th of January when the air war against Iraq began at 3:00 AM local time.

In late January, 6th Fleet generated some action for us as they assigned *USS PHILADELPHIA (SSN-690)*, a *LOS ANGELES* class attack submarine, to give my little task force an ASW exercise. We were assigned an area in the eastern Mediterranean and given a pre-exercise message which laid out the rules. *PHILADELPHIA* was to attack our force and try to sink *RHON* while *SAMPSON* and *SAVASTEPE* defended the oiler and tried to sink *PHILADELPHIA*. I was designated the Officer Conducting the Exercise, or OCE.

We had a great day of ASW and *PHILADELPHIA* was a superb exercise opponent. The submarine had all the advantage as neither the *ADAMS* nor *GEARING* class destroyers were known for their ASW prowess. The CO, Commander Paul Ryan, did a superb job of forcing contact so that we received good training and many opportunities to simulate attacks. In these exercises, the submarine indicates that he has fired a torpedo by launching a green flare while submerged at periscope depth. The surface ships announce torpedo or ASROC attacks over the underwater telephone, or "Gertrude" system.

In this scenario, an *ADAMS* class guided missile destroyer and a *GEARING* class destroyer have almost no chance against a *LOS ANGELES* class submarine. In fact, in a one-on-one fight between a surface ship and a submarine, bet on the submarine every time. Submarines can hide, taking advantage of the mixing of the water column to make detection by active sonar very difficult and they can go extremely quiet to make passive detection difficult as well. The surface ship cannot hide and cannot get quiet enough to escape detection. Speed is life for a surface ship hoping to avoid a torpedo attack and speed equals noise in the water. In a knife fight like this exercise represented, the submarine would always know where both destroyers and the oiler were, while we would lose track of him whenever he wanted to be lost. We had no air support as there were no P-3 Orion maritime patrol aircraft assigned and neither *SAMPSON* nor *SAVASTAPE* was helicopter capable. The best we could do was run the oiler around at top speed, changing his course often to force the submarine to continue to maneuver to achieve a torpedo firing solution. By continually rising above the thermocline layer and taking a shot at the *RHON*, with the accompanying green flare, Commander Paul Ryan made sure that we could re-acquire *PHILADELPHIA* and conduct our own simulated attacks.

I told the Turk to stay with the oiler and every time *PHILADELPHIA* got off a shot we sent the oiler tearing off in another direction and maneuvered *SAMPSON* to cut off the sub, or get off our own simulated shot on the submarine. I stayed in CIC to monitor the action and the plot on the Dead Reckoning Tracer and the XO stayed on the bridge to keep an eye on safety. *SAVASTEPE* never once reported sonar contact on the sub. This was not entirely her fault as by maneuvering at high speed to stay near the oiler, her own ship's noise and water flow on the sonar dome virtually blinded her.

Near the end of the afternoon, we were racing at 25 knots towards the oiler, having lost contact on *PHILADELPHIA*, when the bridge called in to CIC reporting a green flare just off the bow. I raced out to the bridge, looked just forward of the bow, and saw a disturbance in the water directly in front of us and moving from starboard to port. In the instant that I had to think about it, I ordered right full rudder to avoid running over the submarine which I assumed to be just under the surface directly in front of *SAMPSON*.

We passed over the disturbed water turning sharply to starboard and I thought to myself that *PHILADELPHIA*'s sail must have been just under the surface at periscope depth after his last simulated torpedo firing. We called a halt to the exercise over Gertrude. *SAMPSON*, *RHON*, *SAVASTEPE* and *PHILADELPHIA* came to safety course, parallel so nobody would be crossing anyone else, and *PHILADELPHIA* raised her mast from periscope depth to talk to me on the secure radio circuit.

I said, "That was great training, thanks for forcing contact and giving us a chance. I guess we got pretty close right there at the end."

Paul Ryan said, "Yeah, you were in my baffles and I didn't see you coming until after I shot at the oiler and turned to starboard."

I had a mental image of the geometry in my head. He was between us and the oiler, we were racing towards the oiler, he couldn't see us because we were directly astern where his bow-mounted sonar is blind, and he turned to starboard not port!

"I saw the water moving and I thought you were passing in front of me starboard to port, that's why I turned right."

"No, I was at full power, diving for the deep after turning to starboard—north."

Then it hit me, I hadn't seen the water disturbed by his sail moving across my bow right to left, I had seen the prop wash from his screw driving him deep and moving the sub left to right. I had turned toward him, not away. Neither of us will ever know how close we came, but I am sure I passed right over him in that turn.

We were back to Antalya again on February 13th, and this time there was a Russian *YUG* class AGOR, or ocean research ship, the *DONUZLAV*, at the pier in front of *SAMPSON*. The Soviet Union had officially dissolved only eight weeks earlier in December, so there was some uncertainty on my part as to our navy to navy relationship. The Cold War had technically ended, but could we really trust these guys? These "research" vessels had been known over the years to not only conduct legitimate oceanographic survey work, but also to serve as intelligence collectors for the Soviet Union.

I was out having a beer on the pier on the 15th when the CO of *DONUZLAV*, a Russian Navy captain, came down the brow and walked over. I offered him a beer and we chatted about the progress of the air war in Iraq. The Russians were part of the coalition to remove Saddam Hussein from Kuwait, contributing four warships to the embargo. He then suggested we have a friendly volleyball game between the two ships on the 17th which was a Sunday and a day off for the crews.

We organized a volleyball team and on Sunday we met the Russians at the volleyball nets. The *DONUZLAV* captain and I were to serve as the judges on either end of the net. We played two games and the Russians killed us both times. They were really good and executed their set-ups, feints, and spikes like Olympic caliber professionals. We then decided to mix up the teams and play a couple more games with Russians and Americans on each team. These matches were much closer. The détente was palpable.

When it was over the CO invited me over to *DONUZLAV* for dinner that evening. We were due to get underway the next morning and I was wary of a night of vodka drinking, but accepted. That evening I put on my service dress blue uniform, grabbed a bottle of Jack Daniels out of our gift supply as a host gift, and walked down the pier to *DONUZLAV*. It was to be a small dinner, just me, the CO, the XO, who was a commander, and the Operations

Officer, another commander. We started with a tour of the ship and it was apparent that Ops was there because his English was pretty good; better than the CO and XO.

When we settled down to dinner the vodka came out and we began toasting the end of the Cold War, the friendship between our two countries, sailors on the high seas, wives and girlfriends, and on and on. The meal was good, lamb and potatoes, and the vodka kept flowing. When the bottle of vodka was empty we opened the Jack Daniels.

After dinner, the CO brought me into his cabin and showed me pictures of his family and a small book containing his stamp collection. The book was nothing special, but the Russian stamps were beautiful. When I admired it he gave it to me. Feeling the need to reciprocate, I offered them a tour of *SAMPSON*. It was after 10:00 PM and I'm sure the quarterdeck wondered what was up when they saw the four of us weaving down the pier. The CDO, Jim Carr, hustled to the quarterdeck and off we went on a little tour of the ship. If they were still spies they didn't learn anything new, I'm sure.

The next morning, splitting headache and all, we were underway again to patrol south towards Port Said and back north again to return to Antalya. During this time the message traffic indicated that the ground war to liberate Kuwait would soon begin. Saddam Hussein had ignored the final pleas by the rest of the world to pull out of Kuwait. By this time the U.S. and the coalition air forces owned the skies over Iraq and Kuwait. Much of the Iraqi Air Force, which had initially come up to fight, had sought refuge across the border in Iran, their former enemy. Those that didn't had been destroyed.

On the 20th of February, we were just north of Port Said, Egypt, having escorted a large U.S. pre-positioning ship carrying Army equipment to Saudi Arabia, when Sonar reported a passive sonar contact. The SQQ-23 PAIR sonar was advertised to have a passive sonar capability, but I was skeptical.

"How confident are you?" I asked. There were no other surface ships in the area.

"We've got something, Captain, machinery tonals." It was Lieutenant (junior grade) Brad Bailey the ASW Officer.

"OK, go active."

As soon as we started pinging, we gained sonar contact at a range of about 5,000 yards.

"Set condition 1AS." I ordered. 1AS was general quarters for submarine warfare. We reported our contact to 6th Fleet and began to close and track the contact. It was possible that it was one of our own and if so, 6th Fleet would pretty quickly tell us to leave it alone.

This was not a wartime situation, and I had no expectation that we would be attacked, nor did we mean any harm to the submarine. But you never let an opportunity for real world training to pass, especially against a non-cooperative submarine which would be doing its best to evade. We began tracking the sub and setting up for a simulated attack, pinging away on the active sonar. 6th Fleet answered and said it wasn't one of ours and to continue tracking and report. It could be a Russian, I thought, Cold War here we go again.

Fresh from our exercise with *PHILADELPHIA*, we were doing pretty well and pinging away on this guy, whoever he was. Then the XO called in from the bridge, "Captain, we've got a periscope." He gave me the bearing which matched our sonar contact. I guessed that he had tired of our pinging and decided to take a look at whoever was harassing him.

I went to the bridge and as I got there, his sail broke the surface and he came up about 800 yards away. It was a *ROMEO* class diesel submarine, built by the Soviet Union but exported to many client nations, including Egypt. We sent "Alpha, Alpha" (identify yourself) by signal light and in turn identified ourselves and, sure enough, it was Egyptian. I went out on the bridge wing and waved and someone who I assume was the captain, waved back. We then made a big turn away and steamed off to make sure he knew we were through bothering him. I think he got tired of our sonar banging away on him and just decided to come up and end the punishment. Or maybe he was low on battery power.

We reported all this to 6th Fleet and received a nice message in return congratulating us on a job well done. The message went on to say that there was some doubt about the capability of the Egyptian *ROMEO* fleet to get underway, let alone submerge, and our detection had provided valuable intelligence.

On the way north to Antalya we rendezvoused with the U.S. Navy stores ship *USNS CONCORD (T-AFS-5)*, to take on supplies. Lieutenant (junior grade) Corey Keehn, the Gunnery Officer, had the conn for the underway replenishment as we began our approach with a following sea.

When a ship moves through the water, an area of low pressure occurs at the bow and at the stern where the hull displacing the water leaves a little vacuum. When another ship comes alongside for refueling or taking on supplies, a new phenomenon occurs. An area of low pressure occurs between the hulls of the two ships as their movement through the ocean sets up a Venturi effect. If you get too close to the delivery ship, the Venturi effect can take over and suck you in to the side of the other ship, resulting in a collision.

When *CONCORD* was ready, she closed up the Romeo flag and we commenced our approach at 25 knots along her port side. Because of the following seas, both ships were wallowing a little bit and not steering a perfectly straight course. As our bow approached the stern of *CONCORD*, an untimely wallow to starboard caused us to slide into the low pressure area astern of *CONCORD*. Our approach suddenly became a lot closer than the 150 feet we had planned.

Corey dropped speed to match *CONCORD* and used a little left rudder to try open the distance, but we were way too close, maybe only 50 feet, as we moved up *CONCORD*'s side and began to match her speed. Then the Venturi effect took over and we began moving even closer. I took the conn.

"This is the Captain, I have the conn, all engines ahead flank for 25 knots!" I wanted to power out of the situation, get ahead of CONCORD and come around a second time. As the forced draft blowers spun up to meet the steam demand, I looked aft and saw our sailors on the midships replenishment station backing away from the edge of the deck. I estimated only 25 feet separated the two ships. The master on CONCORD did what he was supposed to do, maintain a steady course and speed.

The power worked, we surged ahead and with tiny adjustments of the rudder, we opened the distance. I then realized that once we had opened up to about 200 feet, I could drop speed again, slide back, and gradually ease our way back into 125 feet to begin passing the lines.

I gave the conn back to Corey and he did a fine job the rest of the replenishment. I was on the starboard bridge wing talking on the bridge-to-bridge phone line with CONCORD's master when one of the replenishment rig seamen came to the bridge with a manila envelope addressed to "CO, USS SAMPSON." It was from the master of CONCORD and contained a clean pair of underwear. Ha, ha, very funny.

The ground war in Kuwait began on the 24th and quickly became a rout. It was over in four days; famously 100 hours. Kuwait had been liberated, the Iraqi Army was soundly defeated, and a cease fire declared. We would soon be going home.

We departed Antalya for the final time on February 28th and rendezvoused with the German frigate FGS EMDEN (F-210) who we were to operate with for several days while we made our way to Naples, Italy for a port visit. SAMPSON was scheduled for a week in Naples before heading home and the time pierside would give us a chance to do some much needed maintenance. We were scheduled for a visit by the Board of Inspection and Survey (INSURV) during our Atlantic crossing and I had been diligently reporting all of our various casualties and mechanical deficiencies; so much so that people were worried about the seaworthiness of my ship. I didn't want the INSURV team to come aboard and find a bunch of things wrong that had not been reported. As to the seaworthiness issue, we had a number of structural problems in addition to the weeping fuel oil lines. The forward bulkhead in the forward fireroom had rotted away down in the bilges and I also had a fuel oil tank that was leaking into the bilges. *YELLOWSTONE* had tried to fix that but failed. The ship was just old. Decommissioning was scheduled for June 24th, only four months away. I had specifically requested June 24th because that was the date in 1961 when *SAMPSON* had been commissioned. I thought there was a certain symmetry to a commissioned life of exactly 30 years.

As *SAMPSON* and *EMDEN* sailed south of Crete towards the Straits of Messina and Naples, we conducted a highline transfer and I went across to visit the *EMDEN* CO. *EMDEN* came alongside, we rigged our highline station and I hopped in the boatswain's chair and was hauled across the 125 feet between the two ships. There was much joking among my boatswain's mates about dunking me on the way across, but I stayed dry.

On the 6th of March, we transited the Straits of Messina to enter the Tyrrhenian Sea. I had always made it a practice to go through Messina at 25 knots, just to get it over with. It is a busy strait, with high speed hydrofoil ferries zipping back and forth between Messina on the island of Sicily and Reggio Calabria on the Italian mainland at the toe of the boot. These ferries refuse to give way, regardless of the rules of the road, and are constantly challenging shipping moving north-south through the strait, tooting their whistles and refusing to deviate from course. The slower you go; the more ferries you encounter. As we approached the northern end of the strait and just after we had crossed the bow of one of the hydrofoil ferries, the ship suddenly turned hard to port. Once we corrected to the original course Lieutenant John Steinberger broke out the Sailing Directions for the Straits of Messina and we read about a riptide phenomenon that occurs at the narrower northern end of the strait. It had been so powerful that it had taken 4,500 tons of destroyer going 25 knots and thrown it 60 degrees off course. I also thought about what would have happened if that hydrofoil we had just passed had been a little further north when we hit the riptide.

When we left Naples on March 14th, we were headed home with an arrival date scheduled two weeks later on March 28th, the day before my birthday. We joined up with the rest of the SARATOGA Battle Group in the western Med and transited the Straits of Gibraltar on the 16th, entering the North Atlantic. I peeled SAMPSON off after Gibraltar to go to Rota, Spain to refuel and pick up the INSURV team who would inspect us on the way across the Atlantic. Even though the ship was to be decommissioned, I wanted to put our best foot forward and show them that SAMPSON was still a combat ready ship of the line. I had written a meticulous letter to the senior member of the board, a Navy captain, which would be hand delivered to him on arrival. In it I outlined all of the known deficiencies in the ship. This was a piece of gamesmanship that I had learned during my DESRON 8 days. The idea was to show the inspection team that we knew our ship; hopefully they wouldn't find a slew of problems of which we were unaware.

As we were transiting the Atlantic, Admiral Gee sent a message outlining our procedures for entering port. The ships based in Charleston, Norfolk and Earl would detach a couple of days out, on March 26th, and the Mayport ships, SARATOGA, PHILIPPINE SEA, SPRUANCE, ELMER MONTGOMERY, and SAMPSON, would continue into Mayport for a 10:00 AM arrival. The uniform for entering port would be service dress blue and all ships would man the rail. It was expected that the fanfare would be huge as the country was buzzing with excitement and patriotism following the success of Desert Storm. For me, the best part was the sequence. SAMPSON would lead the group into Mayport. Admiral Gee wrote in his message, "Let's have a greyhound lead us in." Not the carrier, not the cruiser, but the oldest ship in the group on her last deployment.

The transit was uneventful, the weather a little rough but without any storms, and the INSURV inspection proved to be successful from our standpoint. When the final report was issued it reported *SAMPSON* "fit for further service." That wouldn't change anything with respect to decommissioning, but it gave us a sense of satisfaction that we had taken good care of the old lady.

The morning of March 28th dawned clear and bright and as we approached the coast and gained first sight of land we saw that the sky was full of various types of aircraft; news helicopters, small private planes, even the Sea World blimp. At the sea buoy we manned the rails, all hands in their service dress blue uniforms. We were flying our battle ensign and our Super Sam flag. As we sailed between the St Johns River jetties, we saw they were lined with thousands of people, many waving American flags. As we made the turn for the approach to the Mayport basin, we could see that the piers were lined with tens of thousands of people. American flags were everywhere. Banners were all along the fence line welcoming home each of the ships. There were balloons being released into the air, TV satellite trucks, and an Uncle Sam character on stilts. The tug boats in the basin shot red, white, and blue water out of their fire nozzles. Several high school bands were playing on the various piers. It was a carnival atmosphere.

As we backed into our berth, I looked down on the crowded pier from the port bridge wing and picked out Iris with Chris, home from college, and Amy, along with my brother Paul, his wife Cindy holding their daughter Sarah, my god daughter, in her arms, and my old shipmate from *TATTNALL*, Senior Chief Skipper Deas. The crew was perfect, standing at attention and not waving until we passed the word, "Secure from Man the Rail!" over the 1MC. I had thought about playing music as we made the landing; *The Boys Are Back in Town*, by Thin Lizzy, but was glad I hadn't.

As the brow went into place I headed for the quarterdeck to meet Iris who was on the arm of my new DESRON 12 boss, Commodore Mike Miller. Captain John Mitchell had been relieved in December after writing me one of the best fitness reports I ever received and making me the number one CO in the squadron. Commodore Jim Hinkle, as my operational reporting senior during

Desert Shield and Desert Storm, had also ranked me number one among the four commander CO's on whom he reported.

Before we let Iris and Commodore Miller come up the brow to meet me, we let all the sailors who had become new fathers during the cruise leave the ship to meet their new babies; 27 in all, including one set of twins. The wives had put together a tissue paper brow curtain that said, "WELCOME HOME SUPER SAM" on one side and "USS SAMPSON DDG 10, YOU ARE A PERFECT 10," on the other. Against the fence across the pier was a big red, white and blue banner that read, "THEY SAVED THE BEST FOR LAST."

Mike Miller walked Iris up the brow and we exchanged a big hug and a kiss. She looked great in a bright red dress. Chris and Amy were right behind. After that it was pandemonium as everybody streamed aboard or fought their way off to the pier. When things quieted down, it was time to go home. Mayport Road, outside the naval station main gate is about two miles long before it intersects with Atlantic Boulevard. Every foot of that two miles was crowded with more people waving American flags and holding up welcome home signs. It was amazing. When we reached Atlantic Boulevard there was another banner on the overpass that read, "THEY SAVED THE BEST FOR LAST, USS SAMPSON HOMECOMING, WE (HEART) YOU."

We had less than three months to get the ship ready for decommissioning and although we granted well-deserved post-deployment leave, there was plenty of work to do to prepare the ship. Exactly one month after returning from Desert Storm, we were underway on April 29th to go to Charleston, South Carolina and offload all our weapons at the Naval Weapons Station. We remained in Charleston from April 30th to May 2nd, offloading 5-inch ammunition, missiles, torpedoes, and most of the small arms. Friday, May 3rd was the last underway for *SAMPSON* as a commissioned Navy ship. We commenced the real lay-up work the following Monday with the engineering plant forever shut down and various pieces of combat systems gear removed from the ship. By the time she was decommissioned, she was missing the ASROC launcher, all air and surface search radars, the SPG-51 missile fire control radars, and the mast had been topped.

We also began losing crewmembers as the Navy reassigned them to other ships or shore duty. There was a tremendous amount of paperwork to do, including fitness reports for all officers, and evaluations for all the enlisted. The accountable gear which was signed for by me or any of the other officers had to be inventoried and turned in. Discrepancies had to be investigated and a determination made as to what happened. We had moved to a berthing barge, or APL, as the ship became uninhabitable with no air conditioning and no running water.

In early June, we had an awards ceremony as most of the Desert Shield/Desert Storm cruise awards that had to be approved by Rear Admiral Gee or higher had come through. The XO came to see me and said, "Captain, you know you've been put in for a Bronze Star."

"What? That can't be right. Let me see the Awards Manual." I thought you had to kill somebody or jump on a grenade to warrant a Bronze Star. Dave Birdwell brought me the Awards Manual and sure enough, no heroic action was required, only operations in the war zone involving enemy forces.

One of the young sailors who really stood out was Yeoman Third Class Chris Adams. Petty Officer Adams was a brand new third class petty officer, having been a seaman for most of the deployment. As May turned into June, our Chief Yeoman and Chief Personnelman were transferred off the ship, leaving Petty Officer Adams as a one-man Admin Department with a lot of admin yet to be done. He rose to the occasion and did a terrific job. He would play a major role in my career in later years but we had no way of knowing it then.

I was also focusing my attention on the decommissioning ceremony itself. I wanted to put on a class act and I think we did. I invited my old DESRON 8 boss, now Vice Admiral Mike Kalleres, Commander of the Second Fleet, to be the guest speaker. We went about trying to track down all the former *SAMPSON* commanding officers to invite them to the ceremony. Only one, the very first, CDR Forrester W. Isen, was no longer alive. The second CO had been the Commander of the Second Fleet when I was in *NEWPORT NEWS*, VADM Jake Finneran. In the end, nine of 17 former commanding officers made the ceremony.

I also had my own future to worry about. Because I would have only been in command of *SAMPSON* for 11 months when the ship was decommissioned, I was to get a second command, *USS ANTRIM (FFG-20)*, a *PERRY* class frigate. *ANTRIM* would not be mine until late in the year so my first set of orders was to be "stashed" as Chief Staff Officer at DESRON 8 in Mayport. All of this was fine with me.

On June 24th, exactly 30 years after she had been commissioned, we held the decommissioning ceremony. I focused my remarks on the crew. They manned the rails, and, at the appropriate time, they marched off the ship and formed up in ranks on the pier. We hauled down the commissioning pennant, hauled down the colors, which were folded and presented to me, I signed the final deck log entry, and I walked off the ship as the last man.

One of the guests at the ceremony was Ms. Clare Parsons, the daughter of Deak Parsons of ENOLA GAY and Hiroshima fame during World War II, and the great granddaughter of Rear Admiral William T. Sampson. During the ceremony I had Lieutenant Eric Alfaro present her with the oil portrait of Admiral Sampson that had hung in the wardroom for 30 years. I probably was not authorized to do that, but I didn't ask anyone's permission and nothing was ever said.

In 2007, as a Vice Admiral, I had the honor of being the commissioning speaker at the commissioning ceremony in Boston for *USS SAMPSON (DDG-102)*, a new *ARLEIGH BURKE* class guided missile destroyer. Ms. Parsons was at that ceremony as the Ship's Sponsor, and at the pre-ceremony reception the night before, she presented that same portrait to the CO of the new *SAMPSON*, Commander Phil Roos. I can't help but believe that if I had turned that painting in with the other accountable equipment, it would still be sitting in an attic somewhere in the Washington Navy Yard.

After the ceremony, we retired to the Officer's Club on the beach at Mayport and had an all hands party to spend what remained of the ship's Welfare and Recreation funds. A mere two hours after the ceremony, we watched as *SAMPSON* was towed out to sea by *USS HOIST (ARS-40)*, a *BOLSTER* class rescue and salvage ship under the command of Commander Rusty Mirick, who had been in my SOSMRC and PCO class.

SAMPSON was towed to Philadelphia Naval Shipyard where she sat until November 20, 1992 when she was stricken from the Navy list. In December 1994 she was sold for scrap and was scrapped in July 1995.

In July I reported to Captain Joe McCarton, Commander, Destroyer Squadron 8, to serve as his Chief Staff Officer on an interim basis until it came time for me to relieve Captain (select) Steve Sitler as Commanding Officer, *USS ANTRIM (FFG-20)*. I viewed this "stash" at DESRON 8 as a welcome break and a good opportunity to re-orient myself to taking command of a *PERRY* class frigate. *ANTRIM* was one of the DESRON 8 ships. Steve Sitler was very gracious and offered me the opportunity to spend as much time as I wanted to visit *ANTRIM* and to learn the ship.

Between 5-7 September, U.S. Navy aviators held their annual Tailhook convention in Las Vegas. That year it was particularly raucous as, flush with success in Desert Storm, an extra-celebratory mood prevailed. It later came out that there was excess drinking and abuse of women which became a major incident in our Navy. The 1991 Tailhook convention would stain our Navy's reputation for years to come and brought about major changes in our culture, particularly as it applied to women and their roles in the Navy. The effects extended defense-wide to the policies of the Army, Air Force, and Marine Corps as well. Even those of us who were not aviators and nowhere near Las Vegas during the convention were tainted. When I was selected for promotion to captain the following year, I had to sign a statement to the effect that I had not been at Tailhook

91, and that no one who worked for me had been there, before I could be promoted. It was a ridiculous overreaction to the incident, but given the intense political pressures applied by members of Congress, the Navy had little choice but to demonstrate how seriously it was taking the situation.

My orders to *ANTRIM* were cancelled in late September when the promotion zone for the upcoming Captain Promotion Board was released. I had sneaked into the bottom of the zone by five numbers so would be getting looked at during the December promotion board. I had not expected that for another year. Feeling confident that I would be promoted, the Surface Warfare detailing shop decided not to give me a second command as a commander. As a result, instead of the normal two years in a command at sea billet, I would finish with a mere 11 months in command of *SAMPSON* only. I worried about how this might affect my chances for major command, at the captain-level, which was the next milestone in my career, assuming I was promoted to captain. I understood the Navy's rationale: why waste a command on someone who had already "checked the box," and didn't "need" a second command to gain promotion to captain. I was disappointed, as I enjoyed command at sea.

I was nominated to take the job of Surface Operations Officer on the Cruiser-Destroyer Group 12 staff, then deployed to the Persian Gulf embarked in *USS DWIGHT D. EISENHOWER (CVN-69)* and under the command of Rear Admiral John Scott Redd. I would be replacing another friend, Commander Mike Newman, who had been Commanding Officer of *USS BOONE (FFG-28)*. Admiral Redd accepted me for the job and on October 23rd I detached from COMDESRON 8 and went to Dam Neck, Virginia for the three-week Staff Tactical Watch Officer course.

I had Thanksgiving at home with the family before leaving on the 3rd of December to join CRUDESGRU 12 in the Persian Gulf. After 18 years of being home for Christmas, I would miss my second in a row. I hopscotched my way to Bahrain via Philadelphia, Lajes in the Azores, Rota, Spain, Naples, Italy, and Sigonella, Sicily, landing in Bahrain on December 5th. I was pretty tired by the time I arrived and, unfortunately for me, an H-53 helicopter was almost immediately available to fly me out to *EISENHOWER* underway in the Persian Gulf. I was met by a gleeful Commander Mike Newman, introduced to my new boss, Captain Ed Hunter, and met Admiral Redd and Chief of Staff, Captain Frank Herron. It took only a couple of days to turn over with Mike and he happily left the ship to head home. I settled into my routine of planning the ship movements and activities of the 15 or so ships in the Persian Gulf and informing them of plans for the next several days in the daily night intentions message. I enjoyed juggling the many moving parts; assigning ships to continue the maritime interception operations enforcing the embargo on Iraq, arranging port visits and underway replenishments and scheduling the various exercises to keep everybody sharp. It required paying close attention to events and where everybody was operating so as not to direct some activity that was operationally stupid or physically impossible due to time and distance.

The *EISENHOWER* battle group conducted routine operations enforcing the embargo on Iraq and keeping a wary eye on the Iranians throughout January and into February. The group was scheduled to participate in NATO Exercise Teamwork North 92 on the way home in March and I was detailed to lead a team to Dam Neck, Virginia to participate in a pre-sail exercise being run by Commander, 2nd Fleet, Vice Admiral Mike Kalleres. Teamwork North 92 was to be held in the Norwegian Sea and Vjestfjord, again exercising the Cold War Maritime Strategy although the Soviet Union no longer existed. Inertia, I suppose. My team was to consist of the XO's of several squadrons in Carrier Air Wing 7, embarked in IKE, along with a couple of the Group 12 staff officers. The IKE battle group would be shifting from the hot, humid weather of the Persian Gulf to the frozen climes north of the Arctic Circle, a very different operating environment for the ships and the air wing.

Following a weeklong trip to and from Dam Neck, I rejoined EISENHOWER in the northern Red Sea the day before she was to transit the Suez Canal and enter the Mediterranean. *EISENHOWER* pulled into Palma on March 1st and Iris was waiting to meet me. Iris and I spent five enjoyable days in Palma and attended a number of social events hosted by the Palma chapter of the U.S. Navy League. This was when Iris announced that I was never again allowed to go to Palma without her. Those cougars from the Navy League were on the prowl.

Once through Gibraltar and out into the Atlantic, we turned the battle group north for the Norwegian Sea. The battle group, along with NATO allied ships, crossed the Arctic Circle on the 16th of March and entered Vjestfjord on the 17th for three days of exercise operations. The weather was miserable with cold, snow, and high winds and seas, including inside the fjord. When the exercise was over, the *IKE* group crossed the Atlantic and returned to Norfolk on April 2nd. The Group 12 staff boarded a C-9 and flew to Mayport that afternoon for homecoming with the families. Once again, it had only been a month since I had seen Iris in Palma, but of course I had not seen Chris and Amy since before Christmas. I found out shortly after returning to Mayport that I had, in fact, been selected for promotion to captain so the decision by the Bureau of Naval Personnel to not "waste" a second command on me had been validated.

Next up for Cruiser-Destroyer Group 12 was for Admiral Redd to be in charge of a "Mayfly" exercise in May 1992, on the Atlantic Fleet Weapons Training Range off Puerto Rico. Mayfly was a periodic exercise done in conjunction with NATO navies, particularly the Germans, to train against the Exocet missile. The Germans provided the Exocets which were fired from a German ship in the direction of the exercise ships who would try to shoot them down. The Exocets were programmed to flame out and fall into the ocean before they reached the column of exercise ships. Nevertheless, there was some risk as a miscalculation could result in catastrophe if the missile were not shot down. The missiles did not carry live, explosive, warheads, but if one made it to a ship it would do serious damage nonetheless. The French-made Exocet remained the anti-ship missile most feared by our Navy. We had seen what it could do to the British in the Falklands War and what it had done to *USS STARK* in the Persian Gulf.

As Surface Operations Officer, I was responsible for planning the exercise for Admiral Redd's approval. We would have a dozen exercise ships, four U.S., four German, as well as Dutch, British, and Danish ships participating. Admiral Redd and a select portion of the staff would embark in *USS GETTYSBURG (CG-64)*, an Aegis cruiser under the command of Captain John Langknecht, my old CO in *AUBREY FITCH*. Admiral Redd wanted to use ATP-1A, Volume 1, Signal Book signals over the open tactical circuit to direct the movements of all the ships, declare the range "green," and run the exercise. In addition to briefing the operation to all the ships in Roosevelt Roads, Puerto Rico, I was to be the "convoy commander" on the bridge of *GETTYSBURG* to send the radio signals and direct the exercise under Admiral Redd's command.

We flew to Roosevelt Roads on the 18th of May and embarked in *GETTYSBURG*. That afternoon we held a pre-sail brief in the *GETTYSBURG* wardroom where I laid out the plan, including the sequence of the column formation. The Germans laid out the geography as to where the firing ship would be, approximately 20 miles away, just over the horizon. Our column of shooters would steam along on a perpendicular course to the direction of flight of the six Exocet missiles to be fired. Once the range was declared "green" by Range Safety, the German's would fire an Exocet and announce the launch over the radio. Everyone was on their own with permission to shoot as soon as they picked up the incoming missile coming over the horizon.

The Exocet is a tough target. Flying subsonic at about 500 knots, it is a sea skimming missile that flies 7-10 feet above the ocean's surface, making it very difficult to hit with a surface to air missile. The low altitude also means that it is below the radar horizon until it is only 10–12 miles away. At that speed, there is just over a minute to react, and that is with a fully alerted crew that knows the missile is coming and from what general direction. Ships were authorized to take the missiles under fire with guns as well, if they could. Those ships equipped with the Vulcan Phalanx CIWS would have their systems in the full-auto mode as the last line of defense against a rogue missile.

We set sea detail the next morning and made our way to the range where we ordered up the column formation and made final preparations. The Aegis cruisers, like *GETTYSBURG*, had a special fire control setting called "auto-special" which was designed exactly for these quick reaction situations. It removes the human being from the decision process once all the parameters are set for the system. When the AN/SPY-1B radar detects a target meeting the pre-set parameters, the ship's Aegis fire control system fires a missile without human intervention. There is danger in this as the sensitivity of the SPY-1B radar can be over-tuned such that a flock of seagulls or a weather phenomenon can activate the system and send a missile screaming out of the launcher before anyone can react. *GETTYSBURG* was well-equipped to deal with the Exocet, but some of the other ships had more rudimentary fire control systems to include *USS SAMUEL B. ROBERTS (FFG-58)*, a Perry class frigate under the command of my old XO buddy, Commander Joe Sestak.

We spent all afternoon on the range driving the ships around and getting off shots on three of the six planned Exocet missiles. From my station on the bridge it was impressive to watch. The Exocet was hard to see in the daylight, usually a telltale smoke on the horizon was the first visual indication. Almost simultaneous with the visual sighting of the smoke trail, missiles began flying off the rails and out of the vertical launchers and streaking toward the incoming missile. Not all ships saw the missile and achieved a satisfactory fire control solution in time to shoot on each run. On the third missile of the day, late that afternoon, *SAMUEL B. ROBERTS* had a successful intercept; the first time a *PERRY* class frigate had successfully engaged an Exocet with the SM-1 missile. I later talked to Joe Sestak and learned that he had drilled his crew relentlessly to get them ready for this event. This also emphasized how an unaware, not on alert, *USS STARK*, preparing for an engineering inspection and operating outside the exclusion zone in the Persian Gulf in 1987, had almost no chance to defend itself against the two Iraqi Exocets that hit her and killed 37 crewmen. *STARK*'s only hope would have been to have the CIWS in the full automatic mode and ready to fire. For reasons of safety, that was a condition that was only employed in high threat situations when there was a real possibility of a missile attack.

As night fell, we continued firing against targets number four through six. The Exocet was easier to pick up coming over the horizon with the naked eye as the flame could be seen, preceded by an orange glow on the horizon. This is what the lookout on *STARK* would have seen and probably wondered about for a few seconds before reporting a missile inbound. With many oil rigs and natural gas rigs in the Persian Gulf, it is not unusual to see an orange glow and then, as the ship moved closer, a flame on the horizon at night. *GETTYSBURG* was normally first to fire and the speed difference between her SM-2 missiles from the MK-41 vertical launcher and those of the other ships was noticeable. Even if one of the German or other ships launched first, the SM-2 would overtake their missiles, flying an up and over trajectory and be first on the target. The overall exercise was a success, particularly for *SAMUEL B. ROBERTS* and Joe Sestak, and all the Exocets that were not shot down fell harmlessly into the ocean about two miles from our formation.

In June, I took a phone call from Commander Harry Ulrich, then serving as Chief Staff Officer at DESRON 24 in Mayport, to inform me that both of us were on the Major Command list for "CRUDES" command. Harry, a 1972 Naval Academy graduate, was on the same list as me for promotion to captain. "CRUDES" meant that I would either get command of an Aegis cruiser or a destroyer squadron as the commodore. I definitely wanted the cruiser, having thoroughly enjoyed command of *SAMPSON* and feeling somewhat cheated in only having 11 months in command.

In July, Rear Admiral Redd was relieved by Rear Admiral Don Pilling in a ceremony aboard *USS EISENHOWER* in Norfolk. Although based in Norfolk, *EISENHOWER* was the Group 12 designated flagship. In late July, Admiral Pilling took me, Operations Officer Captain Steve Sitler (former CO of *ANTRIM* who I was at one point going to relieve), Intelligence Officer Commander Joe Stewart, and two others on a trip to Key West, Florida to get briefed on our upcoming counter-drug operations at Joint

Interagency Task Force East (JIATF-E). JIATF-E was in overall charge of the multi-agency counter-drug effort in the Caribbean and eastern Pacific, while we, as Commander Task Group 4.1 (CTG 4.1), would be the at-sea commander of the interdiction operations. JIATF-E was commanded by a Coast Guard rear admiral. The night we spent in Key West, Admiral Pilling was invited to dinner with the Coast Guard admiral, so we boys hit the town. We ended up in a topless bar named Pirate Dancer. This name would come in handy later during our operations.

On August 30, 1992, the portion of the staff who would do the CTG 4.1 counter-drug mission, flew to Roosevelt Roads, Puerto Rico and embarked the *LEAHY* class cruiser *USS RICHMOND K. TURNER (CG-20)* who would be our flagship for the first underway period off the northern coast of Colombia. The concept of operations was to array Navy and Coast Guard ships in the Caribbean along the known air routes for drug smugglers running drugs out of Colombia and into Mexico, Nicaragua, Honduras, Jamaica, Puerto Rico or the southern United States. Regardless of the original destination, the end destination for the drugs was almost always the United States. The ships would, in turn, alert aircraft for interception flown by the Drug Enforcement Agency or Customs and Border Protection, or the Coast Guard. Absent an air to air intercept, authorities in the destination countries would be alerted to potentially bust the drug runners upon landing. All of this was coordinated from JIATF-E in Key West. It was a complex and resource intensive operation.

There was a surface transport threat to deal with as well and Navy ships with Coast Guard detachments embarked, or Coast Guard ships themselves, would intercept, board, and search suspicious vessels. We did this for three weeks before returning to Roosevelt Roads to disembark *RICHMOND K TURNER* and embark the nuclear powered cruiser *USS VIRGINIA (CGN-38)* for another underway stint. JIATF-E directed that we set up a concentration of force in one particularly busy area north of Colombia and east of the Panama Canal. The idea was to put heavy pressure on a focused area and see if we could disrupt the drug operations and perhaps get a few busts. Joe Stewart and I drew up the plan and when we presented it to Admiral Pilling we named it Operation Pirate Dancer after the strip club we had visited in Key West. He knew something was up because of our smirks, but he went along with it, and when the Operation Order was published, Operation Pirate Dancer was officially underway.

I had received my orders to attend the National War College at Fort Lesley J. McNair in Washington, D.C. and was scheduled to depart the Group 12 staff in July to begin the course in August. I asked Admiral Pilling to frock me to captain before leaving the staff so I would show up at National War College looking like a captain although being paid as a commander. On the day I detached from the Group 12 staff, Admiral Pilling frocked me to captain in a small ceremony in his office. Before Iris and I made the move to northern Virginia for the war college, my parents drove up to Jacksonville from Winter Park to spend the day. My father was extremely proud of the fact that I had been promoted to captain, but still in doubt that I would go beyond that rank because I had not attended the Naval Academy. He still harbored that suspicion from his own active duty days, that the "ring knockers" would keep an OCS punk down at every opportunity. We nevertheless had an impromptu ceremony at home with him pinning his old captain eagles on the collar of my golf shirt.

October 17, 1970, Orlando Florida. My dad enlists me into the Reserve Officer Candidate program. After the oath, he said, "We got you now!"

May 1973 USS NEWPORT NEWS (CA-148). L-R: Ensign Gary Lankenau, Lieutenant (junior grade) Frank Sorba, me, Ensign Rob Hofmann.

August 1973. On the forecastle of USS Newport News (CA-148). My days as First Division Officer were numbered.

June 2, 1978. Commissioning my brother Steve at Aviation Officer Candidate School, Pensacola, Florida. Mom and Dad look on.

Looper. Flag Secretary, Commander Cruiser-Destroyer Group 12. I learned a great deal that would help me in my next tour as Executive Officer.

December 4, 1986 USS AUBREY FITCH (FFG-34). Happy homecoming with Amy, Iris, and Chris after six months deployed.

August 7, 1990, USS Sampson (DDG-10). A last farewell before setting sail for Operation Desert Shield. Left to right: Chris, Iris, Me, Amy.

Operation Desert Shield, 1990. Taking fuel from USS Saratoga (CV-60) in the northern Red Sea. We conducted 61 underway replenishments during Desert Shield and Desert Storm.

Operation Desert Shield, September 1990. USS Sampson conducts a board and search in the Red Sea.

December 1990, Operation Desert Shield. Alongside USS Yellowstone (AD-41) in Izmir, Turkey. The SLQ-32 antenna lines up perfectly with a Yellowstone life raft canister.

March 28, 1991 USS Sampson (DDG-10). Iris and I leave the ship after a triumphant return from Operation Desert Storm.

May 1991. Family Day cruise aboard USS Sampson (DDG-10). On the starboard bridge wing with son Chris and brother Paul.

June 24, 1991. Decommissioning USS Sampson (DDG-10) at Mayport Florida. The crew marches off the ship 30 years to the day after the first crew marched aboard.

August 6, 1997, USS Cowpens (CG-63). My dad and Iris on the bridge wing in Puget Sound as we sail into Seattle for the Seattle Sea Fair.

Four bells, "Cowpens, departing" swim call in the Persian Gulf. August 1998.

Fore! Keeping the swing grooved by hitting balls into the Persian Gulf. Summer 1998. USS Cowpens (CG-63).

Iris waves from the pilot boat as USS Cowpens (CG-63) enters Darwin, Australia, November 1998.

Waterfight at sea. Iris watches from the VLS deck, USS Milius (DDG-69) as Cowpens comes alongside to douse Milius. November 1998.

October 27, 1999, Pohang Korea, after an AH-64E Apache flight over the Sea of Japan with the U.S. Army 6th Cavalry Division. Happy to be back on land.

Chinhae, Korea, 2000. Office call with Vice Admiral Song, Keong Ho, Commander, Republic of Korea Fleet.

Honolulu Hawaii, April 2003. Greeting Rear Admiral (General) Zhou Borong for Maritime Military Consultation talks at U.S. Pacific Command. Little progress was made.

A light moment with Secretary of Defense Robert Gates at NATO Headquarters, Brussels, Belgium.

October 14, 2009, NATO Headquarters, Brussels, Belgium. Ukrainian Major General Petr Haraschuk presents me with the Order of the Ministry of Defence of Ukraine Medal. I had a soft spot for my colleagues who had previously suffered under Soviet domination.

This poster was used by the Belgium Chapter of The American Overseas Memorial Day Association to publicize Memorial Day activities. The photos are from Ardennes American Cemetery. These events were extremely moving and one of the highlights of our time in Belgium.

Three generations. Mayport Florida, January 15, 2010. My Dad gave me his sword in 1972. I passed it on to Chris to symbolize the changing of the watch.

Going ashore. January 15, 2010, USS The Sullivans (DDG-68). Iris and I leave the ship after 37 years in uniform. I could not have had a better partner.

CHAPTER 18

Getting Purpled

I reported to the National War College on August 16, 1993 to join the class of 1994. The National War College was established in 1946 to replace the Army-Navy Staff College which had operated during World War II. It is a joint professional military education institution checking one of the boxes required by the Goldwater-Nichols Act of 1986 which established criteria for joint experience for all officers seeking promotion to flag rank. Although primarily for military officers, students are also drawn from other agencies of the U.S. government. We were divided up into ten Committees, which could best be described as home rooms.

Fort Lesley J. McNair itself enjoys a rich history. Sitting on what is known as Greenleaf Point at the confluence of the Potomac and Anacostia rivers, it was established in 1791 and is third only to the Military Academy at West Point and Carlisle Barracks in Pennsylvania as the oldest Army post in the United States. The National War College is hosted in Roosevelt Hall, a beaux-arts style building sitting prominently on Greenleaf Point and readily visible to travelers flying in and out of Washington-Reagan International Airport across the Potomac. The building itself exudes class and historical significance and contributes to the sense of academia that the War College hopes to instill in its students.

"Jointness" had been forced on the U.S. military by the 1986 Goldwater-Nichols Act which had been inspired by both the failed hostage rescue attempt in Iran in 1980 and the clumsily executed Grenada invasion of 1983. Both operations had demonstrated that, as powerful as our armed forces were, they were not very good at operating together, or jointly. Too many systems, especially communications and data transfer systems were incompatible. I am a big supporter of the impact that Goldwater-Nichols had on our military. To become "joint" was to become "purple," the result of blending Navy Blue, Army Green, Marine Corps Red and Air Force Blue.

The year at National War College was very enjoyable and I made many friends that I would encounter again and again in the years to come. I enjoyed the classes, didn't do all of the reading, and worked on staying in shape, running, and improving my golf game. It was a remarkable experience, limited only by the individual officer's motivation or lack thereof. I enjoyed the courses, my classmates, the travel, and the opportunity to read history and study world events from the safety of academia.

Much was going on in the world during our time at the National War College which provided fodder for our classroom discussions. In 1992, the U.S. had landed forces in Somalia in a humanitarian mission to stop widespread famine following a civil war which left the country literally ungoverned. That mission evolved into a mission to capture or kill the Somali warlord Mohamed Farrah Aidid after his forces slaughtered a number of Pakistani peacekeeping forces. On October 3, 1993, the famous "Blackhawk Down" incident occurred during a mission to capture Aidid. Many aspects of this operation were the subject of animated discussion at the War College, beginning with the ironic landing of Marines on the beach in full combat gear while media correspondents in khaki pants and polo shirts recorded the event from the safety of the beach. The Marines cannot be blamed for taking advantage of the "assault" as a training opportunity, but the irony was not lost on the American public.

One of the key features of National War College were the regional studies trips during which the class was divided into groups and sent off to learn about the geo-strategic circumstances in various parts of the world. I requested and was picked for the Australia, Singapore and Indonesia trip which we took from April 30th to May 14th 1994. In April, I had been nominated by BuPers to take a job on the Joint Staff in the Directorate for Operations, J-3, in the Joint Operations Division, or JOD, as the head of the Pacific

Division. In my 22 years in the Navy I had never been stationed in the Pacific, and had only been in the region as an ensign on *NEWPORT NEWS*, my War College trip notwithstanding; hardly the credentials that one would think might be desired for the position. Nevertheless, I was selected for the job and thus began a focus on the Pacific theater which would continue for the next nine years. Our class graduated from the National War College on Friday, June 15th, and I reported to the Joint Staff the following Monday.

My 24 months in the J-3 were extremely interesting and rewarding–the best job I had held up to that point in my career with the exception of my time at sea in command of *SAMPSON* or as XO in *AUBREY FITCH*. The JOD was divided into regions which coincided with the four-star combatant commands with regional responsibilities around the globe. My division was aligned with U.S. Pacific Command in Honolulu, Hawaii. Each division was headed up by an O-6 with me representing the Navy, an Air Force colonel heading the EUCOM Division, an Army colonel leading the Western Hemisphere Division, and a Marine colonel running CENTCOM Division. Our boss was a Marine Corps Colonel who reported to the J-33, Navy Rear Admiral Charles W. "Willy" Moore. The J-3 was headed up by Marine Lieutenant General Jack Sheehan. In 1994 and throughout my two years on the staff, the Chairman of the Joint Chiefs of Staff was Army General John Shalikashvili. Lieutenant General Sheehan was replaced by Air Force Lieutenant General Howell Estes, III shortly after I reported aboard.

The JOD was on the "B" ring in the Pentagon, the ring of hallways closer to the center of the building than the prestigious "E" ring on the outer extremity. Across the hall was the National Military Command Center, or NMCC, so often erroneously depicted in Hollywood movies. We operators in JOD routinely transited the NMCC in order to visit our immediate boss, Rear Admiral Moore, or to get to the "E" ring and the J-3's office. The NMCC itself was a large room, populated with cubicles and computers and looking much like any civilian large corporate office area manned by clerks. At its center was the office manned by a one-star officer who was the Deputy Director of Operations, or DDO. The DDO's stood rotational 24/7 watches and were the eyes and ears of the U.S. military on a day to day basis. The DDO's, supported by the watchstanders in the main room, were to monitor military operations throughout the world, take important reports, issue orders when necessary, and keep the military leadership of the United States informed of events day and night. The DDO played a key role in the command and control of the nation's nuclear triad and each watch rotation conducted a daily drill with the U.S. Strategic Command in Omaha, Nebraska and North American Aerospace Defense (NORAD) in Colorado Springs, Colorado. In the DDO's area was a large digital screen fed by the Global Command and Control System, or GCCS, "Geeks" in the vernacular. Hollywood movies often depict this space as being super high-tech with the key leaders watching individual special operations troops advancing on an objective, taking fire, returning fire, and so forth. In 1994, none of this was possible. I recall one operation taking place in the Persian Gulf when Air Force General Estes was the J-3. On the screen was an outline of the Gulf with U.S. naval forces depicted by round friendly force symbology and Iranian naval forces depicted by potentially hostile symbology. On the screen it looked like the Iranians were right next to our aircraft carrier. General Estes became concerned about the apparent proximity of the Iranian forces.

"Sir," I said, "it's the scale, I bet they can't even see each other."

The DDO directed that the sergeant running the GCCS display zoom in. Sure enough, they were more than 20 miles apart. In the Persian Gulf haze often limits visibility to less than 5 to 10 miles.

When I joined JOD, the U.S. was in the middle of dealing with a crisis in Haiti with thousands of Haitians fleeing the country on makeshift rafts and grossly overloaded and unseaworthy boats. The President of Haiti, Jean-Bertrand Aristide, had been overthrown in a military coup by General Raoul Cedras in 1991 and the United Nations Security Council had passed Resolution 841 imposing sanctions and an arms embargo on Haiti. 30,000–50,000 Haitians had been killed during the period of Cedras' military rule which had generated the attempted exodus. The fleeing Haitians resulted in a major interdiction and rescue effort code-named Operation Able Manner, executed primarily by the U.S. Coast Guard and the U.S. Navy. I walked into this crisis in the JOD and was almost immediately made a Crisis Action Team (CAT) Chief in the NMCC. We were standing 12 hours on and 12 hours off watches keeping the leadership informed and passing on military orders to the Commander of SOUTHCOM from the National Command Authority.

By September, with the atrocities on the ground continuing and after an embarrassing incident in which a U.S. Navy ship, *USS HARLAN COUNTY (LST-1196)*, was turned away from Port Au Prince by an unruly mob, the United States was ready to take action to remove General Cedras from power by force with Operation Uphold Democracy. I was on watch the night of the invasion as we watched on CNN while the C-141's lifted off from Pope Air Force base near Fort Bragg to augment the force that was at sea aboard the aircraft carrier *USS AMERICA (CV-66)*. In a great example of jointness and out-of-the-box thinking, *AMERICA* was not loaded with Navy aircraft, but with Army helicopters and Army soldiers, serving as an afloat staging base for the Army invasion of Haiti. General Sheehan was prowling the CAT floor, but he knew something we didn't. President Clinton had secretly dispatched a negotiating team consisting of former President Jimmy Carter, former Joint Chiefs Chairman General Colin Powell, and our Deputy J-3, Major General Jerry Bates, to give Cedras one last chance to surrender power and go into exile, which he did. I later learned that General Bates carried the briefcase containing one million dollars in cash to encourage Cedras to take the deal.

In my own Pacific theater, the ruler of North Korea, Kim Il Sung, died on July 8, 1994. He was replaced by his son, Kim Jong Il, and the younger Kim began threatening South Korea and continuing the ongoing program to develop a nuclear weapon. Thus began a series of provocations which had the United States responding to requests for additional forces from Commander, U.S. Forces Korea.

In August, I had been told by a good friend, Captain Mark Rogers, that I was penciled in for my major command to take command of the Aegis cruiser *USS CHOSIN (CG-65)*, homeported in Hawaii, in the summer of 1996. Iris and I were both excited about this. Me because commanding an Aegis cruiser was the pinnacle for a Surface Warfare Officer and Iris because she would get to live in her beloved Hawaii again. I was pretty excited about the Hawaii part myself.

Life in JOD was never dull as there was always something to generate a crisis; whether it was in the Pacific theater or not, we generally got involved. CENTCOM Division was the busiest as Saddam Hussein, despite his defeat in Desert Storm, continued to be a thorn in the side of the United States and the rest of the world. The sanctions were still in effect and Navy ships were still conducting the Maritime Interception Operations that had begun in 1990 to enforce the sanctions. The United States had launched Tomahawk missiles into an Iraqi Intelligence Center in June of 1993 in response to an Iraqi plot to assassinate former President Bush during a visit to Kuwait.

In my theater on December 17th, we dealt with the North Koreans shooting down a U.S. Army helicopter that had strayed across the DMZ on a familiarization flight, resulting in the death of the co-pilot and the capture of the pilot. We also dealt with a Coast Guard cutter that had picked up a boatload of Chinese in the Pacific trying to make their way to the United States. We went around and round with the State Department trying to figure out what to do with the Chinese who had been moved aboard the cutter because their boat was unseaworthy and in danger of sinking. Finally, we ended up setting up a camp on Midway Island to hold them and feed them until negotiations with China could resolve their fate. Midway was chosen because they would be unable to request asylum as they could if we had brought them to Hawaii or someplace else in the United States. The rationale for choosing Midway was not unlike the rationale for holding prisoners captured in the Global War on Terror, following September 11, 2001, at Guantanamo Bay, Cuba. In July we dealt with the first Taiwan Strait crisis as the Chinese fired short range ballistic missiles into declared closure areas north and south of Taiwan, effectively shutting off trade and causing a major drop in Taiwan's stock market. This would be repeated again in 1996 and result in one of my finer Navy moments on the Joint Staff.

During 1995, when Saddam Hussein was feinting by once again moving forces toward the Kuwait border, the United States responded by moving Army pre-positioning ships to the Persian Gulf. These "pre-po" ships, based in the Pacific and in the Mediterranean, are loaded out with Army equipment; tanks, trucks, artillery and so forth. The idea is that they can be quickly moved to a crisis area and the forces flown in to offload them and use the equipment. The equipment they carry is all heavy equipment and the only practical way to move it overseas is by sea. Having the ships pre-loaded and stationed "at the ready" in the Indian Ocean and Mediterranean puts them closer to potential hotspots. The problem on this occasion was that the true status of each of the ships was not being tracked in the Pentagon. There were supposed to be four pre-po ships at Diego Garcia in the Indian Ocean and when the call went out it was discovered that one was in a maintenance period in California and another was participating in an exercise near Japan.

General Shalikashvili was upset and directed a top to bottom review of the entire global pre-positioning laydown. You would think that this responsibility would fall to the J-4, the Directorate for Logistics. Instead, I was given the task. As he would later during another crisis, General Estes volunteered to take on this project in J3. The rationale was that the status of the ships had real operational implications so J-3 should do the review. Because ships float and I was his Navy guy, I was given the job. It was eye-opening and I spent two months working on it much to the interest of the Army, the Marine Corps, and the U.S. Transportation Command, which was ostensibly responsible for the pre-po ships through the Navy Military Sealift Command. My task was expanded to include all pre-positioning stocks, on land and at sea. I discovered that we had a brigade of equipment in a mountain cave in Norway for the Marines to fall in on and fight the Soviet Union, which no longer existed. This was known as the NALMEB (Norway Air-Land Marine Expeditionary Brigade) and included a vast quantity of cold weather and alpine equipment suitable for fighting in the mountains of Norway. I recommended that it be disestablished over the objections of the Marines. They won that argument, but in the process I had not endeared myself to a Marine Corps lieutenant general who attended the Tank brief when I made my recommendations.

One of the programs I was in charge of as the Chief of JODPAC was the Global Naval Force Presence Policy, or GNFPP. The GNFPP had been created to manage the demand for Navy aircraft carriers and amphibious ready groups (ARG's) with embarked Marine Expeditionary Units (MEU's) which exceeded the Navy's ability to permanently provide. It mandated what presence each combatant commander could count on in his theater, taking into account the necessity for the ships to transit to station, have maintenance performed, and have a reasonable amount of time in home port at the end of a deployment. We had 12 aircraft carriers in the 1990s and it generally took 3 to 4 carriers to achieve the permanent presence of one, 365 days a year, forward in a given theater. This was known as a 1.0 presence. The other services despised this policy because there was not a similar demand for Air Force wings or Army brigades. They felt underappreciated and resented this special status afforded the Navy and Marine Corps. The GNFPP created the perception that the Navy and Marine Corps were special, and more in demand than the Army and the Air Force. The Army and Air Force did their best to create a similar demand, by instituting rotational Army deployments to Kuwait to guard against renewed hostility by Saddam Hussein, and similar rotational deployments of Air Force fighter squadrons, called Air Expeditionary Forces (AEF's) for the same purpose. The AEF for example, could, in theory, substitute for when an aircraft carrier was not present. An Army rotation could substitute for when a MEU was not in theater, although everyone knew they lacked the mobility of a MEU. In truth, nobody bought into these substitutions and what the combatant commanders really wanted were the Navy carriers and Navy-Marine ARG-MEUs because of their inherent mobility and the fact that they could operate freely in international waters and not require shore basing.

One day I was in General Shalikashvili's office with General Estes and Admiral Moore briefing him on the latest edition of the GNFPP when he vented, saying, "Why don't we have this for the rest of the force?" Instead of telling him that the reason was that the combatant commanders weren't demanding the Army and Air Force be present on a continuous or near continuous basis, Air Force General Estes said, "We'll work on it."

I was given the task. Working with my JODPAC team, we invented something called the Global Military Force Policy, or GMFP. In an effort to scope the problem, we focused on something we defined as "low density–high demand" (LD-HD) assets. That is how the carriers and ARG-MEUs were viewed. Low density meaning there simply weren't enough of whatever it was to meet the high demand of the regional combatant commanders.

Working with the services to identify what to include in our LD-HD inventory, we received all sorts of, mostly unwanted, help. Some of it was easy, AWACS, U-2's, RC-135 "Rivet Joints" and Joint Stars for the Air Force for example. But representatives of all the services kept coming up with a variety of insignificant equipment to be offered up as LD-HD and therefore covered by the GMFP. The services no doubt figured that if they could get a particular piece of their equipment designated LD-HD and included in the GFMP, they'd likely fare better in the budget drills and perhaps be directed to buy more. In the end, I briefed it to the Joint Chiefs in the Tank (the special conference room where the Joint Chiefs of Staff meet to deliberate on important issues) and it was signed before I left the Joint Staff. It was my ticket out to go back to sea.

In late 1995, the major command slate came out of PERS-41, the BuPers office responsible for surface warfare and my friend, Captain Mark Edwards, was listed as PCO (prospective commanding officer) of *USS CHOSIN*. In one of my dumber moves I called up Captain Mike Mullen, PERS-41 himself, and said, "What happened to me going to *CHOSIN*?"

Obviously miffed, he said, "Who told you, you were getting *CHOSIN*?"

"Mark Rogers." I said without thinking. Captain Mark Rogers was a good friend from Mayport days, kept his ears plugged into the rumor mill, and was at the time stationed at the White House running the White House Military Office.

"Well he was wrong. Don't worry, you'll get your cruiser." The unspoken message was, don't call us we'll call you.

In March 1996, the China-Taiwan crisis returned with the Chinese once again threatening to fire missiles into the waters around Taiwan. This time the United States decided to respond with a show of force. I was in the office on a Saturday, along with Commander Buz Buzby and Lieutenant Colonel Phil Breedlove when I was summoned to General Estes' office. My division had been working on a wide range of military response options in the event China threatened Taiwan, and General Shalikashvili had been attending numerous meetings at the White House to brief President Clinton using charts which we had built. Because of the time difference between Hawaii, where PACOM is located, and Washington, I spent two nights sleeping on a couch in JOD waiting for the options to come in from PACOM for that day's brief to the President. When I arrived in the J-3 office that morning, General Estes said, "Come on, we're going to see Shali."

We walked into General Shalikashvili's office and I joined General Estes at the table and sized up the crowd: Army General Shalikashvili, Chairman of the Joint Chiefs of Staff; Air Force General Joe Ralston, Vice Chairman, Joint Chiefs of Staff; Air Force Lieutenant General Walt Kross, Director of the Joint Staff; Army Major General Pat Hughes, Director for Intelligence, Joint Staff; Air Force Lieutenant General Howell Estes, Director, J-3; Navy Captain

Bill Sullivan, J-3 JODPAC. Mine was the only Navy uniform in the room with six Army stars and ten Air Force stars.

The Air Force desperately wanted to share in the glory, but couldn't. It had already been decided that the carrier *USS INDEPENDENCE (CV-62)* would sail from Japan to north of Taiwan. That morning after discussing options, the group decided that the carrier *USS NIMITZ (CVN-68)* would leave the Persian Gulf and rush to an area south of Taiwan. The Air Force wanted to backfill *NIMITZ* with an AEF in order to satisfy the 1.0 carrier presence in the CENTCOM area, thus validating their counter to the GNFPP. But, bad news for the Air Force, a regularly scheduled AEF rotation for training was upcoming, and all the gear needed to support the squadrons on the ground in Jordan was slowly steaming across the Atlantic in cargo ships. None of it would arrive in time to relieve *NIMITZ* in the Persian Gulf. Consequently, this group of Air Force and Army generals were forced to agree with my recommendation that the carrier *USS GEORGE WASHINGTON (CVN-73)* leave the Med, transit the Suez Canal, and backfill *NIMITZ* in the Gulf. It was to be an all Navy show. The Air Force was openly disappointed.

So were the Marines who also wanted to be part of the show of force. The Marine Corps Operations Director, a three-star who shall remain un-named, having heard about the meeting, came into my office after the meeting in Shali's office and practically begged me to add the Marine MEU in Okinawa to the mix. It was as if he thought that if I just typed it into the deployment order message nobody would notice and the next day 2,000 Marines and three Navy ships would magically sail out of Okinawa and go hover around Taiwan to threaten the Chinese. I of course had no authority to do this on my own and told him so. Here was a three-star, lobbying me and not somebody higher in the food chain, and also not giving a second thought to disrupting the lives of 3,500 Navy and Marine Corps personnel for which there was no valid mission. I couldn't believe it. This was the same Marine general who went after me after I briefed my recommendation to remove the NALMEB from Norway. We were not on good terms. Once the

Marine general left I sat down at my computer with Buz and Phil looking over my shoulder and personally typed up the order which would be signed out by General Shalikashvili and set all this in motion. It was a great Navy day.

Also in March the next major command slate was published and I saw that I was slated to take command of the Aegis guided missile cruiser *USS COWPENS (CG-63)*, homeported in San Diego, in April 1997. I had always thought to myself, that of all 27 Aegis cruisers in the United States Navy, the one with the most inelegant name was *COWPENS*. I then went down to the Pentagon bookstore and started looking through the Civil War books for the Battle of Cowpens–couldn't find it, must not have been a very important battle. Then I checked the Revolutionary War and there it was. The ship was named after a battle in a cow pasture in northern South Carolina in 1791 which was the first Colonial victory in the south and one of the turning points in the War for Independence. Not bad, but still kind of an ugly name.

One day I was in my office in JOD when big Lieutenant General Howell Estes darkened my doorway; he was about 6'6" tall. He sat down and said, "Bill, where are you in your career? When are you up for admiral?"

"Sir, I haven't had my major command yet so I'm really not eligible."

He said, "You know the Chairman gets to nominate four officers from the Joint Staff to each of the service chiefs for promotion to general or admiral each year. I want him to nominate you."

I was flattered of course, but also realistic, "Thank you sir, but it's not likely to happen until I finish a major command tour."

"When is that?"

"I've got orders to command a cruiser out of San Diego when I leave here. And I would most likely have that command for two years."

"All right, but I'm going to give Shali your name anyway."

And he did, and General Shalikashvili gave my name to the CNO. But, of course, nothing happened; the system is the system and the Navy wasn't about to leapfrog me over a bunch of other officers who had met all the eligibility requirements just because the Chairman of the Joint Chiefs of Staff thought it was a good idea.

On September 18th, 1996, I was officially detached from the Joint Staff to begin the pipeline training for command of *COWPENS*. First up was six weeks of Aegis combat systems training at the Aegis Training Center, Dahlgren, Virginia for something called the Aegis Command Course. For me this was essential because I had never served in an Aegis ship, the most capable and advanced combat system in the world. This was followed by the Major Command Prospective Commanding Officer Course in Newport, Rhode Island.

In late summer of 1996, my son Chris who had graduated from Florida State and was in a manager trainee program with the athletic shoe store Footlocker applied to the Navy for Officer Candidate School. Amy was beginning her senior year at Florida State. We were on the phone with Amy one evening and Amy told Iris and me that Chris was seeing the Navy recruiters and considering joining the Navy. Naturally he had not bothered to share this news with his parents. After Amy had tattled on him I called him up and got the story. It turned out that he had already been to see the officer recruiters and had taken the basic qualification test for Officer Candidate School. The same one I had taken 26 years before and the same one I had administered countless times myself while on recruiting duty. The test has two parts depending on the program for which application is being made. Chris had taken the basic test for non-aviation programs because he thought he wanted to be a Surface Warfare Officer like me. The recruiters told him that Surface Warfare was full for that year and asked him if he was interested in aviation. He did not have 20/20 vision, also like me, so if he went into naval aviation he could not be a pilot, but could be a Naval Flight Officer (NFO), the back-seater in tactical jets or systems operator on other aircraft. He said, "why not?" and took and passed the test. Chris enlisted and was scheduled for Aviation OCS in Pensacola, Florida with a class scheduled to graduate and get commissioned in March of 1997.

On the 24th of February, I checked into the three week Joint Maritime Tactical Command course at the Tactical Training Group Pacific on Point Loma. My old detailer, Captain Dallas Bethea, was the CO. Dallas had also been the second commanding officer of *COWPENS*. I was to be her fourth, relieving Captain Bill Snyder. *COWPENS* was deployed to the Persian Gulf and the plan was for me to meet the ship in Hawaii in April and ride her to San Diego to complete all of the turnover activity before she reached homeport. Change of command was scheduled for April 26th, two weeks after the ship returned from the six-month deployment.

Before all this was going to take place, there was the important event of Chris's commissioning in Pensacola on the 14th of March. I skipped the last two days of the Joint Maritime Tactical Command Course and Iris and I flew to Pensacola. The morning of Chris's commissioning I went on the morning run with his company and then we all went to the ceremony. They allowed me to swear Chris in with the commissioning oath in a private ceremony before the group ceremony in the chapel. He was now Ensign Christopher Sullivan and we were mighty proud. Chris had been accepted into the NFO program but would not learn which aircraft he would be flying until he had completed his basic NFO training. Much would depend on the needs of the Navy, but his performance in the training pipeline would also be a consideration.

CHAPTER 19

Cruiser Command

"**N**ow station the Sea and Anchor Detail, the ship expects to get underway at 0800 for San Diego, Californ-i-a! All guests are requested to leave the ship. Department Heads submit readiness for getting underway reports to the Executive Officer on the Bridge. Now station the Special Sea and Anchor Detail."

Those familiar words sent a special chill up my spine and caused the familiar churn in the stomach. The difference today was that I was only a passenger, the Prospective Commanding Officer to be sure, but a passenger nonetheless in *USS COWPENS (CG-63)*. All of the responsibility for the ship lay with the man I was to relieve; Captain Bill Snyder. I had reported aboard for duty in Pearl Harbor from San Diego, the ship's homeport, the day before on April 3, 1997.

As I stood out of the way on the bridge and watched the crew go through the paces of getting underway, I knew they were also watching me. Sizing me up. *COWPENS* was a good ship with a good reputation and I knew it. I was also watching Bill Snyder, gauging the way he handled himself and handled the crew–and how the crew reacted to him.

Executive Officer Lieutenant Commander Perry Bingham was a hulking 6'7" tall and weighing a good 250–260 pounds. Perry would be my XO for the next nine months and I thought we would make a real Mutt and Jeff pair as he was a foot taller and 100 pounds heavier than me. The crew would have fun with that.

Thus began my indoctrination to "The Mighty Moo," *USS COWPENS (CG-63)*, an Aegis guided missile cruiser, the most advanced surface combatant in the world. I spent the six-day transit to San Diego touring the ship, observing drills, meeting with the Department Heads and Division Officers, Chief Petty Officers and crew as I made my rounds. *COWPENS* was conducting a Tiger Cruise and about 70 family members of crewmembers were aboard for the transit and the experience of seeing a real warship in action.

Captain Ed Moore, the commissioning CO of *COWPENS*, and his successor, my friend Dallas Bethea, had done their best to capitalize on the cow theme associated with the name of the ship. Bill Snyder had continued the practice and I would add my own touches during my tour. The original *USS COWPENS (CVL-25)* was a World War II light carrier which saw considerable action in the Pacific. Her crew nicknamed her "The Mighty Moo" and the new *COWPENS* kept up that tradition. The crew of *COWPENS* was called "The Thundering Herd" and an artistic crewmember had painted a charging bull appearing to burst through the helicopter hangar doors. The cow theme was seen throughout the ship with hamburgers known as "moo-burgers" and large chocolate chip cookies called "cow patties" on the messdecks; the windsock made out of a black and white Holstein cowhide material instead of the required international orange; the Captain's and XO chairs on the bridge covered in Holstein cowhide seat covers; and the wardroom had a supply of Holstein cummerbunds for wear with dinner dress uniforms. Iris got into the spirit and had her Miata outfitted with Holstein seat covers. My callsign was "Wild Bull" and when conversing with the RHIB or the gig via walkie-talkie, they were "Baby Bull." Later, the Command Master Chief, Damage Controlman Master Chief Rupert "Luke" Lucas, bought a large set of longhorn steer horns at a flea market in Imperial Beach and I had them mounted under the bridge windows.

We pulled into San Diego for the big homecoming on the 11th of April and spent the next two weeks making preparations for the change of command ceremony scheduled for April 26th. *COWPENS* was administratively assigned to Cruiser-Destroyer Group 5, under the command of Rear Admiral Pete Long. Rear Admiral Long was to be the guest speaker at the change of command ceremony.

At almost the same time that I was leaving the Joint Staff, Lieutenant General Estes, the J-3, was also leaving to get a fourth star and become the Commander, U.S. Space Command in Colorado Springs, one of the functional combatant commands. He was being replaced by Marine Lieutenant General Pete Pace who would go on to be first Vice Chairman, and then Chairman, of the Joint Chiefs of Staff. Before he left, General Estes told me that he wanted to receive an invitation to my change of command when it happened. I had put him on the invitation list and damned if he didn't show up. This caused a little angst as this 6'6" Air Force four-star general had to be accounted for, walked through the sideboys and rendered honors, and given a prominent seat right next to my father. As had been the case when I took command of *SAMPSON*, my entire family and many close friends made the trip to San Diego for the big day.

On Wednesday of the following week, the SURFPAC Public Affairs Officer came to the ship for an arranged meeting to discuss an idea they had for a story about a Navy ship. He brought with him James Crawley, Military Affairs Correspondent for the *San Diego Union Tribune* and a photographer, Don Kohlbauer. Jim Crawley wanted to write a human interest story about what life is like on a Navy ship.

We met in my cabin along with Perry Bingham and Master Chief Lucas, and they outlined the concept. Jim and Don wanted to ride the ship as much as possible for the next year until we deployed to the Persian Gulf in May of 1998. *COWPENS* was considered a good choice because we had a compressed, 13-month turnaround to undergo a two-month long maintenance period, do all the required work-up training and inspections, and then deploy again to the Persian Gulf. Jim and Don wanted total, unfettered access to the crew in order to tell the story in as unvarnished and straightforward a way as possible. Jim had at one time worked for the *Tallahassee Democrat,* a connection he played up. Don was an ex-Navy Photographers Mate. Both were likeable and enthusiastic about the story. I agreed to everything and told the XO and CMC, "They get total access except in classified spaces." By that I meant everywhere except Radio Central and the cryptologic space. They were welcome to get underway with the ship anytime they wanted and to talk to the crew without interference. They were willing to bunk in crew berthing whenever underway with us overnight and to eat in the wardroom, Chief's Mess, or on the Messdecks, free of charge.

Jim Crawley and Don Kohlbauer rode the ship for my first underway period which included naval gunfire support training at San Clemente Island. Jim, who had never served in the military, was almost giddy with excitement. We had one incident during the firing exercises when a round jammed in Mount 51 under "hot gun" conditions. The Navy defined a hot gun as one that has fired 150 rounds or more in a four-hour period. The rules for dealing with it were pretty straightforward. The danger was that a round jammed in the breech after a misfire could potentially "cook off" and explode due to the heat. The procedures called for cease fire, clear the magazine and mount area, rig firemain water to externally cool the barrel, and point the gun on a safe bearing. The firemain had to be applied for two hours before anyone was allowed inside the mount to manually extract the jammed round.

In consideration of the possibility of an in-bore explosion, I had the forward half of the ship cleared, the firemain rigged, and then I cleared the bridge except for myself. I stayed up there for two hours driving the ship around and keeping Mount 51 pointed at the range on San Clemente until time was up and Chief McDonald and Gunner's Mate First Class Wetzel could clear the round. When the newspaper series was published a year later, this episode was made out to be a big deal and I was accorded hero status for placing my crew's safety ahead of my own. It was nowhere near that dramatic and I had probably been over cautious by clearing the bridge, but that's what sells newspapers.

After an ammunition offload at Seal Beach Naval Weapons Station we returned and tied up at a far southern pier in the industrial section of Naval Station San Diego and began tearing apart the ship for the overhaul. We would be two months at that location, preferable in my view to a drydocking overhaul in a shipyard.

After a post maintenance sea trial and refueling at sea from *USNS RAPPHANNOCK (T-AO-204)*, our next event was to participate in the Seattle Sea Fair, one of the annual good deals for Navy ships. I arranged for my father to come to San Diego and ride the ship to Seattle with me. We also had some Seattle Navy Leaguers aboard and a couple of gentlemen from the city of Spokane, Washington. One of the events to take place in Seattle was for the ship to receive the Spokane Trophy recognizing the best gunnery ship in the Pacific Fleet. My mother and Iris would fly to Seattle and board the ship at Port Hadlock in Puget Sound for the parade of ships. My dad had also asked me to invite some of his Silver Eagle (WWII enlisted pilots) buddies and their wives to ride the ship from Port Hadlock to Seattle.

I had one of the ship's jackets embroidered with my dad's name on it and set him up in the inport cabin. On the transit north from San Diego from the 1st to the 5th of August we refueled twice from an oiler, shot the five inch guns, and participated in an anti-air warfare exercise. Dad had a great time and spent most of it on the bridge in my chair just enjoying being at sea and watching the crew run through their paces.

We tied up at an ammunition pier that is across a small bay on Puget Sound from the town of Port Hadlock for the night of the 5th. The morning of the 6th, hundreds of guests came aboard for the parade of ships into downtown Seattle. *COWPENS* was to be the lead ship with Rear Admiral Bill Putnam, Commander Cruiser-Destroyer Group 3, embarking *COWPENS* for the transit. Admiral Putnam was to be the senior Navy officer for the Seattle Sea Fair festivities. I was up around 4:00 AM the morning of the 5th for the entry into the Strait of Juan de Fuca which separates Vancouver Island, Canada from the state of Washington and leads to Puget Sound some 90 miles east. The scenery was spectacular with the Cascade Mountains to our right and Vancouver Island to the left.

When all the guests were onboard the morning of the 6th, we formed up in a column of eight ships with *COWPENS* in the lead and sailed into Elliot Bay where we were to tie up at Pier 66, downtown. It was a tight berth and the bow of the ship looked like it was practically poking into the windows of the Edgewater Hotel that juts out into Elliot Bay on Pier 67. The same hotel Iris and I were staying in. When we checked into our room, *COWPENS'* bullnose was practically hanging over our balcony. While in our room we were treated to all the ship's announcements, beginning with reveille at 6:00 AM and "taps, taps, lights out" at 10:00 PM.

The Seattle Seafair was very enjoyable and we saw the sights of beautiful Seattle with Mount Rainier in the distance and used the gig for an evening cocktail cruise with our Navy League hosts. Mom and Dad continued on to a Silver Eagles reunion and Iris flew back to San Diego on the 11th when we sailed out of Seattle.

On the afternoon of the 11th, we rendezvoused with *USS CAMDEN (AOE-2)*, took on fuel, and then spent all day on the 12th alongside loading out 5-inch ammunition while we steamed south. On the 18th we pulled into Seal Beach to onload surface to air missiles, vertical launch ASROC, torpedoes, and the remainder of our 5-inch and small arms ammunition.

We were underway on Wednesday the 20th of August for the day long trip down to San Diego and this time we held a Dependent's Cruise and allowed all the families to enjoy a beautiful day at sea while we showed off the ship. Iris came along and brought Kathy Danberg, wife of Captain Bob Danberg. John Carnes, a high school Sea Cadet who had ridden the ship with his unit, brought his mother Pauli for the cruise. Thus began a friendship with Pauli, her husband Ben, and their two boys Joe and John. Ben and Pauli had had no real exposure to the military in their lives and had it not been for John's interest in the Navy and the Naval Academy, we would never have met. Pauli was enthralled with the operation of a Navy cruiser and impressed with the professionalism and skill of the crew.

When I took over command of *SAMPSON* in 1990, we were only five days away from deploying and one year away from decommissioning so the crew was pretty stabilized throughout my tour; we did not see many new faces over that year. The situation in *COWPENS* was different. Over the year we had between deployments, a significant amount of crew turnover would occur. I put into practice something that I only barely had the opportunity to do in *SAMPSON*; interviewing all new sailors reporting aboard and writing a letter to whoever was important in their lives; wives or parents. I was struck by how often there was only one parent that the sailor was willing for me to reach out to; usually Mom. I estimated that 60% of the unmarried sailors I welcomed aboard came from single parent homes.

The letters were handwritten on *COWPENS* stationery, simple, and followed the same basic format:

> *Dear XXXX,*
>
> *I had the pleasure today of welcoming your son/husband XXXX aboard COWPENS. We are happy to have him on the team and look forward to his contributions to the mission effectiveness of this ship. You may rest assured that his safety and well-being will always be my top priority. If you are ever in San Diego, please come visit the ship. I look forward to meeting you in person.*
>
> *Sincerely,*

I sometimes received nice replies from either the parents or the wife, but normally did not. This outreach paid dividends on more than one occasion, but one incident stands out.

One of the young black sailors in Deck Division had been getting into minor trouble and finally, after he was two days late returning from leave at home in Charlotte, North Carolina, his chief had had enough and put him on report. I took him to Captain's Mast and administered the appropriate punishment. He asked me at Mast to throw him out of the Navy, saying he wasn't cut out for this and just wanted to get out and go home. I told him that if I did that he would leave the Navy under less than honorable conditions which would forever be documented on his DD-214. This would haunt him in finding work for the rest of his life. He said he didn't care, he just wanted out.

After Mast, I went down to my cabin and called his mother in Charlotte. She had been one of those who had responded positively to my letter. I told her what had happened and what the consequences would be if I had her son administratively discharged from the Navy.

"You get him to call me! Thank you, Captain!"

I found Master Chief Lucas and told him to grab this sailor, take him to his office and let him call his mother on the U.S. Navy dime. About an hour later, Master Chief Lucas came by to see me to report that this seaman had changed his mind and now wanted to stay in the United States Navy. He was grinning from ear to ear and told me the young man's mother had read him the riot act over the phone.

That young seaman later thanked me for not throwing him out and then announced that his new goal was to earn my trust enough that I would qualify him as Sea Detail Helmsman. Damned if he didn't turn himself around and become one of our qualified helmsmen at sea detail and underway replenishment detail; a position which requires skill and the confidence of the conning officer that his orders are going to be precisely executed.

Every U.S. Navy ship has a "sponsor" who is a woman and is the one given the honor of breaking the champagne bottle on the bow of the ship when she is launched down the ways and into the water for the first time at the building yard. *COWPENS'* sponsor was Mrs. Lucy Mustin, the wife of retired Vice Admiral Hank Mustin who had been Commander, Cruiser-Destroyer Group 2 running the missile exercise when I was Weapons Officer in *TATTNALL* and Second Fleet Commander running the Ocean Safari exercise when I was Flag Sec for Admiral Hank Mauz at Group 12.

I had picked up where my predecessors left off and kept Lucy Mustin advised of the progress of the ship with a personal letter about every two months. When Lucy told me that she was going to be in San Diego the week before Labor Day, I invited her and

Admiral Mustin to visit the ship, have lunch in the wardroom, and ride the ship from the Naval Station to Broadway Pier in downtown San Diego. We were moving the ship to Broadway Pier where we would stay through the Labor Day weekend as the designated "visit ship" for the Naval Academy–San Diego State football game being played that Saturday.

I introduced Admiral Mustin and Lucy to the wardroom and relayed to them my experiences with the admiral, emphasizing his role in demanding warfighting excellence among the ships of the Atlantic Fleet when he was the Second Fleet Commander. Admiral Mustin then made a few inspirational remarks about the importance of what they were doing serving their country in the United States Navy. I think he enjoyed the short ride down San Diego Bay and watching me almost knock down Broadway Pier while making the landing on that old, rickety, wooden pier.

We had some excitement in September as *COWPENS* was chosen to sail up the coast to Monterey, California to serve as the host ship for an event being hosted by the Superintendent of the Naval Postgraduate School, Rear Admiral Marsha Evans. The Postgraduate School was hosting a group known as the Young Entrepreneurs, a group of business people who had made a million dollars in the business world before their 30th birthdays. As part of their program, they would visit the Naval Postgraduate School to learn about postgraduate education for military officers and they would get a tour of *COWPENS*.

We were underway for some local training in the Southern California Operating Areas on Monday the 22nd of September, my 25th anniversary of commissioning at OCS in Newport, Rhode Island. I certainly never dreamed a quarter century before that I would someday command a top of the line Navy warship like *COWPENS*. We took on fuel from the oiler *USNS WALTER S. DIEHL (TAO-193)* the next day and were preparing to head north to Monterey when I took a call in CIC on the secure satellite radio from my boss, Rear Admiral Pete Long.

"Bill, you need to come back into port tomorrow morning to load some special equipment on board. We're making arrangements to have you tie up at the carrier pier on North Island."

"What's up?" I asked.

"The *CONNIE* battle group is returning from the Gulf and we believe the Russians are trailing her with an *OSCAR*. You're getting some special acoustic equipment and some techs to help find her. You're also getting a helicopter from HSL-47."

"*CONNIE*" was the aircraft carrier *USS CONSTELLATION (CV-64)* and her support ships which were returning to San Diego from deployment to the Persian Gulf. An "*OSCAR*" was a Russian nuclear powered submarine capable of launching torpedoes and anti-ship cruise missiles while submerged. We weren't at war with Russia, but this out of area operation by one of their most capable submarines was highly unusual and a major effort was being mounted to gain contact and track this submarine to collect noise signatures and other intelligence. It also wouldn't hurt to let the Russians know that we were on to them.

That night, while we were still at sea I took another call in CIC, this time from Captain Bob "Rat" Willard, the CO of the nuclear powered aircraft carrier *USS ABRAHAM LINCOLN (CVN-72)*. *LINCOLN* was due to deploy to the Persian Gulf about a month after us in June of the next year and they were doing work-up training with an inspection team on board.

Rat said, "Can you come alongside tonight and take fuel from us? It's one of the things we have to demonstrate for our certification."

"Sure, but I refueled this morning. I don't need much."

"That's OK, we just have to send one rig over and pump a little fuel to show we can do it."

"OK, when do you need us?"

"How about 2100?"

"Roger, we'll rendezvous at 2030."

I notified Perry Bingham, and Ops, Don McNeil, and took a look at the display in CIC. *LINCOLN* was about 20 miles away. Off we went.

It was pitch dark, but not too rough when we rendezvoused with *LINCOLN* and set the unrep detail at the port forward refueling station. This would be good training for us as well as *LINCOLN* and the officers were excited about coming alongside the carrier. I had refueled from carriers before, including many times from *SARATOGA* as CO of *SAMPSON* during Desert Shield. Nevertheless, there is a pucker factor when coming 150 feet alongside 100,000 tons of super-carrier, especially at night.

We made the approach, *LINCOLN* sent the rig over without any problem, and we took on about 1,000 gallons of fuel to satisfy the evaluators. When the phone and distance line was over and hooked up I got on the line with Rat.

"Hey man, thanks for doing this."

"No problem, it's good experience for our guys too."

At the time I did not know Rat Willard, but we were later stationed together in Hawaii and he and I and Iris and Rat's wife Donna became good friends and golf buddies. Rat Willard went on to make four stars and commanded both the Pacific Fleet and the U.S. Pacific Command as well as serving as Vice Chief of Naval Operations.

The next morning, we pulled into San Diego and tied up at Pier Juliet at Naval Air Station North Island. A team from the Fleet ASW Training Center was there as was Rear Admiral Long. Admiral Long briefed me on the situation while the techs brought aboard special recording equipment and specially programmed laptop computers to tie into our SQQ-89 towed array sonar system. The *USS CONSTELLATION (CV-64)* battle group was returning from the Persian Gulf via a swing through the northern Pacific and a port visit in Japan. Intelligence indicated that a Russian *OSCAR II* submarine out of Vladivostok was underway in the northern Pacific and probably trailing the *CONSTELLATION* group and simulating war at sea attacks on the carrier. There is nothing illegal about this, but of course the U.S. Navy would want to counter-detect the submarine and be in a position to counter-attack the submarine if necessary, as unlikely as that was. Besides, it was good training. The *OSCAR* was currently undetected by U.S. forces. *COWPENS* was to be part of an ASW barrier with our towed array passive sonar and Light Airborne Multipurpose (LAMPS) helicopter along with other surface and air assets, including P-3C maritime patrol aircraft and the ships and airwing of the *CONSTELLATION* group. The mission was to find the *OSCAR* and hold contact on her while vectoring aircraft to her position to achieve attack criteria on the sub.

"What about Monterey?"

"Oh, you're still going. Get in there on Thursday. The visitors will come out with Admiral Evans on Saturday and you'll get underway to go chase *OSCAR* on Sunday."

Apparently, entertaining the Young Entrepreneurs with a tour of an Aegis cruiser took precedence over finding the Russian submarine tailing our carrier.

We were underway that afternoon with our special equipment and two technicians from the ASW Training Center for the 400 mile run up the coast to Monterey. Once we cleared the sea buoy and were in the open ocean, the helicopter from Detachment 4 of the Sabrehawks of HSL-47 flew out to the ship and landed. HSL-47 Det 4 was to be my detachment squadron for the upcoming Middle East Force deployment, so this was a good opportunity to get acquainted with Lieutenant Commander Mike Phillips, the Det Officer in Charge and his team. The ASW team spent the time on the way to Monterey studying the *CONSTELLATION*'s track and figuring out when and where we would set up our ASW barrier. We streamed the tail and made sure all systems were go for the "Hunt for Red October."

Late in the afternoon of the 25th, we pulled into Monterey Bay and anchored the ship about a quarter mile outside the breakwater. Monterey Bay is not a well sheltered bay as to the northwest it opens to the Pacific Ocean. Once we set the anchor, the ship tended bow in towards the small sailboat harbor and stern out towards the open sea. A swell was running and the ship was rolling quite a bit at anchor. Iris had driven up from San Diego with our golf clubs and I had reserved a room for us at the Naval Postgraduate School BOQ. Iris rode out to the ship on a 70-foot Coast Guard patrol boat that was carrying the Port Officer, a Coast Guard lieutenant commander who would brief us on the rules and regulations for our stay. Because of the swells, we decided to only rig the Pilot's Ladder on the fantail starboard side and not the accommodation ladder. Iris and the Coastie came aboard and we went to the wardroom for the port brief.

After taking care of business I grabbed my clothes for golf and dining ashore with Iris and we headed back to the fantail to go aboard the Coast Guard patrol boat which was hovering just off the starboard quarter. The ship was rolling hard in the swells, sometimes up to 15 degrees, and it was going to be tricky bringing the patrol boat alongside and getting off the ship. The sun had set and it was dark.

The XO, CDO Lieutenant Rich Haidvogel, and the Chief Boatswain's Mate, Chief Daum, were back on the fantail when we arrived; all looking nervous. As the patrol boat came alongside, the ship rolls and swells were resulting in about a 10-foot rise and fall alongside *COWPENS*. We tossed the luggage across and I went first, timing it to literally step straight across to the patrol boat as she rose on a swell. We then dropped and I was looking up about 10 feet to the deck edge of *COWPENS*. On the next rise we were back up at deck level again and I looked Iris in the eyes and saw she looked a little nervous.

"Just get on the ladder" I said, "I'll grab you."

She turned around and stood on the top step of the aluminum pilot ladder, and on the next rise I put my arm around her waist and plucked her off the ladder and swung her to the deck of the patrol boat. Smooth move. Iris later told me that she wasn't really scared until she got on the ladder, turned around, and saw the looks on the faces of the officers and crew.

Sunday morning the 28th, after hosting the Young Entrepreneurs on Saturday, I got up early and Iris drove me down to the pier for the gig ride to the ship. As I stood on the pier, I saw that the ship had swung around and was now pointed out to sea with the stern facing the pier and the break in the sea wall that formed the entrance to the small harbor. There were many private sailboats anchored close to the ship, but this looked like it was going to be a piece of cake—just pick up the anchor, steam straight out to sea, and go find *OSCAR*. How wrong I was to be.

We set sea and anchor detail and began to raise the anchor. Once just past short stay, Chief Daum called up from the fo'csle on his walkie-talkie and said the anchor windlass was bogging down and couldn't raise the anchor. He went up to the bow and looked down and said it appeared something was snagged on the anchor. I had been through this drill before on *SAMPSON* in Alexandria, Egypt so I told them to drop it, letting it free fall, and try it again. Same result, only this time Chief Daum said he could see our anchor and something big was hooked on it.

I sent the XO down to have a look and he radioed back that it looked like an old sailing ship style anchor; a Kedge anchor. He also said he could see chain running away from the anchor which was fouled on the flukes of our anchor and disappearing into the depths.

We tried bouncing it two more times but it wouldn't come loose. I was getting nervous about the position of the ship relative to all the anchored sailboats around us as we tried this so decided I would twist the ship around on the anchor to get the stern facing the open sea and then drag it backwards to give us more room to operate. I needed to drag it backwards to avoid doing damage to our sonar dome. Maybe in the course of dragging the anchor along the bottom whatever had us snagged would come loose. It was a delicate maneuver because I didn't want to do damage to the sonar dome hanging underneath the bow. We twisted the ship using the engines with the anchor chain tending around the stem and managed to swing around without sinking any sailboats. When we were turned 180 degrees we backed one-third and then two-thirds and dragged the anchor with its unwelcome passenger about a quarter mile further out to sea where we tried to pick it up again–still no-go. The anchor windlass would get it up to within sight from the fo'csle and then run out of pulling power.

We had been at this now for about two hours and should have already been out to sea and heading north to set up our ASW barrier along *CONNIE*'s track. I got on the mobile phone and called the CRUDESGRU 5 duty officer and told him what was going on. I also notified the Coast Guard port duty officer that we had a fouled anchor and were having trouble getting underway. Acting on her own initiative, she contacted a local salvage operator who said he'd come out to the ship to take a look.

For the next hour or so, we continued to try to raise the anchor to no avail. I was feeling like our important mission to go find the *OSCAR* was going off the tracks. The salvage operator motored up in his own boat about noon and was brought to the bridge. I told him what was going on and he went down to the fo'csle to take a look for himself. When he came back he had some wild scheme in mind to dive down to the anchor and attach a bunch of inflatable buoys to it and float it to the surface where we could then unsnag it from his workboat. I said, thanks, but no thanks, and sent him home.

I told Chief Daum to prepare to slip the anchor; we'd leave it on the bottom. Anchor chains are designed to be broken apart when necessary and each shot of chain (every 15 fathoms) is connected to the next by a detachable link held together by steel pins. If properly maintained, the steel pins can be knocked out with a marlinspike and a hammer, the link removed and the chain disconnected. Chief Daum hauled around on the anchor one more time until he could stop off the chain with the pelican hooks, remove the detachable link, attach a float on a line to mark the position, and then release the pelican hook to let the anchor and chain free fall to the bottom.

We did all this, the section of chain which was still connected to the anchor, rattled out through the hawsepipe, and we were off on the Hunt for Red October with our little orange buoy marking the spot where our U.S. Navy anchor and unwanted companion lay on the bottom. I had a second anchor so wasn't too worried, and the Navy would later send a salvage tug to Monterey to recover my anchor and deliver it to San Diego several weeks later.

The search for the *OSCAR II* turned out to be fruitless as nobody gained contact over the next two days. I was a little disappointed in the *CONSTELLATION* group as they didn't appear to be very aggressively trying to locate the sub with their own ASW assets.

We gave up the search on the 30th of September and headed south for the next event which was to conduct a ship versus ship war at sea with a Chilean destroyer who would be coming north from Chile to arrive in San Diego on Friday the 3rd of October. *COWPENS* was to be the host ship for their visit and rendezvous with them and lead them into San Diego Bay. First however, the 3rd Fleet staff wanted us to simulate fighting them as they came north from Chile. They had promulgated an exercise message and sent it to *COWPENS* and the Chilean Navy, laying out the rules of engagement for our little war at sea exercise. The rules were pretty simple, try to find the other ship, achieve targeting quality locating data, and simulate taking him under fire with a radio call on a designated satellite circuit. Both ships were to save all the plots of the encounter and the 3rd Fleet staff would compare them and declare the winner.

The Chilean ship was *CS BLANCO ENCALADA (DDH-15)*, a helicopter capable destroyer equipped with the Exocet surface to surface missile system. The Chileans had bought three of these *COUNTY* class destroyers from Great Britain. She could be a formidable opponent with her Cougar helicopters and the Exocet missiles. I was glad we had the HSL-47 LAMPS bird on board for long range detection just as she would be using the Cougars. Our Harpoon missile system would be the weapon of choice to engage them before they got off an Exocet.

After refueling from *RAPPAHANNOCK* we secured all our radars so as to remain undetected by *BLANCO ENCALADA* and headed south. I convened a war council in the wardroom and after looking at the charts, came up with a plan. We had the advantage of knowing that she had to be at the sea buoy off San Diego on Friday morning so we figured backwards as to where along the Mexican coast she would likely be on the day prior. When I looked at the chart I noticed the island of Guadalupe sitting about 150 miles west of the Mexican mainland and around 275 miles south of San Diego.

"Ops, we need a course and speed to get to Guadalupe by Wednesday night. We'll sit on the western side of the island in total EMCON on Thursday and when we think she's passed to the east we'll come at her from the south Thursday night. They'll be looking to the north not expecting us to be behind them."

The wardroom was really pumped by this idea and the word spread through the ship that we were going to nail the Chileans in this exercise. Getting to Guadalupe from north of Monterey by Wednesday night meant a 22 knot run south which would burn up more fuel than we were supposed to but I figured, what the hell, this is supposed to be a war game, you burn what you need to burn.

We ran south all day and night and arrived off Guadalupe just before sun-up on Thursday, October 2nd. As the sun rose I could see that the northwestern side of this volcanic island was rugged and mountainous and did not appear to be inhabited so I brought the ship into about a mile offshore so we would be less likely to be spotted by *BLANCO ENCALADA*. This was a violation of Mexican territorial waters, but I thought we could get away with it off this remote part of the island.

We sat there all day drifting with the engines shut down, calculating when would be the best time to start heading north to look for *BLANCO ENCALADA*. We kept the radars shut down so they couldn't detect our emissions and we picked up nothing on our own ESM gear which suggested, unsurprisingly, that *BLANCO ENCALADA* was also in total EMCON. Our only encounter was with two Mexican fishermen who came alongside wanting to sell lobsters.

Later that afternoon I was on the bridge and looked past the north end of the island and saw a gray, military-looking ship about eight miles away. Oh, oh, it looked like a Mexican patrol boat.

"Cheng, fire up the engines, we gotta move."

We ran away from the island at 25 knots heading southwesterly to keep the island between us and whoever it was until we were 12 miles off the coast and then headed north. If it was a Mexican patrol boat, he never saw us, or if he did, was not interested in giving chase.

We calculated that by then *BLANCO ENCALADA* would have been north of us anyway so we took the ship up to 30 knots and began diagonally closing the Mexican coastline and readying the helicopter to go out and find *BLANCO ENCALADA* so we could Harpoon them and declare victory. My plan was to run up the Mexican coast at high speed just outside the 12-mile limit, calculating that in their search for *COWPENS* they would be least likely to be looking behind them and towards the coast.

It worked and around 11:00 that night, Saberhawk 71 sent locating data back via the Hawklink pencil beam. We fired a simulated two Harpoon salvo at *BLANCO ENCALADA* accompanied by a call on the designated exercise circuit telling them they had been shot. Later, 3rd Fleet confirmed our kill.

Beginning in October *COWPENS* began the very structured series of work-up training events designed to certify Navy ships for deployment overseas. The program was configured to run the ships through progressively more complex evolutions, observed and graded by teams from the Afloat Training Group, Pacific (ATGPAC). The initial series of evaluations were called TSTA I, II, and III, with TSTA standing for Total Ship Training Assessment. Everything from seamanship and damage control through combat systems and engineering evolutions was part of the evaluation process. Mixed in with this were to be missile firing exercises, a work-up period with our helicopter detachment from HSL-47, and an intense engineering assessment called Engineering Certification, or ECERT. Once the three TSTA periods had been successfully completed, the ship would then go through a Final Evaluation Problem or FEP. Once FEP was behind us, we would say goodbye to ATGPAC and begin a higher level of battle group level training in early 1998 beginning with COMPTUEX, or Comprehensive Training Unit Exercise, under the overall direction of Commander 3rd Fleet. COMPTUEX would be followed by MEFEX, or Middle East Force Exercise with the *ABRAHAM LINCOLN* Battle Group. As CO of the senior ship, I was to command PACMEF 98-2, a three ship group consisting of *COWPENS, USS MILIUS (DDG-69)* and *USS THACH (FFG-43)*. *MILIUS* was an *ARLEIGH BURKE* class guided missile destroyer with the Aegis combat system also homeported in San Diego. *THACH* was an *OLIVER HAZARD PERRY* class guided missile frigate homeported in Yokosuka, Japan. *THACH* would join *COWPENS* and *MILIUS* in the western Pacific on our way to the Persian Gulf.

In September, I had been notified that 3rd Fleet had chosen *COWPENS* to be the OCE for a first-ever surface to air missile firing exercise against target drones in the Southern California OPAREA off the coast of San Diego. Up until this decision, all the west coast missile firing exercises were conducted in an area west of Point Mugu, California called the Pacific Missile Test Range. This range was instrumented and allowed the range controllers better visibility into range safety and the presence of possible range foulers, either other ships or commercial aircraft. As OCE, *COWPENS* would assume these responsibilities as well as overall responsibility for planning and exercising the missile shoot. Commander 3rd Fleet, Vice Admiral Herb Browne, wanted to demonstrate that we could safely conduct these exercises in the waters off San Diego and not have to sail 200 miles north to the Pacific Missile Test Range.

My Operations Officer, Lieutenant Commander Don McNeil, was given overall responsibility for the planning while working with representatives of the Pacific Missile Test Range detachment in San Diego. Firing ships would be *COWPENS, MILIUS, USS VALLEY*

FORGE (CG-50), and the Canadian guided missile frigate *HMCS OTTAWA (FFH-341)* with her vertical launch NATO Sea Sparrow missile system. *OTTAWA* was scheduled to be part of the *ABRAHAM LINCOLN* Battle Group for this deployment.

We conducted the exercise on October 21st and it went off without a hitch. *COWPENS* had two successful SM-2 surface to air missile shots against target drones launched from the flight deck of an amphibious ship well over the horizon and each of the other ships also had successful missile firings. When I later accompanied the team from *COWPENS* and the other ships to a de-brief at the Pacific Missile Test Range San Diego office, I quickly realized why in the weeks leading up to the exercise I had seen carloads of my officers and chiefs happily headed off the ship for coordination meetings. The lady de-briefing us, and the main point of contact for Don McNeil and his team, was a stunningly beautiful blonde who began the brief by declaring that we were "all a bunch of studs."

Also in October we had the happy opportunity to promote six of our first class petty officers to chief petty officer. Anytime an enlisted soldier, sailor, airman or Marine is promoted to E-7 it is a big deal, but it is the biggest deal in the U.S. Navy. Only in the Navy does the move from E-6 to E-7 include a distinctive uniform change; from the working dungaree uniform to the officer-like khaki uniform. That distinction has been somewhat diminished in recent years when the Navy adopted the silly blue, gray and black digital camouflage uniform similar in style to the Battle Dress Uniform worn by the other services. Nevertheless, becoming a Chief Petty Officer in the United States Navy is to achieve a level of recognition and respect which is unmatched in the other services at the grade of E-7.

In each command where first class petty officers make the grade and appear on the promotion list for chief petty officer, there is a time-honored tradition of the current batch of chiefs indoctrinating the new chief selectees in their new level of responsibility. In years past this often included a fair amount of hazing, similar but different from the crossing the line ritual when crossing the Equator. Each chief-to-be was required to accomplish a number of tasks to demonstrate his worthiness and of course these came with a certain amount of harassment. A "charge book" was required to be in the selectee's possession at all times and various infractions were recorded in the book. These "charges" were ultimately dealt with on the night before the actual promotion at the initiation ceremony. In years past, each chief-selectee was allowed to choose a junior officer to serve as his "defense counsel" when the charges in the charge book were adjudicated. In 1976, when I was a lieutenant (junior grade) at Navy Recruiting District Atlanta, one of our chief selectees asked me to be his defense counsel. They held the ceremony at the Naval Air Station Atlanta Chief's Club and I dutifully went to defend my chief-selectee. We had not become as politically correct or mindful of alcohol abuse in 1976 as we are today, and it was a raucous affair with lots of drinking involved. When it was my turn to defend my selectee, he was found guilty anyway and not only was he required to drink some nasty concoction out of a prophylactic, so was I for having failed to mount an adequate defense. Which I did, in order to be a good sport.

With this history in mind I talked to Master Chief Lucas, who would be in overall charge of the indoctrination and initiation, and told him to do it right, but don't overdo it. I thought all was well until the morning of the actual pinning on ceremony where the new chiefs would don their khaki uniforms, the fouled anchor collar insignia, and the khaki combination cover of a Chief Petty Officer in the United States Navy. Lucas had told me that the initiation, what had formerly been known as "Hell Night," would take place at the Lakeside VFW post. I was to show up around 10:00 the next morning, as would the wives of the married selectees, for the pinning on ceremony.

When I walked in to the Lakeside VFW, I saw reporter Jim Crawley and photographer Don Kohlbauer sitting in the audience.

"Hey," I said, "didn't know you guys would be here. Good!"

"We've been here all night," Jim said proudly.

Oh shit, Master Chief Lucas had conveniently neglected to mention this little detail when he briefed me on the ceremony. He knew I would have objected on two grounds. First, it's stupid, no matter how much you like and trust the media you're dealing with, to let them observe something like a chief's initiation. It's just asking for trouble. And second, wasn't this supposed to be the private domain of the chiefs; not even officers allowed to participate in the mystic rituals associated with chief petty officer-dom?

I was pissed, and Jim and Don picked up on it. "Don't worry, nothing bad happened," they both assured me.

Nonetheless, when their series ran in the *San Diego Union Tribune* the following May, chapter four was entitled *Making Chiefs* and featured several photographs of what they went through; a pig pile on the floor, wooden stocks, and two of them choking down some horrible concoction for breakfast. The entire series that finally came out of this deal with the *Union Tribune* was overall very positive, but that one chapter really bothered me. I let Lucas know when the ceremony was over that my trust factor in him had gone down a few notches as a result of this particular incident.

The pinning ceremony itself was very dignified and emotional. I said a few words about the role of the Chief Petty Officer in the United States Navy and their responsibility to not only lead the junior enlisted and set a positive example, but also to train "their" junior officers. The new hats were placed on their heads by the wives of those who were married and by the chief of their choice by the single guys. There were many tears.

Throughout the fall as we worked our way through the TSTA training we conducted gunnery, torpedo firings, and numerous engineering and damage control exercises. In November we successfully completed ECERT and had this major engineering challenge behind us. Chief Engineer Lieutenant Commander Ed Lazarski, who had served in the ship as Chief Engineer for almost three years, did a superb job in managing this challenging examination.

Earlier in the year I had been in contact with Lieutenant Commander Terry Culton, my old Chief Engineer in *SAMPSON*, who was in the queue for his Executive Officer assignment, and asked him if he wanted to come to *COWPENS* to be my XO. Terry said yes and was willing to delay his XO assignment for several months to wait for Perry Bingham to finish his full tour. I had two reasons for wanting Terry as my XO. First, I liked his style and his manner of dealing with people. I knew that he would administer the ship with a style of leadership that complemented my own. My second reason was that I trusted him as an engineer and felt that his previous experience would be helpful to me who had made it to major command never having served in the engineering department aboard a Navy ship. This is not to say that I didn't trust Ed Lazarski, I did, but I liked the idea of having my second in command be experienced in engineering to balance my own expertise which was more in operations and combat systems.

In the fall of 1997, Perry Bingham completed his tour and Terry Culton became my XO. I had also maintained contact with the young Yeoman Third Class who had been the last man standing in the Admin Department in *SAMPSON* when we decommissioned the ship; Yeoman First Class Chris Adams. I had watched from afar as Chris Adams advanced through the ranks, going from *SAMPSON* to *USS FORRESTAL (CV-59)* and then to the Blue Angels. In 1997 he was working in the Pentagon and due for orders to sea duty. I brought YN1 (SW/AW) Chris Adams to *COWPENS* in the fall as well. Chris had married a lovely lady, Jenny, and they were in the process of producing daughters at the rate of about one every two years. Because he had served for several years with the Blue Angels and earned his Enlisted Air Warfare pin along with his Enlisted Surface Warfare pin, he came in for much good natured ribbing from his shipmates. He was also a go-getter, and he energized the unofficial First Class Petty Officer's Association in *COWPENS*.

CHAPTER 20

(Near) Collision at Sea

My boss at CRUDESGRU 5, Rear Admiral Pete Long, was scheduled to be relieved in December by Rear Admiral Dan Bowler. I saw that the change of command ceremony was scheduled to occur at sea aboard the CRUDESGRU 5 flagship, the aircraft carrier *USS KITTY HAWK (CV-63)* on the 10th of December. In looking at our own TSTA schedule I saw that we were scheduled for the final phase of TSTA, TSTA III, during the week of 9 December and I had an idea that almost ended my career. Both Pete Long and Dan Bowler were Surface Warfare Officers, but because the flagship was *KITTY HAWK*, they would be doing the ceremony aboard an aircraft carrier; the domain of naval aviators. I sent Admiral Long a Personal For (P4) message and proposed that *COWPENS* rendezvous with *KITTY HAWK* on the 10th and sail alongside so they'd have a real "CRUDES" warship as a backdrop for the ceremony. Admiral Long said, "Sure, as long as it doesn't interfere with your schedule."

I then sent the CO of *KITTY HAWK*, Captain Jack Samar, a P4 proposing the rendezvous and telling him that I intended to take station 300 yards on his port beam during the ceremony. He answered back, "Fine, see you then."

On the 9th of December, we set sea detail and left San Diego for the TSTA III part of our work-up training with the usual gaggle of ATGPAC evaluators on board along with an Army lieutenant colonel who had been assigned to Dallas Bethea's staff at the Tactical Training Group, Pacific. Because we were beginning to jointly work with the Army on linking Aegis radar data to Army Patriot missile batteries ashore in the Middle East, the Army had decided to assign a Patriot qualified officer to Dallas' staff. Dallas wanted the lieutenant colonel to experience some time at sea on an Aegis ship and since he had been CO of *COWPENS* himself, chose us.

On the day of the ceremony, the weather in the Southern California op area was really nasty with heavy seas and a 35–40 knot wind blowing out of the north. We rendezvoused with *KITTY HAWK* about 9:00 that morning without signal and fell in astern at about 1,000 yards. *KITTY HAWK* was steaming on a northerly course, into the wind, in order to recover the Commander 3rd Fleet helicopter which was bringing all the brass out to the carrier for the ceremony. On the helicopter were Admirals Long and Bowler, the ceremony principals, as well as Commander 3rd Fleet, Vice Admiral Herb Browne, and Commander Naval Surface Forces, Pacific Fleet, Vice Admiral Al Krekich.

As we pulled in astern of *KITTY HAWK*, I called on the bridge-to-bridge radio and asked their course and speed. "000 at eight knots," was the answer. We ordered up eight knots to see how that worked. *KITTY HAWK* was visibly pitching as she worked into the seas and the wind. I put the JOOD, Ensign Wes Boose, on the stadimeter to check the range while we also used radar. Within minutes it was obvious that our eight knots was closing on KITTY HAWK's eight knots. We slowed to six knots. After a while, it seemed like our ordered five to six knots was about equal to *KITTY HAWK*'s ordered eight knots.

I again called *KITTY HAWK* and got the XO. The CO was below waiting for the helo with the admirals to arrive. I asked, "What will be course and speed for the ceremony?"

He replied, "We're going to try 270 at five knots and use the island as a lee for the ceremony." The ceremony was planned to take place on the flight deck.

I thought to myself, "Hmm, if at their eight knots I need only five to six to keep pace, what will I need at five?" My guess was somewhere around three, but there is no way to make a linear calculation and this would be cross-sea and cross-wind so would probably be totally different from the physics of what was happening now. On a *TICONDEROGA* class cruiser, bare steerageway (that speed at which the rudders begin to lose effectiveness in controlling the ship) is somewhere around two to three knots.

I didn't say anything–I should have.

The helicopter arrived, the admirals scrambled into the island, the helicopter lifted off, and *KITTY HAWK* began a slow turn to port to set up for the ceremony. Ensign Pat Rogers had the conn. Pat was brand new and this would be his first time to have control of the ship in a close steaming situation. I thought it would be good for his confidence, and besides, I was standing right next to him so what could go wrong? 300 yards is 900 feet and we normally did underway replenishments at 150 feet, sometimes less. There was lots of margin for error.

We followed around in *KITTY HAWK*'s wake and waited for her to settle on course for the ceremony. She finally settled on 260 true at five knots. I was in the process of making a number of mistakes. The first was not suggesting a faster base speed when the XO told me it would be five knots–but I knew they were trying to minimize the wind over the deck for the ceremony so I had kept my mouth shut. This time, wanting to be a hot dog, when *KITTY HAWK* reported herself steady on 260 at five knots, I told Pat to go to 20 knots and begin the approach.

This was my second error in judgment. Normally, before making the approach on the other ship, there is time to settle in behind and compare courses and speeds. I already knew our ordered speed was higher than *KITTY HAWK*'s. Had I sat back for a few minutes I would have also been able to determine if 260 on *COWPENS*' gyro compass was the same as 260 on *KITTY HAWK*'s gyro. More importantly, I might have recognized how much the 35 knots of wind on the starboard beam was crabbing her to port.

The third mistake was starting the approach from 1,000 yards back at 20 knots. Our normal underway replenishment approach on the oiler was 25 knots. Normal underway replenishment speed for the oiler was 13 knots. Difference: 12 knots. We normally started the approach on the oiler from 500 yards. This approach would begin at 1,000 yards and would have a relative speed difference of 15 knots (or more given what we had observed earlier). That may not seem like much, but the extra 500 yards means the ship is going that much faster when you get alongside and the extra three knots of relative speed means that there is more excess speed to deal with in order to slide into station and match course and speed with the carrier. When dealing with 10,000 tons of ship, a few knots makes a difference.

We blew the approach. Came in too fast, started to overshoot badly, and took extraordinary steps not to overshoot too much and look bad. I learned later that none of the senior officers were on the flight deck; all were below in the Flag Mess shaking hands; so the only people I was impressing were the poor sailors on the flight deck dealing with the lousy weather, waiting for the brass to arrive, and wishing the whole thing were over. We were not doing a very good job of impressing even them.

I told Pat to temporarily go to all stop–and then ahead for five knots. Then the weather took over. We were in the port side lee of the carrier and mostly blocked from the 35 knot wind on the carrier's starboard beam. *COWPENS* bridge and forward superstructure were sheltered by the hull and island of the carrier. The after superstructure, however, stuck up above the flight deck of the carrier and was catching the wind. And the wind was crabbing *KITTY HAWK* to port.

All of this took a little while to become apparent on the starboard bridge wing of *COWPENS*; but I did begin to notice the carrier seeming to get bigger while we were working ourselves back into position after overshooting.

About the time that it started to dawn on me that the carrier was getting closer, the helmsman sang out, "Request permission to use rudder as necessary to maintain course."

I quickly looked down at the Rudder Angle Indicator on the bridge wing and saw that the helmsman had on left 15 degrees' rudder. I had a standing order that anytime more than 15 degrees' rudder was necessary to maintain the ordered course; the helmsman was required to request permission from the Conning Officer. This is a pretty standard requirement, because it alerts the Conning Officer to the fact that ship control is getting sloppy. It normally only happens at slow speeds when the rudder is less effective.

Now I knew we were in trouble, but I still didn't want to look bad in front of all the brass (who were still in the Flag Mess). I nodded at Pat to give him permission. I looked aft and saw that the ship had become canted bow in towards the carrier—and the carrier was getting even closer. In reconsidering events after the fact, I decided that the after superstructure, rising above the flight deck of the carrier, was acting like a big sail and getting pushed to port by the wind. Meanwhile, the forward half of the ship, more sheltered by the carrier, was not. And the entire carrier was being blown down on top of us. To add to the danger, we were practically stopped and had poor control with the rudders.

I knew then that we were in serious trouble and now it was all about getting out of it—hot dog approach and looking good be damned—too late for that anyway; we were in extremis. I took the conn from Ensign Rogers (so much for building his confidence) and ordered 20 knots. I left that on for only a few seconds as I listened to the gas turbines *slowly* wind up, and realized 20 knots wasn't even close to being enough. I went to Flank 3.

Flank 3 on an Aegis cruiser is like an afterburner on a jet. It's everything the engines will give you within limits. The Lee Helmsman jams the throttles all the way forward, the computer recognizes what's happening, and the ship's propulsion plant goes to maximum power as fast as it can. You can feel yourself being pushed back by the acceleration.

We began accelerating rapidly but still had a long way to go to get past *KITTY HAWK*'s bow and I had another problem.

Because the wind had been pushing the after part of the ship to port, the bow was now pointing in towards the carrier at about a 5-degree angle. Flank 3 speed was closing the distance between the two ships even faster than the wind was.

I very gingerly put on left five degrees' rudder for a few seconds in an attempt to move the bow more to port. This created its own problem.

A ship is steered by pushing the stern in one direction, which has the effect of pushing the bow in the opposite direction. The pivot point on an Aegis cruiser is up around the bridge area, meaning that as the bow moves to port, one-third of the hull moves left while two-thirds of the hull moves right.

In this case, 225 feet of *COWPENS* was moving away from *KITTY HAWK* while 442 feet was moving *towards* her. That 442 feet was going to be the last to get clear.

After just a few seconds I put the rudder amidships and hoped that our acceleration would carry us past the bow of the carrier before the distance between the two ships went to zero. At this point, I was looking up at the edge of the angle deck of the carrier flight deck. The bridge was going to get by the angle deck, but would the rest of the ship?

About this time, I heard *KITTY HAWK* sound the collision alarm and everybody who was anywhere near the port side of *KITTY HAWK*'s flight deck was running away from what looked like a sure collision.

As we continued to race toward *KITTY HAWK*'s bow, I turned my attention aft where the collision would occur if it happened. The flight deck was looming almost overhead. It looked for sure like the after superstructure would make contact with the angled flight deck.

Just then the bridge reached *KITTY HAWK*'s bow. We were still on a slightly converging course, but really picking up speed. I have no idea how many seconds had passed since I had ordered Flank 3, but it seemed an eternity.

I made a snap decision to turn to starboard across *KITTY HAWK*'s bow. I figured we had enough speed advantage to clear the bow, and I knew that by throwing the rudder right full, the stern would swing out to port and open the distance to the carrier. It was my only hope—the lateral distance was closing too rapidly to get the stern all the way past the bow before *KITTY HAWK* was pushed down on us by the wind.

"Right full rudder," I yelled into the pilot house.

About then, Operations Officer Lieutenant Commander Don McNeil, standing behind me on the starboard bridge wing, said, "We're gonna hit!"

But then those rudders bit in and something happened that I hadn't consciously thought about. When a ship turns, it heels in the opposite direction of the turn. The faster the ship is moving and the more rudder used, the more the ship leans away from the direction of the turn. That's what saved us. In addition to the decision to use all possible speed and to turn across the carrier's bow to move the stern away, the very sharp heel to port pulled that after superstructure out and away from the edge of the flight deck. We slid safely around the bow of the carrier churning up a huge rooster tail wake.

In seconds we were safely across the bow and opening away on the upwind side of the carrier on a reciprocal course. I slowed to 20 knots and continued on around the stern of the carrier in a big circle and came in again on *KITTY HAWK*'s port side, this time at 500 yards. While we were making the circle I called *KITTY HAWK* on bridge-to-bridge radio and told the XO my intentions. The CO was still in the Flag Mess with all the admirals, having missed all the excitement—I later learned that they all looked at each other and wondered what was going on when the collision alarm sounded.

The XO, sounding slightly miffed about the whole episode, agreed with my suggestion that they go to 10 knots and they did. I turned the conn over to the XO once we were safely in position for the ceremony on the flight deck. Terry Culton handed the conn back to Pat Rogers and stayed on the starboard bridge wing to supervise. I sat in my bridge chair and began composing a unit SITREP message to send to COMCRUDESGRU 5, copy to the CO of *KITTY HAWK* to report a near collision. When the ceremony was over, we blasted out of station at Flank 3 and headed off to resume our work-up training schedule.

I was about done with the SITREP when Rear Admiral Dan Bowler, my new boss as of about 10 minutes earlier, called me on the secure radio and said, "I guess we had a close call."

I said, "Yes sir, I'm about to send you a unit SITREP on it."

He said, "Naw, don't send a message, we'll talk about it when you get back to port."

A couple of things happened that afternoon. First, Command Master Chief Lucas came to my cabin all fired up. "We got us a CAPTAIN!" he shouted and shook my hand. He said the whole crew was buzzing about how I had saved the day–forgetting that it was my poor headwork that allowed us to get in a jam in the first place.

Then the Army lieutenant colonel came by to see me. He said he had never seen anything like it (no shit Sherlock, neither had I). He went on to explain how impressed he was by how professionally the two young sailors on the Helm and Lee Helm had reacted to my orders. Had they hesitated on Flank 3, or asked me if I really meant "right full rudder" (especially since all they could see out the bridge wing door on the right was the hull of the carrier), the delay might have been fatal. I thought about that and realized how right he was. I made sure to go find them and tell them what a great job they had done.

Terry Culton came by and suggested that I take advantage of the incident to gather the officers in the wardroom after dinner and talk about it. Good idea. That night I had a rapt audience, including the chiefs, as I walked through the mistakes I had made that allowed the ship to be jeopardized and then what I had done to get out of it and why. It was a good teaching lesson, and preparing for the meeting allowed me to go over it in my mind and think about what went wrong and what went right. It goes without saying that I did not sleep well that night, playing and re-playing the events over and over in my head.

We pulled in that Friday afternoon. *KITTY HAWK* was already back and Rear Admiral Bowler invited me over to *KITTY HAWK* on Monday to discuss it. When I got home that night, I hugged Iris and told her that I had almost collided with the carrier and ruined my/our career.

I went Monday to *KITTY HAWK*. 4 bells, "*COWPENS* arriving." I'm sure that got some interesting comments around the ship. "Watch out for that guy, he'll run right into you."

I sat down in the Flag Cabin with Admiral Bowler, Jack Samar and the XO. The admiral said, "Tell us what happened." I went through the whole sequence of events and mea culpa'd for not doing anything when I recognized the problem with the speed difference, for approaching too fast, for not sitting astern of the carrier on 260 long enough to recognize that she was crabbing to port, for staying with the approach too long once it became apparent that *KITTY HAWK* was being blown down on us, and so forth. I didn't make any excuses and I apologized to the CO and XO of *KITTY HAWK* for scaring the hell out of them.

Then Admiral Bowler had the XO stick in the PLAT camera video of what it looked like from *KITTY HAWK*. The PLAT cameras are fixed in place and are for recording what happens on the flight deck as aircraft land, take off, and are moved about. It is routine for an aircraft carrier to run the PLAT cameras 24 hours a day every day to record events on the flight deck.

As the PLAT camera tape rolled I watched as at first the camera which looks out over the flight deck from the island at a slightly forward angle showed nothing but flight deck and water. Then a sailor on the port side of the flight deck began running away from the edge towards the island. *COWPENS* then came into view very close aboard with all flags proudly flying–so close that all I could see was the top half of the superstructure and the masts and radars. By this time the ship is clipping along at a pretty good pace as the bridge moves forward of the end of the angle deck. The Flank 3 order had already been given. A few seconds later I saw the right full rudder kick in and the ship heel hard to port, moving under the bow of the carrier, now with only the masts and a little bit of superstructure visible above the forward edge of the flight deck. The film then switched to a camera looking forward on the starboard side of KITTY HAWK to show COWPENS blasting along off KITTY HAWK's starboard bow, still heeled to port, and kicking up a big rooster tail.

Jack Samar then showed me the Plan of the Day for the next day which had a big cartoon showing people looking down the stacks of COWPENS from the flight deck as we nearly collide along with some wise-ass caption about out-of-control cruisers. Ho-ho-ho, all's well that ends well.

In the end, there were no repercussions for my close call other than some embarrassment on my part for letting it happen in the first place. It received prominent coverage in the San Diego Union Tribune article about the ship and I know reporter Jim Crawley was really sorry he wasn't there that day to give a first-hand account. His article played up the heroic shiphandling to get out of the jam and didn't go into all the mistakes leading up to the heroics. I've had a number of close calls at sea, any of which could have ended my career, but none closer than that.

CHAPTER 21

Welcome Aboard, Ladies!

We had one more underway period in 1997 to finish up the individual ship portion of our pre-deployment training before breaking for the Christmas holidays and moving into the more complex training to follow in 1998; the Final Evaluation Problem, or FEP. Underway for three days with the full complement of ATGPAC inspectors on board, we ran through all the drills and received a final thumbs up from the senior inspector. After topping off on fuel from *RAPPAHANNOCK*, we returned to San Diego on the afternoon of December 17th to stand down for the holidays.

As we were approaching the sea buoy at sea detail around 6:00 in the evening on the 17th, my cell phone rang; it was Iris. Iris said that our daughter Amy and her boyfriend Erick Brenner wanted to have dinner with us at the house. I was tired from the week at sea and the constant activity as we went through the FEP paces and just wanted to go home, collapse into bed, and sleep all night without the phone ringing. But Iris said Amy said it was important.

By the time we got the ship tied up and I huddled with the XO to discuss upcoming events, it was around 8:00 when I got home. We had a nice dinner, cracked a bottle of wine, and I sat there waiting for whatever the big announcement was with my head bobbing as I tried to stay awake. We really liked Erick, who had met Amy when they were both working at Aerotek, a headhunting firm, as new college graduates. Erick had graduated from Lake Forest College near Chicago and come to San Diego to try something on his own before going to Florida to join his father's orange grove business. Amy had come to San Diego after graduation from Florida

State to live with us and look for work. He and Amy had started out as "just friends," going on group dates, but had gradually found each other and fallen in love.

As we were finishing up dinner and I was nodding off, Erick finally cleared his throat and began his speech. He was sweating buckets as he made a very eloquent presentation about his feelings for Amy. It sounded like he was asking for her hand in marriage although the "M" word was never mentioned. What he wanted was to take Amy back to Florida with him as he started his new career with his father. Of course Iris and I interpreted his speech as a marriage proposal and completely overreacted in a positive way. It would be almost a year later before Amy called Iris from Florida and announced that she and Erick were engaged.

When the holiday break ended, *COWPENS* was a little over four months away from deploying to the Middle East Force and ready to enter the Intermediate and Advanced Phase training. We had done well in the previous phases and I was very pleased with the way the wardroom and the crew were working together. Morale seemed high and disciplinary problems were few.

When I was CO of *SAMPSON* I liked to use *Born to be Wild* by Steppenwolf for my breakaway song after an alongside refueling or replenishment. Navy ships typically play music over the loudspeakers as they break away at high speed after an UNREP. I brought *Born to be Wild* with me to *COWPENS* but also liked to let the bridge watch team pick a song. We did so many underway refuelings with the restrictions on refueling inport that we ran through quite a variety of musical choices during my two years in command. Several of the junior officers wanted to play *Like a Virgin* by Madonna as the refueling probes came across but I nixed that idea. Too easy to get in trouble for political incorrectness, even though I did not yet have any women in my crew. That would change soon. We also let the 0400-0800 watch pick music to play over the ship's announcing system at morning reveille while underway. They were pretty creative with that as well. Typically, at 6:00 AM the 1MC speakers would click to life and some rousing wake-up music would blare throughout the ship followed by the standard Navy reveille announcement. Often the song chosen by the watch would have some relation to upcoming events on the ship's schedule for that day. For example, if we were providing escort or plane guard services to an aircraft carrier the theme from *Top Gun* might be the wake-up song. If we were doing anti-submarine warfare that day, the theme from *Jaws* might awaken the crew.

On the 18th of February, we were underway again, this time for Week One Work-ups which was designed to integrate our helicopter detachment from HSL-47 Detachment 4 into the ship's crew. We welcomed aboard Lieutenant Commander Mike Phillips, the detachment Officer in Charge and his detachment pilots, Lieutenant Sean McDonald, Lieutenant Johnny Lee, Lieutenant Colin Smith, and Lieutenant (junior grade) Mike Hillegas along with the 14 enlisted aircrewmen and maintenance technicians that made up the detachment. Week One Work-Ups is a standard training evolution during which the ship's crew and the helicopter detachment would build their teamwork and flesh out the operating procedures for the two SH-60B Seahawk LAMPS helicopters assigned to the ship. Mike Phillips would become a fifth department head, of the Air Department, and co-equal with my Operations, Combat Systems, Engineering, and Supply department heads.

My neighbor across the street in base housing on the Amphibious Base Coronado was Captain Dick Arnold, the 3rd Fleet Operations Officer, and Dick was taking good care of *COWPENS* whenever he could. Our Week One Work-ups would include a trip down and back to Cabo San Lucas, Mexico on the tip of the Baja Peninsula with a five-day port visit in Cabo sandwiched in the middle. Cabo San Lucas was about 800 miles south of San Diego, a leisurely two-day transit each way.

It would be leisurely in terms of the ship's speed, but anything but leisurely for the flight deck crew and the helo detachment. We flew day and night and ironed out the coordination between the ship and the detachment. My crew manned the flight deck, fire party, refueling team and landing signal team, while the air detachment crewed and maintained the helicopters and stationed a pilot who was not flying in the LSO turret to coordinate events on the flight deck. Gone were the days when I was an LSO in *NEWPORT NEWS* and *SEMMES*, standing back on the flight deck in my yellow "float coat," cranial helmet, pants tucked into my socks, and trying to converse with the bridge using sound-powered phones over the noise of beating helicopter blades and howling engines. The bridge team had to become proficient at achieving the proper winds over the deck and ensuring that the TAO and combat systems team had the SPY-1B radar and the Vulcan Phalanx CIWS properly configured.

The SPY radar was so powerful that a helicopter flying close could suffer damage to its electronics and the crew risked suffering radiation injury. It was part of the checklist that the SPY arrays facing the helicopter had to be powered off when the helicopter was within one mile of the ship. There was a lot of teamwork involved for what would become a very routine evolution.

The CIWS was the close in missile defense system for the ship; a 30 millimeter Gatling gun capable of firing depleted uranium rounds at 2,000 rounds per minute to destroy an incoming missile. It was an autonomous system once put in the full automatic mode in a threat situation. The CIWS radar, sitting atop the gun system under a white radome and looking like R2D2 from *Star Wars*, would automatically detect an object flying at the ship that met certain pre-set speed parameters, and, if in the automatic mode, would slew the Gatling gun to the threat bearing and open fire without any human intervention. For this reason, the CIWS was always in standby mode unless the ship was in actual combat and threatened with an anti-ship missile attack. The CIWS could not discriminate between enemy or friendly aircraft. A friendly jet making a high speed pass on the ship would be engaged just as readily as an incoming missile. A helicopter would not be flying at the normal minimum speed set into the system, but there was some evidence that the rapidly rotating helicopter blades might be misinterpreted by the radar software and set the thing off.

I quickly decided that I would trust my watch team to ensure all the appropriate steps had been taken and gave the OODs the authority to declare "green deck" to launch or recover the helicopter without first checking with me. I had a selfish reason for this; I didn't want to be awakened all night long simply to numbly authorize the "green deck" from my rack.

We pulled into the bay at Cabo San Lucas on February 20th and anchored the ship, there being no pier big enough to handle a cruiser. I was advised that the area where we anchored was a "nature preserve" so we had to watch very carefully what we pumped over the side; no sewage, no oily bilge water, and so forth. We contracted for a sewage barge at great expense to the U.S. taxpayer. I watched in dismay from the bridge later that first day as the first sewage barge, having reached capacity, was towed about 300 yards away from the ship by a small tug and the contents dumped into the bay. That was Mexico for you.

Iris flew down to meet me and we planned a nice five days "vacation" in the tropical paradise of Cabo San Lucas. There was deep sea fishing, diving, many golf courses, and numerous bars and restaurants to enjoy in this popular tourist destination. I had some official responsibilities as well, and on February 23rd we hosted a reception aboard ship for various local dignitaries including Vice Admiral Velasquez, Mexican Navy, Commander, Fourth Naval Zone.

One day we decided to take the gig out and try our luck trolling for sailfish or marlin. I invited a group of the chiefs along, as well as Iris, and I served as boat coxswain. Although we caught no fish, we did encounter a pair of gray whales and were able to parallel their course as they headed for the open ocean. Leaving Cabo on the 25th of February we continued Week One Work-Ups on the transit back to San Diego

On Friday the 6th of March, I was home with Iris and watching the 11 o'clock news when a report came across that an SH-60B helicopter from San Diego on a routine training flight to the Naval Air Station, Fallon, Nevada, had crashed in the San Bernardino Mountains. The squadron was not identified and I received no phone calls; but, now having an official command relationship with HSL-47 Detachment 4, I was concerned.

The next morning, I was on the 4ᵗʰ hole at Sea N' Air Golf Course playing with Rear Admiral Tim Lafleur and Rear Admiral Kevin Green when my cell phone rang. It was Iris telling me that Mike Phillips had called and reported that two of our pilots, Lieutenants Johnny Lee and Mike Hillegas, had been on that helicopter that crashed the night before and that all four officers and one enlisted aircrewman on board had been killed. I immediately called Mike and asked what I could do. He said nothing was needed; the squadron was fully mobilized to deal with the tragedy. He expressly asked me not to come over, as one more captain hanging around wringing his hands and shaking his head would not help. HSL-47 held a memorial service on the 12ᵗʰ of March and I attended along with strong representation from the wardroom, chief's mess, and crew. Mike Phillips told me that two new pilots, Lieutenant Bryn Henderson and Lieutenant Ryan Aaron, would join Det 4 for the remainder of work-up training and the deployment.

We had another sea change ahead of us in early 1998; the introduction of the first women officers in the *COWPENS* wardroom. On March 16ᵗʰ, our new supply officer, Lieutenant Commander Susan Randle, and our new navigator, Lieutenant (junior grade) Sarah Wright, reported for duty. The Navy had begun assigning women to Navy ships in 1978, initially aboard destroyer and submarine tenders and other non-combatant ships. By the late nineties, many ships had fully integrated crews with both officer, chief petty officer, and junior enlisted female crewmembers. Because *COWPENS* had not yet had the berthing modifications necessary to accommodate enlisted female crew, we were to begin with officers only. Sarah, a Naval Academy graduate, was coming off the *SPRUANCE* class destroyer *USS KINKAID (DD-965)* where she had recently completed a six-month deployment to the Persian Gulf. It would be a quick turnaround back to the Gulf for her. Ensign Laura Poleshinski, a recent Naval Academy graduate who we planned to make our Repair Division Officer would follow a month later. Susan had previously served aboard ship on a destroyer tender, and as the senior female officer, she took on the responsibility of looking out for the younger women, although neither of them needed any special care. Sarah was an experienced and fully qualified Surface Warfare Officer on her second sea tour, and Laura, a varsity volleyball player at the Naval Academy, was self-confident, energetic, and eager to learn. As Repair Division Officer she was immediately responsible for 15 male sailors and their performance. She hit the deck running and never slowed down, becoming one of my favorites among the junior officers.

We put all three in one four-man stateroom and set up a rotation for the use of the showers and toilets in the one head in officer's country. The first 15 minutes of every hour were reserved for the women and a sliding sign was affixed to the bulkhead to alert anyone entering as to which gender was inside. We had no problems.

I had made up my mind early on not to make a big deal out of this influx of women officers and to treat them just like any other officers joining the crew. No special notes in the Plan of the Day, no "all hands" meeting to tell the crew to clean up their language and not wander the passageways in their skivvies. Most of these sailors had grown up in a gender integrated Navy anyway and this was nothing new. It was the old guys like me, growing up in a Navy with all male crews aboard ship, who bore watching.

The next step in the process of getting ready to deploy was an ambitious two and one-half week underway period during which we would conduct an exercise called "MEFEX," for Middle East Force Exercise, tailored to our upcoming deployment, and then join the *ABRAHAM LINCOLN* Battle Group for their FLEETEX training exercise. Although *COWPENS*, *MILIUS* and *THACH* would not be part of the *ABRAHAM LINCOLN* Battle Group, we would overlap in the Persian Gulf for over three months, and once there under the overall command of the 5th Fleet Commander, there would be no discriminating among who was with *LINCOLN* and who had come separately.

Our missile exercise on the 6th of April at the Pacific Missile Test Range off Point Mugu, California was a success as we, along with *USS SHILOH (CG-67)*, *USS VALLEY FORGE (CG-50)*, *USS*

JARRETT (FFG-33), USS CAMDEN (AOE-2) and the Canadian frigate *HMCS OTTAWA (FFH-341)* had successful shots against a high dive supersonic drone target. This was a piece of cake for the Aegis combat system aboard the cruisers. The real test would come the following day when we conducted the VANDALEX missile firing, the most challenging and realistic exercise event.

The Vandal is a modified Talos missile that flies 30 feet off the water at Mach 2.5. Only the Aegis system was capable of dealing with this target because of the high speed and limited warning time available to human operators on ships without Aegis. The Aegis system featured the "Auto-Special" setting in which certain parameters are entered into the system and once the "Fire Inhibit Switch" is enabled by the Captain or TAO, the system will automatically engage a target meeting the threat parameters, without human intervention. No man-in-the-loop. The system has to be properly tuned, and there is always the danger that the radar will detect an atmospheric anomaly or even a flock of birds and send a signal to the fire control system that launches a missile before anyone can react to stop it. Likewise, a de-tuned system might not pick up the incoming missile in time to get off a shot against this fast moving target. At sea level, Mach 2.5 is about 25 miles a minute.

For the VANDALEX, *COWPENS*, *SHILOH*, and *VALLEY FORGE* were put in a line abreast with me in tactical command as the senior CO. I put *VALLEY FORGE* closest to the threat bearing and made her the guide as she had the MK-26 rail launcher which is slower to react than the MK-41 Vertical Launch systems on *COWPENS* and *SHILOH*. I wanted to give her a clear look down the threat bearing. I put *COWPENS* next and then *SHILOH*. I was in CIC and I left Terry Culton on the bridge to monitor maneuvers for safety. We set a course about 45 degrees off of the estimated threat bearing so that each ship would have a fairly clear radar view of the direction from which the Vandal would come over the horizon.

Once we were in position in a line abreast and steaming at five knots with 500 yards' separation, I began thinking that *VALLEY FORGE* to starboard down the threat bearing might cause a fraction of a second delay in our system detecting the Vandal as it came over the horizon, even with the 45 degree offset.

"XO, Captain."

"XO, aye."

"Drop a couple of knots of speed and let us drop back a little so our ass end is sticking out a little behind *VALLEY FORGE*."

Terry got it right away, "Aye, aye, sir."

The Point Mugu range personnel declared a green range, I turned the Firing Inhibit Switch to enable, and we settled in to wait. The Aegis combat system was now in charge. Each ship had one designated exercise missile so there was going to be one chance only to score a hit. There was also an unspoken competition between the ships to be the one to destroy the target. Through telemetry, the Point Mugu range personnel would know which ship's missile actually destroyed the target even if all three arrived within a fraction of a second of each other.

Suddenly a buzz alarm sounded in CIC and less than a second later a loud whoosh announced the launch of our missile. Looking at the Large Screen Display, I saw the Vandal symbology pop up a second later as well as the symbology for our outbound SM-2. From the bridge, Terry announced missiles away on *SHILOH* and *VALLEY FORGE*. It appeared that our missile hit the target, but until the Point Mugu range operators gave the word, we wouldn't know for sure.

I told Terry to send the signal detaching *VALLEY FORGE* and *SHILOH* to proceed on duties assigned and went to the bridge. It was about 11:00 AM and we had been underway, working hard for two and a half weeks. I decided we could make the 150 mile run to San Diego before 5:00 PM and get the crew into port before overtime at the naval station. We were scheduled to arrive the following morning, but if we could make it, there was no need to keep the ship at sea and the crew away from their families for one more night.

"CHENG, bring all four engines on the line, we're going to make a run for the barn."

I told the OOD to go to max speed on two engines and then to Flank 3 when the other two engines were on the line. I told Sarah Wright, to plot the most direct possible course for home and told Don McNeill to alert Harbor Control that we would be at the sea buoy at 1600.

We took off and then the Point Mugu range operators came on the radio and reported that it was the *COWPENS* missile that made skin-to-skin contact and destroyed the Vandal nine miles from the ship. *SHILOH* and *VALLEY FORGE* also had successful shots with their missiles flying through the debris a fraction of a second later. I went to CIC and congratulated the team as I listened to the engines crank up and felt the ship shudder as she dug in and accelerated.

Lieutenant Josh Lasky called down from the bridge, "Captain, OOD, all four engines on the line, ringing up Flank 3."

"Captain, aye, I'll be up in a minute."

I planned to get on the 1MC and congratulate the crew, not just for the VANDALEX, but for the entire past several months of hard work as we went through all the preparations for deployment. As I thought about what I would say, I thought about the engineers who were so often taken for granted. All the great combat systems on the ship were worthless if we couldn't get to where we needed to be and if we didn't have reliable power, chill water, and all the other auxiliary services for which the engineers were responsible.

As I arrived on the bridge we were up to 32 knots and booming along through a calm sea. I stepped to the 1MC and clicked the mike button.

"Thundering Herd, this is the Captain speaking. We've just been notified by the range controllers that it was our missile that knocked down the Vandal. Congratulations to the combat systems team on executing the most difficult missile firing exercise in our Navy."

I could hear a cheer in the background.

"I also want to congratulate the entire Thundering Herd on all your great work over the past year as we have gotten the ship ready to deploy next month. It's been a challenging, compressed, inter-deployment period and you have excelled at every turn. I'm honored to be your Captain. Now, you may have noticed that we are moving out. Thanks to our engineers, we are at 32 knots and heading to San Diego. I plan to pull in tonight instead of tomorrow, so the next time you see one of the snipes, thank him for making this possible. Let's make all preparations for entering port."

A bigger cheer from more parts of the ship at the news of going in that night.

The following Monday, I took a call from Captain Dallas Bethea. He had an office on Point Loma with a fantastic view looking out at the Pacific Ocean. He told me he had heard that we splashed the Vandal and that as we were heading for home that afternoon he saw us streaking along past Point Loma headed for the sea buoy and "looking good." Dallas had been "Trail Boss #2" in *COWPENS* and had a warm spot in his heart for the ship. He was one of my biggest cheerleaders while I was Trail Boss #4.

We only had a week in port before our final underway before deployment with two purposes. The first was to participate in JTFEX 98-1, a Joint Task Force Exercise with the *ABRAHAM LINCOLN* Battle Group and the *USS ESSEX (LHD-2)* Amphibious Ready Group. The second was to go back to Monterey, California for a two-day port visit so that the Monterey Chapter of the Navy League could adopt the ship. As long as I didn't lose my anchor again this would be a good deal and get us out of the exercise early.

We anchored in Monterey Bay the afternoon of April 17th and on the 18th, the Monterey Bay Council of the Navy League hosted 50 officers and crew from *COWPENS* at a formal adoption ceremony at the Maritime Museum on Fisherman's Wharf. I presented them with a framed and matted painting of the ship and handed out lots of ballcaps. I later received a beautiful picture of the ship at anchor in the bay, near sunset, with sailboats anchored around us from a gentleman named Tom Spitz who had been in Monterey with his family. This began a correspondence with Tom and his son, Scott, which continued throughout the rest of my command and culminated in the entire Spitz family coming to San Diego to meet the ship when we returned from deployment.

On the 1st of May, the XO came to see me to report that our new navigator, Lieutenant (junior grade) Sarah Wright, had told him she was pregnant. Navy rules did not permit pregnant women to go to sea for extended periods of time in the early stages of pregnancy, and not at all in the latter stages. Because we were about to deploy for six months she would be transferred ashore and lost to the ship. She was also not married, but that made no difference in the Navy's eyes when it came to her long-term prospects as a naval officer. The XO and I discussed the possibility that this was done intentionally in order not to deploy considering that she had just returned from a six-month deployment in *KINKAID*. We decided not to go there. She had been performing well and had conveyed no reservations about the situation that her Navy orders had put her in; 12 months deployed in a 16-month period.

I called her up to my cabin to talk it over with her and she apologized for leaving us one officer short on the eve of deployment. She insisted that she wanted to have the baby while also continuing her Navy career. Her biggest concern was Jim Crawley and the *San Diego Union Tribune* story about the ship. The series was due to be published during the final 11 days we were in San Diego before sailing. Jim had been focusing on her more than on Susan Randle or Laura Poleshinski because she was the navigator and a younger junior officer. As a line officer, she could potentially someday command an Aegis cruiser herself. With the loss of Lieutenant (junior grade) Wright, I moved Lieutenant Josh Lasky from Assistant Operations Officer to Navigator. BuPers was sending me another officer from the nuclear cruiser *USS CALIFORNIA (CGN-36)*, but he would not arrive for several months.

Lieutenant (junior grade) Wright was not the only last-minute loss to the ship. We had a Hull Technician sent over to the Naval Hospital at Balboa for psychological testing after he had claimed he would commit suicide if he had to leave on deployment. He had previously tried to get himself exempted for medical reasons. When the docs gave him a clean bill of health he pulled the suicide stunt. It was fine with me to get rid of him. I also had one of the cooks drop something on his foot and break it which required us to leave him behind. I was suspicious of this one as well because he had come to me a month before asking to be discharged from the Navy.

On the 17th of May, the *COWPENS* series began running every day in the *San Diego Union Tribune* under the title *In Harm's Way*. Beginning that morning and every day until the 26th, I eagerly grabbed my morning paper to find out what it said. Jim Crawley and Don Kohlbauer had done a nice job. Our policy of giving them free rein and not trying to censor anything paid dividends and, in the course of riding the ship so often, including to port visits in Seattle, Cabo San Lucas, and Monterey, they had become enamored of the ship and crew and were virtual cheerleaders. I think because they had become such fans of *COWPENS* they lost a certain amount of journalistic objectivity.

This was exemplified when dealing with the sudden departure of Lieutenant (junior grade) Wright. She had spoken to Jim after speaking with me and asked him not to embarrass her by highlighting her loss due to pregnancy. Jim honored her request, glossing over her departure as being "for medical reasons," and lumping her in with a comment that several other crewmembers, all male, would miss the cruise for various reasons. I am convinced that if Jim Crawley's editors at the *Union Tribune* had known the full story, they would have demanded that he include the titillating details in the article. One of the chapters in the series highlighted the arrival of the women officers and featured Sarah conning the ship during a nighttime underway replenishment, complete with close up pictures.

The one chapter that most concerned me included the Chief Petty Officer's initiation. All the rest, including the near collision with *KITTY HAWK* painted me, the ship, the crew, and the United States Navy in a most positive light. Jim and Don would join us in the Persian Gulf in August to report on what the ship was doing "at the tip of the spear" and write one final chapter on our homecoming in November. Jim told me that he was thinking of expanding on the series and turning it into a book. Sadly, Jim Crawley died in 2007 of lymphoma—he never wrote his book.

CHAPTER 22

Flotilla Commander

I slept fitfully the night before the deployment began; not uncommon given the adventure about to begin. By this time in our lives, Iris and I were comfortable with the prospect of my leaving for six months. This was my ninth deployment in 26 years in the Navy. This time was also different because Iris would be flying overseas to meet me in Singapore and Thailand as well as somewhere on the return leg, depending on where the 7th Fleet elected to send us on the way home. Singapore was a mere three weeks away. While she had visited me before, in Malaga, Spain during the *TATTNALL* deployment and Benidorm, Spain and Toulon, France during the *SARATOGA* deployment, she had always had to worry about arranging grandparents to watch the kids. We were now empty-nesters with Chris an ensign in the Navy and Amy living in Osprey, Florida with husband-to-be Erick Brenner.

The morning of the 26th of May, the pier was crowded with family members saying tearful goodbyes as we set sea detail to get underway. Jim Crawley and Don Kohlbauer were there to chronicle our departure for the *In Harm's Way* series. COWPENS and *MILIUS* sailed out of San Diego with me in tactical command of Task Unit 35.8.10 which would be our designation until we crossed the International Dateline and chopped operational control from Commander 3rd Fleet to Commander 7th Fleet. Our first stop was to be Pearl Harbor, Hawaii for refueling on the 1st of June. We were in negotiations with 7th and 3rd Fleet staff for follow-on refueling by oilers between Hawaii and Singapore, but it did not appear that an oiler would be available along our track. The second day out we received confirmation from 7th Fleet that they did not have an oiler available to refuel us so we would be going into Guam to refuel and then transiting the Philippines via the Surigao Strait enroute

Singapore. That night the XO and I had dinner in the Chief's Mess at the invitation of Master Chief Lucas where I took the opportunity to tell them how much I valued their role in running the ship and generally tried to pump them up. I was blessed with a good group of chiefs, some better than others, but no slackards.

On the 28th, I was informed by Chief Pietrusza, our senior corpsman, that Gas Turbine Specialist Second Class Tracey Ledbetter had a scratched cornea, probably from his long-wear contact lenses. Chief Pietrusza told me that Ledbetter needed some medication not carried in our onboard allowance and that he was worried about long-term damage to the eye. I discussed options with Terry Culton and we considered either flying Ledbetter off when we were close enough to Hawaii to use our helicopter, maximum 200 miles, or asking for an air drop delivery from the P-3 that was coming out in the morning to participate in an ASW exercise we were to conduct with USS BREMERTON (SSN-698). The problem with the helicopter option was that we were 1,300 miles from Pearl Harbor and 850 miles from San Diego and Chief Pietrusza didn't think we could wait a few more days before getting the right medicine for Ledbetter. We settled on the P-3 option and I fired off a message to Rear Admiral Woody Sutton, a friend then assigned as Commander Naval Surface Group, Mid-Pacific in Pearl Harbor, requesting that the P-3 air drop the medication when it showed up on station for the exercise with BREMERTON. On the morning of the 29th, our P-3 from Naval Air Station Barber's Point, Hawaii showed up and air dropped the medicine in a floating container close by the ship. We sent one of the helos out with a rescue swimmer who went into the water, picked up the package, and was hoisted back aboard the helo. By late afternoon Ledbetter was showing signs of improvement. I was very pleased with Chief Pietrusza, who knew his stuff and would have a few more opportunities during the cruise to prove it.

On the 1st of June, we sailed through the reefs and up the channel into Pearl Harbor. As is tradition, we manned the rails and rendered passing honors to USS ARIZONA (BB-39) on the way to the pier. Rear Admiral Sutton and his staff provided great support as they energized the local maintenance infrastructure to help us fix a few problems that had emerged during the transit from San Diego. We sent Petty Officer Ledbetter to the ophthalmologist at Tripler Army Medical Center for evaluation and they decided to keep him to make sure the eye was healing properly. He'd catch up with us later.

About an hour before we were scheduled to get underway at 4:00 PM, Ed Lazarski came to see me to report that Number 1 Evaporator Condensate Distillate Pump had failed. We had two evaporators for converting salt water into fresh water for drinking, cleaning, and other uses. The loss of one evaporator would mean a loss of 50% of our fresh water distilling capacity. I didn't want to face 10 days underway between Hawaii and Guam on reduced fresh water so I called Admiral Sutton, told him our problem, and asked for help. Once again he jump-started his staff and they cannibalized a pump from *USS PORT ROYAL (CG-73)*, who was in a maintenance period. Seeing no reason to keep *MILIUS* hanging around, I told CO Commander Jim McManamon to get underway on time and we'd catch up to them. It was 10:30 that night before we set sea detail and got underway to make our way out the channel to the open sea. We steamed at 20 knots for the next day and a half before catching *MILIUS* on the 3rd.

As we sailed west across the Pacific the weather gradually improved, warmer each day, with remarkably calm seas. We were out of the Pacific shipping lanes as we made the 3,800-mile transit to Guam and were rarely encountering another ship as we made our way southwest across the vast Pacific. Although there was plenty of work and training to do, it was relaxing for me as I could count on getting a full night's sleep most nights. As we continued west and the weather became warmer we emphasized the necessity to keep the air conditioning boundaries as tight as possible so as not to let warm, humid air into the ship. This would be very important as we spent the summer in the Persian Gulf where temperatures during the day, even at sea, routinely passed 110 degrees Fahrenheit. A watertight door left open, even for a minute, resulted in condensation on the bulkheads and decks and the escape of precious cool air.

On the 4th of June we crossed the international dateline at 20 degrees, 15 minutes north and 180 degrees' longitude and lost Friday, June 5th. That happened to be Operations Specialist Second Class Thomas Hilligoss' birthday and we jokingly reminded him that the Navy can, in fact, take away your birthday. That same day we also changed operational control from 3rd Fleet in San Diego to 7th Fleet in Yokosuka, Japan and my little two ship task force became Task Unit 75.9.3.

As we continued on to Guam I was made aware by Master Chief Lucas that two of our brothers aboard ship, Fire Controlman Third Class O'Connor and Engineman First Class O'Connor, both from Guam, had parents and other relatives living on Guam whom they had not seen in several years. I sent a message to the senior officer on Guam, Commander, Naval Forces Marianas, and said we wanted to set up a family reunion and to please make sure they could get access to the base and the ship. Since we weren't originally scheduled to go to Guam, our refueling stop there was a welcome surprise for the O'Connor family—not a name I would normally associate with Guamanians.

The day before pulling into Guam, June 10th, we held a frocking ceremony for our 1st, 2nd, and 3rd class petty officers who had been selected for promotion to the next rank. Frocking meant that they would be authorized to wear the uniform and have the responsibility and authority of the next higher rank, but not get the pay until the date that their number came up and they were officially promoted. Unfortunately, we had three men who, under the rules, could not be frocked because they had failed the last physical fitness test.

After the frocking ceremony I held Captain's Call and addressed the crew to answer their questions and keep them informed. The biggest questions were about where we would go on the way home for Pacific port visits. We had sent a message the day prior, making our request of 7th Fleet and had asked for one of three options in order of priority: (1) Sydney, Australia; Noumea, New Caledonia; Hawaii (2) Bali, Indonesia; Darwin, Australia; Hawaii (3) Hong Kong; Manila, Philippines; Hawaii. I was predicting they'd send us the northern route through the Philippines and Hong Kong to save fuel and also thought Bali was a non-starter due to some civil unrest ongoing in Indonesia. I was to be proved wrong.

That same day I gave the ensigns their periodic fitness reports, my judgment of how they were doing and extremely important to their careers. When it was Ensign Laura Poleshinski's turn, she asked me if I wanted to prop the door open while she was alone with me in my cabin. This wasn't Laura being over cautious, it was how the women at the Naval Academy had been coached; not to let themselves get put into a compromising situation alone with a male, especially one senior and in their chain of command. Her offer was as much for my protection as hers. After a second's pause I said no, come in and close the door. Laura was doing great, and had established herself as one of the best ensigns in the wardroom. She was aggressively working on her Surface Warfare qualifications and never missed an opportunity to participate in an evolution where she could learn, whether it was in the engineering spaces, CIC, or on the bridge.

I also called Chaplain Sam Ortega in that afternoon to talk to him about the evening prayer. Sam was a lieutenant and this was his first deployment experience aboard ship. The evening prayer is a tradition aboard Navy ships and on previous ships on which I had served where there was no chaplain, one of the crew served as a lay-chaplain and did the honors on Sunday and during the evening prayer. The evening prayer was one of those events I hated as a watchstander, particularly on those nights that I had the midwatch from midnight to 4:00 AM. It is normally delivered at 10:00 when Taps is sounded and if you're trying to get a couple hours of sleep before the midwatch, the 1MC coming on followed by a prayer interrupts valuable rack time. Sam had not gotten into the right frame of mind for evening prayers and they had tended to be depressing; praying for the safety of our poor, forgotten, loved ones back home, and rambling along incoherently as if he had no prepared text and was making it up as he went. Some nights I wanted to slit my wrists by the time he was done. I told him the evening prayer should be uplifting; it should acknowledge the good work and accomplishments that had taken place that day and should have some relevance to upcoming events the next day. He did better after our talk.

On the 11th of June, we pulled into Apra Harbor Guam and tied the ship up at the pier without using tugs. I let Chief Engineer Ed Lazarski drive and he did a fine job. As Chief Engineer he was normally in Main Control at sea detail and deprived of the opportunity to drive the ship. As a department head he was in line to someday command a ship of his own and deserved the opportunity to gain shiphandling experience.

Since we had a few hours in port to refuel, I decided I would go for a run despite the heat and got in five miles. The road was almost covered by squashed dead brown toads which over-populate the island of Guam. These are big ugly toads, bigger than a softball and almost, in some cases, when squashed flat, as big as a volleyball. When I got back to the ship I noticed that right across the road from the pier was a nice little cove so I went in for a short swim to cool off. When I got back aboard, I told the XO to let those not involved in refueling go across the street and go for a swim. While we were in port, some of the First Class Petty Officers took the three men who had qualified for promotion but failed the physical fitness test and ran them through the test. The run is what they had flunked and the first class ran with them to egg them on - they all passed. I was really proud of them when I heard the news. We frocked them that afternoon after clearing the harbor and securing from sea detail.

We were underway that afternoon for the 1,300 mile run to Leyte Gulf in the Philippines and our transit of the Surigao Strait, the site of one of the great naval battles of World War II and one of the areas where the original *USS COWPENS (CVL-25)* saw action. On the way to Leyte Gulf we showed some old *Victory At Sea* tapes on the closed circuit television system to get the crew interested in the historic waters we would be transiting on the way to Singapore.

The 14th of June 1998 was a magical day at sea for me. We entered the Surigao Strait at about 7:00 AM and spent the whole day transiting the 275 miles of Leyte Gulf, the Surigao Strait and the Bohol Sea before emerging around sunset into the Sulu Sea for an all-night transit across to Palawan Island and the South China Sea. Before entering Leyte Gulf, we passed over the Philippine Trench which is about 35,000 feet deep—almost 7 miles. As we entered Leyte Gulf I took a small glass jar and lowered it over the side to fill with water. I then labeled it and sent it to Captain Mark Rogers, who had been commanding officer of the Aegis cruiser USS *LEYTE GULF (CG-55)*.

It was a beautiful, sunny day and the water was crystal clear. As we passed between the islands I could imagine what it was like during World War II, fighting in these confined waters. The shoreline was a lush, tropical green, with white sandy beaches and thick jungle and palm trees going almost to the water's edge. We were escorted by several schools of dolphins numbering in the hundreds. From the bridge wing I watched them swimming alongside the ship and diving 20 to 30 feet below the surface, yet still visible. In fact, the bottom was also visible about 100 feet down. This was a little disconcerting, but a glance at the fathometer showed we were in no danger.

Signalman Seaman Murdock and Operations Specialist Second Class Lewis read some history over the 1MC for the benefit of the crew and explained the Battle of Leyte Gulf as we sailed the same waters. It was Sunday Holiday Routine so we had a fantail cookout, and, since it was also Father's Day, we had the non-fathers do the grilling on the fantail. The crew was able to lounge around in shorts and swim trunks, enjoy the weather, the scenery, and the Moo-Burgers and hot dogs. Our unofficial ship's band set up and jammed on the after VLS deck. One of their improvised songs was *Anthrax Fever*, sung to the tune of *Cat Scratch Fever* by rocker Ted Nugent. Although this was funny and clever, it foretold an event which had caused some ships difficulties. Because one of the chemical agents which Saddam Hussein was credited with weaponizing was the Anthrax virus, everyone in the 5th Fleet area of operations was required to take the Anthrax vaccine. The need for the vaccine and the potential side effects had become controversial and some ships had encountered sailors who refused to be vaccinated. Our test would come soon.

Another *COWPENS* tradition was to occasionally have movie night on the forecastle, projecting the movie on the large flat superstructure below the bridge, like a drive-in theater. As it got dark and after we were into the Sulu Sea, we showed the crew's choice: *Blazing Saddles*. At least I was told by Master Chief Lucas that the crew had voted for *Blazing Saddles*; somehow I think the Chief's Mess rigged the survey.

As to movies, I made one censorship decision early in the cruise, banning *Boogie Nights*. I had been half watching it in my cabin one night while doing paperwork and I thought it was borderline pornographic. It was supposed to be a parody of the porn industry of the 80s, but with Susan Randle and Laura Poleshinski on board I thought it was inappropriate. I told the XO that *Boogie Nights* was no longer authorized for showing in *COWPENS* and the word got around the ship. The "underground plan of the day," which was published irregularly by a couple of enterprising crewmembers, had great fun with my censorship. I knew about it but the crew didn't know that I knew. I found it hilarious. They would poke fun, in a good natured way, at events or members of the crew. I found it enlightening as well.

That day spent sailing through those Philippine waters remains one of my all-time favorite days at sea. I wished that I could somehow share it with Iris. In addition to the sheer natural beauty of the water, the dolphins, and the Philippine islands, there were the navigational challenges and the joy of watching my crew, who worked so hard, enjoying a fun day off. It was great to be the Captain.

The run across the Sulu Sea is about 425 miles and we exited the Balabac Strait between Northwest Danger Shoals and Great Danger Bank just before sunset on the 15th, entering the South China Sea. Things got really busy that night as we drew closer to

Singapore and the merchant traffic entering and leaving the Malacca Strait picked up considerably. From the Balabac Strait to the Singapore Strait is about 1,000 miles, passing north of the island of Borneo. The Singapore Strait leads to the southeastern end of the Malacca Strait, a 500-mile-long strait separating the Malaysian Peninsula from the Indonesian island of Sumatra and connecting the Pacific and Indian Oceans. At its narrowest point, the Phillips Channel south of Singapore, it narrows to about a mile and a half and considering that over 50,000 ships per year transit the strait, represents a major chokepoint. One quarter of the world's traded goods pass through the Malacca Strait.

The night of the 17th, I got very little sleep as the bridge and CIC team worked to avoid all the shipping we encountered. I tucked *MILIUS* in 1,000 yards astern so she could follow in our wake and let us run interference for her. I'm sure Jim McManamon didn't get much sleep either as a ship we would avoid astern of us might very well end up on a collision course for *MILIUS*. I had to be up at 4:30 for the entry into the Singapore Strait and then the Johor Strait which runs around the north side of the island nation of Singapore and separates it from Malaysia. The Johor Strait would take us to Sembawang on the north side of Singapore where the United States Navy had a small base and where Admiral Steve Loeffler, Commander Logistics Force, Western Pacific, had his headquarters. Iris would be waiting for me in the morning as we tied up.

Early the morning of the 18th of June, we entered the Singapore Strait and made the turn up the Johor Strait past the huge commercial Changi Airport. We picked up a harbor pilot at the entrance to Johor, a young Singaporean who didn't have much to say, and as it turned out, wasn't much help with the navigation. It is about an 18 mile run through the Johor Strait to reach Sembawang and about halfway there a torrential downpour came out of nowhere and reduced visibility to almost nothing. The crew on deck for sea and anchor detail got soaked and we were reduced on the bridge to navigating by radar for about 10 minutes until the rain stopped. The Singaporean pilot did nothing to assist with the navigation. When the rain stopped, the sun came out bright and hot and the temperature and humidity must have both been 100. Singapore is only about one-degree north of the Equator. Within minutes, everyone who had been soaking wet was dry again; that is, until they started sweating in the heat and humidity.

As we approached Sembawang, I saw that there was little or no current and no wind so we tied the ship up at the wharf without using tugs. There on the pier was Iris, waving up at the bridge along with Deborah Loeffler. Iris's flight had landed around midnight the night before and Steve and Deborah had been kind enough to pick her up and let her spend what was left of the night at their quarters. Iris and I would take a room at the BOQ for the duration of our five-day stay.

The first three days were busy with official functions beginning with my office call on Rear Admiral Loeffler. The next day we hosted a formal luncheon in the COWPENS wardroom for Admiral Loeffler in honor of Rear Admiral Richard Lim, Chief of the Republic of Singapore Navy, his Vice Chief, Rear Admiral Larry Loon and his wife, and Colonel Lui Tuck Yew, Republic of Singapore Navy Fleet Commander. The galley crew in the wardroom did a great job although Mess Specialist Chief Guiterrez got drunk sneaking sips of wine in the wardroom pantry while lunch was underway. I let it pass.

At the lunch I presented the Singaporean admirals and Rear Admiral Loeffler with souvenir bottles of COWPENS wine. Before leaving San Diego I had devised a scheme to bring along some COWPENS label wine. I put Ensign Dude Underwood in charge of the labels and then went to Trader Joe's and bought three cases of red wine that cost $1.99 a bottle. It wasn't for drinking, but for display purposes. Dude was his real name, the one on his birth certificate. I met his parents after the cruise when we went to his wedding in China Lake and I think they were still enjoying the 60s.

We designed a label with a picture of the ship, a note from me, and a brief history of the Battle of Cowpens. We made it vintage 1991, the year of the ship's commissioning and called it "Captain's Special Reserve." Before an event where I planned to present our guests with a commemorative bottle, I would soak the old label off in my sink, dry the bottle and apply one of Dude's *COWPENS* labels. I always cautioned the recipients not to drink it.

USS THACH (FFG-43) joined my task group in Singapore under the command of Commander Tom Goodall, sailing from her homeport of Yokosuka, Japan. Our schedule had us leaving Singapore on the 23rd of June, transiting the Malacca Strait, and arriving in Phuket, Thailand the next day. Iris would remain overnight the 23rd in Singapore and catch a flight to Phuket on the 24th. I had been kidding her about earning her Southeast Asia Campaign Medal with Gold Oak Leaf Cluster for this trip. We transited the Johor Strait, the Singapore Strait, and entered the Malacca Strait that morning. My strategy for Malacca was much the same as my strategy for Messina; go fast, avoid all the merchant ships, and get past One Fathom Bank before dark. A fathom is six feet and One Fathom Bank was aptly named. I gave *MILIUS* and *THACH* the tactical signal to "maneuver independently to avoid shipping" to give each CO the flexibility to handle the strait as they saw fit. I certainly didn't want to tie their hands by setting up some rigid formation. They followed my lead and rang up 25 knots all day for the transit. We burned up a lot of fuel and I expected to hear about it from the 7th Fleet staff when we submitted our monthly fuel consumption report.

On the morning of June 24th, all three ships anchored in Makham Bay on the east side of the small peninsula which is home to Phuket, Thailand. On the western side of the peninsula is the Patong Beach area where all the tourist beaches and resort hotels are located and the scene of such devastation and amazing video when the tsunami hit in 2005. Iris and I would be staying in a hotel on the Patong Beach side of the island. Phuket would prove to be a great liberty port for the crew with its beaches, bars, restaurants, and night life, not to mention inexpensive prices when compared to Singapore. The Thai people are wonderfully friendly and accommodating. The only downside was the timing. We had been in Singapore for five days only two days before with no payday in between; many of the crew were low on funds.

On the morning of June 29th, I gave Iris a kiss goodbye and went to the ship for sea detail and our underway with the next stop being in the Persian Gulf some 3,200 miles further west. We were planning on her meeting the ship on the return trip in November, but we didn't yet know where that would be.

As we were at sea detail and ready to weigh anchor, I took a call from Tom Goodall on *THACH* reporting that his Disbursing Officer, a lieutenant (junior grade) was AWOL and had cleaned out the safe. Tom said his XO and Chief Master-at-Arms were ashore looking for him and that he would get underway as soon as they returned to the ship. I told him to report it up his administrative chain of command as well as to 7th Fleet and to include the U.S. Embassy in Bangkok.

As we sortied from Phuket on June 29th, the size of my little task group grew with the addition of the oiler *USNS WALTER S. DIEHL (T-AO-193)* and *USNS NIAGARA FALLS (T-AFS-3)*, a stores ship. The weather center in Guam called us on INMARSAT later that afternoon as we headed west through the Andaman Sea on the way to the Bay of Bengal and the Indian Ocean to warn us of some expected bad weather. It was southwest monsoon season in that part of the world and the weather was typically poor with high winds and seas. In some areas 20 foot seas were predicted and I studied the charts with Don McNeil and Josh Lasky to consider cutting closer to the Indian coastline to avoid or at least minimize the bad weather.

On May 11th, the Indians had conducted three underground nuclear weapons tests, following that up on the 13th with two more. It was the first time since 1974 that India had conducted such a test and it strained relations with the United States. The Indian test site, in Pokhran in the northwestern desert state of Rajasthan, was only about 90 miles from the Pakistan border. The Paks followed up with nuke tests of their own on May 28th and again on the 30th. With that test, Pakistan officially entered the sphere of nuclear capable nations, joining the United States, Russia, France, Great Britain, China and India. Although the world had long known that Pakistan was capable and had been developing a nuclear weapons program, it wasn't until these tests that it became official. Israel remained outside the "official" list, as did North Korea. The United States was concerned about a possible escalation. The two countries had fought three wars since their independence from Great Britain in 1947, mostly over the disputed territory of Kashmir. The reason I considered all of this is that a close sail-by of a small U.S. Navy task group might be misunderstood as some deliberate gunboat diplomacy rather than simple weather avoidance. I didn't want to inadvertently cause an international incident and resolved to make sure 7th Fleet knew our intended track well ahead of time so they could intervene if necessary.

The next day Jim McManamon called to tell me that he had a sailor with a history of heart problems who was experiencing chest pains. They had been in INMARSAT discussions with the doctor aboard *USS TARAWA (LHA-1)* which was in Phuket. The doctor wanted to see him as soon as possible. Jim was suggesting that he might have to turn back and race towards Phuket to save this sailor's life. We were about 400 miles west of Phuket, well outside helicopter range.

In *COWPENS* we put our heads together and came up with a plan. *THACH* was still about a hundred miles behind us and racing to catch up after the unsuccessful search for the Disbursing Officer. We told *THACH* to turn around and start heading towards Phuket again. We told *MILIUS* to also turn around and start closing *THACH* and to prep the sailor for a helicopter ride. *MILIUS* had a helicopter deck but did not have a hangar and was not capable of embarking her own helicopter detachment. *THACH* had her own detachment of SH-60B helicopters. I considered sending *MILIUS* back with one of my helicopters, but without a hangar, that would be less than ideal and this way we could take advantage of the 100 miles closer that *THACH* already was to *TARAWA*.

We launched Saberhawk 73 who flew to *MILIUS*, picked up the sailor and the *MILIUS* corpsman and delivered them to *THACH* 100 miles further east. *THACH* refueled Saberhawk 73 and sent her back to us and when *THACH* reached 200 miles, the maximum permissible, from *TARAWA*, she launched one of her helos to

TARAWA. By 10:00 PM that night we had word that the sailor was aboard *TARAWA*, resting comfortably, and apparently out of danger. He would have to make his way to Bahrain to rejoin *MILIUS*. Meanwhile, my little task group was now spread out over 400 miles of ocean.

The next day, we refueled from *WALTER S. DIEHL* and then detached her to head towards Phuket. Along the way she would refuel *MILIUS*, running to catch up with us, and then *THACH*, even further behind and also running at 25 knots to catch up. *THACH* had continued east to 150 miles from *TARAWA* to recover her helicopter after it had landed and refueled on *TARAWA*. 7th Fleet was not going to be happy with the gas guzzlers of Task Unit 75.9.3.

By the 2nd, *THACH* was still 140 miles behind, *MILIUS* having rejoined on the 1st. We had turned the corner around the southern tip of the island nation of Sri Lanka and were now in the Laccadive Sea between India and the Maldives. By nightfall the southwest monsoon was beginning to make itself felt, the seas were building, the wind was up, and there were periodic heavy rain showers.

At 6:00 AM on the 4th of July, we officially departed the 7th Fleet area of responsibility and "chopped" (change of operational control) to 5th Fleet based in the Gulf at the island nation of Bahrain. *THACH* caught up with us in the morning so we were complete once again. On the 5th we rendezvoused with *USNS YUKON (T-AO-202)* but because the weather was so bad decided to postpone the underway replenishment until the next day when hopefully it would improve as we entered the Gulf of Oman and gained the lee of the Arabian Peninsula. *THACH* was at about 45% fuel and bouncing around in the heavy seas. Winds were 25-30 knots and seas were 10-12 feet. When I discussed this with the master of *YUKON*, he said his run down from Fujairah in the UAE where he had topped off on fuel had been pretty rough once he left the Gulf of Oman and entered the North Arabian Sea.

On the 6th, conditions improved as we entered the Gulf of Oman and we were able to get all three ships refueled and do our vertical replenishment with *NIAGARA FALLS*. The weather improved markedly during the night. I had had a tough time sleeping with all the movement high up in the superstructure where my cabin was located one deck below the bridge. Like a pendulum, the higher up, the more movement there was associated with a 10 or 15-degree roll. The temperatures also climbed to over 100 degrees. The master of *YUKON* told me that when he was in Fujairah taking on fuel the temperature on his flight deck was 140 degrees Fahrenheit.

On the 7th of July, we transited the Strait of Hormuz and entered the Persian Gulf in the configuration and readiness posture we had trained for during work-up training. It was an uneventful transit with all of the expected interactions occurring with both the Omanis and the Iranians. The Strait of Hormuz Traffic Separation Scheme is designed to minimize the chance of collision among the many ships transiting into or out of the Persian Gulf carrying roughly 35% of the world's seaborne oil trade. On the north coast is Iran and on the south coast is the United Arab Emirates and Musandam, an exclave of Oman. At its narrowest point the strait is 21 miles wide and the traffic separation "lanes," inbound to the north and outbound to the south, are separated by a two-mile wide "median." Transiting Hormuz involves transiting the territorial waters of both Iran and Oman under the transit passage provisions of the United Nations Convention on the Law of the Sea.

Upon arrival in Mina Sulman, Bahrain we tied up pierside and conducted turnover briefings with the 5th Fleet staff at the Administrative Support Unit (ASU) Bahrain. The 5th Fleet Commander, Vice Admiral Tom Fargo, was traveling so I did not have an opportunity to call on him before we were to depart on the 10th. Admiral Fargo was to be relieved by my old boss on the Joint Staff, Vice Admiral Willy Moore. Underway on the 10th of July we proceeded north to the northern Persian Gulf where the Maritime Interception areas were located in the area northeast of Kuwait, south of the Um Qasr waterway where the Tigris and Euphrates Rivers empty into the Persian Gulf and southwest of the Faw Peninsula. It was in this area that 5th Fleet had set up patrol areas named after major league baseball stadiums. We were assigned to "Fenway."

On the way to Fenway, we rendezvoused with the Royal Navy oiler *RFA BRAMBLELEAF (A-81)* and topped off on fuel. The Brits were actively involved in enforcing the UN sanctions on Iraq, but by 1998, they and the United States were the only ones. A British frigate, the Type 23 *HMS GRAFTON (F-80)*, and the Type 42 destroyer *HMS YORK (D-98)* were part of the MIO force. The coalition put together by President Bush for Desert Storm had been slowly diminishing as various European nations lost interest in the effort. Some, notably France and Germany, had been accused of violating the terms of the sanctions by trading with Iraq in goods and services which were prohibited under the cover of the UN Oil for Food Program, UN Resolution 986. I marveled myself at the apparent futility of the effort and the fact that seven years after I had conducted the first Red Sea boarding during Desert Shield in *SAMPSON* we were still at it, expending resources to keep Saddam Hussein contained. All the while, Saddam continued to resist, occasionally taking shots at our aircraft enforcing the no fly zones, and threatening Kuwait and Saudi Arabia with provocative troop movements.

We arrived in Fenway on the 11th and received our first tasking which was to guard the sanctions violators who had already been boarded and searched and determined to be in violation. Fenway was about 30 miles south of the Iran-Iraq border and we had five violators under guard. In addition to preventing them from escaping, we were responsible for daily health and comfort" visits to ensure the crews had enough food and water and that nobody was ill. On the very first visit, Josh Lasky's team found a chart showing smuggling routes along the Iranian coast. We confiscated it to add to the evidence package.

The guidance for MIO had changed since our training in San Diego earlier in the year with the addition of the requirement to be prepared to conduct "non-compliant" boardings, including at night. Sanctions violator tactics were to exit the Um Qasr waterway and move northeast into Iranian territorial waters before getting caught.

Once in Iranian territorial waters, our rules of engagement prohibited us from going after them. They would hug the Iranian coastline until further south in the Gulf and then make their move into international waters and go to wherever their customers were for the illegal cargoes. It was simply not practical to shadow them with a cruiser or destroyer in hopes of bagging them when they made their move. Often, their customer was Iran itself and once the cargo was transferred to an Iranian flagged ship or reached an Iranian port, it was game over. The non-compliant boardings were for those ships that refused to stop and cooperate. The ship had to have a low enough freeboard so that a boarding team in a RHIB could scramble over the side, storm the bridge, and force the master to stop. These were generally to be done at night to gain the element of surprise.

Another challenge of operating a ship like *COWPENS* in these waters was navigation. There are many places where the water shallowed to less than the 30 feet that *COWPENS* drew. Most of the time in Fenway there was only about 25 feet of water under the sonar dome. Racing around at high speed only exacerbates the danger because of a phenomenon known as "squat." When a ship is in shallow water, speed can be dangerous because, as the ship moves faster over the bottom, a Venturi effect occurs between the hull and the bottom, literally sucking the ship lower in the water. I gathered all the officers together in the wardroom on the way to Fenway and discussed these considerations. To illustrate my point, I told them that in most of the Persian Gulf, if you tipped the 667-foot-long *COWPENS* on its nose on the bottom, everything aft of the bridge would be sticking out of the water. The other point I emphasized was safety. No sailor's life was worth whatever benefit was to be accrued by catching one of these sanctions violators and turning them over to the authorities.

Between the 11th and the 16th of July, we boarded and searched eight ships and conducted several health and comfort visits for the detainees held in Fenway. All of the ships we boarded were found to be in compliance and were released on their voyages, but that did not mean things were not interesting. One of the "986" ships had gone into Iraq full of grain, which was in compliance with the sanctions, but when he came out empty we were obliged to board him again to make sure he wasn't smuggling contraband. While empty his sides represented a 30-foot climb for the boarding team. To make matters worse, his pilot ladder hung down only to about six or seven feet above the water, making it very difficult for the boarding team to get a foot on the bottom rung from the RHIB. It was also rough, so the team had to use the swells to gauge the best time to make their move as the RHIB rose up alongside. All of this emphasized the day to day risk of injury or death to our Navy crews enforcing the UN sanctions.

On the 12th, we began our required series of Anthrax shots. Everyone in the CENTCOM theater was required to take the shots because of the fear of Iraq, or even Iran, weaponizing the Anthrax bacteria and using it against us. The shots had become controversial within the military after some reports had suggested it was just as dangerous to get the shots as it was to be infected by an Anthrax attack. And the shots were 100% going to happen; the attack probably wouldn't. Strict guidance had been issued stating that service members who refused the shots were subject to disciplinary action and if they still refused, they would be administratively discharged under "other than honorable" conditions. There was a lot of misinformation about the Anthrax shots, most of it coming from the homefront in newspaper articles, news magazines and programs like *60 Minutes*. I took the first shot to set the example. Doc Pietrusza told me that he had heard rumblings that two or three crewmembers might refuse. In the end however, everybody took the shot. Mine raised a ping pong ball-sized knot on my left arm.

On breaking away from *USS NIAGARA FALLS* following an underway replenishment on the 14th, we spotted a white speedboat adrift in the middle of the ocean. We took the ship over for a closer look and saw that no one was aboard this 28-30-foot Scarab speedboat with three giant 250 horsepower outboard engines. It looked like the kind of boat used throughout the Persian Gulf to smuggle cigarettes, drugs, and other contraband. We put the RHIB in the water with Chief Daum onboard and he boarded the boat. Inside were a cooler with some Pepsis and water, eight ten-gallon gas cans full of gas and 18 one-liter plastic containers of oil. The key was in the ignition and when Chief Daum turned it, the engines fired up. The Chief drove it around a little bit but later told me that he was afraid to really open it up. It was so powerful he was afraid it would flip.

I had the crew attach a line and we took it under tow behind the ship as we headed towards Fenway. We were due for a port visit in six days in Dubai, United Arab Emirates, and I had plans to try to sell the boat and apply whatever we could get for it to the ship Welfare and Recreation Fund. I figured the engines alone were worth $50,000. We could pay for everybody's cruisebook from Welfare and Rec and still have money left over. I thought we could do our board and search operations with the boat towed behind. It would only get dicey if we had to do a high speed chase or some other radical maneuvering.

Then the 5th Fleet lawyers got involved. I had reported the find in my evening situation report and laid out my intentions to sell. The lawyer said we could only keep it if the owner can be shown to have abandoned it. How were we going to prove that? It looked like it had drifted away from its mooring, perhaps in a storm. I was informed that we'd have to turn it over to somebody when we got to Dubai, although who exactly wasn't clear. There were no registration numbers on the sides although there must have been some kind of manufacturer's serial number somewhere. I was disappointed, as was the crew, because I had told them my plan over the 1MC. Master Chief Lucas said everyone was excited by the idea. Now I was regretting my decision because for the next six days we'd be towing this thing around behind us; we had no way to lift it onboard and store it on deck.

The problem took care of itself that night. At 3:30 the next morning, the OOD called me to say that the after lookout reported that the Scarab had rolled over on its side. We stopped the ship and I got out of bed and went to the fantail to take a look. The boat had rolled over somehow and now was floating vertically with only about two feet of the bow sticking above the surface of the water. Apparently an air pocket in the bow was keeping it afloat. The ocean was flat calm and we had been poking along at five knots through the night so it must have been slowly taking on water. We pulled it in as close as we could and cut the line. Chief Daum was there with me and we discussed shooting holes in the bow with an M-14 to let the air out so that it would sink and not be a hazard to navigation. While we were having this high level discussion, the boat slowly sunk out of sight and went to the bottom like the *TITANIC*. My cash cow was gone—easy come easy go. I dutifully reported the sinking to 5th Fleet and I wonder if they thought I was lying because I didn't like the answer from the previous night.

On the 16th of July, we were about to board the container ship *M/V NOURA*, registered in Aqaba, Jordan, when an Iranian *KAMAN* PTG came sailing through Fenway and approached *COWPENS*. The *KAMAN* class PTG is a small guided missile patrol boat, built in France. It carries a 76 MM gun mount, a 40 MM anti-aircraft gun, and most importantly, the C-802 surface to surface missile. Although dwarfed by *COWPENS* at about 150 feet and 275 tons, these were formidable little ships which, like a hornet, could deliver a nasty sting. This same *KAMAN* had had an earlier confrontation with *MILIUS* while *MILIUS* was attempting to stop a possible smuggler in the area which Iran claimed as territorial seas. Jim McManamon on *MILIUS* had had a bridge radio disagreement with the captain of the *KAMAN* about the territorial seas issue. Unfortunately, in my view, the Commander of Destroyer Squadron 50 stepped in and told *MILIUS* to depart the area and let the suspect vessel go, essentially siding with the Iranians from his perch ashore in Bahrain. I thought this was stupid, lending credence to the Iranian claim, and once again demonstrating the downside of all our modern day communications capabilities.

As a precaution, I went to CIC, sent Terry Culton to the bridge to be my eyes, and we called away the SCAT team (manning the 50 caliber machine guns and 25 MM chain gun) and manned Mount 51. I thought about going to General Quarters but rejected the idea as an overreaction. The last thing I wanted was for the

Iranians to see my crew scrambling all over the ship to battle stations as if it were December 7th at Pearl Harbor. He ended up passing harmlessly by at about 2,000 yards and then turned north towards Iran and sped away.

We began the boarding of *NOURA* late that afternoon and it was a grueling job for the boarding team which began the effort in 109 degree temperatures and had the task of inspecting over 180 containers. They dragged themselves back aboard at around 1:00 the morning of the 17th after we cleared the ship to proceed to Umm Qasr, Iraq. I went back to the fantail to greet them as they came aboard and shake their hands. They were exhausted and drenched in sweat.

But the night was not over. At 3:30 the OOD called to tell me we had detected a 300-foot oiler which was running south at 20 knots and would not answer us on bridge-to-bridge radio. I went to the bridge and we took off in pursuit while continuing to challenge him over the radio and flashing our signal lamps to get his attention. He then made a course adjustment towards Kharg Island that suggested he was trying to escape into Iranian territorial waters. We quickly overtook him at 30 knots, positioning the ship off his port quarter in order to herd him to the west and open waters while we called away the boarding team, the SCAT Team, and made preparations to launch the helicopter. I hated doing this at 3:45 in the morning; everyone was already tired, including me, but it was our mission and we had to do it.

I was thinking that this could be our first non-compliant boarding and I didn't like the way it was shaping up. Boarding a ship from a RHIB at 20 knots is no easy task and very dangerous. As we drew closer I could see he was riding high in the water; his freeboard might be too much for the boarding team. As we closed to within a couple hundred yards, he finally answered the radio. He claimed he was in ballast and had just come out of Khor-e-Musa, Iran, was enroute to Fujairah, UAE, and the master was down in his bunk asleep. If what he said was true he was not a candidate for boarding, having come from Iran, not Iraq. He then altered course away from Kharg Island. We didn't know if that was because of where we had positioned *COWPENS* or if it was a routine course change for Fujairah.

Don McNeil was the TAO in CIC and he ran the Aegis tapes backwards to see when he had first shown up on radar and sure enough, he was telling the truth, he had come out of Khor-e-Musa. Just as I was getting that report the master came to the bridge and got on the radio. He explained that he had just dropped off the pilot and come up to speed for the run to Fujairah when we showed up. I explained to him why he looked suspicious, especially his watch officer's refusal to answer the radio even when it became obvious we were chasing him. He acknowledged this, apologized, probably smacked the watch officer on the side of the head, and offered to stop if we still wanted him to. I said no, not necessary, and wished him a safe voyage. I felt bad that we had rousted everyone for no reason, but once again, it was our mission and had to be done. When I finally crawled out of the rack at about 9:00 that morning, our schedule began to change. Originally we were going to escort one of the sanctions violators being held in Fenway to Kuwait to turn over to the Kuwaiti Coast Guard, our government having been successful in convincing the Kuwaitis to take custody. Before we could begin that tasking, we were called by 5th Fleet and directed to depart the MIO area and rendezvous with the aircraft carrier *USS STENNIS (CVN-74)* and pick up duties as her shotgun. At the same time, we would be taking over as Gulf Air Warfare Commander, responsible for all anti-air warfare activity in the Persian Gulf. A short time later a new schedule came out and instead of going to Dubai, a great place for liberty, we would be going to Jebel Ali on the 20th. Jebel Ali was about 20 miles south of Dubai, within striking distance, but not convenient for the crew. On the plus side, it has a very large harbor and we would be able to go pierside.

We went south to the central Persian Gulf and rendezvoused with *STENNIS* around 6:30 in the evening. They immediately put us in plane guard station and we commenced racing around at 30 plus knots because there was no wind and they were conducting flight operations. It was even hotter in the central Gulf than it had been further north in Fenway and much more humid. As shotgun, we normally positioned ourselves about 5 miles on the Iranian side of the aircraft carrier while she steamed back and forth in her carrier operating area launching and recovering aircraft. When in shotgun it was more relaxing for me than planeguard because of the distance from the carrier, but we were still racing around at over 30 knots. The fuel gauge was dropping quickly.

On the night of the 18th, at about 7:00, the forward air conditioning units began tripping off-line due to low flow and our combat systems equipment began overheating. I called Admiral Suggs on *STENNIS* and told him what was happening and recommended he shift air warfare commander to another Aegis ship, which he did. As the equipment continued to overheat we had to shut down all radars and HF communications equipment as well as the computers supporting the Aegis combat system. I went down to Auxiliary Machinery Room Number 1 which housed the forward air conditioning plants and spoke with Chief Engineer Ed Lazarski and Terry Culton. Ed showed me that the sea suction strainers for the AC plant were full of sea life, mainly mussels and other shellfish which had so clogged the strainers that the cooling water was cut off, causing the units to trip off the line. Without the AC, the flow of chill water so vital to our electronics was interrupted. Chill water is vital to the ship combat systems which generate tremendous heat because of the power produced. Ed said that he thought that all the running around we had been doing for the past 24 hours chasing *STENNIS* had caused the normal growth on the hull to break off and be sucked up by our sea suction system. I originally thought we might have sucked up some plastic bags or fishing nets, but when Ed showed me the bouillabaisse in Aux 1, I knew he was right.

Once we cleaned the strainers, everything returned to normal and we resumed our Gulf Air Warfare Commander duties. We then got ahead of the problem in the after AC plant with a systematic strainer cleaning effort that kept the combat system fully functional. In the course of this we had learned a lesson about cleaning the hull–if you can afford the gas, racing around at 30 plus knots for extended periods will help.

On the 19th, we received the Chief Petty Officer selection board results and were delighted to learn that eight of our first class petty officers had been selected for promotion to Chief Petty Officer. Among them was Yeoman First Class Chris Adams who I had brought to *COWPENS* from the Pentagon and had been Yeoman Seaman Adams when I was CO of *SAMPSON*. I was thrilled for him and proud of him. Some of the selectees were among the ones who had taken the physical fitness test in Guam with the younger sailors who had failed it and urged them on to passing scores. I was glad to see their unselfish leadership rewarded. Of course, some equally outstanding first class petty officers were not on the list and that was disappointing; everybody can't make it. After a five-hour delay sitting outside the ship channel into Jebel Ali, we pulled in on the morning of the 20th. Jebel Ali is a huge commercial port 20 miles south of Dubai on the Persian Gulf side of the United Arab Emirates. It is entered via a very narrow but straight 6-mile-long shipping channel dredged out of the shoals which are clearly visible on both sides. Once inside the breakwater there is another 3-mile-long inner harbor with two huge slips projecting out to the north. Each of these slips is about a mile and a half long and a quarter mile wide. There is plenty of room inside and probably over a hundred ships could be handled throughout the complex.

The weather conditions were calm so, although we had embarked a British harbor pilot, I chose to tie the ship up without using tugs or the pilot. He moved aft on the bridge wing and watched with his walkie-talkie at the ready in case we got in trouble and needed the tug which was standing by. Lieutenant Steve Rancourt, the Damage Control Assistant, had the conn and he did a nice job.

The ambient temperature in Jebel Ali was 107 degrees and our meteorologist, AG1 George Williams, estimated the apparent temperature, accounting for humidity, at 125 degrees. The "feels like" temperature. Later that day I went for a run in the port and managed about two miles before I quit; it was just too hot and humid.

Our four-day port visit in Jebel Ali was shortened by one day when 5th Fleet ordered us to get underway on the 23rd to head to the North Arabian Sea south of Pakistan to be in position for "Pony Express" operations to use our SPY-1B radar and Aegis combat system to track an expected Pakistani Tarmuk Short Range Ballistic Missile launch. There continued to be great interest in learning what we could about the ballistic missile capabilities of both India and Pakistan since their tit-for-tat nuclear tests a couple of months earlier.

We did, however, make the most of our days in port although for security reasons and because of a lack of a Status of Forces Agreement, or SOFA, between the U.S. and the UAE, liberty for the crew was pretty constrained. There was a Seaman's Club in the Jebel Ali port with a swimming pool, locker rooms and a bar so that is where most of us went when off duty. There was also a Seaman's Club in Dubai run by two British ex-patriates, Marty and Jane Hoyle, called the Dubai International Seaman's Center. This place had become an institution in the Gulf and the walls were covered with ship plaques and pictures of ship commanding officers from all nations. We added my picture and a *COWPENS* plaque to the collection during a wardroom party we held on the 22nd to say goodbye to Chief Engineer Lieutenant Commander Ed Lazarski, Navigator Lieutenant Josh Lasky, and Gunnery Officer Lieutenant (junior grade) Wes Boose. I was fulfilling my promise to Josh that I would let him go early to get ready for SEAL training in San Diego. The hardest farewell speech was Ed Lazarski's; he had been a good Chief Engineer for 42 months. When it was my turn to talk about Ed, I talked about the special relationship that develops between a ship captain and his engineer and pointed out to the others that for the engineers, every day is showtime, unlike in combat systems and other areas where the crew can gear up for big events.

We were underway the morning of July 23rd to rendezvous with *USNS YUKON* for fuel and then transit the Strait of Hormuz to head for our Pony Express station outside the Gulf. Ensign Laura Poleshinski had the conn for the underway and this time we didn't invite the pilot aboard or ask for a tug to stand by. Laura, who was by then establishing herself as perhaps the most motivated and energetic of the junior officers, did a great job and I could tell by the sparkle in her eyes and the look on her face that she was thrilled to get the opportunity. Marty Hoyle from the Dubai International Seaman's Club came down to the harbor on his Harley-Davidson motorcycle with an American flag strapped to the back and rode up and down the pier to bid us farewell.

Arriving on station in our assigned position about 300 miles east of Oman and 25 miles south of Pakistan, we commenced Pony Express operations. The Aegis combat system and SPY-1B radar were capable of tracking space tracks via a special program tape that was inserted into the Aegis computer system specifically for that purpose. The SPY radar in its normal configuration could track an air target out to 256 nautical miles. That 256-mile distance was a result of the computer software, not the electromagnetic capability of the radar. For Pony Express operations the normal Aegis program tapes were removed and the special tapes inserted which did not limit the range at which the radar could process a target its electrons were powerful enough to reach out, touch, and detect upon return. On *COWPENS* our code name for setting the combat system up for this mission was "Spotlight."

The reason for the 256-mile maximum range in the normal configuration is that for anti-air warfare against manned aircraft or missiles there was simply no reason to have greater range. Our own missiles could only fly about a third of that distance and to be seen above the radar horizon at that range an aircraft or missile would have to be at extremely high altitude. With the software filtering out any returns beyond 256 miles, much more computing power was focused on targets inside 256 miles, giving the radar system greater fidelity.

The downside to configuring the system for Spotlight was that the ship lost its anti-air self-defense capability. If a ship came under unexpected air attack it was defenseless using the SM-2 missiles. For that reason, in a hot war scenario where an anti-ballistic missile tracking capability was desired, the ship in Spotlight mode would have an escort, or shotgun, in normal anti-air warfare mode ready to defend against air attack. Today, the Navy is developing something called the Air and Missile Defense Radar which will be capable of doing both missions at once; track space tracks while also defending the ship against air attack.

During Pony Express operations the intelligence community would send an alert when they thought we were in the window for a Pakistani missile launch. I had been designated Commander Task Group 57.5 responsible for the operation with *MILIUS*, stationed 140 miles to our east off the coast of Karachi, Pakistan, under my tactical command. When we got the word, both *COWPENS* and *MILIUS* would set up the Aegis systems for space tracking and wait for something to happen. Which, it never did.

The crew began referring to Pony Express operations as Groundhog Day because each day was a mirror of the one before with the exception of whatever training or events we injected into the routine. On the 30th of July we received a planning message indicating that when we returned to the Gulf there was to be a MIO surge operation and I was going to be designated the commander of the operation. The concept was to use U.S. Navy MK-V patrol boats, U.S. Navy Special Forces, and the Kuwaiti Coast Guard in a coordinated effort to interrupt UN sanctions smuggling in the shallow waters along the Iraq and Kuwait coast where our big cruisers, destroyers and frigates could not go. The British would also be participating and operating under my tactical command. *COWPENS* would be embarking a colonel from SOCCENT, the U.S. Central Command Special Operations Command, to coordinate the Special Forces involvement. We later learned that we would be relieved of Pony Express duties on the 5th of August by *USS VALLEY FORGE (CG-50)* in order to re-enter the Gulf, do a short port visit to Bahrain, and then go north for the MIO surge.

The morning of the 4th of August, Chief Corpsman, Doc Pietrusza came to see me with an unusual medical emergency. One of our third class Damage Controlmen, who I will not name to spare him any further embarrassment, had come to see him complaining of severe pain in his left testicle. Doc Pietrusza had examined him, consulted his references, and come to the conclusion that this poor fellow had something called "torsion testicle." The books said that torsion testicle occurs when the testicle gets twisted and the blood supply gets cut off. The book further advised that treatment within six hours was the standard, otherwise the testicle could possibly be lost. Chief Pietrusza had proven his worth already this deployment and I trusted his judgment.

I called the bridge, ordered all four engines on line and we headed east towards Muscat, Oman, 300 miles away. Terry Culton got on the satellite radio and advised 5th Fleet of our situation, told them we were leaving our Pony Express station and asked them to coordinate diplomatic clearance for our helicopter in Muscat, and to pre-arrange medical support for when the helicopter landed. We rolled the helo out on the flight deck and got her ready to launch when we got to 200 miles from the coast.

I went to Sick Bay to see the petty officer and assure him that we were doing all we could to get him to a hospital as fast as possible. He was in a lot of pain and scared. Don McNeil called from CIC and said he had the 5th Fleet doctor on the satellite radio and she wanted to talk to the Chief Corpsman. Chief Pietrusza left the petty officer in the care of one of the junior corpsman and went to CIC while I went to the bridge. We had the satellite radio speaker patched into the pilot house. Ensign Laura Poleshinski was on watch as JOOD.

We listened as this female Navy captain doctor described to Chief Pietrusza just exactly how to cradle this petty officer's testicles in his hand to help relieve pressure and ease the pain. There were smirks going around the bridge, including from Laura, and I am assuming throughout 5th Fleet. We were on the 5th Fleet Administrative Net which is monitored throughout the fleet, including by ships inport.

At exactly 200 miles from Muscat we launched Saberhawk 73 with the petty officer on board in a stretcher. We later learned, through the 5th Fleet staff, that he had been seen at the Royal Omani Air Force hospital and the doctors had determined that it was not torsion testicle but some kind of inflammation. I told Chief

Pietrusza not to worry about the misdiagnosis and that we had done the right thing. He caught all kinds of crap in the Chief's Mess with various chiefs complaining that their balls ached and would he please cradle them in his hands.

We went through Hormuz on the night of the 5th of August and re-entered the Persian Gulf. It was a long night and I didn't get off the bridge until about 2:30 in the morning. The phone kept ringing with contact reports until I got up at 6:00. Once back inside the Gulf the heat was once more oppressive; it almost made me long for Ground Hog Day in the North Arabian Sea.

The morning of the 7th, I flew over to *ABRAHAM LINCOLN* who had entered the Gulf and replaced *STENNIS* while we were on Pony Express operations. I met with Rear Admiral Bill Putnam, Commander Cruiser-Destroyer Group 3 and my friend, Captain Jim Stavridis, Commander Destroyer Squadron 21, to discuss the upcoming MIO Surge operation. One of the big goals was to involve Kuwait in the operation; perhaps even more important than actually catching any smugglers. The Kuwaitis were very tentative militarily and understandably wary of anything that might inflame relations with Iraq and Saddam Hussein. It was, after all, only eight years after Iraq had invaded and occupied their country. While on *LINCOLN* I heard about a terrorist attack on the U.S. Embassies in Nairobi, Kenya and Dar es Salaam, Tanzania.

CHAPTER 23

Striking Back at Terrorism

O n August 7, 1998, near simultaneous explosions rocked the
U.S. embassies in Dar es Salaam, Tanzania, and Nairobi,
Kenya killing 224 people including twelve Americans. The
world saw horrific pictures of the devastation and the dead and
injured being removed from the rubble. President Clinton promised
retaliation.

We tied up the ship at Mina Sulman in Bahrain the morning
of August 8th, and I went to Commander 5th Fleet headquarters to
pay a call on Vice Admiral Charles W. "Willy" Moore, Jr., the new
5th Fleet Commander. Vice Admiral Moore had been my boss in J-3
at the Pentagon and I looked forward to seeing him in Bahrain. He
had taken command from Vice Admiral Tom Fargo while
COWPENS was operating in the North Arabian Sea. Willy Moore
had always been one of my favorite guys for his irreverent sense of
humor.

When I arrived at 5th Fleet headquarters, the staff was in
absolute uproar orchestrating the relief response to the embassy
bombings. In a quirk of the Unified Command Plan, Kenya fell in
the Central Command area of responsibility while Tanzania was in
the European Command area. Although the two bombings were
very likely related, and the two countries shared a common border,
two different Commander's, or CINC's, would be responsible for
responding with a relief effort.

I ended up spending an enjoyable three hours sitting in Vice
Admiral Moore's office, swapping sea stories and catching up on old
times while he directed the efforts of his staff which were organizing
a team to go to Nairobi. At one point, Admiral Moore said to me,
"We think this guy Osama bin Laden is responsible for this. We

believe we know where he is and if we can tie it to him, we're going to go after him."

I pressed for details. Admiral Moore told me that bin Laden had a terrorist camp in Afghanistan and if retaliation was ordered, we'd attack him with a Tomahawk strike. Now I was really interested since I had 36 Tomahawk Land Attack Missiles, or TLAMs, in my MK-41 VLS launcher in *COWPENS*.

Admiral Moore then said, "If we get the go ahead, you'll be one of the shooters." I told him we'd be ready and then he said, "This is real close hold, you can't tell anybody."

Later that afternoon, I went back to the ship and got my strike leadership team together in my cabin. No way was I going to keep this news to myself. If we needed to conduct extra training to make sure we were ready, my key leaders needed to know so that they would be focused; not going through the motions just because the Captain wanted to hold more training. I told them what Admiral Moore had told me and that we needed to make sure our Strike Team absolutely had their act together. I explained to them the sensitive nature of the information, but also authorized them to tell the necessary junior officers and senior enlisted personnel so that they would understand the urgency. We then speculated on where the launch baskets would be. Afghanistan is a land-locked country, so we'd be flying Tomahawks over Iran or Pakistan to get to wherever this camp was. We estimated that we'd most likely shoot over friendlier Pakistan than risk a misunderstanding with Iran.

Of course, our next assignment following the port visit to Bahrain was for *COWPENS* to serve as On-Scene Commander for the MIO surge operation in the northern Gulf and we had to get ready for that as well. The idea was to get the Kuwaitis and the U.S. MK-V's up close to the Shat-al-Arab waterway where they could intercept Iraqi sanctions violators trying to sneak along the coast in shallow water and avoid capture until they could make it into Iranian territorial seas.

In Bahrain, we embarked *San Diego Union Tribune* reporter Jim Crawley and photographer Don Kohlbauer for a five-day underway period. Jim and Don had managed to convince the editors at the paper that, having written the eleven-part series on *COWPENS*, which had run before departing San Diego, they needed to write a story from the Gulf to report on how things were going. We got underway from Bahrain on August 13th and proceeded north to the MIO areas to begin the surge operation. It was brutally hot and humid as we set sea detail to depart Bahrain; Jim and Don were getting a good welcome to the Persian Gulf in August. Jim was especially excited to be going to sea to report on "his" ship.

While making preparations for the operation to begin, we had received a series of updated Tomahawk missions via Extremely High-Frequency Mission Data Update. 5th Fleet had also been running an unusually high number of Tomahawk exercises. All of the launch baskets for the exercises were in the North Arabian Sea, south of Pakistan.

Arriving in the northern Gulf on the 14th, we positioned the ship right at the Kuwait 12-mile territorial sea limit to await the arrival of the U.S. SOCCENT representative, Air Force Colonel Jim Connors, two U.S. MK-V patrol boats and the Kuwaiti *NAJA* and *COUGAR* patrol boats. *COWPENS* was to embark Colonel Connors and a Kuwaiti Flotilla Commander, also a colonel. Everybody showed up except the Kuwaitis. We went ahead with a briefing in the wardroom which included the CO of *THACH* and the CO of the Canadian frigate *HMCS OTTAWA (FFH-341)*. Because the Kuwaitis were a no-show, there were many unanswered questions. Jim Connors was on the phone with the Embassy in Kuwait City trying to find out what was going on, but getting nowhere. Finally, about 7:00 PM a pair of Kuwaiti *COUGARS* arrived and we were able to get some training done. No sign of the Kuwaiti Flotilla Commander. "Insha'Allah," as they say in the Arab world.

About 7:45 the evening of the 16th, we received the 5th Fleet Night Orders, which directed *COWPENS* to conduct a MIO surge turnover with *VALLEY FORGE* on the 17th and then proceed to the southern Persian Gulf. I couldn't yet tell the entire crew what I knew, and I certainly couldn't tell Jim Crawley and Don Kohlbauer from the *Union Tribune*, but things had been percolating while we were trying to get the Kuwaitis interested in the MIO surge.

On August 15th, *USS ELLIOT (DD-967)* had been detached from MIO duties and sent through the Strait of Hormuz to the North Arabian Sea. *ELLIOT* was Tomahawk capable. *USS SHILOH (CG-67)* and *USS MILIUS (DDG-69)* were already on station in the North Arabian Sea on the same Pony Express operations we had been conducting south of Pakistan. Again, both ships carried Tomahawks. In an unusual twist, *USS HAYLER (DD-997)*, who was entering the 5th Fleet for the first time to relieve *USS BRISCOE (DD-977)*, had been turned around two days earlier just south of the Strait of Hormuz and was en route the Red Sea whence they had just come. *BRISCOE*, who should have been on her way home to Norfolk, had been ordered to loiter in the Red Sea.

It was evident strike preparations were underway; we ships just weren't cut in on the details. We knew that forces, all Tomahawk capable, were being positioned for a possible strike, we just weren't privy to the detailed planning and dialogue. I also had the problem of the presence of two newspaper reporters on board who would have to leave early. They knew something was up, they didn't know exactly what—but they could guess. My Strike Team personnel all knew as they had been training daily on Tomahawk scenarios generated by 5th Fleet. It's pretty tough to keep a secret on a ship, so when I got on the 1MC and told the crew we would be relieved in the morning by *VALLEY FORGE* for a special mission, the ship was buzzing with rumors of action soon to come.

I met with Jim Crawley that evening to tell him that he and Don would be leaving first thing in the morning on the Desert Duck, the 5th Fleet SH-3 logistics helicopter. I told him that I couldn't say what we were headed off to do but did tell him this, "Jim, remember when I told you that our mission here was to be an instrument of national policy. Well, we're going to go do our mission." I could see that it was killing him that he had to leave; so far his underway time in the Gulf had been kind of a bust. We had sent him up in our LAMPS helo to observe some MIO operations; boarding and searching merchant ships going in and out of Iraqi waters, but no real excitement had occurred.

On the morning of August 17th, we watched *VALLEY FORGE* sail into view, conducted a quick turnover of the MIO surge plans and then headed south into the Gulf. I received further instructions from CTF 50 to prepare for a routine nighttime transit of the Strait of Hormuz the night of August 18th. Once south of the traffic separation scheme in the Gulf of Oman, we were to set total EMCON (no radars, no radio transmissions) and proceed to a point about 200 miles south of the coast of Pakistan to await the word to close to our launch position.

The XO and I decided we should secure all outgoing email to prevent a security leak by one of the troops eager to describe his adventure. Security was necessarily very tight. The purpose of this strike was to catch Osama bin Laden in his camp and kill him. If word leaked, he could be spooked and evacuate.

BRISCOE and *HAYLER* were in position in the Red Sea off the coast of Sudan. This made sense as Sudan had long been suspected of harboring terrorists and there was a Sudanese connection to bin Laden. When he had been exiled from Saudi Arabia, he had set up his operations in Sudan before moving to Afghanistan. *SHILOH, ELLIOT, MILIUS* and the attack submarine *USS COLUMBUS (SSN-762)* were already in position in the North Arabian Sea. *SHILOH* and *MILIUS* were in their Pony Express stations, *COLUMBUS* was submerged somewhere (even we didn't know exactly where), and *ELLIOT* in a more southerly position about 20 miles east of where we were headed. The idea was to maintain the pretense of business as usual for *SHILOH* and *MILIUS* and keep the presence of the rest of us unknown so as not to tip our hand. The Pakistanis had been conducting daily surveillance of the Pony Express ships so we wouldn't be moving them to their launch baskets until nightfall. Although Pakistan was a friend of the U.S., it was well-known that their Inter-Services Intelligence Directorate (ISID) was sympathetic to the Taliban who ruled Afghanistan after the Soviets left in 1989. The Taliban, who had taken over control of Afghanistan in the vacuum created by the departure of the Soviets and the lack of real interest by the United States, were providing a safe haven for Osama bin Laden and his Al Qaeda organization.

We took on fuel and stores from *CAMDEN* the evening of August 17th and made an uneventful transit of Hormuz the night of August 18th. Once south of the traffic separation scheme we set total EMCON and turned out all the lights. We operated Saberhawk 76 in EMCON as well, using only the Hawklink to communicate. The Hawklink travels on a 1-degree pencil beam and is virtually impossible to intercept. I ended up getting a lot of calls that night from the bridge as they encountered merchant traffic headed into the Gulf. Operating without radar, the watchstanders were guessing at ranges and on those occasions when I came to the bridge to take a look, I decided that they had a tendency to under-estimate the ranges. Better than *over*-estimating ranges I suppose.

By the evening of August 17th, we had received orders from CTF 50 to secure all off-ship communications, such as email, for security reasons, a step we had taken the day prior. These same orders authorized me to brief the crew on our upcoming operations. I got on the 1MC after dinner and explained our mission, giving them all I knew about the embassy bombings, Khobar Towers, and the connection to Osama bin Laden. Coincidentally, that evening on the SITE TV system, the evening news was from August 7th, the day of the embassy attacks. We had received the latest SITE TV tapes during our replenishment from *CAMDEN*. All three major news networks led with the story, showing video of the destruction and of the dead and injured. ABC did a piece on bin Laden, labeling him the primary suspect and describing his activities. A reporter had recently interviewed him in his Afghan hideaway. Osama bin Laden had effectively declared war on the United States by issuing a fatwah. A fatwah is a declaration of Islamic orders, in this case for a crusade or holy war. In so doing, he drew no distinction between the U.S. military and American civilians. Other reporting showed President Clinton vowing revenge. From my perspective, the timing of the news reports was pure serendipity. Everything reinforced what I had told the crew on the 1MC. I was concerned that at least some members of the crew might harbor misgivings about the morality of our mission. That concern proved to be unfounded and I think that the video and reporting were part of the reason why.

As before, when we left the Persian Gulf and the confined waters of the Gulf of Oman and entered the North Arabian Sea, the weather was much cooler with highs in the mid to low 90s, a southwest breeze and higher seas. The area we had chosen to wait to approach our launch basket was out of the major shipping lanes and far enough from the coast of Pakistan that we encountered no shipping or the Pakistani maritime patrol aircraft. They were otherwise occupied keeping an eye on *MILIUS* and *SHILOH* and presumably unaware of *COWPENS*, *ELLIOTT*, and the submerged *COLUMBUS*.

5th Fleet cancelled the Tomahawk training exercise which had been scheduled to occur on August 19th. We thought perhaps our National Command Authority had decided against the strike for any of a number of reasons. It was also possible that intelligence indicated that our target was not at the training camp or that some additional targeting was required. As I was the senior CO, *COWPENS* had been designated Local Area Launch Controller by CTF 50, who was still in the Gulf aboard *LINCOLN*. In the event of a communications failure between CTF 50 and the shooters in the North Arabian Sea, I would be responsible for executing the launch plan for all five ships assigned the Afghan targets. We had trained for this and I was confident that the Strike Team could hack it. Our missions would not be backed up by another ship. These targets were so far inland that only the Tomahawk Block III missile could reach them. With limited numbers of Block IIIs in theater and a large number of aimpoints, some missions would not have a backup loaded on another ship. The idea is to achieve a specific time-on-top of the target so if one ship has an internal failure or a missile failure, the backup shooter has to be ready to quickly fire a backup missile to achieve the same end result.

The Tomahawk missile is a unique weapons system. When a ship deploys with Tomahawk missiles, the missiles sit stupid in the MK 41 launchers. A ship deploying to the Persian Gulf will sail with a package of data transport devices (DTD's) loaded with pre-planned missions for the Gulf. These missions are planned at two facilities in the United States called Cruise Missile Support Activities, or CMSA's. One is in Norfolk, Virginia and generally supports the European Command and the Central Command and the other is at Camp Smith, in Honolulu, Hawaii and supports the Pacific Command and the Central Command.

Mission planners at the CMSA are given a list of targets and aimpoints and are charged with planning a mission for one Tomahawk missile to go from a point at sea to the aimpoint. They did this using a computer system and mensurated satellite imagery (mensuration is geometry applied to the computation of lengths, areas, or volumes from given dimensions or angles) to guide the missile from the first pre-planned waypoint at sea to the aimpoint, or target. Using the imagery, they identify landmarks on the ground to help the missile navigate and also to avoid running into mountains, radio towers, tall buildings and other obstructions before reaching the target. The firing ship's responsibility is to get the missile from its firing position to the first pre-planned waypoint without also hitting oil rigs, other ships, or other obstructions. The firing ship is also responsible for figuring out when to shoot to achieve the desired time-on-top. New missions can be received after the ship sails via regular communications paths under a system called Mission Data Updates (MDUs). MDUs are loaded electronically into the DTDs, which, in turn, load a specific mission plan into a specific missile. Once loaded via the DTD, each missile sits in the launcher with a specific point on the face of the earth as its target, waiting for the signal to launch.

All of the missions for this strike near the town of Khowst, Afghanistan had to be loaded via MDU because they were not in the standard 5th Fleet package. Nobody had planned for launching Tomahawks into Afghanistan. On this deployment had I been told that I would be firing Tomahawk missiles and asked to guess where, I would have been hard-pressed to come up with Afghanistan. Iraq or Iran, yes, perhaps Syria or even Sudan or Somalia. Maybe even

North Korea if some crisis erupted there, but Afghanistan would be way down the list.

By the 19th, we had received all the MDUs for this strike. *COWPENS* was carrying only ten Block III missiles and would fire all ten. Altogether, 57 missiles were to be fired into the terrorist camp. Because of the process, we had no way of knowing precisely what our targets were. The ship's job was to get the missiles to the pre-planned waypoint on time and without colliding with each other on the way, after that, the CMSA planned flight paths would take over and deliver the missiles on time to their individual targets.

At 4:30 PM, August 19th, we received a message from Commander 5th Fleet telling us to set Weapons Posture One for Tomahawk. This required that we roll all the Tomahawk canister Safe/Enable switches in the magazines to the enable position. Because Tomahawk is a deliberate attack weapon, ships don't routinely sail around with the canisters enabled for safety reasons. Unlike, for example, the SM2 surface to air missiles, which must always be ready to fire in an environment like the Persian Gulf, there will always be time to go through these steps before a Tomahawk is launched. Setting Weapons Posture One for Tomahawk suggested that the action might occur sooner rather than later. We had not yet received a Launch Sequence Plan so did not know exactly when the strike was to take place.

At about 7:30 the evening of August 19th, the Launch Sequence Plan came in. Time-on-top of the target was set for 9:30 PM local Afghanistan time, August 20th. We calculated a two hour 20-minute time of flight for the missiles which meant we needed to be in position and ready to shoot in about 24 hours.

I again picked up the 1MC and told the crew the timeline. I had promised to keep them informed, and I didn't want people staying up all night so they wouldn't miss something. There was palpable electricity in the air; understandably so. The ship was about to go into combat and launch an attack on a declared enemy of the United States.

At 6:00 AM August 20, 1998, I awoke to a musical medley at reveille. We were in a remote section of the North Arabian Sea, out of the shipping lanes, so I had slept well during the night. That morning I was treated to the theme music from the movie *Apocalypse Now,* followed by *We Will Rock You* by the group Queen.

At 9:30, we briefed the launch plan in the wardroom. I agreed to let personnel without specific firing or ship control stations watch from the O-3 level amidships and O-4 level CIWS decks. We also decided to launch Saberhawk to get some video and pictures of the launch. The overall plan from CTF 50 was for *COWPENS* to take tactical control of *SHILOH, ELLIOT* and *MILIUS* upon completion of the launch and proceed to a rendezvous position off the coast of Oman. *COLUMBUS* would launch submerged and remain so, and having launched then slink off to wherever submarines go when they don't want to be found. We put out a message to the three surface ships assigning them 4-Whiskey grid sectors centered on the rendezvous point. A 4-Whiskey grid is a simple method of assigning ships an area within which to operate freely when they don't need to be gathered close together for mutual support.

The ballet was to play out in a manner which would not alert the Pakistanis that something was about to happen. So far, *COWPENS* and *ELLIOT* had remained undetected far to the south. *COLUMBUS* was submerged and undetected although we knew her location from the Launch Sequence Plan. *SHILOH* was 40 miles south of the western coast of Pakistan in her Pony Express location. *MILIUS* was 30 miles south of Karachi, in her Pony Express position. The Pakistanis had locating information on *SHILOH* and *MILIUS*, but they had been there for two weeks so aroused no additional suspicion. Pakistani Atlantique ATL2 maritime patrol aircraft had been making daily reconnaissance flights on the Pony Express ships and *MILIUS* had been visited a time or two by Pakistani Navy units out of Karachi. All of the Pakistani naval and air activity had been during daylight (they generally didn't operate at night) so the plan was for *SHILOH* and *MILIUS* to head south to their launch positions after sunset.

Don McNeil, who had been the TAO on watch the night before during the 2000–0200 watch, reported that we had picked up a U.S. military aircraft IFF signal squawking a code indicating a 4-star officer was aboard. The aircraft had originated in the vicinity of Oman and appeared headed to Pakistan. We were to find out later that the plane carried Vice Chairman of the Joint Chiefs of Staff, Air Force General Joe Ralston, sent on a secret mission to alert the Pakistanis to the upcoming strike. We would be violating Pakistani airspace with our missiles and it would not do to have Pakistan mistakenly think it was under attack by American ships. CTF 50 had issued guidance on what to say over the bridge-to-bridge radio if Pakistani naval units approached or questioned us before or during the launch. Our reply was to the effect that we were operating in international waters and meant no harm to the people or country of Pakistan.

To conceal the movement of the firing ships from Pakistani surveillance, *COWPENS* and *ELLIOT* would remain in total EMCON and move north to the launch positions south of the Pakistani coast so as to arrive no more than two hours before launch. *SHILOH* and *MILIUS* would remain openly operating in their Pony Express positions until darkness when the last Pakistani surveillance flight would have returned to base. At the appropriate time, they would set total EMCON and move to their assigned launch points. When everyone was in position, we would have five ships more or less in a line 60 miles south of the Pakistani coast and spaced about 20 miles apart. From west to east would be *COLUMBUS, SHILOH, COWPENS, ELLIOT,* and *MILIUS*.

At 11:55 we received word from CTF 50 that the go/no-go decision would come at 4:00 PM local. That would be 8:00 AM local in Washington, D.C. and suggested that perhaps there was some last-minute hand-wringing over the strike. Certainly, any intelligence suggesting that Osama bin Laden was not at the camp would cause a delay. The intelligence indicated, however, that he was there, and that a meeting was taking place so that some key figures in the terrorist world might be there with him.

At 12:15 PM we received our Indigo Firing Message and set Condition II Strike. At 3:15 PM we received the first message which attached a name to the operation: INFINITE REACH.

4:00 PM came and went with no word as to a go/no-go decision. We did have the Indigo message which authorizes firing, but a call from Rear Admiral Putnam saying, "It's a go." would have been nice. Despite being the senior officer and ostensibly in charge of the firing ships, I resisted the urge to call Admiral Putnam on the secure satellite radio and ask questions; our orders to shoot on time had not been countermanded.

The first missile would be away at 7:10 PM, after dark in that part of the world. At 5:10 PM we began to spin-up the missiles, meaning warm-up and circuit checks to ensure they were ready. We positioned the ship such that we would enter the launch basket precisely on time for the 7:10 PM launch. Despite the potential for distraction, and calamity in the event of an emergency, we launched Saberhawk 76 at 6:40 PM and positioned her forward of the bow with a movie camera to capture the launch. The missiles would come out of the MK 41 VLS and head off the starboard side, drop their boosters about four miles from the ship, kick in their turbo-jet engines, drop down to a cruise altitude of about 500 feet, and head for the first pre-planned waypoint. The helicopter would be safe hovering forward of the bow. The missile launch sequencing and routing were designed to ensure no fratricide from the missiles running into each other since they all had the same pre-planned waypoint, yet allow them to all arrive at their assigned targets on time. The real risk I was taking was if the helicopter developed a mechanical problem and had to be recovered at precisely the wrong time. We couldn't fire missiles while recovering the helo. I got away with it and we had some great footage but had it gone wrong I would have been in real trouble, especially since no ship had been assigned to back up our shots.

At 7:08 PM, sitting in the Captain's Chair in CIC, I rolled the Firing Inhibit Switch (FIS) key to allow the launch. Over the intercom circuit, I announced, "FIS is green." This enabled the entire system and turned responsibility for executing the launch plan over to the Strike Team. Precisely at 7:10 PM we began the launch sequence, which went flawlessly. From first to last missile was about 20 minutes. Some things can go wrong during a Tomahawk launch which is not the fault of the crew. Missiles can fail to function properly and fall harmlessly into the ocean. Things can go wrong during, in this case, the two-plus hour flight to target. If the planners at the Cruise Missile Support Activity haven't done their job well, the missile can fly into a mountain or some other obstruction; Khowst is in an especially mountainous area near the border with Pakistan. I later learned that all ten of COWPENS' missiles reached their intended targets. At least one missile of the 57 failed in flight and crashed in a remote area of Pakistan.

Most of the crew not on watch gathered on the O-3 level "weight deck" where the free weights were stowed, or on the O-4 level CIWS deck. They got quite a show as our ten missiles were launched. They could also see the glow of flame from the missiles launched by SHILOH and ELLIOTT 20 miles away to our east and west. From CIC, I watched the launch on our black and white TV cameras and heard the WHOOOSH as they left the launcher. In COWPENS, the bridge was responsible for reporting a successful transition from boost phase to cruise flight with the code words "Happy Trails." More of the cow theme at work.

Mike Phillips and the helicopter crew had the best seats in the house and they captured some great footage. Thankfully nothing went wrong and as soon as the launch was complete we landed them and started our move to the west. Immediately after all ships had launched their missiles, COWPENS took tactical command of the surface ships and directed everybody to their pre-assigned 4-Whiskey Grid positions at 25 knots, while maintaining total EMCON.

We raced through the night to the 4-Whiskey Grid positions which were about 200 nautical miles away to the southwest, off the coast of Oman. The position had been chosen to be away from the launch point, but not so far that if there were to be a re-attack, we'd be close enough to get back. Although *COWPENS* was out of Block III missiles and, therefore, unable to re-attack the target, a couple of the other ships, notably *SHILOH*, had been loaded out with more Block III's and had rounds remaining.

We tuned in the BBC around 11:00 PM and heard the initial reports of the strikes into Sudan and Afghanistan and heard President Clinton addressing the nation and explaining why the attacks were conducted. The camp in Afghanistan was identified as the Zhawar Kili al-Badr Terrorist Camp—I wondered if they had a sign out front.

The next day, the Paks found us with their Atlantique maritime patrol aircraft despite our maintaining radio and radar silence. No big deal really, but the plan had been to remain undetected so that information such as numbers and names of the firing ships would not become public knowledge. It was pretty easy for the Pakistanis to find us given that they had watched 57 missiles fly across their coast and could figure out where they came from. All they had to do was expand the search from that point.

We also learned that there had been a near simultaneous Tomahawk strike on a suspected terrorist-associated chemical weapons facility in Sudan by *BRISCOE* and *HAYLER*. When that attack was later determined to have been based on poor intelligence and probably not an appropriate target, I was glad that *COWPENS* had been assigned the Afghanistan targets. The firing ships cannot be faulted for decisions made at much higher levels. Nevertheless, it was more satisfying to know that Osama bin Laden had been our target.

After it was all over, we cleaned up the burn marks on the launchers and congratulated ourselves on a job well done although we had no idea yet of the results of the attack. We would eventually get a look at satellite imagery of the target area or there would be intelligence reporting, based on human intelligence, as to what had happened in Khowst. We did know that we had made history as the first surface ships and submarine to attack a land-locked country. Later press reporting revealed that much of the world did not know that it had been Tomahawk missiles conducting the attack. There was erroneous reporting about stealth bombers, carrier-based aircraft, or U.S. Special Forces raiding the camp.

One year later, when I was attending the CAPSTONE course for new flag officers in Washington, D.C., I received a briefing on our strike at CIA Headquarters in Langley, Virginia. In this briefing, we were told that based on the best intelligence available, the strike had been correctly planned for a time that Osama bin Laden was hosting a meeting of key Al Qaeda leaders at the camp. For reasons unknown, but most likely a tip-off from somewhere in the Pakistani ISID, bin Laden, and his key operatives slipped away before the missiles arrived—possibly even while they were in flight. There were, nevertheless, still people at the camp and we did cause casualties, but we'll never know exactly who and whether any important Al Qaeda figures were among the dead. I am convinced that General Ralston's visit to Islamabad the day prior, while well intentioned, blew the cover on the operation and ISID individuals sympathetic to Al Qaeda and the Taliban tipped off bin Laden, enabling his escape.

In 1998, Tomahawk strikes were relatively unusual. Because this was a terrorist target, there was resistance to naming the ships that had conducted the attacks for fear of retaliation, including on family members in homeports. The firing ships were directed not to send out any press releases or in any way publicize our role in the attack. I sent a message back to Admiral Bowler in San Diego and asked him to contact Iris if there were elevated threat warnings somehow related to the strike. The *San Diego Union Tribune* story had featured Iris as well as me so her recognition factor was higher than normal for the wife of a cruiser CO. There was a precedent for this. In 1988, after the cruiser *USS VINCENNES (CG-49)* accidentally shot down an Iranian Airbus in the Persian Gulf, the Captain's wife was attacked by a pipe bomb placed in her private automobile in San Diego. No one was ever caught and it could not be conclusively proven to be in retaliation for the Airbus incident, but that was the theory.

I saw the satellite photography battle damage assessment pictures from our strike at 5th Fleet Headquarters in Bahrain during a later port visit that summer of 1998. I knew that our targets were mostly small wooden structures and huts. In later years, particularly after 9/11, Operation INFINITE REACH was roundly criticized as yet another ineffective response to terrorism by the Clinton administration. Happening as it did during the Monica Lewinsky affair, it was also criticized as a diversion to draw attention away from the President's personal problems. A *Wag the Dog* kind of deal as in the Dustin Hoffman movie. The fact that $57 million dollars' worth of cruise missiles was expended against a bunch of wooden huts and canvas tents in the middle of nowhere in Afghanistan was also subject to criticism.

I have often reflected on that criticism but have never let it bother me. On *COWPENS,* we did what our nation asked us to do. It is not for the crew of the ship to second guess the decisions made at the highest levels of our government, or to feel regret that, for reasons beyond our control, the operation did not achieve its intent. We put our missiles on target, on time. Knowing what I know today, I don't believe the strike was a presidential diversion from domestic difficulties. We apparently came within hours or even minutes of taking out bin Laden and perhaps other key players, like Khalid Sheik Mohammed, who later attacked us on 9/11. I have often wondered how history might have changed had we, in fact, been successful on August 20, 1998.

CHAPTER 24

Homeward Bound

We awoke the morning of August 21st to a changed world in the Persian Gulf region. Because of the strike and the potential for retaliatory terrorist attacks, U.S. Central Command raised the threat level throughout the region and 5th Fleet cancelled all currently scheduled port visits for Navy ships. For those based ashore, as in Bahrain, liberty off base was curtailed and heightened security was evident at the gates and other points. I thought that we might not set foot on land until we arrived in Australia in October.

When we arrived at our loiter point in the 4-Whiskey grid I inquired as to intentions at CTF-50. Guidance was to remain covert (this was before the Pakistani Atlantique flew by) and that the plan was to send *COWPENS* and *MILIUS* through Hormuz one night and *SHILOH* and *ELLIOTT* the next. Once inside the Gulf, *COWPENS* was to pick up escort duties for *ABRAHAM LINCOLN* and *MILIUS* was to escort the big deck amphibious ship, *USS ESSEX (LHD-2)*. 5th Fleet was working on a plan to re-load Tomahawk missiles for the firing ships. The most likely option was in Bahrain after the missiles were flown into theater by Air Force C-5A heavy lift aircraft. In the meantime, we were hearing that Saddam Hussein was once again acting up in Iraq by making threatening gestures towards Kuwait and Saudi Arabia. Some guys never learn.

The overall reaction of the crew to the strike had been very positive, although at that time we had no idea of the results. I was told by Master Chief Lucas that one or two crewmembers had expressed misgivings about what we had done. That was probably to be expected and it would likely get worse once reports began to emerge that innocent civilians had been killed or injured; whether true or fabricated. There was bound to be some collateral damage and we heard that one or two missiles did not make it to the target. I took every opportunity when addressing the crew to emphasize that we were now engaged in a new kind of warfare against an enemy that knows no borders, has no standing military or government, and does not hesitate to kill innocent civilians. We learned that all military facilities back in the U.S., in Europe, and in Asia had been put on a heightened state of anti-terrorist alert. We were receiving but not sending emails, the security ban was still in place, and I had heard from Iris and knew that she knew we were undoubtedly involved. She had already thought through the possible implications for her.

At around 5:00 PM I called CTF-50 again. I was in tactical command of four ships and everybody was curious about the next move. CTF-50 Ops, Captain Dave Ziemba said we should plan to remain in the North Arabian Sea for "a few more days" and that we might wait for *HAYLER* to arrive from the Red Sea and join our group. I knew *HAYLER* was in Djibouti refueling so that translated to another three or four days hanging out in the North Arabian Sea. Because they were leaving four of the most capable ships outside the Gulf, I thought that a re-strike must be under consideration.

During this time, we began to hear reporting that bin Laden may not have been at the camp when the missiles arrived and that there were collateral casualties. I thought the collateral damage was to be expected, but was disappointed to hear that the primary target may have escaped. I reflected on whether or not I, and the ship, had participated in the killing of innocent people while executing our mission. In all likelihood if the Zhawar Kili al-Badr Camp was an established facility, there would have been family members living there. There was no way to know so I put it out of my mind. The purpose of a forward deployed Navy is to be ready to act in the national interest and that is what we had done—our duty.

An hour and a half after my conversation with CTF-50, we were directed to take *MILIUS* and head for the Strait of Hormuz, leaving *ELLIOTT* behind under the tactical command of Captain

Steve Bush in *SHILOH*. Clearly CENTCOM and 5ᵗʰ Fleet were in a state of flux, trying to figure out what next after the strike. Off we went with a mid-morning August 22ⁿᵈ transit of Hormuz, an underway replenishment with *CAMDEN* and then a rendezvous with *LINCOLN* for escort duties next on the schedule. We joined up with *LINCOLN* on the 23ʳᵈ, relieved her shotgun, *USS JARRETT (FFG-33)*, and chased her around until 2:00 AM on the 24ᵗʰ when we got word to turn shotgun back over to *JARRETT* and close to within 30 miles of Bahrain to receive a visit by Vice Admiral Willy Moore, Commander 5ᵗʰ Fleet.

Arriving in the vicinity of the Bahrain Bell, which marks the beginning of the roughly 30-mile-long channel into Mina Sulman, Bahrain, we received the "Desert Duck" helo with Admiral Moore and assembled the crew on the fo'csle so that he could address them. He did a great job, pumping them up for the good job they had done on the Tomahawk strike and making some really cogent points. He told them how much confidence the President had in them by going on television and addressing the nation before he knew the results of the attack. He talked about the new era of warfare that the United States was entering, and emphasized that we were, in fact, at war, something I had been telling them as well. Finally, he said port visits were off the schedule for an indeterminate time for security reasons and I don't think anybody was either surprised or unhappy. With that done we headed back to the carrier operating area to resume shotgun duties for *LINCOLN*.

On the 25ᵗʰ, just before lunch, we received a distress call from a Chevron tanker, the *M/V SAMUEL GINN*. The ship's master had suffered an apparent heart attack and the First Mate was on the bridge-to-bridge radio requesting assistance. I received permission from CTF-50 to head towards *SAMUEL GINN* to render assistance and off we went at 30 knots. We began moving Saberhawk 76 out of the hangar to possibly pick the master up and fly him to a hospital in Bahrain, but *LINCOLN* had a helicopter already airborne which we vectored to the tanker. *LINCOLN*'s helo arrived overhead but could not find a safe place to land. The tanker had no litter for hoisting the master up to the helo and the helicopter, already airborne when the call came, had no litter on board.

Once again we called on Doc Pietrusza, had *LINCOLN'*s helicopter come to us, and loaded the chief into the helo along with a litter. By now we had joined up on *SAMUEL GINN* and were riding alongside watching as Chief Pietrusza was lowered to the deck. By the time he got to him, the master was dead. The crew told him they had stopped administering CPR about ten minutes earlier. Chief Pietrusza radioed back via walkie-talkie that the master had stopped breathing and his eyes were fixed and dilated.

We discussed the situation with CTF-50 and it was agreed that *LINCOLN'*s helo would take the body to *LINCOLN*, where a real doctor could examine him and decide what next. The First Mate radioed us and said the master's wife was aboard, not uncommon on these big merchant ships, and she wanted to accompany the body. I relayed this to CTF-50, got the OK, and a second *LINCOLN* helo was dispatched to pick her up and fly her to the carrier. About an hour after all this, CTF-50 radioed me, said the master was indeed dead, and asked me to notify *SAMUEL GINN*, which I did. While all this was going on, the 5th Fleet staff was in contact with the shipping company in San Francisco and coordinating disposition of the body. We headed back to *LINCOLN* and later that afternoon got Chief Pietrusza back. Chief Pietrusza had had an interesting cruise; between heart attacks, torsioned testicles, scratched eyes, and the assorted crushed fingers and banged heads, he'd been busy.

That night while we were escorting *LINCOLN*, a freak storm blew in off the coast of Iran which was unlike anything I had seen at sea. We had just finished the nightly operations and intelligence brief in the wardroom around 6:30, which included a benign weather brief by Aerographer's Mate First Class Williams, when I took a call from the OOD reporting what looked like a huge sandstorm on radar coming off the coast of Iran. I went to the bridge and looked at the SPA-25 radar repeater. The whole northeast quadrant of the scope was whited out with the whited out portion moving southeast towards *COWPENS* and *LINCOLN* at about 40 knots. The weather at our position was calm and clear. From the way it painted on radar I too thought that it was a sandstorm.

LINCOLN was conducting flight operations and had a number of aircraft in the air so we called them and reported what we were seeing. The wind began to freshen and the sea began to develop whitecaps, and then it hit like a hurricane. It was not a sandstorm but a violent front with heavy rain, lightning, and winds gusting to 70 knots. We brought everyone inside the skin of the ship and called *LINCOLN*, five miles downwind, and warned them of the violence of the storm. The wind ripped the bridge wing awnings away and bent the stanchions.

LINCOLN began recovering aircraft as we raced into planeguard station a thousand yards astern. The rain, lightning and wind were unlike anything I had seen. *LINCOLN* had to "bingo" six jets into Kuwait and one of their helos had to recover on *MILIUS* to refuel and ride out the storm. The violence lasted about an hour but the lightning show went on until 11:00. We stayed in planeguard until all the aircraft that had landed in Kuwait returned to the ship along with the helo from *MILIUS*. Years later when I was living in the Washington, DC area, a storm front moved through the area with hurricane force winds. The local weather reporters called it a derecho. I had never heard of a derecho, which is a straight line (derecho is Spanish for straight) windstorm associated with a fast moving band of severe thunderstorms. As I reflect back on that night in the Persian Gulf, I think that what we experienced was a derecho.

Because of the restrictions on port visits, 5th Fleet and CTF-50 found themselves with more ships available for MIO operations than they needed and began looking for creative ways to give the ships some downtime without going into port. I called Dave Ziemba on the secure satellite radio and told him that I could use a couple of days at anchor to do some repairs to one of the steering units and to allow new Chief Engineer Jeff Bernasconi to inspect the reduction gears which had indications of gasket particles showing up in the strainers. Jeff also needed to change out the foam on the engine intakes which had become clogged with sand, like a car air filter. Dave arranged for *MILIUS* to pick up *LINCOLN* escort duties and I was free to do whatever I wanted.

We looked at the charts and decided to anchor the ship in 140 feet of water in a position north of the Cyrus Oilfield and south of the Ardeshir Oilfield which would put us outside the main shipping lanes. We did this on August 29th and although we had to continue flying the helicopters for routine surveillance, we were looking forward to two days of relative quiet and a chance to do some maintenance that couldn't be done while racing around chasing the carrier.

Swim call was in order, and that afternoon we put the RHIB in the water with a gunner for shark patrol and let the crew not on watch go back to the fantail and swim. We rigged the pilot ladder for climbing out of the water and everybody had a great time, including me. I did a few watermelons off the starboard side bitts and enjoyed the swim in the calm, warm waters of the Gulf. Swim call is one of those high risk, high reward events. There is always the chance that someone will get hurt, and in waters like the Persian Gulf there are unfriendly creatures, notably sharks and sea snakes. Sharks are rarely seen at sea, and I had never seen one in the Persian Gulf. Sea snakes, on the other hand, were quite common and often seen from the bridge swimming just below the surface. Sea snakes are air breathers, without gills, so they have to come to the surface to take a gulp of air, making them easy to spot. Most of those I've seen in the Gulf are ugly, yellow bellied, with brown markings and three to five feet long. They are venomous with the poison being similar to that of cobras, which makes them very dangerous if provoked to bite.

While we were swimming on the starboard side of the ship, we allowed the fisherman to fish off of the port side fantail. We realized that this might not have been the best decision when Chief Gunners Mate McDonald pulled up a mackerel that had been neatly sliced in half while on the hook by something bigger with clearly very sharp teeth; perhaps a barracuda, also found in those waters.

Adjusting the schedule, we set up swim call hours and fishing hours which did not overlap.

Departing our anchorage on the 31st of August, we followed that up with five days of routine MIO operations in the northern Gulf in an area designated MA-3 East. The weather was extremely hot and Petty Officer Williams reported apparent temperatures of 133 degrees and 136 degrees on successive days. 136 degrees was as high as his scale went. There was little excitement during this period, as we conducted routine boardings on five 986 ships as well as health and comfort inspections on the vessels being held for disposition. One of them, a gasoil dhow, had pumped all 28,000 gallons of his gasoil cargo into the ocean during the night. When Ensign Al Licup and his boarding team questioned the master about it, he claimed the owner had radioed him and directed that he do it. There is a theory that smugglers who get caught and held for disposition have figured out that if they manufacture an oil leak, the environmentally conscious Americans will let them go home to get it fixed rather than pollute the ocean. I think they were on to something because that was not an unusual occurrence.

Leaving MIO on September 4th, we headed south to rendezvous with *LINCOLN* for more shotgun duties. I had a young petty officer, an Engineman Third Class named Coker, who was in the process of applying for a Navy ROTC scholarship and thought that if he received a commission he might like to be a Navy pilot. I radioed Captain Tom Kilcline, the Carrier Air Wing 14 commander, or CAG, in *LINCOLN*, and arranged for Petty Officer Coker to spend a day on the carrier to learn about life as a naval aviator. Tom was an F-14 pilot and whenever he was up flying and *COWPENS* was close by he'd call us up, request a fly-by, and go screaming by the bridge. I could look down into the cockpit from the 65-foot-high bridge wing while giving him the finger, which he happily returned.

We learned a little later that 5th Fleet had decided that it was now safe to let the ships into port and that we would be going to Bahrain on September 17th. It had been almost a month since the Tomahawk strike and nothing had happened by way of retaliation. We were also getting within striking distance of completing our time in the Gulf. The schedule called for us to transit Hormuz for the last time the night of October 9th and head for Australia. Our first port visit would be in Darwin in the Northern Territory on October 22nd followed by a port visit in Townsville on the east coast, inside the Great Barrier Reef.

LINCOLN had loaned us a photographer's mate to take pictures for the cruise book, including portraits of all the new people who had arrived since we departed San Diego. We had the promotion ceremony for our eight new chiefs on September 16th and after refueling from *USNS YUKON (T-AO-202)*, we cut some Flank 3 figure eights in the ocean with the photographer up in Saberhawk 73 taking pictures to commemorate the new chiefs. He took a great shot of the ship pulling away from *YUKON* at Flank 3 which ended up on the cover of the Pentagon's *Joint Force Quarterly* magazine about two years later.

We had had an unfortunate incident while inport Bahrain wherein several of the Engineering Department petty officers had drunk too much at the club and created a disturbance in the berthing compartment when they got back to the ship. When they were confronted by sober, senior petty officers and told to shut up and hit the rack, one of them, a second class Gas Turbine Specialist, had been disrespectful and took a swing at one of the first class petty officers. A few days later we held Captain's Mast and although the whole story was convoluted and confused, with some unclear memories, it was clear that this petty officer had been the main antagonist. I knew this particular petty officer; he had never been in trouble before and was a good, hard worker. His divisional and departmental chain of command attested to his good performance and explained his actions as being the result of too much alcohol, which it clearly was. But, you can't allow fights among the crew and junior petty officers being disrespectful to senior petty officers who are acting responsibly, so I threw the book at him: busted him to petty officer third class, restricted him to the ship for 45 days and assigned extra duty for 45 days. The Captain has to send a signal to the crew in situations like this one, and I did.

When the unpleasant Captain's Mast was over, I went back to my cabin and thought about it some more. This petty officer had 14 years of honorable service, was married, and had four children. The restriction and extra duty meant no liberty before we hit Hawaii on the way home and working extra hours in the evening on whatever crummy detail the Chief Master-at-Arms came up with after consulting with his fellow chiefs. He could survive all that. The bust, however, was going to cost him $510 a month. I was worried about the impact on his family in San Diego. Moreover, if he didn't get promoted again to petty officer second class in the next year, he was facing the possibility of separation from the Navy before he had earned his retirement benefits because of something called High Year Tenure.

I called the XO, Chief Personnelman Herbert Daugherty, and Disbursing Clerk Bernard Posey up to my cabin and told them that nothing was to leave the ship. No paperwork on the bust and no adjustment to his pay. I swore the three of them to secrecy. Under the rules, I had four months to re-instate a sailor to his previous paygrade on my own authority and I planned to do it before we returned to San Diego. The sailor would not realize that his pay was not being cut because almost all of it was being direct deposited at home and he was receiving a very small amount on the ship which would not be affected. I didn't want the individual to know so that he would think the worst had happened.

The next day I called him up to my cabin and told him to trust me; that I would take care of him. He was distraught over the whole situation and very shaken. He had not yet written his wife or emailed her and told her what had happened and that too, was heavy on his mind. I didn't let on; if he told his wife, so be it. In some ways that would be part of the punishment. Over the next few weeks I made a point of talking to Chief David Yeager, the Chief Master-at-Arms, to see how this sailor was doing on the extra duty assignments. Chief Yeager said he "was working his ass off" and had a good attitude. That just reinforced my decision.

Our final four-day visit in Bahrain before departing the Gulf and heading for San Diego via Australia and Hawaii was to be the

4th to the 8th of October. We held a PACMEF 98-2 party at the club with *MILIUS* and *THACH*. Each ship had their ensigns put on a skit which poked fun at the other ships and at operations in the Persian Gulf in general. As the "Commander" of PACMEF 98-2, I took a few good natured shots from *THACH* and *MILIUS*.

We were scheduled to leave on the 8th and then rendezvous with *LINCOLN* for an INFINTE REACH awards ceremony aboard the carrier where selected members of the crew of each firing ship would get a medal pinned on by Secretary of Defense William Cohen. Even though, as far as we knew, we hadn't killed Osama bin Laden, the INFINITE REACH Tomahawk strike was considered a success because the ships had all performed well and we had struck back at those who planned and executed the African embassy bombings. Admiral Putnam's staff had selected the individuals from each ship who were to fly to the carrier for the ceremony, a mixture of officers and enlisted from various elements of the Strike Team.

Underway from Bahrain on the 8th of October with spirits high because we were leaving the Gulf, we rendezvoused with *LINCOLN* on the 9th and transferred our INFINITE REACH awardees to the carrier where Secretary Cohen pinned medals on Lieutenant Curt Goodnight, Ensign Adam Jackson, Fire Controlman First Class Murphy, Gunner's Mate First Class Castillo, and Fire Controlman Third Class Wells. We sent *THACH* on ahead through Hormuz since she was not involved in the strike. Once the awardees were back on board, I put *MILIUS* in station astern and raced through Hormuz around midnight to catch up to *THACH* and rendezvous with *YUKON* to top everyone off on fuel.

From the Strait of Hormuz to the Australian port of Darwin is about 6,600 miles. We had almost two weeks of steaming across the Indian Ocean ahead of us before seeing land again. A tropical disturbance we had been watching generated some rough weather on the 12th of October which had the ship taking some 30 degree rolls. Half the crew had come down with sea sickness and were barely functioning so we went ahead and declared holiday routine and let everybody who wasn't on watch hit the rack. As it turned out, the day before, the First Class Petty Officers had held their fund raising raffle for "Captain for a Day" and Fireman Madison, one of our young gas turbine technicians from Main Propulsion Division, had won and declared holiday routine as one of his first orders. He was also going to get to sleep in my inport cabin that night and be served dinner in the cabin by the wardroom mess attendants. He had designated steak and lobster as the meal for the day on the mess decks. With everybody sick, steak and lobster were going to be a waste. I thought about having the OOD's call him in the inport cabin every 15 minutes throughout the night and report something but that would have been mean. Madison later appeared before me at Captain's Mast for disobeying an order and showing disrespect to a senior petty officer. Bet he wished he was Captain for a Day that day! I placed him on restriction and extra duty but made sure he was finished before his father boarded the ship in Hawaii for the Tiger Cruise.

Also on October 12th, we officially departed the 5th Fleet area of responsibility and entered 7th Fleet waters. I now officially resumed duties as the commander of Task Unit 75.9.3 responsible for *COWPENS, MILIUS* and *THACH. THACH* would soon be leaving us for a port visit in Bunbury, about 100 miles south of Perth on the west coast of Australia. She would then transit independently back to her homeport of Yokosuka, Japan.

We crossed the Equator on the 15th of October at 00 degrees north and 085.34 degrees' east longitude, and had the requisite crossing the line ceremony, complete with the arrival of Davey Jones in the person of Boatswain Mate Chief Daum and his Royal Party. We had some skits on the fo'csle which ranged from awful to hilarious and I was glad that nobody got out of line. Unlike my earlier crossings, this time there was no beauty contest. The skit contest was judged a tie between MP Division which did a funny skit about trying to fix a leaking valve, and the First Division "Dancers." Both women officers, Susan Randle and Laura Poleshinski, were slimy pollywogs and willingly participated with the rest.

The weather turned beautiful once we were near the Equator with flat, almost oily, calm seas. Tom Goodall and THACH had been detached earlier leaving only *COWPENS* and *MILIUS* in TU 75.9.3. The nights were spectacular with millions of stars visible. I often went to the bridge wing after taps and sat in my chair watching the sky. Shooting stars were quite common because the ambient light was so low, making them easy to spot. The seas were so calm that schools of dolphin were painting on the surface search radar miles away. On the afternoon of October 16th I saw something I had never before seen at sea. We were steaming along at 20 knots in a flat calm sea. I was out on the starboard conning platform which sits aft of the bridge and extends out beyond the bridge wing so that the conning officer can get a good look along the side of the ship when docking or undocking alongside a pier. As I looked forward of the bow, I saw a large, dark brown object in the water about 100 yards ahead and just to port. I ran through the Signal Shack to the port side just as we came abeam of it and saw a giant squid or octopus shooting away from the side of the ship and spewing out a big cloud of dark, chocolate brown ink. He looked like he was about as big as a washing machine. It was quite a sight. I initially thought it was a squid because the octopus is a bottom dweller living in relatively shallow water, whereas the giant squid roams the open ocean and deep waters. However, there is a species of octopi that swims in the open ocean and I don't think the squid squirts ink so it must have been a very large octopus.

We had some spectacular sunrises and sunsets as well with the clouds turning a thousand different shades of blue and gray, turning to pink and orange as the sun set. We often had 100 off duty sailors on deck watching and taking pictures. There were too many clouds for the Green Flash, but I was convinced that if we had a clear sunset we would see it. The Green Flash is an optical phenomenon, normally only seen at sea when there is a clear horizon with no clouds or haze. It appears as a green spot just above the sun or a green puff, lasting only a second, at the point where the sun has just set. In the light color spectrum, green is the last color that is visible to the human eye as the sun's rays curve over the horizon during sunset. Iris does not believe it is real, but I have seen it more than once.

On one of those beautiful days, I went up in Saberhawk 76 to re-enlist Boatswain Mate Second Class Studer. Studer was one of the boatswain mates on the flight quarters detail and since the helicopters had kept him up many nights manning flight quarters to land, refuel, and re-launch in the middle of the night, he thought it only fitting that he disrupt their day for a helicopter ride. While we were up we flew around the ship and the water was so clear that we could see completely under the hull, the sonar dome perfectly visible as the ship knifed through the calm seas.

I was up on the bridge around 4:30 the morning of October 22nd as we sailed through the Beagle Gulf to make the approach on Darwin Harbor. It was difficult to identify the lights as we approached this unfamiliar port in the dark and I was intensely involved in the safe navigation of the ship. As the pilot boat approached in daylight I saw Iris in the cockpit ready to board the ship with the pilot. We had planned on her meeting me in Darwin and I knew that she should have arrived the day before, but I didn't expect her to talk her way onto the pilot boat to come out and meet the ship. The Aussies are such great people though, that I really wasn't surprised. She clambered up the pilot ladder ahead of the pilot, came to the bridge and gave me a big hug and a kiss. She looked great in khaki pants and a San Diego Padres tee shirt. She then sat in my chair as we brought the ship in and tied up at the pier.

Then things got interesting. There are two naval piers in Darwin, each about 900 feet long, sitting end to end. The westernmost pier was occupied by two Australian *PERRY* class guided missile frigates, *HMAS NEWCASTLE (FFG-06)* and *HMAS CANBERRA (FFG-02)*. *COWPENS* and *MILIUS* were to tie up on the easternmost pier with *MILIUS* outboard *COWPENS*. *MILIUS* had tied up outboard *COWPENS* on previous occasions, but always with large Yokohama fenders between the two ships. As I stood on the starboard bridge wing and watched *MILIUS* enter the harbor, I looked down and saw three small fenders being moved into place by a little workboat.

"Where's the Yokohamas?" I asked the pilot.

"All we got are in use, Mate. Back there." Pointing at the two Australian frigates.

"Shit. XO, call Weps and tell him to get every fender we've got on the starboard side."

I then called Jim McManamon on bridge-to-bridge radio and told him there were no Yokohamas available to go between us and to get every fender he had ready to go. The *ARLEIGH BURKE* and *TICONDEROGA* class hulls do not line up well together because of the rounded, beamy, shape of the *ARLEIGH BURKE*'s and the fairly straight sides of the *TICONDEROGA* class.

Iris was now sitting in my starboard side bridge wing chair watching this little drama unfold.

Our guys scrambled around getting the fenders ready, tying some off in strategic locations, while others were carried at the ready by two or more sailors to position them at the last moment where it looked like they would do the most good. The same drill was underway on *MILIUS*.

As *MILIUS* crabbed into us with the help of a tug, Iris looked over the side, surveyed the situation, and said, "This isn't going to work."

Just what I needed: 26 years' experience, two ship commands, many years at sea, and my wife informs me that we're all screwed up.

But she was right. *MILIUS* made contact and we went skin-to-skin in about three places. There was no significant damage except when *MILIUS'* SLQ-32 antenna made contact with some railings on our O-3 Level. The railing broke and the fiberglass housing of the SLQ-32 sustained some damage.

Iris and I had a great visit together in Darwin although I had the usual official business associated with a foreign port visit. Iris had flown to Sydney, spent a day and night there before catching the long 2,000-mile flight north to Darwin. When I left Darwin on the 27th, she would fly to Townsville on the east coast and wait for us to arrive there. That first day in Darwin was busy with the obligatory official calls on local officials. In and around these official obligations, Iris and I managed a day on the Adelaide River Crocodile Tour where the crocs leap out of the water to grab chickens being dangled from poles as we cruised the river in a tourist boat. Swimming around Darwin was discouraged because of the salt water crocodiles and the "box stingers," a dangerously poisonous species of jellyfish. The pilot told me that they had pulled 68 salt water crocodiles out of Darwin Harbor that year, some 15 to 20 feet long. We bought some Australian wine and in the one evening that was completely free we took XO Terry Culton to dinner and then rendezvoused with the wardroom for some dancing and drinking at an Irish pub called Kitty O'Shea's. Rich Haidvogel led a boisterous group dance to *Kung Fu Fighting* by Carl Douglas. The dinner with Terry was at a restaurant on the other pier which featured the local delicacy the Australians called "bugs." When served, bugs look like lobster tails but if you saw them coming out of the water you would think they were giant ocean dwelling centipedes. It was best not to see them alive.

In preparing for the trip from Darwin to Townsville I had studied the charts and read the *Sailing Directions* for the transit of the Torres Strait which is the path north of Australia and south of Papua New Guinea connecting the Arafura Sea to the west with the Coral Sea to the east. At its narrowest, the Torres Strait is 93 miles wide. The challenge lies in the shallow water and many reefs and shoals. For a ship with a 30-foot draft like *COWPENS*, it was required that a Torres Strait Pilot be hired to guide the ship through because it was necessary to "ride the tides" as you went, in order to have enough water. At some points we would only have 6 feet of water under the sonar dome. I was more than happy to comply and Jim McManamon in *MILIUS* did the same.

I said goodbye to Iris the morning of the 27th, and welcomed our Strait Pilot on board as we departed Darwin Harbor, transited the Beagle Gulf and Clarence Strait and entered the Arafura Sea. The pilot was very friendly, no surprise there, and he offered to play tour guide during the trip by getting on the 1MC and describing the history of the area. These waters were explored by the legendary British Captain James Cook who mapped the lands and waters from Australia to Hawaii until his death at the hands of Hawaiian Islanders in 1779. Captain Bligh of *Mutiny on the Bounty* fame was another explorer some years later than Cook. The pilot also offered to guide us inside the Great Barrier Reef on our way south to Townsville. Once we were out into the Arafura Sea I detached *MILIUS* to proceed independently to her next port visit in Mackay, further south of Townsville on the east coast of Australia. I was sure Jim McManamon was happy to be on his own for a while. We would rejoin again in Hawaii.

On the 30th, after conducting a five-inch gun shoot in the Coral Sea to work out the kinks and show our Strait Pilot some ordnance, we conducted our transit of the Great Barrier Reef, entering through One and a Half Mile Pass, circumnavigating Lizard Island, and exiting via Cook's Passage. Because the Great Barrier Reef is an environmentally sensitive and protected area we had to ensure that absolutely nothing was discharged over the side while inside the reef.

That morning, testing me, the pilot asked, "Captain, would you like to cross the reef at high tide or low tide?"

"High tide I guess; looks like the water's deep enough either way."

"Wrong answer Mate, you want to go through at low tide, that way you can see the reefs on either side of the pass."

I really hadn't thought about it that way. But he was right; you could see the waves breaking on the reef on either side of the pass which made it easy to judge the best course to shoot through in the center.

At 4:30 AM on the 31st, we again crossed the Great Barrier Reef at Palm Passage and entered a long narrow channel into the harbor at Townsville. Again, Iris was there to meet me, having spent the night in a hotel in town, afraid to go out by herself, and dining on snacks purchased in the hotel lobby. She came aboard at a refueling pier and rode the ship as we moved to our final berth and backed into a slip barely longer than the ship.

While we were refueling, Terry Culton came to see me.

"Captain, So and So and So and So want to have a Wiccan ceremony aboard ship tonight, it's Halloween."

The two sailors were a Third Class Operations Specialist in the *COWPENS* crew and an Operations Specialist Seaman from *MILIUS* who I had taken aboard at Jim McManamon's request because he was in a relationship with one of Jim's female sailors. Jim wanted to break up this little romance. *MILIUS* had been fully modified for a mixed gender crew, unlike *COWPENS*.

"Hell no," I said.

But Terry was prepared and had brought the Chaplain's Manual with him.

"Chaps says we have to let them, it's one of the recognized religions."

"You're shittin' me!"

"No sir, see, right here."

"Son of a bitch. What the hell are they gonna do? I don't want 'em burning down the ship."

"Chaps will be there with them to supervise."

"Good grief, where?"

"In the Ship's Library."

I had to let the two Wiccans do whatever it is that Wiccans do on Halloween night. Just as the Navy had to provide the opportunity for Catholics, Protestants, Jews and Muslims to practice their faith at sea, we had to make accommodations for the Wiccans too.

During our visit in Townsville we took care of our official obligations, including a lunch in the wardroom for the mayor and local military dignitaries, and had time for some more Australian sightseeing. Iris and I went snorkeling inside the Great Barrier Reef and toured Magnetic Island, so named because it apparently had a "magnetic" effect on Captain Cook's compass when he explored the area in the 18th century. The island lies about five miles offshore of Townsville and is a major tourist attraction in the area. We had a nice dinner and said goodbye for another week and a half until she would again meet me in Hawaii with her good friend Kathy Danberg.

Iris and Kathy were going to ride *MILIUS* for the Tiger Cruise from Hawaii to San Diego. Although we were allowed to have mixed male and female Tigers aboard ship, the rules in 1998 specified that no spousal, fiancé, or boyfriend-girlfriend relationships were permitted in the same ship. Mothers, fathers, sisters, brothers and so forth were allowed, but no shacking up. Jim McManamon had very graciously agreed to let Iris and Kathy ride *MILIUS*, while I had invited son Chris, ensign, USN, and brother, Paul, to ride *COWPENS*.

By this time the crew fully expected to see Iris during *COWPENS* port visits. She had met the ship in Monterey twice, Seal Beach two or three times, Seattle, Cabo San Lucas, Singapore, Phuket, Darwin, Townsville, and would be there again in Pearl Harbor. In fact, when we had first pulled into Bahrain, one of the Operations Specialists serving as a bearing taker on the starboard bridge wing, Operations Specialist Third Class Lee Reinhart, had turned to me and said, "Captain, are you sure we're in the right place? I don't see Mrs. Sullivan."

When we left Townsville on November 4th, we were really finally headed home to San Diego via a four-day stop in Pearl Harbor to offload our remaining 23 Tomahawk Block II missiles; the ones without the range to reach Khowst, Afghanistan. Our missiles would be transferred to *USS OLDENDORF (DD-972)* who would be headed to the Persian Gulf within a few weeks. We would also embark about 80 "Tigers" for the transit to San Diego. *MILIUS* was to stay in Mackay an extra day and then follow us into Pearl Harbor the day after to offload her Tomahawks for transfer to yet another ship.

We had rough weather transiting the Coral Sea as we passed through the Great Barrier Reef and began the 5,000-mile journey to Hawaii. On the 6th we passed just north of the island of Guadalcanal in the Solomon Islands which was much larger than I had expected from reading my World War II history. We went by Savo Island and "Iron Bottom Sound" where another sea battle had taken place and looked north up "The Slot" where the Japanese Navy had sailed at night to bombard our Marines on Guadalcanal. It was another opportunity to impress upon the crew the history in these waters and the great traditions of the naval service.

With *MILIUS* no longer in company, I was still technically the Commander of Task Unit 75.9.3 and PACMEF 98-2, but we sailed alone. This allowed us to really relax the watchstanding requirements to let officers and crew get more rest and take care of routine administrative matters. I was sure that Jim McManamon would enjoy his nine days of independent steaming without the damn cruiser and its more senior CO 1,000 yards away and in tactical command. He'd depart Pearl with us for the transit to San Diego and return once again under my thumb.

The more relaxed pace also allowed us to knock out the qualification boards for our youngest officers and enlisted to earn their Surface Warfare Officer and Enlisted Surface Warfare Specialist pins. This was especially important because *COWPENS* was scheduled for a major overhaul period in the shipyard beginning in March and the underway opportunities would be very limited for those who had not yet qualified. One of those who qualified was Ensign Laura Poleshinski who had been very aggressively working on her qualifications since the day she reported aboard. Typically, we would have a pinning ceremony in the wardroom at the evening Operations and Intelligence Briefing and I would pin the new device on the officer with everyone else looking on. My procedure was to undo the top button of the uniform shirt and put my left hand inside to fasten the clips that hold the pin on from inside the shirt. The afternoon after Laura's successful qualification board I asked her how she wanted me to handle her pinning.

"Just like you do everyone else, Captain," she said in typical Laura fashion.

That evening, we had two sets of SWO pins to present, Laura and Ensign Al Licup. I did Al first and did it like I always did. I could sense the anticipation in the room as I moved to Laura, undid her blouse, and stuck my hand inside just as I had for Al. Laura just smiled. The pockets are pretty high on the women officer's khaki shirts.

At around 8:00 PM on the 9th of November, we crossed the International Dateline and left the 7th Fleet area of operations, entering that of 3rd Fleet. My Task Unit designation changed from CTU 75.9.3 to CTG 35.8.3. We had adjusted our course to cross the International Dateline exactly on the Equator which would make the crew "Golden Shellbacks," a more specialized designation. I was on the bridge as we approached and, watching the GPS, we made a hard turn at the end to try hit it right on the nose, not that anyone would ever know the difference. The CIC watch ran an Aegis printout of the exact moment and it showed our position to be 00 degrees, 00 minutes, 00 seconds North Latitude and 179 degrees, 59 minutes, and 59 seconds East Longitude. Not bad, 1/60th of a nautical mile off - about 100 feet.

Crossing the International Dateline going east in a ship also gives you two consecutive days with the same date, in this case November 10th. The XO and I decided to make that day holiday routine and gave the crew two consecutive holiday routine days. We also made a big deal out of giving Petty Officer Hilligoss back his birthday which he had lost on the 4th of June when we crossed going west.

I had one pleasant detail to take care of before we arrived in Pearl Harbor. I brought the second (now third) class petty officer that I had busted after the fight in Bahrain into my cabin to give him some good news. On the night of the 12th, before we pulled into Pearl, I told him that I had never sent the paperwork off the ship following his Captain's Mast. His pay had never been docked and his wife had never seen a change in her allotment. The Bureau of Personnel knew nothing about it. I told him to start wearing his second class petty officer crow immediately and that as far as I was concerned it was over. I was afraid that while we were in Hawaii he would have his Service Dress Blue uniform re-striped for third class because that was the uniform we would wear into port in San Diego. I also told him that I would never say anything to his wife about what happened; how he handled that was up to him. I felt that he had paid enough of a price; 45 days of extra duty, no liberty in Australia, and the humiliation of going to Captain's Mast and getting busted. He had no doubt agonized over his family situation and his future in the Navy. Besides, the whole story of what happened that night was confused by fuzzy alcoholic recollections of events and this was a 14-year sailor with a clean record and a wife and four kids at home. I thought he was going to kiss me when I told him all this; he was so relieved. Several months later after I had relinquished command of COWPENS, I was at the Navy Exchange on Coronado when I ran into this sailor and his family. His wife gave me a look that would melt your heart and said, "I know what you did." Talk about feeling good about handling an ugly situation.

That evening we held our navigation brief in the wardroom for the entry into the naval magazine at Lualualei which is a channel that branches west off the main Pearl Harbor channel. I told Pete Patterson, our relatively new Navigator that I wanted to be awakened at 4:30 for the approach and that we should enter the main channel just after sunrise. I wanted to get an early start on offloading our Tomahawk missiles. Once that was done we'd move the ship into the main naval station basin and tie up for the duration of our stay.

Pete did not have a good morning. First he forgot to call me, probably because he was trying to figure out why it was so dark outside. When I did get to the bridge it was still pitch black. We had called Harbor Control and told them where we were and they responded, "You're early." Pete had miscalculated sunrise by an hour, so now we were entering the channel in the dark. The pilot came out to meet us and my pal Captain Hank Sanford from Destroyer Squadron 8 came out with him. Hank was now the Commanding Officer of Naval Station Pearl Harbor. I apologized to the pilot for them having to scramble around to take us early while shooting dirty looks at Pete. The fact that the base CO was coming out to meet the ship probably helped motivate the port services team to scramble to accommodate the early arrival.

Once the missiles were offloaded, we moved the ship from Lualualei to the naval station. As we passed Hospital Point I saw Iris and Kathy Danberg on the lawn behind base housing waving to the ship. They had stuck plastic cups in the chain link fence to spell out **ALOHA COWPENS**.

We manned the rail and rendered honors as we passed the *ARIZONA* Memorial as is Navy custom. The battleship *MISSOURI (BB-63)* had been put in place as a museum just forward of the sunken *ARIZONA* since our last visit. I thought it fitting that we now had in one place the primary reminder of how Japan started the war in 1941 and the place where they signed the surrender documents in Tokyo Bay in 1945. Before *MISSOURI* arrived, I had always thought that it was a little unbalanced. This way the millions of Japanese tourists who visit Hawaii had a little reminder of how things worked out.

We left Pearl Harbor the morning of the 17th with our 80 Tigers on board, including Seaman Kyllo's 74-year-old grandfather and the father-in-law of Damage Controlman Second Class Weeks who was a retired Air Force major general. I gave the general my inport cabin. We had sent about 80 of our crew ahead to San Diego to make room for the Tigers. This "advance party" would stand most of the inport watches immediately after our arrival. I let Jeff

Berlasconi get the ship underway from the pier without the help of tugs while his father proudly looked on.

On a typical Tiger Cruise, each guest sleeps and eats in the equivalent bunks and messing areas as their sponsor; officers in staterooms and the wardroom, chiefs in the chief's berthing and mess, and enlisted in the berthing compartments and the messdecks. Tigers are allowed free roam of the ship with the exception of classified spaces and are allowed to stand watches and accompany their sponsors on routine duties and evolutions. Each Tiger is issued a Personnel Qualification Standards booklet and given a number of evolutions to observe or participate in to get "signed off." Of course we generate a schedule that facilitates all this including opportunities for the Tigers to fire small arms and steer the ship.

We put *MILIUS* in station 1,000 yards on the starboard beam so the Tigers on each ship would have something to look at besides water as we steamed towards San Diego. We fired the guns and put on demonstrations with the helicopter. Unfortunately, the regulations did not permit us to give the Tigers a ride in the helicopters, but Chris, as a commissioned naval officer, was able to hop in Saberhawk 76 and go visit his mom on *MILIUS*. We did "leapfrogs" with *MILIUS* allowing both ships to practice underway replenishment approaches on the other and we made sure that all the junior officers with Tigers aboard got a chance at the conn. The most popular event was "Repel Boarders." This was a water fight between the two ships as we came alongside *MILIUS*. As the Officer in Tactical Command, I made sure *COWPENS* was on the upwind side. The engineers had all six fire pumps on the line and *COWPENS* thoroughly doused *MILIUS*. *MILIUS* however, surprised us with a "spud gun" which fired potatoes back at us. Jim McManamon was careful to order his crew not to shoot anywhere near the SPY radar arrays lest a potato cause a million dollars' worth of damage. When we broke away, Jim called on bridge-to-bridge and requested a rematch with the positions relative to the wind reversed. I denied his request.

On the morning of November 21st, I intruded on the traditional wake-up song, going to the bridge before reveille and playing the Florida State fight song instead. FSU and Florida played their annual grudge game that day and fortunately, the Seminoles won 23-12. I had a number of Gator fans in the crew, but also some Seminoles.

Our last full day at sea was Sunday, November 22nd and we observed holiday routine interrupted only by refueling from *USNS RAPPAHANNOCK (T-AO-204)*. The Tigers really enjoyed this evolution and the crew didn't mind the disruption to holiday routine. Very few people slept soundly that night with the excitement of homecoming the next day.

Homecoming on the 23rd was a joyous occasion as they always are. Rear Admiral Dan Bowler came aboard to welcome us home but very graciously left the ship as soon as practicable so as not to be in the way of all the reunions. *MILIUS* followed us in and tied up astern of *COWPENS*. It was a little odd for me to walk down the pier and watch Iris come in on *MILIUS*; a little role reversal. PACMEF 98-2 was officially over. Over the preceding 181 days we had spent 140 days at sea, had steamed 37,097 nautical miles, and had visited five foreign countries.

Among those on the pier for our arrival were the Spitz family who had sent me the beautiful photograph of *COWPENS* at anchor in Monterey Bay, and with whom I had begun a friendly correspondence. Jim Crawley and Don Kohlbauer from the *San Diego Union Tribune* were also there to record the end of the cruise and write one final chapter for the *In Harm's Way* series.

CHAPTER 25

Ready to Fight Tonight

I finished my command of *USS COWPENS* on the 12th of February 1999, when Captain Bill Mason relieved me in a ceremony at Naval Station San Diego. Bill would take the ship through a year-long overhaul and then deliver the ship to Yokosuka, Japan where *COWPENS* would replace *USS MOBILE BAY (CG-53)* as part of the Forward Deployed Naval Forces. The two ships would conduct a "crew swap" with the *COWPENS* crew sailing back to San Diego on *MOBILE BAY,* and the *MOBILE BAY* crew taking over *COWPENS.* Crew swap allowed the Navy to bring home the forward deployed ships for much needed maintenance and upgrades without a wholesale transfer of some 700 officers and sailors back and forth across the Pacific, thereby saving money.

Before that change of command, however, I welcomed aboard my third Executive Officer, Lieutenant Commander Roy Kitchener, and said farewell to my loyal and trustworthy XO, Lieutenant Commander Terry Culton. Roy would prove to be a superb officer and I would have enjoyed working with him as my second in command for longer than the six weeks we had together. We also had one more significant underway period, visiting Acapulco, Mexico for a four-day visit in mid-January. Iris joined me for that port visit as well, and we had a nice time as she continued her "follow the fleet" program.

When we pulled into San Diego on the morning of January 26, 1999, it marked my last time at sea in command of a U.S. Navy ship. I had orders to detach from *COWPENS* and report to the Navy Surface Warfare Officer's School, SWOS, as the commanding officer. CO of SWOS was a plum assignment and many previous commanding officers had gone on to be promoted to rear admiral.

For my final sea detail in command on that January morning, our newest female officer, Ensign Kristi Lemkueller, had the conn. As we sailed by the city of San Diego we looked ahead to the Coronado Bridge to see the *STAR OF INDIA* under tow heading for the bridge on its way to the Broadway Pier area where she was a tourist attraction. The *STAR OF INDIA* is the world's oldest active sailing ship, built in 1863. This three-masted barque was one of the world's first iron-hulled ships.

"Kristi, let's slow down and let the *STAR OF INDIA* get under the bridge before we get there. I don't want to be known as the guy who sunk the *STAR OF INDIA* on his last sea detail."

Safely tied up and with my last sea detail under my belt, I looked forward to a change of command and the new challenge of commanding SWOS. However, something happened which changed everything. My phone rang around 10:00 PM in mid-December. It was Chief Warrant Officer Jim Morris who had been my Cryptologic Officer in *COWPENS* in 1997 and had transferred ashore to the Naval Personnel Command in Millington, Tennessee.

"Is your name William Daniel Sullivan?" he asked without preamble.

"Yep."

"Congratulations sir, you're on the one-star list. Don't tell anyone I told you."

Jim had been a recorder during the Rear Admiral, Lower Half, Selection Board so knew the results. He wasn't supposed to tell me, but he did. I told Iris immediately of course but otherwise kept this fantastic news to myself. I was selected for promotion to rear admiral; something completely beyond my wildest imagination 26 years earlier when I had received my commission in Newport, Rhode Island.

Over the next several weeks I nervously awaited a second source of confirmation from one of my buddies who was already a flag officer. I expected to hear at least a hint from someone like

Dave Stone who had made it the year before, or Jay Foley who had made it two years earlier, or Rear Admiral Tim LaFleur who was in San Diego and with whom I sometimes played golf. No one called. They were all more disciplined than Chief Warrant Officer Morris. The Chief of Naval Operations, Admiral Jay Johnson, had put out the word regarding selection board result leaks. As we got near my change of command with Captain Bill Mason, my orders to command the Navy Surface Warfare Officer School in Newport, Rhode Island were changed assigning me temporarily to the staff of Commander Naval Surface Force, Pacific as a Special Assistant to Vice Admiral Ed Moore. The orders went on to describe my status as "awaiting further orders." No explanation was given, but that was confirmation enough, despite the lack of any congratulations from my friends.

When the list was finally released and therefore safe to talk about, I began discussions with retired Navy Captain Bob Erskine who served as the "Flag Matters" assistant to the Chief of Naval Operations. Each time we talked, Bob dropped hints that I was going to be sent to Korea as Commander, U.S. Naval Forces Korea (CNFK) in Seoul. Iris was not thrilled by this possibility, having never been to Korea and having a negative perception of what it would be like to live there. Eventually Bob told me that I was, in fact, going to be CNFK and relieve Rear Admiral Chris Cole in October 1999. First, I would attend the CAPSTONE course required of all newly promoted flag and general officers.

Because I was going to an overseas assignment where I would be expected to interact on an equal footing with the admirals in the Republic of Korea Navy, not to mention their Army, Air Force and Marine Corps generals, I was eligible for "frocking." My father may have been the most amazed recipient of this news. Amazed but proud he was, and he bragged about my promotion to everyone. Likewise, Iris's parents, Norm and Mae Stutzer, were equally proud and probably just as amazed as my dad that the knucklehead who married their daughter while still in college had made it to flag rank.

A week after frocking, I began my new flag officer life by detaching from the temporary assignment at SURFPAC and heading to Washington for the six-week Flag and General Officer CAPSTONE course. The idea behind CAPSTONE was to prepare all recently selected or promoted flag and general officers for their new responsibilities with a thorough, if quick, education about the other services, the regional and functional combatant commands, the Joint Staff in the Pentagon, and the Congress. All of the combatant commands located in the United States were visited by the entire class, consisting of about 30 new admirals and generals from all the services. Each service had an opportunity to showcase its capabilities during these field trips. A regional studies program rounded out the course which included a two-week trip outside the country to visit with the relevant combatant commanders and meet with the militaries of the countries in the region. For this, the class was divided into three groups of ten and led by a retired four-star officer. Because I was under orders to command U.S. Naval Forces Korea, I was "ordered" to take the Pacific trip. From August 7th to 21st, my group flew in an Air National Guard KC-135 tanker to Seoul, Korea; Kuala Lumpur, Malaysia; Singapore; and Kadena Air Base in Okinawa and Yokota Air Base in Japan; finishing up at U.S. Pacific Command in Honolulu. We were originally scheduled to visit China, but earlier that year, in May, the United States had accidentally bombed the Chinese Embassy in Belgrade, Yugoslavia during Operation Allied Force. Three Chinese reporters were killed and a major diplomatic kerfuffle ensued. In the investigation following the bombing, it came out that the B-2 stealth bomber aircrews had put the bombs exactly on target but the building they hit had been improperly identified. The intended target, the Yugoslav Federal Directorate for Supply and Procurement, was right down the street. The CIA had misidentified the embassy as the intended target and provided the aircrews with the wrong coordinates. Kuala Lumpur was substituted for Beijing on our trip as a result.

Finishing CAPSTONE, Iris and I returned to San Diego and made the move to Seoul with stops in Hawaii and Tokyo on the way. Arriving at Seoul's Gimpo (formerly Kimpo) Airport, just west of downtown Seoul, we were met by the aide I would inherit briefly from Chris Cole, Lieutenant Harvey Ebersole and my new Korean driver, Bobby Yu. Harvey stayed on for a couple of months to provide me with some continuity until Lieutenant Bill Blacker arrived to take over. When Bill was transferred near the end of my tour, he was replaced by Lieutenant Pete Kim, a Korean-American naval officer and Naval Academy graduate. Because Pete looks Korean, he caused some confusion among the Koreans who often began babbling at him in Korean before realizing he was an American. I also met my Korean aide, Lieutenant Kim, Sae Han, Republic of Korea Navy. The ROK Navy had been providing the Commander, U.S. Naval Forces Korea with a Korean officer to help facilitate dealings with the ROK Navy since CNFK was established following the Korean War. It was considered a plum assignment for a young ROK naval officer and many had gone on to achieve high rank, including the then ROK CNO, Admiral Lee, Seo Young. During my two years in command, I received two more ROK aides, Lieutenant Ji, Soo Young who replaced Lieutenant Kim, and then Lieutenant Jai Joon You whose father was a ROK Rear Admiral and had at one time also been the CNFK ROK aide. All three of these fine young Korean naval officers went on to have successful careers.

I also arranged for Yeoman Chief Chris Adams to join me in Korea as my Flag Writer. The same Chris Adams who had been a seaman in *SAMPSON* and had served with me as a first class petty officer and chief in *COWPENS*. A Flag Writer is a special yeoman, part of the personal staff, who takes care of administrative details for the admiral he serves. Many flag officers use their Flag Writers to draft personal correspondence and speeches for them and to arrange travel orders and other details. Often a Flag Writer will follow the same admiral from job to job. That would be the case with Chris for as long as I rated a Flag Writer. Chris would go on to make Senior Chief Petty Officer while we were in Korea and later become a Master Chief, the highest enlisted paygrade.

One of the benefits of being "CNFK" was a dedicated house, Admiralty House, on the U.S. Army's Yongsan Garrison, complete with a white painted anchor in the front yard, and a Mess Specialist assigned to prepare meals for official entertaining, take care of my uniforms, and generally take care of the house. Our first Mess Specialist, or MS, was Chief Gloria Almaro, a delightful lady and a wonderful cook. When she was transferred several months into my tour, she brought in and trained Mess Specialist First Class Jerry Manrique, who also did a fantastic job.

During the week before I replaced Chris Cole in an official Army-style ceremony on the 5th of October 1999, I made all the rounds with Chris to get introduced to the heavies, both American and Korean. The change of command was attended by Admiral Dennis Blair, Commander, U.S. Pacific Command (then still known as CINCPAC) and was done in fatigues, with an Army-style ceremony on the parade grounds in front of USFK Headquarters. By Army-style, I mean the speakers all faced the assembled troops on the parade grounds with their backs to the invited guests in the stands behind them. In a Navy change of command ceremony, the guests and the troops are all on the same side of the podium and the speakers speak to their faces.

Our two years in Korea was an immersion in Army culture. We wore fatigues every day except when CNFK unilaterally declared a "Navy Day" and we wore our khaki, blue, or white uniforms. The fatigues were symbols of the "ready to fight tonight" philosophy of life in South Korea. The million-man North Korean Army, 70% of which was positioned on the DMZ a mere 35 miles north of Seoul, had the ability to launch an artillery attack with little or no warning. We found the Army to be much more rank conscious than the Navy. When I had gone through the orientation course for brand new admirals, Admiral Don Pilling, the Vice Chief of Naval Operations, had told us, "One and two-star officers call each other by their first names. One and two-star officers never call three and four-star officers by their first names unless invited to do so and then only in private." I took this knowledge with me to Korea and as I was introduced around to the Army brass I assumed the same familiarity with the two-star Army generals I met. I got some strange reactions.

In addition to my headquarters on Yongsan, CNFK also had a small outpost in Pohang, Korea on the east coast, manned by about 20 Marines and commanded by a Marine lieutenant colonel. There were magazines at Pohang containing wartime ammunition stocks and it was the Marines job to maintain them as well as support visiting U.S. Navy ships and aircraft. In Chinhae, on the southern tip of the peninsula west of Pusan, was a small U.S. Navy base run by a Navy commander. This base was co-located with the ROK Fleet Commander's headquarters and existed to support visits by U.S. Navy ships.

As CNFK I was the peacetime Naval Component Commander for the Army General serving as USFK, General John Tilelli. During wartime, Commander 7th Fleet became the naval component commander and CNFK became the on-peninsula naval liaison. Because I was the Navy component commander on the peninsula, Iris and I were included in all the high level dinners and social engagements with the Koreans, up to and including with the President of South Korea, Kim, Dae Jung. It turned out to be a great way to start off as a newly minted flag officer. Because of the joint and international responsibilities of the job, as a frocked one-star I was entitled to some of the perks normally reserved for three and four-star officers; a car and driver, an aide, a mess specialist assigned to the quarters, and official representation funds for official entertaining. Despite her initial trepidations, Iris quickly grew to love our time in Korea.

South Korea is a beautiful country with lush green mountains and rivers and a long and beautiful coastline. To the south lies the island of Cheju-do which the Koreans consider their own version of Hawaii. Unquestionably, our fondest memories of Korea were of the Korean people themselves. We made many Korean friends and have stayed in touch with them over the years. The Koreans have a reputation as a tough people, who can be difficult in negotiations; but once you make a Korean friend, you have a friend for life. The Koreans had lived through a rough 20th Century, but South Korea had emerged as one of the "Asian Tigers," with a booming economy, large, modern cities, and successful industries, especially shipbuilding, electronics, and automobiles.

The U.S. military presence in South Korea, there to defend the country from the belligerent North Koreans, was not always welcome. Especially when there had been some incident involving a U.S. service member and a Korean national, there were often demonstrations outside the gates of Yongsan. When this happened, the gates were locked down and the Korean riot police showed up in their Bluebird school busses to keep the peace. They would emerge from the busses in full riot gear with shields and batons and were not hesitant to crack a few heads to keep the crowd from storming the gates. South Korea has a mandatory service requirement, like our old draft. Young men were required to either join a branch of the military for one year or join the government police. Many of the riot police were these conscripts doing their one year of service. A student could be rioting in the streets one month and find himself wielding a baton against his fellow students the next.

As delightful as our two years in Korea were, it was not without its challenges. With the DMZ only 35 miles north of Seoul, much of the capital city was in the range of North Korean long range artillery. Under General Tilelli, and his successor, Army General Tom Schwartz, it was emphasized that we were in a wartime situation and could never afford to lower our guard. There were the occasional incursions by North Korea, including the grounding of a YUGO class mini-sub in 1996 which was involved in infiltrating commandos into South Korea and a summer 1999 sea battle in the Yellow Sea during which a North Korean patrol boat was sunk by the ROK Navy. After we left Korea in 2001, there were more incidents including another Yellow Sea battle in 2002 during which the ROK Navy lost a patrol boat, and yet another small battle in 2009 which cost North Korea another patrol boat. The North Koreans retaliated in March 2010, torpedoing and sinking a ROK corvette, *ROKS CHOENAN*, and killing 46 ROK sailors. Later that year, North Korea fired 170 rounds of rockets and artillery at Yeongpyeong Island, killing four South Koreans and wounding 19. The USFK command and the South Korean military were heavily army oriented and I would take some delight in reminding the general in charge that all the most recent crises had taken place at sea.

Intelligence indicated that in addition to a massive rocket and artillery barrage as the opening salvo of any attack on South Korea by the North, there would be a two pronged, east and west coast attack on the South Korean coastline. Hundreds, perhaps thousands of high speed air-cushioned craft or small boats would attempt to land forces along the South Korean coastline to infiltrate behind the DMZ. The United States and South Korea had developed a creative tactic to counter this threat. The concept had U.S. Navy cruisers, destroyers, and frigates with embarked LAMPS helicopters directing attacks over water by U.S. Army 6th Cavalry Brigade Apache AH-64 attack helicopters. The Apaches would be directed to enemy naval units by the LAMPS helicopters which had a far superior command and control capability with reach-back to the Navy ships. The Apaches were equipped with Hellfire missiles, designed to attack enemy tank forces on land. The Hellfire was considered an ideal weapon to employ against the North Korean landing craft and patrol boats.

In 2000, during the annual Foal Eagle combined exercise between the U.S. and ROK militaries, this tactic was being exercised in the Sea of Japan. As the U.S. naval commander in Korea I was expected to be an expert advisor to General Schwartz on the employment of the Apache helicopters in concert with the Navy. I flew to Pohang to take a familiarization ride in an Apache and see for myself how this tactic was being exercised. I joined an Apache squadron at the Pohang airfield, was briefed on the mission, and assigned to an Apache piloted by an Army warrant officer. They dressed me out in the flight suit with all the required survival gear and we boarded the helicopter. The Apache is a two-seat aircraft, with the weapons operator sitting in the very nose of the aircraft and the pilot sitting behind in a seat that is raised above that of the weapons operator to afford better visibility. The cockpit is very cramped and as I climbed in and strapped in with the assistance of the crew chief I thought to myself that if I had to get out in a hurry it would be very difficult.

We launched and headed out over the ocean to join the exercise in progress. Over the intercom I discussed the tactics with my pilot and learned a few things about the Apache and how it could be employed over water. The disconcerting news was that the Apache was not equipped with an automatic system intended to keep it from flying into the water while cruising as was the case with our LAMPS helos. This feature is very important at night when the horizon and the surface below is not visible. The Apache is equipped with a radar altimeter, but a multi-tasking pilot conducting an engagement might not have time to keep an eye on it. Note to self, don't do this at night. We continued east over the ocean and began seeing U.S. and ROK Navy ships. We were about 50 miles from land and jammed into this tiny cockpit I was hoping that nothing went wrong that would require that we ditch. I then started quizzing my pilot about the ships we were seeing; U.S. Navy *ARLEIGH BURKE* destroyers and *OLIVER HAZARD PERRY* frigates, along with ROK Navy *KDX-I* destroyers, *ULSAN* frigates and *POHANG* corvettes. He couldn't tell one from the other. He couldn't even tell a ROK ship from a U.S. ship unless we were close enough to see the flag. I thought to myself, "How are these guys going to know who to shoot at unless there is a LAMPS helo right with them to tell the good guys from the bad guys?"

The unpredictability of North Korea under Kim Jong Il, the son of the original leader, Kim Il Sung, lent credence to the "ready to fight tonight" philosophy. Military dependents in Korea were required to have their paperwork in order for an evacuation and to keep a "go kit" ready for a hasty departure in the event of war. Everybody, including family members, was issued gas masks. Most Army and Air Force personnel assigned to Korea were on unaccompanied one year tours and not allowed to have family join them. The annual turnover of personnel necessitated continuous training and education. Once a year a realistic evacuation drill was conducted which required all dependents to physically muster with their paperwork and supplies as if they were ready for evacuation. A small number were evacuated to Japan each year to test the system. Iris participated in these drills along with every other family member allowed to live in the South. After sizing up the operation at the Yongsan gymnasium, Iris announced that when things started to heat up she would be buying a business class ticket to Hawaii rather than being evacuated to Japan in a military transport.

North and South Korea regularly dropped leaflets on either side of the DMZ for propaganda purposes and it was not unusual to walk out the front door in the morning and find a tattered leaflet on the sidewalk depicting an evil American soldier bayoneting a North Korean baby. A trip to the DMZ at Panmunjom was an eye-opening experience as the North and South stared each other down across the line. Even more sobering was a visit to the tunnels dug under the DMZ by North Korea to infiltrate soldiers across the border as part of an invasion. Four of these tunnels had been discovered along the DMZ which attested to the seriousness of the threat. Nobody knows how many tunnels remain undiscovered in the mountainous terrain of the DMZ.

The story of the Korean Peninsula in the 20th Century was a sad one and we met many Koreans who related tales of their families being forever ripped apart by the end of World War II and the Korean War. Japan occupied and annexed Korea in 1910, brutally controlling the entire peninsula until their surrender at the end of World War II. While the Soviet Union had been key to defeating Nazi Germany in Europe, it did not declare war on Japan until the summer of 1945 after the German surrender and when it looked pretty certain that Japan would be defeated. When American planners were considering the magnitude of accepting Japan's surrender in all of the parts of Asia that it still occupied, including Korea and Manchuria, they realized that there simply were not enough American troops to safely and effectively accept the Japanese surrender. An arbitrary line was drawn across the Korean Peninsula at Latitude 38 degrees north, chosen because the capital of Seoul would lie on the American side, and responsibility for north of 38 degrees was given to our new ally in the Pacific, the

Soviet Union. Subsequently, the Soviets set up a Communist government in the north and installed Kim Il Sung as the leader. The Americans set up a quasi-democracy in the south under anti-Communist first president Syngman Rhee. Because of tensions over these developments, the 38th parallel became an impassable border and thousands of family members separated on either side never saw each other again.

I was treated very well by the ROK Navy and enjoyed my time visiting their ships. A highlight was the opportunity in the spring of 2000 to go to sea with the ROK Navy and visit the island of Pyeongyang in the Yellow Sea, the same island that would be shelled by the North ten years later. Traveling to Pyongtaek on the west coast, I went to sea aboard the ROK corvette *JECHON (PCC-776)*. At sea we rendezvoused with the small "PKM" patrol boat which delivered me to Pyeongyang-do. The island was home to a ROK Marine battalion ready to do battle with the North Koreans, including having the beaches protected by obstacles to prevent amphibious landings reminiscent of the beaches of Normandy on D-Day.

Given a tour of the defenses by the ROK Marine brigadier general, I was amazed to see Harpoon missiles in canisters on the island and a trailer with a Harpoon control console inside and an SPS-10 surface search radar on the roof. The ROKs planned to launch Harpoons from the island against North Korean naval ships sailing south through the West Sea. I wondered how they would target only enemy warships amid all the fishing boats and commercial steamers in those waters. The Harpoon is an uncontrolled missile after launch. Once the radar seeker comes to life, the missile goes after the first radar return it finds. That night PKM-322 took me to rendezvous with the ROK Navy's newest and most capable destroyer, the KDX-I class *KWANGGAETO THE GREAT (DDH-971)* to spend the night. The next morning, we rendezvoused with PKM-367 to finish the trip with the sea detail back to Pyongtaek. Throughout I was impressed with the seamanship, shiphandling, and cleanliness of the ROK ships.

The U.S. Army also took good care of us in Korea and I was able to rustle up a Blackhawk helicopter or a C-12 for trips around the peninsula on official business virtually any time I asked. This was yet another perk not normally afforded a one-star officer, but the Army was used to it and had the assets with a full aviation brigade on the peninsula. If I was going on official business which included Iris, which was often the case, she was entitled to fly as well, and came to really enjoy the helicopter rides as a great way to see the country from low altitude. I will admit however, that there were times when I got a little nervous, especially when the weather moved in. All helicopter flights were by necessity under visual flight rules and navigation often involved following highways while consulting road maps. Listening to the pilot and co-pilot on the intercom circuit could be disconcerting:

"What road is that down there?"

"Ummm... I think its Highway One."

"See those power lines up ahead?"

"No, where?"

"We better climb."

"That looks like a bad thunderstorm up ahead."

"We better try to go around."

"Ok, how high are the mountains around here?"

The big event in Korea in 2000 was the beginning of the 50th Commemoration of the Korean War which began on June 25, 1950 when Communist North Korea launched a surprise invasion of the South. Events were scheduled to coincide with key events during the war on the 50th anniversary of each event. It was very much a "commemoration," not a "celebration," as there was nothing about this war to celebrate except some battlefield successes. In 2000 the key events were the beginning of the war on June 25th, the commemoration of Task Force Smith on July 5th, and the Inchon invasion on September 15th. For each of these commemorations, large groups of American Korean War veterans traveled to Korea to participate, especially if they had personally been involved in specific events such as the Inchon landing. For many of these veterans it was their first time back in Korea since the war. When they left, South Korea was a devastated country, primitive in almost every regard, and utterly destroyed by the fighting. The people were mainly peasants in a rural, agrarian society. The South Korea that these veterans saw in 2000 was a bustling, modern, and energetic society with towering modern skyscrapers and fancy hotels in all the major cities. The most common refrain heard from these veterans was, "Now I know what I was fighting for."

On October 12, 2000, *USS COLE (DDG-67)* an *ARLEIGH BURKE* class destroyer was hit by a suicide boat during a refueling stop in the harbor of Aden, Yemen. Seventeen sailors were killed and 39 injured. At the morning meeting with the USFK staff, the J-2 (Intelligence Officer), Brigadier General James "Spider" Marks showed pictures of the damage. As the naval expert in the room, I was called on to give my assessment to General Schwartz. I told him it was no accident and that the damage appeared to be the result of a large shape charge detonated against the hull above the waterline.

"How did they let a suicide boat get right next to the ship?"

"Sir, you have no idea what it's like in these shit-hole ports. There is no order. Small boats are running all over the place. Some are coming alongside to make arrangements for supplies, or garbage disposal, or to handle lines. Some are just beggars looking for hand-outs, and some are merchants trying to sell brass pots or rugs to the crew."

In October of 2000, *USS COWPENS*, was scheduled to visit Pohang, Korea and I arranged a one-day visit to go see the ship. *COWPENS* was now homeported in Yokosuka, Japan having crew-swapped with *USS MOBILE BAY (CG-53)*. Captain Bill Mason, who had relieved me, taken the ship through an overhaul, and then to Japan, had been replaced by another officer. My visit was somewhat disappointing as only five crewmembers were holdovers from my

411

tenure and the mood in the ship was not the same. It was the *MOBILE BAY* crew; the *COWPENS* crew having sailed *MOBILE BAY* back to San Diego. The *MOBILE BAY* crew simply had not embraced all the "cow" themes we had adopted to make the best of an inelegant name. It was great to see my old sailors, but they told me something was lacking; the old spirit was gone.

About a year and a half into my two-year assignment in Korea the Chief of Naval Personnel, Vice Admiral Norb Ryan, visited Korea and we hosted him for dinner at Admiralty House. As we were having drinks before dinner, Admiral Ryan informed me that I was on the list to get command of an aircraft carrier battle group. He didn't know which one or when, but I was in the queue. This was fantastic news and exactly what I had hoped would be the next step in my career. The selection rate from one-star to two-stars was about 50%, and those who didn't continue to serve in operational, at-sea billets were likely not to make the cut for the next rank.

A few months later, with no official word yet as to when or where my battle group command would happen, Admiral Dennis Blair, the Commander at CINCPAC in Hawaii, made a visit to Korea. His protocol officer called my office a week before the visit and told my aide that the admiral wanted to have dinner with me and Iris. Great, I said, I'll invite General Schwartz and perhaps the ROK CNO and we'll have a nice dinner at Admiralty House. The word back from his staff was "no, he just wants to have dinner with you and your wife." This was very odd. Normally when a four-star officer travels a great distance to a foreign country with whom the United States has significant interests and there are other four-star officers in command there, his schedule is crammed with official events. A private dinner with a lowly one-star is simply impractical. But, whatever the admiral wants. I knew Admiral Blair, but not particularly well. We had sat at the same table at a Navy Ball in Washington with him and his wife Diane during which I had managed to tip over a glass of red wine which went all over the table cloth but fortunately not on anyone's dinner dress white uniform. Apparently that faux pas had been forgotten.

That evening, again over drinks before dinner, Admiral Blair said, "Bill, I want you to come to Hawaii and be my J-5." The J-5, a two-star billet, was the regional combatant commander's Director for Strategic Plans and Policy; a key member of the staff.

I hesitated a couple of beats, and then blurted out, "What about my battle group?"

"There's plenty of time for that," he replied.

I then thanked him for the offer and his confidence in me and said, "Of course. When!"

"This fall when your tour here is up."

Iris, of course, was thrilled. She had been looking forward to going to Hawaii four years earlier when I thought I was going to be CO in *USS CHOSIN (CG-65)*. But I knew the window for battle group command was a small one and that if I went to CINCPAC for a couple of years, even if it enhanced my chances to get a second star because of the billet, I'd likely be outside the window to go back to sea. It's hard to say no to a highly respected four-star admiral and that was Dennis Blair. I learned later from Admiral Tom Fargo, my CINCPACFLT boss as CNFK and later to succeed Admiral Blair at CINCPAC, that he and Admiral Blair had discussed my future and decided that I could be lost in the shuffle way out in Korea and by slotting me into the J-5 billet at CINCPAC they would raise my visibility and increase my chances for promotion. Turned out they were right.

One other event worth mentioning that occurred in 2000 was the election of George W. Bush as the 43rd President of the United States on November 7, 2000–sort of. November 7th was election day in the United States (November 8th in Korea) but as readers will remember, the final outcome was not known until December 12th when the Supreme Court put an end to the wrangling and appeals and recounts over Florida's 25 electoral votes. In Korea, and I am sure in many other countries around the world, there was an undercurrent of amusement, and perhaps a little sangfroid at the uncertainty and legal maneuvering taking place in the U.S. We had taught the South Koreans how to create a democratic form of government and over the years lectured and cajoled them as they evolved their system to achieve their own democracy. Here was the United States, a beacon of democracy, passing judgment on the rest of the world, and dispatching "election monitors" to far flung corners of the world to ensure fair and honest elections, struggling with its own outcome. Nobody would say it outright, but there was a certain amount of satisfaction, I suspect globally, in watching this struggle play out in America.

As we drew nearer to the second anniversary of our arrival in Korea, things fell into place and a date was set for me to be relieved by Rear Admiral Gary Jones. The date for the change of command had been set for September 7, 2001 and by coincidence, the U.S. Navy CNO, Admiral Vern Clark, was scheduled for a visit to Korea so I arranged to have Admiral Clark speak at our ceremony. The week prior, Iris and I had squired Gary and Tammy Jones around for all the office calls and social events just as Chris and Cathy Cole had done for us. One thing I had resolved to do differently however, emboldened by the fact that my CNO was in attendance, was to have a Navy style change of command in Summer White uniforms and with a stage and podium *facing* the audience, albeit still on the parade ground. We did it right with sideboys for the official party and a ship's bell, just as we would have done aboard ship.

It was a sad departure from Korea as we bade farewell to many close friends, particularly among the Koreans. The hardest however was saying goodbye to my personal staff who had supported Iris and me so well. Driver Bobby Yu and his wife had been with us the full two years and we had spent countless hours together. ROK Navy aide, Lieutenant Jai Joon You (aka "JJ") and his delightful wife, as well as my U.S. Navy Aide, Lieutenant Pete Kim and his wife Jean, had been a terrific team. Finally, our house Mess Specialist, Petty Officer First Class Jerry Manrique, had spoiled both Iris and me for any future house MS we might later be so fortunate to have. We had tears in our eyes as we hugged and said goodbye before going through passport control at Incheon Airport on September 8, 2001. They were all there to say goodbye.

CHAPTER 26

9/11 and the Pacific

I was under orders to report to United States Pacific Command at Camp H.M. Smith in Honolulu, Hawaii on the 16th of September. That gave Iris and me a week of leave before assuming my duties and relieving Rear Admiral Steve Smith as the PACOM J-5. I would have been content to spend that week on the beach at Waikiki and the golf courses of Oahu, but Iris had other plans. There is an organization of women golfers that every year sponsors a ladies' golf tournament called the Military Dependents Golf Tournament. Each year a different military installation plays host to the tournament and in 2001, that tournament was being hosted at Fort Knox, Kentucky from September 9th to 13th. Iris had begun playing in this tournament some years before with a contingent of ladies from Army-Navy Country Club and was signed up for the 2001 team. Husbands were welcome to join their wives for the event and play other courses in the area during the week. Despite the attractive option of remaining in Hawaii for a week of R&R, I agreed to go. As an added benefit, my friend Major General Steve Whitcomb, having left Korea before me, had recently taken over as the Commanding General of Fort Knox, and we would get to see him and his wife Cathy. Steve had arranged for us to stay in a VIP guest house on post.

Flying out of Incheon Airport on September 8th, we arrived in Hawaii the morning of September 8th because of the International Dateline. According to the clock, we landed before we left. We unloaded luggage at the home of Captain Buz Buzby, my former colleague in the J-3 Joint Operations Division (JOD), and his wife Gina. Buz was Commander, Destroyer Squadron 31 and living in quarters on Ford Island. That same evening, we caught another flight and made our way to Fort Knox on the 9th of

September. That Sunday night was a kick-off reception at the golf course on Fort Knox which would host the ladies' tournament. Monday the 10th was set aside for a practice round with the actual tournament taking place over three days, September 11th through 13th.

The morning of September 11th Iris headed off to the tournament golf course in our rental car and I walked over to the other golf course on Fort Knox to play a round that had been arranged for the husbands of the tournament ladies. Just before I teed off, I was in the pro shop and heard something on Fox News about an airplane crash in New York. With no time to hang around to see what had happened, I went to the first tee and teed off with three other husbands.

The 4th tee at the course we men were playing is alongside the fence between the golf course and the Gold Depository at Fort Knox. I had only seen it on TV and in the James Bond movie *Goldfinger*. Just as we finished teeing off, a golf cart zoomed up and we were told that the course was closed and we had to leave.

"What's up?" we asked.

"Not sure, some kind of terrorist attack in New York."

I thought back to the Fox News report I had seen in the pro shop as we got back into our carts and headed to the clubhouse. Not knowing the extent of the plot, the Fort Knox Gold Depository was considered a potential terrorist target as were many other sites across the United States. When we arrived at the clubhouse we went inside and watched the news in the snack bar, arriving in time to see the footage of the first and second airplanes hitting the World Trade Center towers, and then to hear of the third airplane hitting the Pentagon. We later heard about the plane that went down in Pennsylvania. It was obvious that this was a coordinated terrorist attack. What next, nobody knew. I wondered about Iris and her golf tournament and whether they had also been pulled off the course so I headed back to our guest quarters.

Shortly thereafter, Iris returned and we spent the rest of the morning and afternoon watching in disbelief as the two World Trade Center towers collapsed along with the ensuing news coverage. The ladies golf tournament was cancelled and everyone began making plans to get home. Most drove because all air traffic in the country had been shut down. Fort Knox was in lock-down and nobody could come or go from the post without a good reason. Iris and I had no options for getting to Hawaii with air travel secured so we moved in with Steve and Cathy Whitcomb and spent the next three days watching the news and planning our trip back to Hawaii amid much uncertainty.

When we finally caught a flight out of Louisville on September 14th we made it as far as San Francisco before being held overnight. The next morning, we caught a flight to Honolulu on American Airlines, one of the airlines that had been targeted by the Al Qaeda terrorists. There was a powerful moment before takeoff when the captain made an announcement from the flight deck. I am paraphrasing here because I don't remember the exact words, but it went something like this:

"Welcome ladies and gentlemen aboard flight XXX to Honolulu. We are thankful that you chose American Airlines for your travel. We are all very aware of the events of the last several days. I can assure you that your safety is the top priority of American Airlines. We all now realize that we are in this together and that our safety depends on our collective defense. To reinforce this, my co-pilot, and I will walk through the cabin to reassure each of you that your safety is our top priority."

The Boeing 777 is a wide-body aircraft with two aisles down the length of the passenger compartment. The captain and the co-pilot then slowly walked the length of the passenger compartment, one in each aisle, and made direct eye contact with each passenger. I had no doubt as to exactly what they were doing—profiling their passengers.

My turnover with Steve Smith was understandably chaotic. In the wake of the 9/11 attacks every combatant command

417

worldwide was establishing updated security procedures and assessing the terrorist threat in their respective areas of responsibility. For those combatant commands on U.S. soil, new plans, procedures and rules of engagement were being developed to counter a hijacked or rogue airliner. The Donald Rumsfeld led Pentagon was demanding plans and proposals and issuing updated guidance almost daily.

In Hawaii, the difficulty of stopping a hijacked airliner from smashing into downtown Honolulu or any of the many military installations on the island was self-evident. Aircraft taking off and landing at Honolulu International Airport flew right by downtown Honolulu and the adjacent Hickam Air Force Base and Pearl Harbor. When Donald Rumsfeld was asked in Congressional testimony following 9/11 what he was doing to protect the Pentagon from another attack, he responded, "My gosh, 50 airplanes a day fly right by my window landing at National Airport!"

When George Bush was elected President and began assembling his cabinet, those of us in the military were quite pleased and expecting the best. Dick Cheney as Vice President was considered a staunch ally of the Pentagon, having served admirably as Secretary of Defense during President George H.W. Bush's presidency and during Desert Shield and Desert Storm. Likewise, retired General Colin Powell, former Chairman of the Joint Chiefs of Staff during that same period, the new Secretary of State, was viewed as a pro-military leader of the diplomatic corps. Selecting Donald Rumsfeld as Secretary of Defense was a surprise move, but again, his prior experience as Secretary of Defense during the Ford administration caused us to believe we would have an experienced hand running the department with favorable results. Finally, President Bush named the lesser known Condoleezza Rice as his National Security Advisor. Though lesser known to the general public, Dr. Rice was well-known and respected in military circles for her intellect and was considered an expert on the Soviet Union. The conventional wisdom was that smoother sailing was ahead for the Pentagon following the drawdown that had occurred during the Clinton administration following the collapse of the Soviet Union.

Donald Rumsfeld wasted little time in disabusing us of the notion that happy times lay ahead. His experience as Secretary of Defense in the 70s had convinced him that he had to quickly and forcefully assert his control over the uniformed military and re-establish the preeminence of the Secretary of Defense. Believing that the generals and admirals had run roughshod over previous Secretaries and that the Pentagon was a bloated bureaucracy that wasted money by the billions, he set about establishing his authority by questioning everything. Programs that had been moving along swimmingly suddenly came in for close re-examination. Donald Rumsfeld thought that the uniformed military was still planning to fight the Soviet Union and had not adapted to the realities of the 21st Century. In many respects I think he was right.

9/11 turned everything on its head. After years of practically ignoring attacks on the United States launched under the overall direction of Osama bin Laden's Al Qaeda terrorist group, 9/11 collectively slapped us across the face and awakened the same sleeping giant that the Japanese attack on Pearl Harbor had awakened in December 1941. Even the 1998 Tomahawk attack on bin Laden that I had been proud to lead in *COWPENS* was widely viewed as a half-hearted, low risk response to the embassy bombings in Kenya and Tanzania.

The rapidity with which the United States moved from having no military plans on the shelf for Afghanistan to the commencement of operations to remove the Taliban from power and chase down Osama bin Laden, which began on October 7th 2001, was truly remarkable. At Pacific Command, we were in support, with naval and air assets from the Pacific theater, but not directly involved. We did however participate, as did every other combatant command, in a series of wargames to help formulate planning for a "Global War on Terror." As the PACOM J-5, I traveled to Washington several times to represent Admiral Blair at these war games, code-named "Precision Cyclone."

My first direct involvement in the conflict came when the Japanese Chairman of the Joint Staff Council came to Hawaii in

October to visit Admiral Blair and offer Japan's assistance to our efforts in Afghanistan, code-named "Operation Enduring Freedom." The Chairman of the Japanese Joint Staff Council is the equivalent of the U.S. Chairman of the Joint Chiefs. He brought with him his J-5, Rear Admiral Yoji Koda. The four of us sat down in Admiral Blair's office and General Yuji Fujinawa said, "We want to know how we can help."

The problem was the Japanese constitution, which was written after World War II and designed to prevent Japan from ever again becoming a military hegemon in Asia. It was called the Japanese *Self Defense* Force for a reason. Their constitution effectively prevented the Japanese military from operations other than defense of the homeland. Most notably, it prevented "collective self-defense."

General Fujinawa went on to say that the military wanted to support the U.S. but that the constitution and the Parliament, or Diet, placed severe limits on what they could do. They had to be careful. Admiral Blair turned to me and said, "Bill, you and Admiral Koda go sit down and figure out what can be done."

Yoji and I went to my office and he explained to me what they thought they could do without violating the constitution and getting in trouble with the Diet. He said that whatever we came up with would have to be briefed to and approved by the Diet and they would disapprove anything that came close to resembling offensive operations by the Japanese Self Defense Forces, or JSDF. The JSDF could not provide military support to allies not engaged in defending Japan.

Admiral Koda proposed having the Japanese Navy send an oiler and two escort destroyers to the North Arabian Sea where U.S. Navy carrier forces were providing air support to the effort in Afghanistan. The fuel they provided our ships would be free of charge. He also proposed forward deploying some P-3 aircraft to the region to provide surface surveillance for their little task force. He explained that the P-3's could not provide surveillance for the U.S. Navy because that would be seen as directly supporting the

American combat operations. However, he implied, wink, wink, once their Navy received approval for the mission and sailed over the horizon, they might have "more flexibility."

I quickly agreed to both ideas and told him that we would need all the support in the region we could get and had already engaged in discussions with India to make use of their ports to refuel and repair our ships. We knew that the U.S. Central Command was having similar discussions with Pakistan.

Admiral Koda then dove into the details and I realized how serious this Japanese constitution issue was. We had a far ranging discussion that included how to define the war zone so that their ships could remain clear and whether or not providing fuel to ships or aircraft that then attacked Afghanistan would be a violation.

Eventually Yoji became satisfied that as long as the plan was presented to the Diet in such a way as not to cue them to these issues, it would probably fly. We went back and briefed Admiral Blair and General Fujinawa and they approved what we had come up with. It took a couple of months for the Japanese to work it through their system and get the Diet's approval, but they got it done. A three ship task force of one oiler and two destroyers sailed to the North Arabian Sea and commenced refueling operations with our ships. The Japanese continued this deployment, rotating ships in and out, for over five years. They never charged us a dime. Rear Admiral Yoji Koda sent me a nice autographed picture of the three ships sailing in formation. He went on to earn three stars and become the Japanese Maritime Self Defense Force Fleet Commander.

As 2002 began and the Global War on Terror continued, primarily in Afghanistan, the Rumsfeld Department of Defense began to think about the worldwide optics of the United States seemingly perpetually in a state of war, or at least conflict, in the Middle East. It was supposed to be a global war on terror, but we seemed anchored to the Middle East, and now, Southwest Asia. Admittedly, that was where all the troubles seemed to emanate from, but surely, there was someplace else with a terrorism problem that affected American interests. Of course we had for many years been assisting the government of Colombia in its struggle with the Revolutionary Armed Forces of Colombia–People's Army. In Spanish, the Fuerzas Armadas Revolucianarias de Colombia, or FARC. But that had more to do with the "War on Drugs" than the "War on Terror." In the Pacific theater the government of Sri Lanka had been fighting an insurgency against the Liberation Tigers of Tamil Eelam, also known as the Tamil Tigers, since 1983. But that was purely an internal struggle with no U.S. national interests at stake.

In the Philippines however, one of the several militant Islamist separatist groups based in and around the southern Philippines caught the attention of the U.S. government. The Abu Sayyaf group had, since the early 1990s, been carrying out a bombing, kidnapping, assassination and extortion campaign in what they described as their fight for an independent Islamic province in the southern Philippines. Among those kidnapped in a 2001 raid on a resort on the island of Palawan, were Martin and Gracia Burnham, an American missionary couple, and Guillermo Sobero, a Peruvian-American tourist. Sobero was later beheaded. In 2002 the U.S. State Department classified the Abu Sayyaf as a terrorist group and put them on its list of Foreign Terrorist Organizations. There were also loose connections to Al Qaeda, primarily through funding. The group began associating itself with Al Qaeda, like so many others did, after 9/11.

This was close enough for the Department of Defense and planning began for Operation Enduring Freedom–Philippines. We had found a theater outside the Middle East but we were still dealing with a Muslim adversary. The U.S. needed a good Christian terrorist group to go after in the War on Terror to balance things out, but there didn't seem to be any around. The Irish Republican Army, although still technically in existence, had renounced its violence campaign in the early 1990s. In January 2002 I was dispatched to Manila to meet with the Director of National Defense, Angelo Reyes, and the Philippine military leadership, to cobble together a plan for the United States to assist the Philippines in defeating the Abu Sayyaf. Still sensitive to the history of the United States and the Philippines dating back to the Spanish-American War, our annexation of the Philippines, and the presence of major U.S. bases in the Philippines until 1992, the Filipinos would allow training assistance, intelligence support and logistics support only. No U.S. troops would actually fight the Abu Sayyaf, and no permanent U.S. bases would be permitted.

This was fine with Secretary Rumsfeld who ran hot and cold on the Operation Enduring Freedom–Philippines concept. The island of Basilan was the main home of the Abu Sayyaf, along with the nearby islands of Jolo and Sulu. These islands lie about 500 miles due south of Manila at the southern end of the Sulu Sea. In January and February 2002, I made three separate trips to Manila to hammer out the terms of reference with the Philippine military for our assistance. In between trips to Manila, I went back to Washington to participate in a wargame called "Primary Knight." This was my first indication that planning was underway for Iraq. Primary Knight was not about invading Iraq, rather it was a risk assessment exercise, designed to assess that *if we did invade Iraq*, where else in the world might we be vulnerable because forces had been diverted to the Iraq effort. As the representative for the Pacific, I had the most input because the Pacific theater featured the two most likely crises outside the Middle East–a North Korean provocation or a Chinese invasion of Taiwan.

In early March, I was in Washington to participate in a second edition of the Primary Knight war game, centered on a U.S. invasion of Iraq to remove Saddam Hussein from power. As I played my part in representing Admiral Blair and Pacific Command interests at these events, I became more and more convinced that we were serious about doing something in Iraq. Particularly among the civilian Defense Department participants representing Secretary Rumsfeld, there seemed to be a mindset that 9/11 had changed everything and we were no longer going to ignore tin pot dictators who thumbed their noses at the United States and the rest of the world. We had seen the consequences of not striking until struck first, and we didn't like it. This became the concept of "pre-emptive defense" and I fundamentally agreed that an imminent threat should be dealt with beforehand rather than after absorbing the first blow. That said, I did not feel that Saddam Hussein and Iraq represented an imminent threat to the United States; certainly not to the level requiring an invasion. It was true that ever since Desert Storm, Saddam Hussein had been a nuisance. Several times in the mid-nineties he had moved forces and threatened Kuwait and Saudi Arabia, causing the United States to send forces to the region to deter him. He had been thumbing his nose at UN sanctions since 1991, making life difficult for International Atomic Energy Administration inspectors, and occasionally taking shots at our aircraft patrolling the UN mandated no fly zones. By 2002 the only countries seriously observing the UN sanctions and committing forces to enforcing them were the United States and Great Britain. American and British ships were still doing Maritime Intercept Operations at sea 12 years after Desert Shield, tying up Navy resources and putting our sailors at risk every day. In his State of the Union speech in 2002, President Bush articulated the notion of an "axis of evil," naming North Korea, Iran and Iraq. The implication was obvious; we were tired of fooling around with these guys and were going to do something about it. Of the three, Iraq represented the easiest target.

Between March and June 2002, I was on the road almost constantly. I had brought Senior Chief Chris Adams with me to PACOM from Korea as my Flag Writer and I kept him busy cutting travel orders and arranging flights. Iris was loving living in Hawaii but it seemed like I was never home. In March I also traveled to San Francisco to participate in meetings on the U.S. - Japan security relationship. In April I went to China for the annual Military Maritime Consultative Agreement meetings, back again to Tokyo for Northeast Asia Cooperative Dialogue meetings, back again to Tokyo in May for Defense Trilateral Meetings, and then to Canberra, Australia for Australia–U.S. Staff Level meetings.

The U.S.–China Military Maritime Consultative Agreement meetings were an annual event that alternated hosts between China and the United States. Abbreviated MMCA, the meetings were a

U.S. initiative to establish better communications between Chinese and American military forces in the air and on the sea, and to establish certain protocols to reduce the chances of an incident. During the Cold War we had a similar agreement with the Soviet Union called the "Incidents at Sea" agreement, or INCSEA. As the PACOM J-5 it was my job to take a team to China and lead the negotiations with my Chinese counterpart. We started in Beijing and then moved to Shanghai were I was given the "great privilege" of touring one of their *LUHAI* class destroyers. In visiting our Embassy in Beijing before the meetings began, I was informed that the Chinese "rear admiral" assigned to lead the Chinese delegation, PLA Navy Vice Chief of Staff Rear Admiral Zhou Borong, was really an Army general. They dressed him up in a naval officer's uniform, but he didn't know much about naval matters. He had been chosen because he spoke and understood English reasonably well. He was supported by a team of People's Liberation Army–Navy (PLA-N) officers who provided the real naval expertise. Rear Admiral Borong was just a figurehead. This charade gave an indication of just how serious the Chinese were about hammering out an agreement: not very. We couldn't get them to agree to the simplest things, like communications drills at sea to reduce the chances of a misunderstanding. In 2003, we hosted that year's MMCA in Hawaii and the same team came, including "General-Admiral" Borong.

While all this was going on, Operation Enduring Freedom–Philippines was progressing on the island of Basilan, with our military assisting the Philippine Army with intelligence, training, and logistics support. The Filipinos, however, were not having much success in eliminating the Abu Sayyaf. As was typical of these efforts, we also lavished the island of Basilan with humanitarian assistance in order to "win the hearts and minds" of the mostly Muslim islanders. Part of the strategy was to have Navy SeaBees, our Navy construction battalion arm, build a ring road around the island and a pier to enhance commerce and improve the livelihood of the natives. The idea was to convince the island population that the central government in Manila had their best interests at heart and they should not support the separatist Abu Sayyaf group. The Philippine military was not satisfied with the progress of this effort and wanted more robust U.S. military assistance. As a result, we began cooperative planning for "Operation Balikatan."

Meanwhile in June I went to Washington twice for another war game and for meetings on the Pacific with our State Department colleagues and then to Singapore for a seminar war game and Annual Staff Talks Mid-Term Review. The bi-lateral meetings in the Pacific were numerous and required constant attention. Fortunately, I had a good staff that divided up the countries in theater so that I had experts to take with me on each trip to brief me on what I was supposed to say and to know. My Deputy J-5, Air Force Brigadier General Ray Johns, and I divided up the responsibilities to spread the pain. At issue was ensuring the right level of attendance at these various meetings. The Asian nations are very rank conscious and it would be considered an insult and a diminishment of relative importance to send a one-star officer to a meeting hosted at the two or three-star level. There were some things that only Admiral Blair could cover, some for me to cover, and some that Ray could cover. Further complicating this dynamic was the reluctance of the Asian nations to agree to multi-lateral meetings. There is no equivalent to NATO in Asia. A rough equivalent, the Southeast Asia Treaty Organization (SEATO) had been established in 1954 but disbanded in 1977. The problem with SEATO, which was intended to collectively provide defense against Communist expansion in Southeast Asia, was that the Asian nations would not trust each other in military matters. They preferred to deal with other nations in one-on-one, or bi-lateral, forums.

In May, Admiral Blair retired and was replaced by Admiral Tom Fargo, a submariner who had been the four-star Pacific Fleet Commander before being picked to head Pacific Command. I had known Admiral Fargo since the days when I was a captain in J-3 on the Joint Staff and he was the one-star Director for Operations, J-3, at U.S. Atlantic Command (USACOM) in Norfolk. As Commander, Pacific Fleet he was also based in Hawaii and was the officer responsible for executing our plan to defend Taiwan from a Chinese invasion. He was well suited to move from Pacific Fleet to PACOM.

Operations Plan 5077 (OPLAN 5077) was the plan to help defend Taiwan from an invasion by China, generally assumed to consist of a massive missile attack, followed by an air attack, and culminating in a cross-strait amphibious invasion. As the J-5, I was responsible for maintaining and updating this plan. When Donald Rumsfeld had taken office as Secretary of Defense he had mandated a top to bottom review of all such operational plans from each of the combatant commanders. As he was with the operation of the Pentagon in general, he was convinced that the military's planning for contingencies across the globe was mired in the past. He believed that military commanders would always ask for much more force than they actually needed to execute an operation and that the uniformed military was guilty of "old-think." This predisposition was to play a major role in events leading up to March 2003. Amid everything else going on, Operation Enduring Freedom–Philippines, Iraq planning, and the many bi-lateral nation-to-nation talks and conferences, we were constantly refining OPLAN 5077.

Having worked through the details with the Philippine military during a mid-July visit, we were ready to propose a more aggressive approach to dealing with the Abu Sayyaf, although still without American forces directly engaged in the fighting. The task now was to gain approval for this plan from Secretary Rumsfeld, and by extension President Bush, and then present it to Philippine President Gloria Macapal-Arroyo. For this new, more aggressive plan, I was teamed with Marine Major General Joe Weber, Commanding General, Third Marine Division, on the island of Okinawa, Japan. It would be Joe's Third Marines who would augment the Army Special Forces already working with the Philippine military.

Meanwhile, the drumbeat towards war with Iraq continued. While only peripherally involved myself, primarily in assessing the potential impact in the Pacific, I watched as in Washington we seemed to be moving inexorably toward an invasion. As early as September of 2002, the force buildup had begun and the talk now became about "when," not "if." The WMD argument was not just talk however. Military planners honestly believed that Saddam Hussein possessed and might use chemical weapons against advancing American forces. He had deployed poison gas against Iranian forces during the Iran–Iraq War and later used it to help put down a Kurdish uprising in the north of Iraq. Recognizing that all advancing troops might have to don chemical protective gear, talk turned to the need to launch the invasion in the cooler winter or early spring months; by May it would simply be too hot for soldiers to wear the gear for any length of time. Sustaining a buildup through the summer to await cooler weather in the fall was also seen as impractical. Circumstances were driving military planners towards a timeline based on weather, regardless of events on the diplomatic front.

In early September I traveled to Washington with Admiral Fargo for his brief of OPLAN 5077 to Secretary Rumsfeld. It did not go well. We had been warned that it was difficult to get through a whole brief with Rumsfeld because he would spend a huge amount of time challenging the going in assumptions that formed the basis of any recommended plan. In writing a plan for responding to a crisis, you have to first agree on a basic set of assumptions; the conditions that lead to the crisis, the actions of the enemy, the actions of third party nations, and so on. Once that is agreed, then a plan of action can flow logically. Nobody believes that any given crisis is going to actually follow the script, but without the basic conditions articulated, a plan has no meaningful foundation. Rumsfeld loved the mental gymnastics of challenging and questioning every assumption and making the briefer defend every position. Admiral Fargo handled himself well, but because of time constraints and the constant interruptions and questions, we never got beyond the opening assumptions. It was extremely frustrating and I questioned whether he really wanted to hear a plan that he would have to put his signature to. In my discussions with fellow J-5's around the globe, I learned that our experience was not uncommon.

One question that came out of the meeting was the issue of how much support we could expect from our allies in the region.

Would Japan, Korea and the Philippines let us fly combat sorties from their airfields for example? The defense of Taiwan was a U.S. commitment, not theirs. Would they risk antagonizing China and perhaps being drawn into a war?

I was dispatched to Tokyo in mid-September to brief U.S. Ambassador Howard Baker on OPLAN 5077 and get his opinion on Japan's actions. He was very friendly, very interested in the subject, and appreciative of the fact that we sought his opinion. He was uncertain, however, as to what the Japanese would allow, and like everything else in the plan, felt that it all depended on the circumstances leading to the Chinese aggression. Back to the assumptions.

Every year the United States and Australia have high level meetings called Australian–U.S. Ministerial Meetings, or AUSMINS. The location alternates back and forth between Canberra and Washington and the centerpiece is a joint meeting between the U.S. Secretaries of State and Defense and the Australian Ministers of Foreign Affairs and Defence. In 2002, the meetings were hosted by Washington at the State Department. Admiral Fargo and I went to sit in. On the 25th of October we gathered on the 7th Floor of the State Department for the four-way meeting between the key players. By this time the war drums were pounding loudly and what to do about Iraq and how much support could be expected from Australia was dominating the discussion. For whatever reason, Colin Powell had to miss this portion of the meeting and UN Ambassador John Bolton filled in for him. It was at this session that I heard one of the dumbest things ever said by a senior diplomat.

Ambassador Bolton was rolling out the pictures of the supposed Iraqi mobile chemical weapons labs for the benefit of the two very skeptical ministers from Australia. It was clear from their comments and expressions that, in their minds, these chemical chuck-wagons hardly justified war. Finally, one of them said, "What if the inspectors don't find any evidence of WMD?" At the time the IAEA inspectors had been thrown out of Iraq but the UN was moving towards a resolution that would get them back in.

Bolton blurted out, almost petulantly, "We've already got Congressional authority to use force."

I was stunned. He had just told them it didn't matter what the inspectors found, we were going to invade Iraq. It also implied that we didn't really care what the Australians thought either.

In September, President Bush had traveled to the United Nations in New York and urged the assembly to confront and disarm Saddam Hussein and back previous UN resolutions ordering disarmament. On November 8th the UN Security Council unanimously adopted Resolution 1441, calling on Iraq to comply with previous resolutions by disarming and re-admitting the IAEA weapons inspectors or face "serious consequences." On November 18th, United Nations weapons inspectors, led by Hans Blix, arrived in Iraq. Hans Blix, a former Swedish Foreign Minister, was head of the International Atomic Energy Agency. This was followed in January of 2003 by Hans Blix telling the Security Council that Iraq had not genuinely accepted demands to disarm and "should cooperate more."

On January 31st 2003, having received Secretary Rumsfeld's approval to proceed, I flew to Manila once again to this time brief Philippine President Gloria Macapal-Arroyo on our Operation Balikatan. Checking in to our hotel on the 2nd of February we watched the footage on the lobby television of the space shuttle *COLUMBIA* disintegrating as it re-entered the earth's atmosphere. All seven astronauts on board were killed as *COLUMBIA* was destroyed over Texas. It was February 1st in the United States.

On the 4th of February, Joe Weber and I briefed President Macapal-Arroyo and her national security team, including Minister of Defense Reyes, with whom I had established a good relationship. She was a tiny lady, under five feet tall and impeccably dressed in a bright red business suit. She listened intently to the brief, and when we finished she said, "When can we start?"

"Well, Madam President, I will return to Hawaii and report on this meeting and then Admiral Fargo will inform Secretary Rumsfeld and President Bush of your approval."

"We are ready to start tomorrow. Next week."

From the palace we went to the Embassy to brief Ambassador Frank Ricciardone and for me to call on the secure telephone and brief Admiral Fargo. I then left Manila the next day to return to Hawaii. When I arrived at work on Friday I went to see Admiral Fargo. He said, "Something's up in Washington. The Secretary isn't so sure he wants to do Balikatan."

"What, after we briefed the president and got her approval?"

"I don't know what's going on. He seems to have changed his mind."

Somewhere, somebody had poisoned the well. I felt betrayed and felt bad about how this news would be received in the Philippines. The Philippine military was excited about the plan and looking forward to more robust assistance from the United States. President Arroyo had not hesitated to approve the concept.

As things turned out, we never executed the plan briefed to the President of the Philippines. Instead we created a more robust exercise program and called it Balikatan to smooth over the fact that we had backed out of the deal so carefully negotiated with the Philippine Armed Forces. American presence was always a source of political drama in the Philippines and the Balikatan exercises became a reason for the occasional demonstration in front of the palace or the U.S. Embassy.

While I was flying back to Hawaii after the Arroyo briefing, Secretary of State Colin Powell was in New York on February 5th presenting his now famous evidence of concealed WMD to the UN Security Council. The same mobile "WMD labs" shown to the Australians were trotted out and shown to the Security Council. Not surprisingly, there was skepticism about the conclusiveness of this presentation.

On the 19th of March 2003, the United States initiated hostilities against Iraq in Operation Iraqi Freedom. As the news of the commencement of hostilities was reported by the networks, I was in my office at PACOM Headquarters in Hawaii, watching the television just like everyone else. As I watched the coverage, I thought to myself, "I can't believe we're really doing this." Not that I should have been surprised given all the various planning conferences I had attended in Washington, and having been privy to certain classified information. Seeing it actually unfold, however, hit home in a way that all the meetings and planning sessions never had. The sheer enormity of what we were doing was sobering. I thought to myself that, as far as I knew, this was the first time in modern U.S. history that we had invaded another country absent an act of war initiated by that country. In the past we had either retaliated for a direct attack on the United States or its territories or forces, or had gone in to help a friendly country defeat an aggressor. Admittedly, we had become engaged in wars and military action under some flimsy circumstances, but always there had been a rationale which could be trotted out by way of explanation; a casus belli.

The sinking of the battleship *USS MAINE* in Havana Harbor in 1898 provided the impetus for the United States to go to war with Spain in support of the Cuban revolt and led to our involvement in the Philippine Revolution and the American-Philippine War in 1899. The Mexican-American War of 1846–1848 was the result of Mexican incursions following the U.S. annexation of Texas in 1845. Our involvement in Vietnam was the result of our Cold War containment of the Soviet Union and the belief that we were saving the South Vietnamese, and our own interests, from being overrun by the Communist North Vietnamese. The Tonkin Gulf incident of August 4, 1964 served as the casus belli for direct military action by the United States against North Vietnam.

All that said, despite the persistent irritant represented by Iraq under Saddam Hussein, Operation Iraqi Freedom felt different. It was a pre-emptive invasion to remove Saddam from power before he could do more damage and potentially use or proliferate weapons of mass destruction. 9/11 had created the aforementioned mindset among the Bush administration that we were no longer going to sit back and take the first punch. The origins of the invasion of Iraq extended to the years prior to the Bush administration, although this fact was conveniently forgotten later by those who opposed the war. In October 1998, during the Clinton administration, the Iraq Liberation Act made regime change in Iraq official U.S. policy. This act passed 360-38 in the House of Representatives and by unanimous consent in the Senate. When President Bush came into office he inherited a low-level conflict with Iraq which had been ongoing since the end of Desert Storm.

Many claims have been made that "Bush lied" about WMD in Iraq as justification for the war. The Clinton administration had also highlighted the threat of WMD from Iraq, and every western intelligence service held the position that Saddam Hussein possessed WMD in the form of chemical weapons. Further, it was intelligence consensus that he aspired to develop his own nuclear capability. In the wake of 9/11 and with the concept of "pre-emptive defense," the idea of letting this cancer metastasize in Baghdad was anathema to the Bush team. In my opinion there was adequate justification to excise the cancer sooner rather than later, but the Bush team erred in over-emphasizing the WMD angle. By April 3rd, U.S. forces had seized control of Saddam International Airport, changing the name to Baghdad International Airport, and by April 9th had seized control of Baghdad, ending the regime of Saddam Hussein. Saddam however, remained on the loose.

Sometime in early April I took a phone call from Air Force Major General Mike Dunn, the Joint Staff Vice J-5. I had known Mike in Korea where he had served as the Deputy Chief of Staff at USFK, and of course in his role as Vice J-5.

"Hey Bill, they're looking around for someone to replace me this summer and right now you look like the top candidate."

"Oh yeah, where are you going?"

"I can't say yet, but I've been nominated for a three-star position. So head's up, you may be coming to Washington."

The next time I saw Admiral Fargo I told him about the conversation with Mike. He didn't really react, so I figured he knew before me that I was being considered. The CNO would not have thrown my name into the ring without talking to Admiral Fargo about it beforehand. The Vice J-5, technically the Vice Director, Strategic Plans and Policy Directorate, was a nominative two-star position and when an opening came up, all four services would be given the opportunity to nominate an officer for consideration. Without my knowledge, the Navy had nominated me.

CHAPTER 27

Iraq, Iraq, Iraq

I reported to the Joint Staff, J-5, the Directorate for Strategic Plans and Policy, on June 23rd, 2003. Unlike during my previous Pentagon tours, I was now on the prestigious E-Ring, second floor. I had a window looking out towards the Potomac River and the monuments beyond. My immediate boss was Army Lieutenant General Walter F. "Skip" Sharp. Air Force General Dick Myers was the Chairman of the Joint Chiefs of Staff and Marine Corps General Pete Pace was the Vice Chairman. The J-5, Plans and Policy, and the J-3, Operations, necessarily worked very closely together and my previous experience in J-3 was helpful in adjusting to my new duties. The J-3 was Air Force Lieutenant General Norton "Norty" Schwartz, and his deputy, my counterpart, was Army Major General Stan McChrystal. It was a talented and cohesive group, the J-3 and J-5 working together much better than they had in my earlier tour as part of the J-3. J-3–J-5 cooperation was essential as the policy deliberations and decisions which were handled by the J-5 often translated into deployment orders and other operational impacts orchestrated by J-3.

By the summer of 2003, things were beginning to spiral out of control in Iraq. The invasion and collapse of the Saddam Hussein regime had gone reasonably quickly. A combination of factors, however, had led initially to civil unrest and finally to a formidable insurgency. Policy decisions made in the run-up to the invasion, coupled with the absence of a well thought out post-hostilities plan, had resulted in incoherence in the mission for our troops once the main combat effort was over. We had watched on the 1st of May from Admiral Fargo's office in Hawaii as President Bush made his memorable S-3 VIKING flight out to the carrier *LINCOLN* off San Diego and spoke to the nation from the flight deck under the now infamous "Mission Accomplished" banner. I believe that the banner was more the ship's doing than the White House. The *LINCOLN* was returning from a combat deployment and their mission *was* accomplished even though the war was far from over.

I stepped into the Vice J-5 position in the midst of a Pentagon and an administration scrambling to figure out how to get things on track in Iraq. One of the key responsibilities of the J-5 was to attend White House Situation Room meetings to represent the Chairman at National Security Council meetings. It seemed like there were 20 meetings a week and 15 of them were on Iraq.

The National Security Council, or NSC, was established as part of the National Security Act of 1947 which also established the Joint Chiefs and the Chairman, the Department of Defense, the Central Intelligence Agency, and created the U.S. Air Force out of the Army Air Corps. Its stated purpose was to provide national security advice and assistance to the President on national security and foreign policy matters and to coordinate the efforts of the "interagency." The interagency, a widely used but ill-defined term, consists of all elements of the U.S. Government with an interest in any given issue requiring coordination and cooperation across agencies. There were several layers of the NSC process designed to provide the President the best possible advice and recommendations without involving him personally at each step. My involvement was at the Deputies Committee which was chaired by the Deputy National Security Advisor; Steve Hadley. I often attended Deputies Committee meetings as the principal Joint Staff representative even though the four-star Vice Chairman of the Joint Chiefs was the designated attendee. I found Steve Hadley, a friendly, organized, and lawyerly gentleman, to be an effective chair at these meetings, giving everyone their opportunity to speak, summarizing the action items well, and generally keeping an even keel. I would also periodically accompany the Chairman or Vice Chairman to the higher level meetings; the Principals Committee and National Security Council. Condoleezza Rice chaired the Principals Committee and President Bush presided over the National Security Council.

It is difficult to describe the intense time pressures that the Chairman and Vice Chairman were under on a daily basis. If I were to be the number two at a Principals Committee meeting, I would meet the Chairman or Vice Chairman at their office and literally brief them on the meeting while walking to the car and during the drive to the White House. It was not uncommon for the conversation to begin, "What are we going to talk about at this one, Bill?" Their schedules were so jammed that they had little time to sit and read the papers beforehand, or to have a huddle with senior staff and iron out what position to take on a given issue. Likewise, when I was the Joint Staff representative for a Deputies Committee meeting, I would get briefed an hour beforehand by the action officer responsible for the topic du jour. Often there was no time to seek clarification from higher authority on a questionable point which was likely to be discussed.

At National Security Council meetings President Bush was a different man than the one that often caused me to cringe when watching him give a speech or do a press conference on television. He was focused, decisive, and asked good questions. He was also fun, and enjoyed poking fun at people around the table, particularly Steve Hadley in his second term after Steve had replaced Condoleezza Rice as National Security Advisor. At one meeting he had great fun at the expense of Donald Rumsfeld over the news that some entomologist had discovered a new species of dung beetle and had named it after Rumsfeld.

Dealing with Donald Rumsfeld in the Pentagon was a hit or miss adventure and that carried through to his staff, particularly in the Policy shop under Doug Feith. It was not unusual to gather in Secretary Rumsfeld's outer office to have a meeting and hear somebody ask his secretary, Delonnie Henry, what side of the bed he had gotten up on that morning.

As time went on I spent a significant amount of time with Secretary Rumsfeld. Often when Ministers of Defense from foreign countries would call on him in his office, I would be detailed as the duty Joint Staff officer to sit next to him in my dress uniform and participate in the meeting, although I was rarely asked to say anything of significance. The Secretary kept everyone off balance; at times as friendly, charming and smiling as could be, and at other times cranky, irritable, and short with everybody. It all depended on the answer to that "which side of the bed" question.

At one meeting I was the senior Joint Staff representative and trying to explain something to him. He kept interrupting me with questions, throwing me off my game. At one point while I was trying to complete one thought while dealing with one of his interruptions, he, said "Speak in complete sentences." It was an embarrassing moment, but I pressed on. I observed this same style and rudeness on many occasions, even involving four-star officers or senior civilian members of his staff.

Secretary Rumsfeld was famous for managing the Pentagon through his "snowflake" memos. They were called snowflakes, even by him, for the way they flew out of his office and around the building as if in a blizzard. If he had a thought, or a question, he would jot it down on a small piece of paper, his secretary would type it up, and it would be sent either to his own staff or down to the Joint Staff where it would enter the action tracking system before landing on the desk of whoever was deemed the right person to take it for action. More often than not these were one or two sentence memos, without context. If more than a few days went by without an answer, another snowflake would emerge on the same subject, but often worded differently. This version would also get a tracking number and be sent to the appropriate office; sometimes to a different office than the previous version. Donald Rumsfeld found this bureaucracy, which he was guilty of exacerbating, extremely frustrating and wasteful.

In truth, on the Joint Staff, we were often our own worst enemies. If asked a simple question, like, "What color is the chair?" the Joint Staff machinery would insist on a comprehensive answer which included the material covering the chair, how many buttons held the cover in place, how long the legs were, where the chair was manufactured, and what other colors were available. Responses also had to include all the necessary "chops" by other organizations with a stake in the answer. If he asked a simple naval question like, "how many aircraft carriers are in the Persian Gulf today," the answer had to be chopped by the Navy staff before it flowed back up the Joint Staff chain of command and back to OSD. By the time it made its way back to Rumsfeld's inbox, the answer might very well have changed.

As 2003 wore on and the situation in Iraq continued to worsen, the effort in Afghanistan was put on the back burner. On July 22nd, Saddam's sons, Uday and Qusay, were killed by U.S. forces, but Saddam Hussein remained on the loose. Despite the overriding focus on Iraq, there were still meetings to be held and decisions to be made on other issues, most notably about turning command of Operation Enduring Freedom in Afghanistan over to NATO. The Bush administration, however, was almost singularly focused on Iraq. After all, the justification for our invasion of Afghanistan was widely accepted; not so much the decision to invade Iraq. Saddam Hussein was still at large and the evidence of WMD was scant.

After much diplomacy and hand-wringing, NATO was handed command of the Afghanistan mission on August 11, 2003, marking its first major operation outside of Europe in the 54-year history of the alliance. The diplomacy involved convincing the other 18 NATO nations to assume responsibility for the mission. Even though NATO is commanded operationally by an American four-star, at the time Marine General Jim Jones, and the Commander of the NATO International Security Assistance Force (ISAF) would also be an American or British general, Secretary Rumsfeld had many doubts about the ability of NATO to get the job done. He had been U.S. Ambassador to NATO from 1973-1974 and had a good understanding of what a wishy-washy body it could be. Convincing NATO involved convincing Europe that ISAF would be a humanitarian, peacekeeping mission, not a war. That is the way the governments of Europe, and Canada, presented the mission to their people. This would come back to haunt us in years to come.

The Joint Staff, as it had been in the 90s when I was a captain in J-3, was a fascinating place to work. It was even more so as a two-star admiral and the number two officer in the J-5. On a daily basis I was exposed to the workings of our government national security apparatus at the highest levels. As General Norty Schwartz once commented to me, "It's a hell of a civics education." It is also a real meat-grinder.

On a typical weekday I was in the office no later than 6:15 AM. The Chairman held a meeting with his Directors at 6:30 AM in order to be ready for his meeting with the Secretary of Defense at 7:00 AM. Most evenings did not end until 7:30 or 8:00 PM. Because of the grind of the daily schedule, there was no time to re-group, discuss the day's events, and start thinking about the next day until after 6:00 PM.

There were pleasant travel aspects to the job as well. As I had done in the Pacific, there were several opportunities to represent the U.S. military in high level bi-lateral meetings with our friends and allies around the world. As the Vice J-5, I was also the U.S. military representative to something called the U.S.–Canada Permanent Joint Board on Defense (PJBD). This group was established in 1940 and meets twice a year, alternating between the U.S. and Canada, to conduct studies and provide policy recommendations to the respective governments. It is co-chaired by politically appointed American and Canadian co-chairs. My first PJBD meeting was in Quebec City, Canada, a beautiful, walled city on the banks of the St. Lawrence Seaway. There were two days of meetings and two nights of socializing at all the PJBD sessions. My Canadian counterpart was also a Rear Admiral, Drew Robertson, and we became good friends. Neither of us ever knew what became of PJBD recommendations, as the co-chairs forwarded them by letter to the President and Prime Minister, respectively, where I believe they ended up in the circular file.

Similar to the PJBD was something called the Inter-American Defense Board, or IADB, for which I was also the U.S. representative. The IADB included all of the nations in the western hemisphere from Canada in the north to Chile and Argentina in the south. This included all the tiny island nations in the Caribbean. The IADB made the PJBD look like a real dynamo. Most of the other representatives were the military attaches of their respective countries, living in the Washington, D.C. area and participating in the IADB as a collateral duty. Some of the South American countries, however, detailed a one or two-star officer to Washington specifically to represent them on the IADB. We met once a quarter and accomplished nothing except having a nice lunch after the meeting. I thought it a waste of time and money. I wondered what these specifically detailed South American generals did the rest of the time.

On December 13th Saddam Hussein was captured near Tikrit, Iraq, his hometown. In Baghdad, Ambassador Paul Bremer, head of the Coalition Provisional Authority (CPA) made the famous announcement, "We got him!" This brought a certain amount of closure but did nothing to stabilize the country. The relationship between Paul Bremer and Donald Rumsfeld was an interesting one and provided real insight into Secretary Rumsfeld. When the Saddam statue fell in Baghdad and a rump government was established, Paul Bremer was designated by President Bush to head up the CPA. Rumsfeld argued that Ambassador Bremer should report through him, as Secretary of Defense, not through Secretary of State Colin Powell. His argument was that the Defense Department was providing the preponderance of force in the country, and military personnel were performing, out of necessity, most of the civilian ministry type of duties that one would normally expect the State Department and other government agencies to provide. This was true. Paul Bremer, however, had been appointed by the President and that was who he was going to report to. This resulted in a number of pronouncements and policy decisions emanating from Baghdad that caught Secretary Rumsfeld, his presumptive boss, by surprise. The now famous edicts to disband the Iraqi Army and the policy of de-Baathification caught Washington by surprise; at least the Pentagon. Disbanding the Iraqi Army turned thousands of young men loose with no jobs. Frustrated, they soon joined the insurgency. The Baath Party was Saddam Hussein's political party. To survive in a position of authority in Saddam Hussein's Iraq, Baath Party membership was a must. By throwing Baath Party members out of their positions following the invasion, Paul Bremer and the United States deprived post-invasion Iraq of the very techno-crats necessary to continue a functioning government.

Doug Feith, the Under Secretary of Defense for Policy, USDP, was my most consistent OSD partner in preparing for and attending Deputies Committee meetings. Doug was an interesting character, and one of the most disliked on the Rumsfeld team. Considered one of the key "neo-cons" who got us into Iraq in the first place, he did not enjoy a good reputation within the interagency. Personally, I liked Doug. He was always a gentleman to me and treated me with respect. One of the initiatives of the Rumsfeld Pentagon was a global posture re-alignment. Again, Donald Rumsfeld felt that the way our forces were distributed around the world, particularly in Europe, was "old-think," postured to fight the Soviet Union and not reflective of the 21st Century global environment. Inertia had kept 200,000 troops in Europe long after the collapse of the Soviet Union. Likewise, he believed that the South Koreans were far more capable militarily, not to mention economically, than their enemies in North Korea. Why, he would ask, did we still need 38,000 U.S. military tied down on the Korean peninsula? Why were we still operating navy and air forces out of Iceland where they had been strategically positioned to counter a Soviet naval breakout through the choke points represented by the Greenland–Iceland–United Kingdom gap? Once briefed on our global force disposition, Secretary Rumsfeld zeroed in on three enduring deployments that he thought would be low hanging fruit. The naval and air forces in Iceland, the peacekeeping troops in the Sinai Peninsula, and an Army Blackhawk helicopter detachment in the Turks and Caicos Islands were all seen as unnecessary holdovers from a bygone era. The aforementioned Iceland forces, consisting of Navy P-3 Orion maritime patrol aircraft, Air Force fighters and search and rescue helicopters, along with a staff and all the requisite support personnel were successfully pulled out over the protestations of the government of Iceland. Likewise, the Army helicopter deployment to the Turks and Caicos, there to support the U.S. counter-drug effort, was terminated and the six helicopters made available for general use. Secretary Rumsfeld was not, however, successful in pulling the United States out of the

Multinational Force and Observers mission in the Sinai. Established after the Camp David Accords were signed in 1978, the Multinational Force and Observers mission resulted from an agreement between the United States, Egypt, and Israel to set up an observer force to monitor the agreements outlawing force buildups by either Egypt or Israel along the Sinai border. It went into effect in 1981 and twenty-three years later Secretary Rumsfeld thought it had outlived its usefulness and was no longer necessary.

Doug Feith had never been to Asia, presumably, even as early as 2003, the theater of most importance in the 21st Century. I was chosen to accompany Doug on a tour of Asia, at the same time executing one of the periodic engagements with the Chinese. In addition to the regular meeting with the Chinese, the purpose was to brief our friends and allies on the global posture re-alignment. It was a fantastic 12 day trip, although we spent more nights airborne in the Air Force Gulfstream G-5 than we did sleeping in hotel rooms. Between the 4th and 16th of February 2004 we traveled to Anchorage, Alaska; Beijing; Canberra, Alice Springs, Katherine and Darwin, Australia; Singapore; Misawa, Japan and back to Washington. After the formal meetings with the Chinese in Beijing we were visiting allies and the theme of the trip was to pitch the idea that the United States did not necessarily want large bases full of U.S. military personnel overseas, rather we wanted access to places overseas from which our forces could operate in a crisis. The bumper sticker was "Places not Bases."

At the same time that these events were taking place, the U.S. government was tackling the concept of fighting a global war on terror. This was different than planning to fight the Soviet Union, where forces and capabilities could be quantified and countering forces planned for, fielded, and positioned. In fighting terror, we were fighting a tactic, not a force or a country. One of the questions to be answered was: who is the enemy? In the wake of 9/11 it was pretty easy to identify Al Qaeda and Osama bin Laden, but a global war encompassed various splinter groups and loosely associated sympathetic terrorist organizations, most of whom had no designs on the United States. The Abu Sayyaf group in the

Philippines fell into this category, yet we were still assisting the Philippine government in dealing with them.

If there is one thing the military is good at that the rest of the government is not, it is in writing a campaign plan (the exception being a political campaign plan). Following the 9/11 attacks, the federal government had taken a number of significant steps, most notably creating the Department of Homeland Security and the Transportation Security Agency (TSA), and creating a new combatant command to defend the United States (Northern Command). The creation of the Director of National Intelligence (DNI) would come later in 2004 after the 9/11 Commission Report was issued in July. But in terms of developing a coherent strategy that laid out the ends, ways, and means of a campaign to combat terrorism, the government was floundering.

Recognizing a need, we took it on in the Joint Staff J-5 to articulate a strategy. We stood up a new division within J-5 for combating terrorism and put some of our best minds to work on the problem. We invited other elements of the government to participate, but received little support. One of the reasons, I believe, is that throughout the government, but particularly in those agencies with national security portfolios, the Rumsfeld Pentagon was despised. Part of it was Donald Rumsfeld's style, an arrogance which transmitted to the lower levels of the OSD staff, and part of it was a belief that these were the same people who had gotten us bogged down in Iraq and were in the process of mismanaging that adventure.

We ended up creating a briefing which was very well received. It began by laying out the history of attacks against the United States, culminating on 9/11, and explained how we had ignored them, dealt with them as law enforcement issues, or simply not connected the dots and realized that we had a motivated enemy plotting against the United States and the western world. The brief went on to explain how technology had made it easier for our enemies to communicate, spread their message, and recruit, and how the weapons at their disposal had become increasingly more lethal. In identifying the enemy, we were forced to state the obvious: Islamist Extremists. Nobody in the administration wanted to characterize this as a war on Islam, but the facts pointed to Islam as the religion which produced the vast majority of terrorists. We took pages from radical websites and used them to demonstrate the goal of re-creating an Islamic Caliphate that mirrored the reach of the Ottoman Empire that prevailed from 1299 to 1922. Some websites envisioned a Caliphate that covered the globe. We identified the conditions which led to radicalization, most significantly poor governance, lack of opportunity and meaningful education, and radical teachings. Finally, we articulated a strategy that was centered not on military conflict, but on building partner nation capacity and bringing all elements of national power, soft and hard, to bear on the problem.

I ended up being the spokesman for this unclassified brief and once it spread on the internet I was receiving invitations to present it everywhere from the University of Southern California and Mississippi State University, to Capitol Hill, to groups visiting the Pentagon, and to the John F. Kennedy School at Harvard, all of which I did.

If the administration had any positive WMD outcome to report following the invasion of Iraq, it might have come from Libya. On December 19, 2003, Libyan president Muammar Qaddafi stunned the world by renouncing Tripoli's weapons of mass destruction programs and welcoming international inspectors to verify his pledge. Inspectors from the United States, Great Britain, and international organizations worked to dismantle Libya's chemical and nuclear weapons programs, as well as its longest-range ballistic missiles. On February 26, 2004, the United States lifted a travel ban on Libya which had been in place for 23 years. The Bush administration credited the pre-emptive invasion of Iraq for convincing Qaddafi that he might be next. That quite possibly was the case. Intelligence reporting later suggested that Iran may have taken a pause in its nuclear weapons program around the same time; presumably for the same reasons.

This same thinking found its way into a revision to the Unified Command Plan in 2004. The Unified Command Plan, or

UCP, divides up the world among the United States geographical combatant commanders. In 2004 there were five, Pacific Command, European Command (which also had responsibility for Africa with the exception of Egypt and the Horn of Africa down through Kenya), Southern Command, Northern Command (created after 9/11), and Central Command. The combatant commanders are the nation's warfighting commanders in their respective regions. They are also responsible for military to military engagement, as I had been doing for Pacific Command while serving as J-5. For reasons intended to avoid awkward situations, India was assigned to Pacific Command while hated enemy Pakistan, sharing a border, was assigned to Central Command. The idea was that the Pacific Command commander could be friendly and supportive of India at the same time that the Central Command commander was doing the same with Pakistan. If one commander was responsible for both nations, he would be trusted by neither. In the eastern Mediterranean, or the Levant, a similar approach was adopted. Israel, Lebanon and Syria, bordering the Mediterranean Sea, were assigned to European Command. Egypt, although neighboring Israel, residing on the continent of Africa, and also bordering the Mediterranean, was assigned to Central Command. This reflected Egypt's status as the leader of the Arab world, all the rest of which, with the exception of Syria and Lebanon, was in the Central Command region.

As the situation in Iraq deteriorated throughout 2003, intelligence indicated that insurgents from throughout the Islamist world were given easy access to Iraq through neighboring Syria. Many of those Jihadists killed or captured fighting the United States and its coalition partners in the Iraq insurgency had entered Iraq across the Syrian border. Despite diplomatic entreaties to halt the flow, the Bashar al-Assad government of Syria was seen as doing little or nothing to help. The Rumsfeld Defense Department came up with the idea of modifying the Unified Command Plan out of cycle and moving Syria and Lebanon from the European Command theater to the Central Command theater. Their rationale was to send a not too subtle message to the Syrians that they were now in the crosshairs of our warfightingest combatant command.

Watch out or you could be next, we'll just keep going west. This adjustment was made but it did not make an appreciable difference on the ground.

In April we began getting hints that something bad had occurred in the Baghdad Correctional Facility, Abu Ghraib Prison, which was under U.S. control. I did not see the pictures until they were aired on the television news program *60 Minutes* on April 28th. The story is well-known and not worth repeating here, but the impact of the pictures of a rogue group of West Virginia National Guard soldiers abusing Iraqi prisoners was a huge embarrassment to the country and to the U.S. military. In the days following the *60 Minutes* program there was a notable deflation of morale in the Pentagon. We all felt tainted by the scandal.

In May, the world was treated to the horror of the decapitation of an American civilian contractor in Iraq, Nicholas Berg. Nicholas Berg had been abducted and his decapitated body discovered on May 8th. On May 11th a video was released graphically showing Berg being beheaded with a knife while being held down by four masked men shouting "Allahu Akbar." It is widely believed that Abu Musab al-Zarqawi, who later became the acknowledged leader of Al Qaeda in Iraq, wielded the knife. The group claimed that the beheading was in retaliation for the events at Abu Graib prison.

One of the highlights for me in 2004 was the opportunity to travel with Secretary of State Colin Powell as a substitute for the Assistant to the Chairman (ACJCS), Vice Admiral Jim Metzger. Jim was finishing his tour and preparing to retire from the Navy and a three-day trip to Brazil would have been an inconvenience. I was detailed to accompany Secretary Powell on the trip as "Acting ACJCS." We left Washington on October 4th aboard the Secretary's C-40 aircraft, a specially configured Boeing 737, and flew to Sao Paolo, Brazil. Secretary Powell invited me up to his private cabin in the C-40 for a chat. Having been Chairman of the Joint Chiefs himself he was familiar with the role of the ACJCS and my role as the Vice J-5. He could not have been nicer; kind and welcoming. The signals I received from the State Department personnel on the trip were nothing but positive; they absolutely loved Colin Powell.

The morning of the 5th, Colin Powell spoke at an American Chamber of Commerce breakfast in Sao Paolo and I sat at a table with a number of American businessmen. The presidential election was a month away, with Senator John Kerry challenging George W. Bush for the office. The Americans at our breakfast table turned to me when Powell was done and said, "Can you convince him to run for President?"

Leaving Sao Paolo, we flew to the capital of Brazil, Brasilia, for meetings with the President, Luis Inacia Lula da Silva, popularly known as "Lula," and his senior cabinet members. Upon leaving Brasilia we detoured by the island of Grenada. In September, Hurricane Ivan had gone across Grenada and devastated the country. The Grenadians were asking for U.S. assistance and Colin Powell wanted to get a first-hand look at the situation while the aircraft was refueled. We flew around the area of the capital, St. George's, to view the damage before landing. Grenada has two things going for it: nutmeg and tourism. The nutmeg trees had been virtually wiped out, uprooted or stripped of their leaves and nuts. The hotels had suffered serious damage along with many homes and businesses. When we landed, I trooped along with the rest of the staff to accompany Secretary Powell to his meeting with the Prime Minister and his cabinet. It was a sad affair. The nutmeg crop had been nearly completely wiped out and, as was explained, nutmeg trees take years to grow and mature so that they are productive. Ivan had hit Grenada as a Category 3 hurricane and 90% of the homes, mostly wooden shacks, had been destroyed. The tourist industry was virtually destroyed as well. The Prime Minister and his cabinet were all blacks, dressed in open collar shirts and trousers, the women in colorful dresses. Half of the men were wearing sandals. It was truly a third world experience and my heart went out to these desperate people who saw in Colin Powell somebody they could trust and put their hope in. For his part, Secretary Powell listened carefully but made no firm promises.

I do not know what level of aid the United States ultimately provided to Grenada. Too many other events transpired as the year closed out and the plight of Grenada fell off my radar scope. On

November 2ⁿᵈ, George Bush was re-elected President of the United States and on November 14ᵗʰ Colin Powell resigned as Secretary of State. Condoleezza Rice was named the next Secretary of State and Steve Hadley was elevated to National Security Advisor. At the Pentagon, Donald Rumsfeld and Paul Wolfowitz stayed on but Doug Feith left as USDP to be replaced by Ambassador Eric Edelman, a former Ambassador to Turkey and former NSC staff member.

In December 2004, Donald Rumsfeld was speaking to a group of soldiers in Kuwait preparing to move into Iraq. He was questioned by one of the troops about the lack of up-armored vehicles available in the war zone to protect soldiers from the improvised explosive devices (IEDs) which had become the weapon of choice for killing Americans. The soldier went on to say that the troops were being forced to improvise with scrap metal and sandbags in order to increase the survivability of their vehicles, primarily the High Mobility Multipurpose Wheeled Vehicle, or Humvee. There simply were not an adequate number of up-armored Humvees in the inventory. Caught off guard, Secretary Rumsfeld famously said, "You go to war with the Army you have, not the Army you want or wish to have at a later time." This dismissive statement created a firestorm of negative publicity.

Around the Pentagon were stationed about six Humvees manned with soldiers and .50 caliber machineguns. These vehicles had been put in place shortly after 9/11. One day I had finished my lunchtime run and as I was cooling off outside the Pentagon Athletic Center my curiosity got the best of me. I walked into the River Entrance parking lot and asked the corporal manning the machine gun if this was an up-armored Humvee.

"Yes sir," he said.

"Are they all up-armored?" I asked, waving my arm at the others in sight.

"Yes sir."

After showering and returning to my office I was on the phone with Ian Brzezinski, Deputy Assistant Secretary of Defense for Europe and NATO, and I told him what I had learned. Ian was the son of Zbigniew Brzezinski who had been Jimmy Carter's National Security Advisor from 1977 to 1981.

"Rumsfeld is gonna get crucified if the press finds out he's protecting the Pentagon with up-armored Humvees while our soldiers in Iraq are getting killed while driving around unprotected," I said.

"Shit, you're right, thanks!" and he hung up.

Within days those Humvees were gone, never to be replaced. Hopefully they were shipped to Iraq, but more likely they went back to whatever National Guard unit was then providing the troops around the Pentagon.

2004 ended with a bang—literally. On December 26th, a magnitude 9.1 earthquake, the third largest ever recorded on a seismograph, occurred on the Indian Ocean floor about 100 miles west of the Indonesian island of Sumatra. The earthquake triggered a series of devastating tsunamis along most of the land masses bordering the Indian Ocean, creating waves as high as 80 feet and killing approximately 230,000 people in 14 countries. In the days that followed a massive humanitarian effort was launched, led in large part by the U.S. Navy which sent all available assets, including the aircraft carrier *ABRAHAM LINCOLN*, to the area. Helicopters quickly became the most valuable asset, supported by Navy ships on which to land, refuel, and from which to deliver humanitarian supplies. In what I thought was an extremely shortsighted move by the government of Indonesia, our helicopters and relief aircraft were not allowed to base on Indonesian soil, and our ships were required to stay outside the 12 mile territorial seas limit. The Indonesians were still angry about the military to military clamps that had been put on our relationship by the Leahy Amendment following abuses by the Indonesian military in putting down unrest in East Timor. It was difficult to fathom these restrictions while we were providing massive amounts of humanitarian relief and putting our people at risk. These things are never as straightforward as they seem.

Among the more notable trips I took as the U.S. representative for bi-lateral military to military talks were two trips to Mexico City, a trip to Santiago, Chile and Buenos Aires, Argentina, a trip to Rome and multiple trips to London for talks on the Iraq War.

In January 2005, I led a team to Mexico City for talks with their Army leadership and I took Iris along to enjoy the social aspects and see Mexico City, at 21 million people in the greater metropolitan area, the most populous city in the western hemisphere and fifth largest in the world. The Mexicans rolled out the red carpet for us and we had an enjoyable time, but the Mexican military officers were very difficult to deal with and not eager to agree to much in the way of military to military cooperation. The Mexicans still resent the United States annexation of Texas in 1845 and the resulting Mexican-American War of 1846-1848 which gave us California, Arizona, and New Mexico. This was made quite clear to me as I toured the Mexican War College and gave a speech to the War College class. As part of my tour they escorted me to a stone gazebo set out in a courtyard and directed my attention to the ceiling. Painted, Michelangelo-style, on the ceiling were three maps. One, labeled "the past," showed Mexico's territory before the war; including California, Arizona, New Mexico, and most of Texas. The second, labeled "today," depicted the current border with the United States. The third, labeled "the future," looked a lot like "the past."

One of the initiatives of the Bush administration was something called the Proliferation Security Initiative, or PSI. The PSI was intended to be a voluntary, cooperative, international effort to stop trafficking in weapons of mass destruction, their delivery methods, and associated materials, primarily to keep them out of the hands of terrorists or rogue states. The idea came about after the Spanish boarded an un-flagged North Korean ship, the *SO SAN*, and found 15 SCUD missiles on their way to Yemen. The ship had to be released, much to the embarrassment of Spain, when it was discovered there was no international legal basis to seize the cargo. Following the *SO SAN* fiasco, the United States launched a diplomatic initiative to sign up as many countries as possible to this informal collaborative effort and by 2005 about 60 countries had signed on. A meeting was to be held in March of 2005 at U.S. Strategic Command (STRATCOM) Headquarters in Omaha, Nebraska, of something called the Operational Experts Group. The OSD section responsible wanted someone in uniform to chair the meeting and I was picked. Reluctantly, I went to Omaha along with a team of civilians from OSD and chaired the meeting. It was a grueling day as I tried to herd cats from 21 "voting" countries and another 30 or so "observer" countries to emerge with a statement that everyone felt comfortable signing. By the end of the day I had become a virtual dictator, overruling numerous "happy to glad" editing recommendations. But we got it done. The PSI still exists, and the last time I checked, 102 nations had signed the guiding principles.

Also in 2005, I was given a task by General Myers to work with my Canadian counterpart, Rear Admiral Drew Robertson, to figure out what the future of NORAD should be. One of the outcomes of the 9/11 attacks was the establishment of a new four-star combatant command with responsibility for the defense of the United States. Established in April 2002, Northern Command, or NORTHCOM, was charged with military support to civilian authorities, and protecting the territory and national interests of the United States within the contiguous United States, Alaska, Canada, Mexico and the air, land and sea approaches. Established in 1957, NORAD is a combined U.S. and Canadian command, based at Peterson Air Force Base in Colorado Springs, Colorado, responsible for aerospace warning, air sovereignty and defense of the United States and Canada. The creation of NORTHCOM called into question the division of responsibilities between the two commands, and perhaps the need for NORAD. Additionally, the Canadians were in the process of re-organizing their military to include the creation of Canada Command with responsibilities similar to those of NORTHCOM. Supported by a team of American and Canadian staff officers, Canadian Rear Admiral Drew

Robertson and I met in Colorado Springs in July for three days to discuss what, if anything, needed to be done to NORAD to reflect the new realities brought about by the creation of NORTHCOM and CANADACOM. We came up with a range of options, from do nothing to eliminating NORAD, with a number of variations in between. Among them was the recommendation to expand NORAD's charter from aerospace to include the sea approaches and concurrently change the name to North American Defense Command. I made my report to General Myers and Drew made his to General Ray Henault in Canada. As I write this, NORAD is still NORAD, the do nothing option having carried the day.

Meanwhile, world events continued to churn, resulting in numerous meetings in the White House Situation Room that did not have anything to do with the war in Iraq. On February 10th, North Korea announced that it possessed nuclear weapons, claiming that a nuclear capability was required to defend against United States "hostility." In Beruit, Lebanon, the former Prime Minister, Rafik Hariri, was assassinated on February 14th in a suicide bombing. The Syrian government was implicated in the attack and over the next couple of months public outrage became something known as the Cedar Revolution. Finally, under international pressure and following UN Security Council Resolution 1559, Syria announced that it would withdraw its 14,000 troops from Lebanon. Syria had occupied Lebanon for 29 years, beginning in 1976 as the result of the Lebanese civil war. The United States responded positively to this development and, at the White House, meetings were held to determine how to assist the government of Lebanon in developing its own security forces for sovereign defense and domestic law enforcement. Despite the withdrawal of Syrian forces however, the anti-Israel and anti-U.S. terrorist group Hezbollah continued to call Lebanon home and effectively ran the southern half of the country. This would have implications for both the United States and Israel in 2006.

My last military to military engagement trip in 2005 was to South America to meet with Chilean and Argentine counterparts to discuss a range of issues. Arriving in Santiago, Chile with my J-5 team on the morning of Sunday, November 13, we conducted two days of cordial discussions with the Chilean team led by their J-5 equivalent, an Air Force major general. From Santiago we flew across the Andes mountain range to Buenos Aires and had the same type of meetings with the Argentines, this time led by an Argentine rear admiral. The highlight of that visit was a dinner and horsemanship show in a large arena where the history of Argentina was enacted, largely on horseback. The main point being that the Spanish introduced horses to Argentina and the Argentines became extremely proficient horsemen, outriding the Spanish to win their independence. The horsemanship was exceptional. Although our military to military relationship with Argentina was a good one, the Argentines had not forgotten our support to the British during the Falklands War in 1982.

On September 30, 2005, Chairman of the Joint Chiefs, General Dick Myers, finished his term and retired to be replaced by the Vice Chairman, General Pete Pace. General Pace became the first Marine to serve as Chairman of the Joint Chiefs. Navy Admiral Ed Giambastiani became the new Vice Chairman. Earlier in 2005, my boss, Lieutenant General Skip Sharp, had moved to become the Director of the Joint Staff, being replaced by Air Force Lieutenant General Gene Renuart. Gene had previously been the J-3, or Director of Operations, at U.S. Central Command in Tampa. I had met Gene on several previous occasions as he accompanied General John Abizaid to the Pentagon to brief Secretary Rumsfeld and the Joint Chiefs on the war in Iraq.

2006 was to be a busy year for a number of reasons, not least of which was the deteriorating security situation in Iraq. On February 22nd the al-Askari Mosque in Samarra, Iraq, one of the holiest sites in Shia Islam, was bombed and nearly destroyed. Al Qaeda in Iraq was blamed for the bombing which set off a wave of Sunni - Shia violence resulting in the deaths of thousands of Iraqis and the bombing of more mosques, both Shia and Sunni. Debate raged in Washington as to whether Iraq was devolving into civil war. The Bush administration argued that what was happening in Iraq did not meet the criteria of a civil war. At the Pentagon, an on-the-record session with Pentagon and other media correspondents was scheduled to address the question of whether or not Iraq was in a civil war. Assistant Secretary of Defense for International Security Affairs Peter Rodman was the OSD representative and I was to be the Joint Staff representative; the guy in uniform to add credibility to the Pentagon position. This put me in an awkward position and in preparation, Peter and I did some research into the definition of a civil war. The Merriam-Webster Dictionary defined a civil war as "a war between opposing groups of citizens of the same country." That sounded an awful lot like what was happening in Iraq. Another definition described civil war as being "a war between factions or regions of the same country." That definition didn't support the administration's position either. Finally, we found some scholarly opinions to the effect that the intensity at which civil disobedience becomes a civil war is contested by academics. It was pretty flimsy, but boiled down to the idea that civil war was in the eye of the beholder. What was happening in Iraq was not about one group trying to create a separate state, as in the U.S. Civil War, or overthrow the incumbent government. Rather it was random violence along religious, Shia and Sunni, and ethnic, Arab and Kurd, lines. We made our case to the press based on those grounds. Regardless of the label, Iraq was spinning out of control and Washington was struggling to deal with it.

One of the key tasks for success in Iraq was building up the Iraqi security forces such that they would be able to protect the country and preserve stability inside its borders. The centerpiece of the United States military effort, in addition to defeating Al Qaeda in Iraq, was the training and equipping of Iraqi military and police forces. This was a mission never envisioned in the run-up to the war and one for which our military was, quite frankly, ill-prepared. Training foreign police forces is supposed to be the province of the U.S. State Department, but State was not up to the task from a manpower standpoint. Unlike the military, the other agencies of the U.S. government cannot simply order their people to go in harm's way. This was a problem that plagued our efforts throughout both wars, in Iraq and Afghanistan. While many courageous and dedicated civilians volunteered to serve in both Iraq and Afghanistan, many were young and relatively inexperienced.

Twice in 2006 I was dispatched to the halls of Congress to testify before committees on the progress of our train and equip mission in Iraq. On both occasions I was accompanied by Eric Edelman, the Under Secretary of Defense for Policy. Eric and I would prepare together for the hearings and we worked hard to have a grasp of the facts and answer the questions as accurately and as honestly as we could. Despite our noble intentions, there was an unspoken expectation, especially for Eric, that we would defend the efforts of the Defense Department and the military. As a rule, all members, from both parties, treated me, in uniform, with courtesy and respect. The Democrats saved their ire for Eric. He was, after all, representing the hated Donald Rumsfeld, and by extension, the despised Republican President Bush.

By far the most antagonistic and outright hostile member was Congressman Dennis Kucinich from Ohio. Ignoring the stated purpose of the hearing, he castigated Eric Edelman for things which had nothing to do with training and equipping the Iraqi security forces, attacking him for events occurring in his previous role as a member of the White House National Security Council staff in the first George W. Bush administration. It was nothing more than political grandstanding, having no bearing on the day's topic. I left the hearings even more disillusioned with our elected officials than before.

In the summer of 2006, Fidel Castro, the longtime Prime Minister and President of Cuba, became seriously ill with an acute intestinal disorder. There was much speculation that the Cuban leader, who had long had an adversarial relationship with the United States and had outlasted nine American presidents, was on his death bed. The Bush administration saw the pending death of Castro, and the expected leadership vacuum, as an opportunity to support the downtrodden people of Cuba and facilitate the establishment of a democratic government in Havana. An interagency meeting was called at the State Department to mobilize all elements of the U.S. government to be prepared to support the common citizens of Cuba during the unrest which was anticipated when Castro died. Secretary of State Condoleezza Rice chaired the meeting. I went to represent the military and sat at the table as the only participant in uniform.

Secretary Rice kicked off the meeting saying, "The President has made it U.S. policy that there will be a democratic Cuba by the end of his term. The purpose of this group is to organize the U.S. government to be prepared to step in and assist the people of Cuba in achieving freedom and democracy when Castro dies."

I thought to myself, "What? A free and democratic Cuba before Bush leaves office?" I watched heads nod around the table and wondered if anybody else thought this was pie-in-the-sky thinking. Assignments were passed out and the military was given the task of assisting the other government agencies as necessary to achieve this lofty goal. The going in assumption was that there would be political unrest and a power struggle for control upon the announcement of Castro's death. Presumably the downtrodden Cubans, tired of the failed Communist government of Fidel Castro, would rise up against the elites and fight to establish a democratic government in Cuba. This struggle would likely result in a humanitarian crisis and by providing humanitarian assistance and political support, the United States would win the hearts and minds of the common people and facilitate their ultimate triumph.

Secretary of Commerce Carlos Gutierrez, a Cuban-American who fled Cuba with his family in 1960, was charged with preparing the humanitarian aid part of this strategy. He asked for military support for advice and logistics assistance in order to pre-stage this humanitarian aid to be ready for the crisis when it began. A week later, I went to Secretary Gutierrez's office at the Commerce Department for a preliminary meeting on exactly how to make this happen. Secretary Gutierrez started with the idea that we could use Guantanamo Bay, Cuba (GITMO) as the staging ground for humanitarian relief supplies in order to be ready to go when the trouble started. It was clear that, despite being born in Havana, his grasp of Cuban geography was weak. He didn't know where GITMO was. I showed him a map. GITMO is in the far southeastern part of the island, over 500 miles from Havana, which is in the northwest part of Cuba. Moving supplies from GITMO to where they would most likely be needed, in and around Havana, would be problematic. I pointed out that Havana was a lot closer to Homestead Air Force Base in Florida, about 200 miles away, and only about 100 miles from Key West. Besides, if staging humanitarian supplies was the plan, Homestead or Key West would save a lot of headaches associated with the terrorist prison at GITMO, would be a lot cheaper, and could more easily support the personnel necessary to manage this relief effort. Secretary Gutierrez was very appreciative of our assistance and adjourned the meeting with enough knowledge to take some preliminary ideas back to Secretary Rice. We never had another meeting and on July 31st, Fidel Castro peacefully handed the reins of power over to his brother Raoul. No uprising or humanitarian disaster occurred and, as I write this, Fidel Castro is still alive and George Bush is no longer President.

On July 12, 2006, war broke out between the Lebanese Hezbollah and Israel. It began when militants from the group Hezbollah fired rockets at Israeli border towns as a diversion for an anti-tank missile attack on two Humvees patrolling the Israeli side of the border fence. The ambush resulted in the deaths of three Israeli soldiers and the capture of two. Five Israeli soldiers were subsequently killed in an unsuccessful rescue attempt. Israel responded with air and artillery attacks on Hezbollah positions inside Lebanon. The war lasted until September 8th, when Israel lifted its naval blockade of Lebanon. Both sides came under heavy international condemnation for killing civilians, Israel more so than Hezbollah. The U.S. backed Israel in the conflict and re-armed Israel with precision weapons when their stocks ran low. At the same time, the Syrian government under President Bashar al-Assad was re-supplying Hezbollah with rockets and other weapons. I accompanied General Pace to several White House Principal's Committee, and one NSC meeting with the President, to discuss the ongoing conflict.

At one of these meetings, how to deal with the Syrians re-arming Hezbollah across the border was being discussed. A suggestion to conduct U.S. airstrikes on Syrian convoys or to drop some key bridges connecting Lebanon and Syria to make the convoys more difficult was made. The idea of cratering Syrian runways to prevent airlifting supplies was also considered. This would be an act of war against Syria. After an uncomfortable pause, National Security Advisor Steve Hadley moved the conversation in another direction. The idea was not addressed again in my presence and needless to say, we never did take that action. Neither did the Israelis, not wanting to drag Syria into the war.

On August 9, 2006, General Pace and I attended a secure video-teleconference meeting in the Pentagon of the Homeland Security Council meeting taking place in the White House Situation Room with the British homeland defense team videoing in from London. Donald Rumsfeld and Eric Edelman were at the table from OSD. Michael Chertoff, the Director of Homeland Security, and Fran Townsend, President Bush's Assistant to the President for Homeland Security, chaired the meeting on the U.S. side. As this was a Homeland Security Department meeting, we were not asked to contribute, merely to listen in. It was fascinating.

The British had uncovered a plot to blow up commercial airliners flying between the United Kingdom and the United States and Canada using liquid explosives; a new tactic. Nine or ten flights were targeted. The British were not ready to make the arrests, preferring to wait and see if they could further penetrate the cell and identify more conspirators. They contended that an attack was not imminent and that tickets had not yet been purchased. The U.S. side was urging them not to wait; to make the arrests immediately before somebody got through security and blew up an airplane. There was also a spirited discussion about whether or not to warn the airlines and the Federal Aviation Administration. This was more interesting than the issue of the timing of the arrests. What if something happened and it became known, which it would, that officials knew of the plot and didn't warn the airlines? What would issuing a warning do to the airline industry? How many tickets would be cancelled out of fear of a terrorist attack? In the end, the U.S. side prevailed and the British executed the arrests that night. Shortly thereafter, the Transportation Security Administration issued the rules about carrying liquids aboard flights which we continue to follow.

On October 9, 2006, the North Koreans detonated their first nuclear weapon in a test in North Hamgyong Province on the northeast coast. This came after announcing their intention to test six days earlier. With this test, which may have been a partial dud, North Korea officially joined the list of nations with a nuclear weapons capability, although a primitive one and without a means of delivery. As usual, there was international outrage and a United Nations Security Council Resolution imposing limited military and economic sanctions, but no real repercussions for North Korea. North Korea has since conducted three more tests, in 2009, 2013, and 2016, the various sanctions and diplomatic entreaties having been to no avail. At the time, many speculated that Kim Jong Il, having been lumped together with Iraq and Iran in President Bush's "axis of evil," and having seen what happened to Saddam Hussein, had redoubled his efforts to gain a nuclear capability as a deterrent. In fact, when supporting the UN sanctions, South Korean Prime Minister Han Myeong-sook told the South Korean Parliament that South Korea would not support any UN sanctions which contained military measures against North Korea in response to the test. It appeared that Kim Jong Il had achieved his deterrent goal.

Over the course of my three and one-half years as the Vice J-5, the Navy had been good enough to submit my name in nomination for several jobs that would result in my promotion to three-stars, a vice admiral. What few people outside the military realize is that the last time an officer goes before a promotion board is when he or she is being considered for two-star rank. All three and four-star positions in our military are by appointment to specific billets. All three and four-star appointments are temporary and only for the duration of an assignment to a position that carries that rank. In order to retire at the three or four-star rank, an officer must have served honorably at that rank for at least three years and have that retirement rank approved by the Secretary of the Service; Army, Navy or Air Force. All three and four-star officers are permanent two-stars and temporary three or four-stars. All officers nominated by their respective services for promotion to three or four-stars must be approved by the Secretary of Defense, the President, and then confirmed by the U.S. Senate.

In the case of the Navy, the Chief of Naval Operations could decide he wants an officer to fill a three-star Navy position and then nominate that officer to the Secretary of the Navy and then to the Secretary of Defense to go through the confirmation process. If the CNO wants to nominate a naval officer for a joint three-star position, he submits that officer's name to the Chairman of the Joint Chiefs, as will the Army, the Air Force and the Marine Corps. From there the Chairman makes his selection and then begins running the process up the chain through the Secretary of Defense. All joint jobs are open to all the services although there are some that naturally devolve to a particular service. For example, the Commander of Pacific Command has always been a Navy admiral.

While I was the Vice J-5, Admiral Mike Mullen was the CNO, and Admiral Mullen tried on three occasions to get me selected for joint three-star positions. First it was to be the U.S. Representative to the NATO Military Committee in Brussels, Belgium. On that occasion, a Marine, Lieutenant General Ed Hanlon, got the nod. Ed had attended the Marine Corps Basic School with General Pace and Supreme Allied Commander Europe (SACEUR) Marine General Jim Jones. The fix was in; besides, I had only been the Vice J-5 about a year when that opportunity arose. Next, the CNO nominated me to be the Vice Commander, U.S. Northern Command in Colorado Springs. However, in 2004, Admiral Tim Keating was picked to command NORTHCOM. In the joint world two officers in the same uniform are not named number one and number two at a joint command. That didn't work out either and an Army officer got the job. Finally, the CNO nominated me to replace Lieutenant General Mike Dunn as the President of the National Defense University at Fort McNair in Washington, D.C. I had relieved Mike as Vice J-5. Again I was beaten out by a Marine, Major General

Frances Wilson. I sensed the hand of General Pace in that one as well.

In January of 2006, I talked over my options with Iris. I had enough time in grade as a rear admiral to retire as a two-star. I appreciated the fact that the Navy had nominated me for the joint billets they had and also appreciated why they weren't going to make me a three-star Navy fleet commander. I had been almost entirely in joint billets since being promoted to rear admiral and, because I had gone to Pacific Command instead, I had not commanded a carrier battle group. It was very rare to pick an officer to command a fleet who had not commanded at sea as a flag officer. I also didn't want to be the oldest two-star in the Navy, waiting around for some three-star to fall on his sword so I could rush in and take his place. Together we decided I should go see Admiral Mullen and tell him I intended to retire.

In early February, I called the CNO's office and said I wanted to see Admiral Mullen on a personal matter. Not surprisingly, his calendar was full so he invited me to come by his quarters after work. I did and we sat down in the living room and I told him that I appreciated his support, but I had decided that I didn't want to wait around forever hoping to get promoted. I would be putting in my retirement letter. He then told me that General Pace wanted me to take the NATO Military Representative job in Brussels. This was news to me. I went on to say I wasn't sure I wanted to wait around for another eight months for Ed Hanlon to leave.

Later that week, after the last meeting of the day, I sat down with General Pace in his office and told him about my conversation with Admiral Mullen. He confirmed what Admiral Mullen had told me and went on to say that he couldn't guarantee I'd get the job; Secretary Rumsfeld would have to agree. I said I'd stick around but asked him to let me know immediately if I wasn't going to get the job so I could get on with my life. He agreed and I went home to tell Iris about the conversation. The idea of delaying my transition to civilian life on the uncertain prospect of getting promoted and sent to Brussels was still troubling us. I had been commissioned already for almost 34 years and I wasn't getting any younger.

Iris and I took a week's leave and went with our group from Army-Navy Country Club to an all-inclusive resort in the Dominican Republic at Punta Cana to play golf. One of the group was retired Army Major General Dick Beltson, several years older than me and then fully retired. I told Dick what had transpired and that I was still deciding whether or not to wait around for the Brussels job.

"What? Are you crazy? Turn down a chance for a third-star? You gotta do it. Do you know how many guys would give their left nut for this opportunity?"

Iris and I talked some more on a walk on the beach at Punta Cana and decided Dick was right. We'd stick it out on the Joint Staff until a decision was made on Ed Hanlon's relief.

CHAPTER 28

NATO

In April of 2006, I was in Tokyo to participate in the Northeast Asia Cooperation Dialogue, a "track two," meaning unofficial, forum for security discussions among the United States, Japan, China, Russia, South Korea and North Korea. Dr. Susan Shirk of the University of California, San Diego, chaired these meetings which were attended by a mix of academics, civilian security experts, and military. I was the U.S. military representative. Very early on the morning of the 12th of April my phone rang in the hotel room. It was my boss, the J-5, Air Force Lieutenant General Gene Renuart.

"Congratulations, you got the job."

"Brussels?"

"Yep, Rumsfeld signed off on it."

"Thanks, sir." I rolled over and went back to sleep. It was 3:00 AM in Tokyo and 7:00 PM the 11th of April in Washington.

Deciding to wait had been the right decision. Pending confirmation by the U.S. Senate, I would get promoted to vice admiral and go to Brussels, Belgium, headquarters of NATO, and represent the United States on the NATO Military Committee. Each of the 26 NATO member nations sent a civilian ambassador to NATO to sit on the decision-making body, the North Atlantic Council (NAC), and a senior military officer to sit on the Military Committee. Military Committee representatives were called "MilReps" in the vernacular.

I was familiar with the role of the MilRep, who reported directly to the Chairman of the Joint Chiefs, because in his weekly reports and visits to Washington, the MilRep always kept the J-5 cut in on what was going on. Often the MilRep would seek advice from the J-5 on an issue rather than bother the Chairman. Marine Lieutenant General Ed Hanlon, who had aced me out two years' prior, was the incumbent and scheduled to depart Brussels in November 2006 to retire from the Marine Corps. His predecessor had been Air Force Lieutenant General Tim Kinnan. The Navy had not held the position since the early 90s when it had been a four-star billet. The very first MilRep, after NATO had been created in 1949, had been Army General Omar Bradley of World War II fame.

Created in 1949 as the Cold War between the West and the Soviet Union heated up, NATO began with nine Western European countries plus the United States, Canada and Iceland. In 1952 Greece and Turkey joined, followed by West Germany in 1955. The last of the Cold War core of 16 countries to join was Spain in 1982. Pundits often claimed that NATO was designed after World War II to "keep the Americans in, the Soviets out, and the Germans down." Following the collapse of the Soviet Union, NATO began to collectively look for a raison d'être. Significant reorganization had taken place between 1992 and 2006, including the disestablishment of the second of two warfighting commands, Supreme Allied Commander Atlantic (SACLANT), based in Norfolk and commanded by an American admiral. SACLANT existed to defeat the Soviet Navy at sea and that no longer seemed necessary. SACLANT was reconfigured and re-missioned as Allied Command Transformation (ACT) with the mission of experimentation and the development of new strategies, tactics, and technologies.

Ed Hanlon wanted to be home for Thanksgiving in 2006 and I didn't want to go to Brussels until after Thanksgiving. Ed left on schedule and on the 21st of November I was promoted to Vice Admiral in a ceremony in the Pentagon. Ed and I did our passing of the baton in absentia. General Pace presided over my ceremony in the Hall of Heroes, and my Mom and Dad put on my new shoulder boards. Iris helped me on with the new jacket with the new stripes.

Pete Pace did a magnificent job at the ceremony, acknowledging my Dad's service and Iris's father's service, including his POW status. Iris's mother was too ill to make the trip from Orlando and Chris was not there due to operational requirements.

After spending the Thanksgiving holiday with Amy and Erick and the grandkids in Charleston, South Carolina, Iris and I flew overnight to Brussels, arriving the morning of December 1st. We were met by my new aide, Commander Steve Hoffman, my driver, Army Sergeant Tom Cook, and the rest of my security detail. We spent the day in-processing at the U.S. Embassy, the Army Garrison, and at NATO Headquarters, before being driven to the house in the little village of Jezus Eik, just outside the Ring Road around Brussels. Jezus Eik, which translates to "Jesus Oak" from Flemish, was built around a 12th Century church. Legend had it that there was an oak tree where the church now stood that was believed to have magical healing powers. As people traveled to touch the oak in order to be healed of their illness, a small town, a church, and restaurants grew up in the area. It was a quaint little town and many good restaurants were within walking distance of the house.

The house was a spectacular old Belgian chateau with a wonderful downstairs living room with a large fireplace and large dining room that featured a table that could seat 16 comfortably and 18 with a little crowding. It was set back on a well-protected, wooded lot in an upscale neighborhood. In the basement was a control room where the in-house security detail maintained a 24-hour watch, one on duty during the day and two at night. The fenced in yard was well covered with security cameras and the house was rigged with intrusion sensors, duress alarms, and a safe room.

The security detail was a holdover from the 1970s and 80s when there had been two significant terrorist attacks against American generals serving in Europe. In 1979, the SACEUR, General Alexander Haig was attacked in Mons, Belgium. In 1981 Brigadier General James Dozier was kidnapped by the Red Brigade terrorist group in Italy. At the time, General Dozier was Deputy Chief of Staff at NATO's Southern European Land Forces in Verona, Italy. When these attacks occurred, the U.S. MilRep was a four-star officer and it was decided that he needed a security detail to prevent something similar happening to him. Over the years, including after the position was downgraded to three-stars, the security detail remained. I thought it was unnecessary and I never felt threatened in any way, but it was a great convenience. The team consisted of 16 Army security trained personnel, led by a Warrant Officer and a Sergeant First Class. The car was an up-armored BMW 750 with a 12-cylinder engine and puncture-proof tires. A chase car always accompanied the BMW with a driver and armed security guard inside. Anytime Iris and I, or just me, went anywhere for an official event, one of the team did advance reconnaissance of the site. There was never any question about where to go when we arrived.

Over the course of our three years in Brussels we became very close to the Army soldiers who made up our security detail. Some rotated in and out during our tour, but most formed a core group that was with us almost the entire three years. It was easy to get to know them well. I always offered to help them with orders or career situations by endorsing their requests or writing letters of recommendation, but often wondered whether an endorsement by a naval officer, even an admiral, would really help. In one case though, I really came through.

Sergeant John-Michael Brady was a very squared away soldier with a lovely wife and a son in his early teens. In 2009 he applied for a commission through the Army's officer candidate program. The Army had a procedure in place which, as I understood it, virtually guaranteed acceptance into the program if a soldier received an endorsement from a general officer in his chain of command. Sergeant Brady didn't have an Army general in his chain, he had me. I wrote the endorsement and he sent it in with his application. When the list came out, Sergeant Brady's name was not on it. Disappointed, he came to my office to tell me. I expressed my condolences and told him not to give up and to try again next year.

In the meantime, the detachment officer in charge, Chief Warrant Officer John Corley, made some phone calls to the Army personnel people and discovered that Sergeant Brady's record was never put before the board. He had never been considered. As he dug into it with the personnel office he discovered that an administrative error had occurred when Brady's package arrived and was put in the stack with the others who had the general officer endorsement. Apparently confusion arose about whether or not an admiral counted. In the process, Brady's package got pulled from the pile and never made it before the board, either as a general officer endorsee, or otherwise.

When Warrant Officer Corley told me the story, I decided to do something. The Vice Chief of Staff of the Army was General Pete Chiarelli. I had become friends with Pete when he was Defense Secretary Gates' Military Assistant as a lieutenant general and he had traveled with Gates to NATO meetings. I wrote Pete an email and told him that an injustice had been done to a deserving soldier, describing the screw up over the Navy admiral endorsement. I acknowledged that Sergeant Brady may or may not have been selected anyway, but because of the confusion over my endorsement, he never got a look. Pete wrote right back and said, "Stand by, I'm on it."

I don't know exactly what Pete did, but a special board was convened and about three weeks later we were notified that Sergeant John-Michael Brady would be attending officer training. Today John-Michael Brady is an officer in the United States Army. Last I heard he was a captain. And I am proud of what I did.

When we arrived in Brussels there were 26 member countries in NATO. Following the end of the Cold War, the collapse of the Soviet Union, and the "independence" of the Warsaw Pact countries and the Baltic States, NATO began to expand eastward. In 1999 NATO expanded to 19 countries with the addition of Poland, Hungary, and the Czech Republic, all former Warsaw Pact nations (the Czech Republic as Czechoslovakia), much to the consternation of the Russians. In 2004, NATO expanded again with the addition of Estonia, Latvia, Lithuania, Slovenia, Slovakia (the other half of what had been Czechoslovakia), Bulgaria, and Romania. Estonia, Latvia, and Lithuania, the Baltic States, had been annexed as part of the Soviet Union after World War II. To our great credit, the United States had never acknowledged the legitimacy of the Soviet claim (just as the United States should not recognize the legitimacy of the

Russian annexation of Crimea in 2014). The Baltic States remain eternally grateful for this principled stand by the United States and for our assistance and encouragement for their accession into NATO.

Slovenia had been part of the former Yugoslavia and Slovakia had been the other half of Czechoslovakia until they decided to peacefully separate on January 1, 1993. Bulgaria and Romania, both bordering the Black Sea, had been core members of the Warsaw Pact and under the thumb of the Soviet Union. I recalled visiting Constanta, Romania in 1984 aboard *USS BIDDLE (CG-34)* and being harassed by a Bulgarian patrol boat as we sailed south for the Bosphorous on the way out of the Black Sea. My Dad had told me about his carrier cruises to the Mediterranean in the 1950s and his squadron having World War III targets assigned in the Romanian oil fields.

Russia very much resented the expansion of NATO eastward into its sphere of influence. Nevertheless, the Russians kept an Ambassador and a MilRep (a Navy vice admiral), in Brussels who participated in quarterly meetings with NATO in something called the NATO-Russia Council.

The U.S. Ambassador to NATO was Victoria "Toria" Nuland, a career foreign service officer. Toria was the only woman ambassador in this boy's club and she acquitted herself extremely well. Smart, quick on her feet, and articulate, she was an effective ambassador and represented the United States well. I coordinated very closely with all three U.S. Ambassadors to NATO during my tenure because it was essential that we not send mixed signals to the rest of NATO in our respective forums. If there was a disagreement over an issue, we worked it out internally, going to Washington if necessary rather than espouse two different viewpoints publicly. There were few disagreements during my three years in Brussels. For one thing, the U.S. Ambassador to NATO has a dual reporting chain, to the Secretary of State and the Secretary of Defense. The MilRep reports to the Chairman of the Joint Chiefs, who in turn reports to the President but also the Secretary of Defense. I liked Toria personally and she and her husband, the author and commentary writer, Bob Kagan, became good friends. Toria was replaced by Kurt Volker in 2008 and Kurt by Ivo Daalder in 2009 when the Obama administration took over. I enjoyed a good working relationship and an enjoyable social relationship with all three of the ambassadors with whom I served.

Toria was fluent in Russian and routinely had one-on-one lunches with the Russian Ambassador to NATO, to which I accompanied her. The Russian MilRep, Vice Admiral Kunetsnov, also attended these lunches. Invariably the main topic of conversation was the U.S. missile defense plan for Europe. The Bush administration was moving forward to place a radar site in the Czech Republic and ten Ground Based Interceptor (GBI) missile silos in Poland. Despite the intent of the system being to protect the United States and Europe from a ballistic missile launched from Iran, the Russians didn't like it.

I did not care for Russian Admiral Kunetsnov, supposedly a submariner, but in my opinion more of a spy. He had last served at sea in the early 1980s and had spent most of his time since involved in arms control issues. We had had a private meeting in his office and he had complained bitterly about the U.S. missile defense plan for Poland and the Czech Republic. When we parted ways, he gave me a bottle of vodka shaped like a ballistic missile with *Red Army Vodka* on the label. When we later met again in my office, I reciprocated with a bottle of Jack Daniels–boy did I wish I had a bottle of booze shaped like a Ground Based Interceptor.

The Russian Ambassador was a real piece of work. If you looked up Russian Mafia in the dictionary, you would likely find his picture. Big and burly, he had greasy gray hair pulled back into a small ponytail and always wore the light sensitive eye-glasses that seemed to be more dark than not, even indoors. He usually wore a black suit, a black shirt and a black or gray necktie. In a previous assignment he had headed up the Russian border guard organization. As we sat at his table in his residence having lunch, he continually drank vodka while he and Toria debated the merits of the U.S. missile defense plan. He had a young interpreter translate back and forth although he understood English perfectly. Toria, perfectly understanding her words being translated into Russian, would correct the interpreter when he misrepresented what she had just said. This was highly amusing although I felt sorry for the interpreter and for what might happen when the meeting was over.

My first meeting of the Military Committee was the Monday after we arrived in Brussels. Two of the MilReps I already knew as they had been their country's military attaches in Washington while I was Vice J-5. British Vice Admiral Anthony Dymock had been an acquaintance and Iris and I had attended an official dinner at his residence in Northwest Washington and had met his wife Lizzie. Likewise, French Air Force Lieutenant General Pascal Vinchon and his wife Carine had become friends in Washington. When Pascal left the French Embassy, Iris and I had gone to his farewell party at the French Ambassador's residence.

The Chairman of the Military Committee was Canadian Air Force General Ray Henault. The Chairman is an elected position by a vote of all the Chiefs of Defense of the NATO members and had always come from within their ranks. Ray had been Chief of Defense of Canada when I was working with Rear Admiral Drew Robertson on the future of NORAD project. An American is never the Chair of the Military Committee by agreement, since an American is always the SACEUR, responsible for NATO operations. The Deputy Chairman of the Military Committee is always an American in order to play a role in the nuclear capability decision-making within NATO. When I arrived, it was Air Force Lieutenant General Tom Baptiste. He would soon be replaced by Army Lieutenant General Karl Eikenberry who was coming out of command of the NATO forces in Afghanistan, ISAF. Karl had relieved me in 2003 as the Pacific Command J-5. Small world.

Two other MilReps were at their first meeting that day, Danish Army Lieutenant General Knud Bartels, and Norwegian Army Lieutenant General Harald Sunde. We three became fast friends and formed an informal group called the "1 December Club" because we had all arrived in Brussels to take up our new positions on December 1st. Knud later became the Chief of Defense of Denmark and then was elected as the Chairman of the NATO

Military Committee. Harald later became the Chief of Defense of Norway. Clearly, the exalted position of NATO Military Representative meant a lot more in Europe than it did in the United States.

At NATO Headquarters there are a number of meeting rooms, but the main one features an oval shaped table at which sit all of the representatives of whichever body is in session, the NAC or the Military Committee. The countries are arrayed around the table in alphabetical order in English; therefore, I always sat next to the British MilRep (United Kingdom–United States). Since we were in agreement about virtually everything, this was convenient for whispering back and forth during meetings and aligning our positions. Alternatively, if we had conflicting guidance from Washington and London, we could figure that out before either one of us spoke up and put the other one in an awkward position.

All of the discussions at the formal meetings were simultaneously translated in both English and French. Almost all discussions were in English, but the French were under orders to only speak French at a formal meeting. Often the Belgian, the Dutch, or the Luxembourg MilRep would make an intervention in French. As a Canadian, General Henault was required to speak both English and French and he occasionally spoke in French to demonstrate his neutrality. Almost everyone but me spoke two or three languages fluently. I had semi-convinced the Spanish MilRep, Vice Admiral Jose Trevino Maria Ruiz, that I spoke some Spanish so he would email me jokes in Spanish which I never understood. He still does.

The dynamics of the Military Committee were interesting. I quickly learned that when the United States representative speaks, everyone pays close attention. The United States is the powerhouse in NATO and what we say matters, especially to the newer members who rightfully credit the U.S. with taking down the Soviet Union and freeing them from the Communist shackles under which they had lived for two generations. Though the U.S. was universally respected in NATO, our policies were not necessarily applauded, especially when it came to Iraq.

In particular, the French, Germans, Italians, Spanish, Dutch, and Luxembourg very much disagreed with the decision to invade Iraq. Most of the rest, although less vocal, also considered it a huge mistake. The Polish were the ones who most supported the U.S. in Iraq and sent a significant contingent of troops to help, ultimately commanding one of the sectors. The other eastern Europeans kept their own counsel or helped in small ways, largely out of loyalty to the nation that had helped garner their freedom.

ISAF in Afghanistan was another matter. After the 9/11 attacks, nobody begrudged the United States the decision to invade, defeat Al Qaeda, and remove the Taliban from power. As time passed, however, they felt as if they had been deceived when the United States turned its attention to Iraq and handed off responsibility for Afghanistan to NATO and ISAF. As mentioned before, most of the western European nations who agreed to the transfer of command expected the mission of ISAF to be more humanitarian and nation-building than combat. It was on that basis that they convinced their parliaments and their populace that it was the right thing to do. When the body bags started coming home, public opinion turned against the mission.

One of the foundational reasons for initiating combat in Afghanistan for the United States was to eliminate the safe haven that had permitted Osama bin Laden and Al Qaeda to plan for and train for their terrorist activities. The existential threat perceived by the United States was not shared by most Europeans, not even after the Madrid and London bombings. Of course the British were with us, and they had been touched not only by the London subway bombings, but by the liquid bombing plot and the Richard Reid shoe-bomber plot. Most of the rest of the Europeans felt that they had been suckered into ISAF under false pretenses so that we could focus our resources on Iraq. Moreover, they felt that our actions in the Middle East were creating more terrorists than we were killing. I'm not sure they weren't right.

When I arrived in Brussels, Marine General Jim Jones was SACEUR, but his term was up and he was relieved one week later by Army General John Craddock. I had known General Craddock in the Pentagon when he was Rumsfeld's Military Assistant and then the Commander of U.S. Southern Command in Miami. Also, after the 2006 mid-term elections in the United States, Secretary of Defense Donald Rumsfeld resigned and President Bush appointed Bob Gates, former Director of the CIA, as his replacement.

I came to know Secretary Gates very well during my time in Brussels as he was the Secretary of Defense throughout my tour. Three times a year NATO holds a meeting of Defense Ministers called Defense Ministerials and Secretary Gates always attended, although reluctantly. The three meetings were hosted once in Brussels and the other two times in another country. On the State Department side, the same thing occurred, called Foreign Ministerials. Every other year NATO held a summit which the heads of state of each country attend. Because General Pace, and later Admiral Mullen, were so busy, they chose to let me represent them at these meetings. The result was some great travel which always included Iris; NATO did not do trips without a spouse program.

I first met Secretary Gates at a Defense Ministerial in Seville, Spain in February 2007. Because General Pace chose not to attend, I was the senior military advisor during the meetings and sat in on all the discussions and preparatory sessions. I found Secretary of Defense Bob Gates to be very level-headed, pragmatic, and reasonable. Serious about his responsibilities, he nevertheless kept a sense of humor despite his frustrations with the NATO bureaucracy and the often scripted exchanges that took place at the Defense Ministerial meetings. At one meeting in Partnership for Peace format, the Defense Minister from Kazakhstan had just made an intervention and Gates turned to me and said with a smile, "Looks like Genghis Khan made a pass through Kazakhstan." The Kazakhs have very Mongolian-like features.

In November of 2008, after Barack Obama had been elected the next President of the United States, we were together for a Defense Ministerial in Tallinn, Estonia. It was generally assumed that Secretary Gates, who had reluctantly agreed to serve as Secretary of Defense for President Bush, would step down with the arrival of the Obama administration. When the meetings ended, Secretary Gates headed to the airport in Tallinn to depart for Washington. It was protocol for the MilRep, the NATO Ambassador, and the U.S. Ambassador to the country hosting the meetings, to say farewell to the Secretary of Defense at the airport as he prepared to board his airplane. I shook his hand, and gave him one of my U.S. MilRep challenge coins.

"Sir, this may be the last time I see you before you leave office. It's been a pleasure."

He smiled, took the coin, and said thanks and good luck. Of course, President Obama asked him to stay on as Secretary of Defense in order to provide continuity while the nation remained at war in both Iraq and Afghanistan. When I next saw Secretary Gates in Brussels for another meeting in early 2009 I jokingly asked for my coin back since he hadn't left office. Later that year, in October, I attended my last Defense Ministerial in Bratislava, Slovakia. By then I had my plans in place to retire and leave Brussels the coming December. At one of our morning meetings in the hotel in Bratislava I gave the Secretary a new coin and told him this was my last Defense Ministerial. This coin, I explained, had been updated to include the flags of Albania and Croatia who been admitted to NATO during the 2008 NATO Summit in Bucharest, Romania.

"You may not have been able to escape, but I am," I said. He really did not enjoy the NATO meetings, feeling that they were too scripted and little really was accomplished in the formal sessions. The real work was done on the margins through networking and in one-on-one meetings with his counterparts where real agendas could be discussed outside the public eye.

The social schedule at NATO was extremely full; it was not unusual for Iris and me to attend a dinner hosted by one of the other MilReps or Ambassadors two or three nights in a week; once in a while four. We hosted a dinner at our quarters on average every two weeks. We also hosted dinners for the staff and anytime one of the PSD soldiers was transferring to a new duty station.

The expansion of NATO to include the former Warsaw Pact countries made for some interesting exchanges since, at one time, we had been Cold War enemies. In particular, two of my good friends from the Baltic States of Lithuania and Estonia had been fighter pilots in the Soviet Air Force. Lithuanian Air Force Major General Edvardus Mazeikas had been a MIG-29 pilot based in Vladivostok. Estonian Major General Vello Loemma had been a MIG-21 pilot based in Ukraine. The Soviets were careful to base Baltic State officers far from their homelands in order to minimize the chances of a coup or other uprising. Edvardus told me that they would go on high alert in Vladivostok whenever the 7th Fleet carrier ventured into the Sea of Japan. He described things from the Soviet side as they sent their fighters out over the Sea of Japan, were intercepted by our carrier-based fighters, and escorted as they closed on the carrier.

It also took a while for the reality of our new ally status to be reflected in all of the NATO systems. One particular example was quite amusing. The Military Committee made a familiarization trip to the NATO AWACS base in Geilenkirchen, Germany. Before going for a flight in two NATO E-3A AWACs, we were given a brief in the headquarters by the commander of the AWACS wing. During the brief they told us how the NATO AWACS had recently been upgraded with all the newest software. Once airborne, we headed north over Denmark and then back south to be dropped off in Brussels. I was in the aircraft with my Polish counterpart, Lieutenant General Mieczyslaw Cienuch. As we flew north, the tactical display in the aircraft showed all the ground based radar sites in Poland using the symbol for "unknown assumed hostile." The much ballyhooed software upgrade still showed Poland, NATO member since 1999, as bad guy territory. Mieczyslaw and I had a good laugh over that one, but I wonder if he really thought it was funny. I should add that Mieczyslaw also went on to become the Chief of Defense of Poland.

On four occasions during my time in Brussels Iris and I were invited on an official visit by the Chief of Defense of one of our NATO allies; arranged by my MilRep counterpart. Again, this reflected the status of the United States among our NATO allies. Such offers were not, to my knowledge, tendered to most of the MilReps of other countries. Each of these trips was unique in its own way and worthy of some description.

The first of these visits was to Latvia, courtesy of the Latvian MilRep, Army Major General Raimonds Graube. Riamonds and his wife Baiba, had found out while talking to Iris that her grandmother had been born in Latvia, in the Baltic Sea coastal town of Liepaja, 120 miles east of the capital, Riga. Together we flew to Riga where Raimonds had arranged an official schedule for me and Baiba would arrange tours and shopping for Iris. They rolled out the red carpet with meetings for me with the Chief of Defense and Minister of Defense, nice dinners, an opera performance and a tour of military facilities. Visiting the Baltic States really brought home the cruelty of the Soviet dominance from Stalin's re-annexation in 1940 until their independence in 1990 (Lithuania) and 1991 (Latvia and Estonia). The Baltics had enjoyed independence following the collapse of Czarist Russia following the Bolshevik Revolution of 1917, until Stalin's re-annexation.

The hatred for the Soviet Union, and now the Russians, is palpable throughout the Baltic States. When relating a historical fact, our hosts would inevitably begin, "In the Soviet time..." Baiba's story was compelling, and apparently not that unusual. Her father had been a merchant seaman and when Germany invaded the Soviet Union in Operation Barbarossa in June 1941 he had the misfortune of being in port in Hamburg, Germany. He and the rest of the "Russians" in the crew were arrested and sent to prison for the duration of the war. When he was released after Germany's surrender and returned home to Latvia, he was arrested by the Soviets for having been in Germany throughout the war. Talk about Catch-22. He was sent to the Siberian gulag for 12 years before being allowed to return home to Riga. In all three Baltic countries there are museums relating the history of the Soviet domination. In Vilnius, Lithuania the museum is in one of the old prisons where political prisoners were held and tortured. It is pretty gruesome.

Raimonds arranged for us to drive to the main military airfield outside Riga along the Daugava River which runs through the city. The airfield had been a Soviet fighter and bomber base during the Cold War. When the Soviets withdrew after Latvia's brief struggle for independence in 1991, they trashed the airfield on the way out the door. The buildings and hangars we saw were in terrible disrepair with broken windows and disconnected piping everywhere. The runway was cracked and potholed and had grass and weeds growing up through the cracks and holes. Raimonds said that the Soviets left all of their military facilities, which were now Latvia's, in similar condition. We boarded a VIP configured Russian MI-17 HIP helicopter for the flight to Liepaja. We let Iris and Biaba sit next to the big picture window to enjoy the flight over the Latvian countryside. A female Latvian Army crewmember (in a dress and heels!) was on duty to serve soft drinks, coffee or tea during the flight. As we approached the helipad at Liepaja, Iris saw an American flag and a blue three-star flag flying from the flagpole.

She turned to Raimonds and me and said, "What American facility is here?"

"That's for you," Raimonds said.

Liepaja had been a major Soviet Baltic Sea submarine base and, like the airfield, had been left in bad disrepair by the Soviets. The Latvians had very little in the way of naval capability, only a couple of minesweepers and salvage ships.

Overall, our visits to the Baltic States were the ones which touched us the most emotionally. These people had only been free of Soviet domination for a little over 15 years when we visited. In Major General Raimonds Gruabe's case, he had been one of the heroes of the standoff with the Soviet Union which ultimately resulted in independence. He became Latvia's Chief of the National Guard from 1998 to 1999 and Chief of Defense from 1999 to 2003. When he left Brussels as the MilRep, he once again served as Latvian Chief of Defense. At one meeting in Brussels I was sitting next to Admiral Mullen and he was reviewing Raimonds' biography.

He leaned over and said, "He went from Chief of Defense to MilRep?"

"Some countries get it right," I said. He just laughed.

In May of 2008, Iris and I were invited on an official visit to Norway by General Svere Diessen, the Norwegian Chief of Defense; arranged by my good friend Lieutenant General Harald Sunde. We arrived in Oslo on the 16th of May and stayed in a lodge next to the famous Holmenkollbakken ski jump, built in 1892 and home to the 1952 Winter Olympics. May 17th is Norway's National Day, the date in 1814 when the Norwegian Constitution was signed. That morning we awakened to see snow falling on the mountaintop where the lodge and ski jump was located and to be greeted by Harald and Solvi in traditional dress. We had an enjoyable day in Oslo, finding a position near the palace to watch the parade of Norwegians in traditional dress file by and be acknowledged by King Harald V.

The purpose of our trip was for me to better understand Norway's security situation and for Iris and Solvi to have fun together shopping, touring and eating. Harald had arranged a spectacular itinerary, designed to understand Norway's geo-political situation and the challenges associated with the Arctic to the north and Russia to the east. He had arranged a small military passenger aircraft to fly us from Oslo 500 miles north to Bodo at the mouth of Vjestfjord. Vjestfjord was the huge fjord on the west coast bordering the Norwegian Sea where the United States had planned to position aircraft carriers to fight the Soviet Union as part of the Maritime Strategy of the 1980s. It was also home to Norway's Northern Command, inside a huge underground complex built into a mountain which I toured with Harald while Iris and Solvi toured and shopped. From Bodo we flew north the next day to Kirkenes, as far north and east as you can go in Norway along the Russian border. Kirkenes is another 400 miles further north of Bodo at about 70 degrees' north latitude, well above the Arctic Circle. Kirkenes is only five miles from the Russian border and is a tough, dirty seaport on the Barents Sea.

Harald chose Kirkenes so that I would better understand the security situation along Norway's border with Russia. Here was where the Norwegian Border Forces had their main focus; from Kirkenes in the far north to the border with Sweden in the south. There is a small marker in the woods at the intersection of the borders of the three countries. In one of the observation posts we looked through the large "big-eye" binoculars across the border to the Russian factory town of Nikel. The contrast was startling; in many ways reminding me of the contrast looking across the DMZ into North Korea from South Korea. Nikel was a huge, dirty, gray, factory town, practically barren of trees. A mere five miles west across the border, Norway was lush and green. We did not see any people moving around the streets of Nikel or going into or coming out of the factories.

That evening came the highlight of the trip. We stayed in a small lodge on the banks of a large fjord. Just before sunset, the proprietors, a husband and wife, suited us up in survival suits and loaded us into a Zodiac. The husband was dressed out in a wetsuit and scuba tanks. We motored out into the fjord and went about a mile from the lodge. The diver went over the side and his wife piloted the Zodiac as we followed his bubbles along the sheer wall of the fjord. After 20 minutes or so, his hand broke the surface holding up one small King Crab. Giving us a few seconds to ponder what this portended for dinner, he then thrust up his other hand with about nine large King Crabs in his grasp. We loaded them into the boat, took pictures holding them, and headed back to the lodge.

While his wife prepared dinner we drank white wine and watched a film about the King Crab industry in Norway and how the crabs were migrating from the Bering Strait across 3,000 miles of ocean north of Russia to the coast of Norway. We then had a spectacular dinner of fresh caught King Crab and wine.

The next day we made the 950-mile flight south to Oslo for one last night before leaving Norway. One of the side benefits of the trip was to gain an appreciation for the size of Norway, one of the richest countries in the world due to abundant natural resources, most notably oil and natural gas deposits in the Norwegian Sea and the Arctic Ocean. Norway has a 16,000-mile coastline, factoring in all the fjords. What is hard to appreciate, from looking at a map, is how far east it curves from the southern tip up to the Russian border at Kirkenes. If you drew a line due south from Kirkenes, it would intersect Cairo, Egypt.

In 2009, we made two more official trips at the invitation of the Chiefs of Defense of Slovenia and Croatia. Croatia, along with Albania, had been admitted to NATO at the 2008 NATO Summit in Bucharest, Romania.

Brigadier General Anton "Toni" Turk, the Slovenian MilRep, arranged a trip to Slovenia to coincide with the grape harvest at his small vineyard in the hills of the Dolenjska Region, southeast of the capital, Ljubljana. Technically, my host was the Slovenian Chief of Defense, Major General Alojz Steiner, but Toni and his wife Zora squired Iris and me around. First I had to earn my fun time by speaking to the students at the Slovenian War College in Maribor in the far east of the country. Slovenia is a small nation of only 7,800 square miles and just over 2 million people; part of the former Yugoslovia. Toni and Zora took us north to the lakeside town of Bled, just south of the border with Austria. Bled was one of the favorite vacation spots of Josip Broz Tito, the authoritarian president of Yugoslavia. Glacial Lake Bled is famous for its tiny island and Bled Castle. The only way to get to the island is by specially configured boats which are rowed out to the island in a unique way by oarsmen who have passed down the profession for generations. The boats hold about a dozen passengers, sitting on benches, and are rowed with a single long oar from the rear. The oarsman propels and steers the boat with a figure-eight type motion. The older oarsmen have gnarled, clawlike hands from years of rowing back and forth to the island.

Next on the itinerary were the massive caverns of Postojna, the largest caverns in Europe. The real fun came when we arrived at Toni's small vineyard in Dolenjska. We had a spectacular day harvesting the red grapes. Toni and Zora's entire family was there as well as neighbors from home and the surrounding vineyards. Iris and the ladies cut the grapes from the vines while I joined the men in hauling the grapes in a large bucket strapped to my back down the hill to where the mechanical grape crusher was manned by the official vintner. Zora and her daughter prepared food all day and each trip down the hill with a basket of grapes was rewarded with a glass of last year's wine and a slice of ham or cheese from the table.

Our final trip was to Croatia in the fall of 2009. Croatia, yet another part of the former Yugoslavia, had been admitted to NATO in 2008. Major General Drago Lovric had become a very good friend, both while Croatia was awaiting membership and then after being voted membership in Bucharest. Croatia, like many of the Balkan nations, had fought a bitter war for independence with the Yugoslav National Army and Serbian paramilitary forces beginning in June of 1991 and lasting four years. Drago had been one of the fighters in that war along with the Chief of Defense, General Josip Lucic'. These were tough guys.

Iris and I flew to the capital, Zagreb, and then were driven to the coastal town of Split, some 160 miles away. In Split we stayed in Navy quarters and had a nice dinner hosted by General Lucic'. Looking at him I had no doubt that he had been a fierce fighter in Croatia's war for independence. The next day I had my official responsibilities and spoke to a group of naval officers that had been assembled in an auditorium for my talk, followed by a tour of one of their corvettes.

After touring Split, and running into Admiral Jim Stavridis who had replaced General John Craddock as SACEUR in July, we headed 100 miles south down the Dalmatian coast to Dubrovnik to a villa that had at one time been one of Tito's many vacation spots. Drago had to depart the program at Split to take care of Jim Stavridis, so for the rest of our stay we were escorted by Colonel Darko Bijuklic, Drago's Deputy MilRep in Brussels. We were treated to unbelievably generous hospitality on the part of the Croatians. They opened Tito's old villa up just for us, brought down staff from Zagreb, and asked us in the morning what we wanted for dinner that night. They then went out and bought the supplies and served a wonderful dinner, complete with Croatian wines, out on the terrace overlooking the sea. The villa was on the Adriatic coast in a fenced off, isolated area. It had been shelled by the Yugoslav Navy during the war for independence and the area around the swimming pool was permanently damaged with numerous shell craters in the cement pool deck and sea wall. We were given a tour of the underground tunnel system which ran for almost a mile and was designed to allow Tito to escape if ever the villa came under attack.

Each of these four trips was special and unique in their own way. In every case, the host nation wanted to show off their country, explain their security situation, outline their military goals and objectives, and most importantly, gain the support of the U.S. Military Representative. It was also a way to express appreciation, especially in the Baltics, Slovenia, and Croatia, for the role the United States had played in gaining their freedom and supporting their admittance to NATO.

In early September 2007, the Red Switch phone in my office rang. It was General Pete Pace, the Chairman of the Joint Chiefs.

"Bill, in a few hours the Secretary of Defense is going to announce that I will not be continuing as the Chairman."

I was stunned. The Chairman of the Joint Chiefs normally serves four years, but his initial appointment is for only two years. It is very unusual for the President not to nominate him for the second two-year term.

He went on, "I wanted you to know before you heard it on the news, and I didn't want your Military Committee colleagues to find out before you did."

"OK sir, thanks for the heads up. I don't have to tell you that I'm disappointed."

"The President and Secretary have decided that they don't want to fight through the confirmation process. A vote for Pete Pace would be a vote for the Iraq War. They just don't want the fight."

By this time our involvement in Iraq had become enormously divisive, in the Congress and in the country. The "surge" decision had been made, but the surge troops were only just getting into theater and no positive outcome was yet apparent. I was disappointed and felt bad for General Pace. It would be personally embarrassing not to be nominated for the second term, and I really liked him as a person, as a leader, and as a boss. When the announcement was made public, I learned that my CNO, Admiral Mike Mullen, would be the next Chairman of the Joint Chiefs. At the same time, Vice Chairman Admiral Ed Giambastiani would also be stepping down to be replaced by Marine General James "Hoss" Cartwright. Once again, in a joint organization, two military officers from the same service at the top is never done; Admiral Ed Giambastiani had to go coincident with the appointment of Admiral Mike Mullen.

In the spring of 2007, the Prospective Commanding Officer of the next ship to be named *SAMPSON, USS SAMPSON (DDG-102)*, Commander Phil Roos, contacted me about the ship's commissioning ceremony, scheduled to be held in Boston in November. He asked if I would be interested in serving as the commissioning ceremony principal speaker since I had been the last commanding officer of *USS SAMPSON (DDG-10)*. Of course I said yes and once the request had been approved by Secretary of the Navy Donald Winter, I had the job.

For financial reasons, Iris and I had different flights from Brussels to Boston. With my aide, Commander Steve Hoffman, I flew through Frankfurt, Germany while Iris flew direct to Washington, D.C. and then to Boston. Our flight was delayed due to fog in Frankfurt and we missed our Boston connection, traveling instead through Charlotte, North Carolina. On arriving in Boston we had no luggage. I had traveled in blue jeans with my uniforms in the checked baggage. Once in Boston I notified Commander Roos and he found an officer, Chief Engineer Lieutenant Bob Heeley, about my size, to loan me a business suit. I went to the pre-commissioning ceremony reception the night before in the Chief Engineer's blue suit and red tie, a shirt I bought in Boston, and the shoes I wore with blue jeans on the flight. If my uniforms didn't arrive, I would do the ceremony in the suit and just explain the lost luggage situation. At 2:00 AM the morning of the ceremony, the hotel staff banged on my door and delivered my suitcase—crisis averted. Steve Hoffman however, did not get his luggage until two days after we were back in Belgium. I was lucky. At the reception the commissioning coordinator from the Bath Ironworks Shipyard in Maine told me that they didn't have official records to prove it, but they believed that this was the first time that the de-commissioning commanding officer of the last ship of the name was still on active duty and able to act as the commissioning officer for the next ship of the same name.

The 3rd of November featured a nor'easter with sideways rain throughout the ceremony. I sat on the ship exposed to the weather next to Senator John Kerry who had made a last-minute decision to participate and say a few words. I made the keynote speech, and, when it was time to man the ship and set the watch, I presented the ceremonial looking glass to the first in port Officer of the Deck, Ensign Christina Douglas. My brother Paul and his son Matt were in the audience, up from Tallahassee because Florida State was playing Boston College that night in Chestnut Hill. Although we had tickets, Iris and I elected to watch the game from the comfort of our hotel room, having been soaked enough during the ceremony. Florida State won, beating then number two ranked BC 27–17 in a downpour.

In April 2008, NATO held its regularly scheduled biennial summit in Bucharest, Romania and Admiral Mullen decided that he was too busy to attend. As the MilRep I would go and represent him as the senior military advisor to President Bush, Secretary of State Rice, and Secretary of Defense Gates. As always, there was a spouse program associated with the summit and Iris accompanied me to Bucharest.

The Romanians had effectively cleared out the city to ensure tight security while all these world leaders were in town for three days. The main thoroughfares were blocked off and armed security guards lined the streets from the airport to the center of town. We were told that most businesses were told to close and that the government had arranged free train and bus transportation out of town so citizens could more easily leave for a forced vacation in the countryside. We could never get away with this in the United States.

All of the meetings were held in the outrageously ornate Palace of the Parliament which had been the palace of Nicolae Ceausescu, the authoritarian Communist dictator of Romania from 1967 to 1989. He and his wife were executed following the December 1989 revolution. The Palace of Parliament is the world's largest civilian building, most expensive administrative building and world's heaviest building. The Pentagon is the only larger building in the world, hence the "civilian" qualifier.

There were three major outcomes of the 2008 Bucharest Summit. Albania and Croatia were granted admittance to NATO, Macedonia was denied admittance, and Russian President Vladimir Putin complained about the U.S., Poland and Czech Republic missile defense plans during the NATO-Russia Council meeting. Despite the vocal support of almost everybody for admitting Macedonia, the Greeks blocked it because they objected to the name that Macedonia had chosen for itself when it gained its independence from Yugoslavia in 1991. In NATO it only takes one country to block anything. In fact, because of Greek objections, in every NATO document Macedonia was referred to as "FYROM," the Former Yugoslav Republic of Macedonia. It was U.S. policy, and one that I religiously followed, to call them Macedonia when speaking about them; not "FYROM."

Both General Pace and Admiral Mullen, like Secretary Gates, were put off by the structured nature of the discussions when the NATO Military Committee met in "Chiefs of Defence," or CHODs, format. In truth the Military Committee is made up of the chiefs of defense of each of the member nations. Those of us serving as MilReps were just that, representatives of our respective chiefs of defense, permanently assigned to deal with the daily routine of NATO business and report back to our bosses in the home country.

As with the defense ministers, the quality of discussion in CHODs sessions varied widely depending on the nation doing the talking. Most of the newer, eastern European nation's chiefs of defense were operating under strict instructions from their capitals and had little or no wiggle room to freelance in open debate around the table. They often read verbatim prepared statements when it was their turn to talk, regardless of what had previously been said. The older and more westernized member nations on the other hand were represented by officers who engaged freely in open debate with the self-confidence of knowing that they had the free rein to think on their feet and appropriately represent the interests of their countries. Part of the reason that the newer member nations were less nimble in discussions was the fact that, except for French, all discussions were in English. I had great respect for my Military Committee colleagues, as well as CHODs and ministers, who could listen to a discussion in English, formulate their thoughts, and then present their country's case in English. I certainly could not have done the same thing in another language. For the eastern European former Warsaw Pact nations, their second language growing up was most likely Russian, not English.

The major event in NATO throughout my tour was the war in Afghanistan, a NATO operation since 2003 under the name "ISAF" for International Security Assistance Force. The Commander of Allied Command Operations, SACEUR, General John Craddock, was the overall commander of the operation. When I first arrived in Brussels ISAF was in the process of transferring command between British Lieutenant General David Richards and American General Dan McNeil. David Richards was the last British officer to command ISAF as beginning with General McNeil, an American four-star general would continually be in command. The United States provided the bulk of the troops, most of the logistics support and firepower, and did most of the fighting. That is not to say that other nations did not contribute in a meaningful way, they did, but as with all things NATO, it was American military might which made the difference. Some small nations, like Belgium, took on relatively small and safe missions, such as defending the airport at Kabul. Others, including non-NATO contributors like Macedonia, defended the ISAF Headquarters compound in Kabul.

The more capable nations took on bigger responsibilities; but took them on unevenly. Afghanistan was divided into four main regional commands. The Americans commanded Regional Command East, along the border with Pakistan and considered the most dangerous and volatile. The British and Canadians alternated command of Regional Command South, based in Kandahar and a close second to the East in volatility and Taliban activity. The Germans commanded Regional Command North, based in Mazar-e-Sharif, a relatively quiet sector. Finally, the Italians and Spanish shared command of Regional Command West, based in Herat, close to the Iranian border. Several other nations assumed significant responsibilities in sub-sectors of the four major commands, notably the Polish, the Dutch, Denmark and France.

I wanted to get to Afghanistan sooner than the Fall 2007 scheduled Military Committee trip in order to see for myself what it was like, so I asked General Craddock if I could tag along with him in late January when he made a trip to review the situation. We left the airbase in Cheivres, Belgium on January 28th in his C-40, a specially configured Boeing 737. In order to maximize his time on the ground, General Craddock decided to remain overnight in Baku, Azerbaijan, in order to shorten the next day's flight time and leave time that day for meetings and briefings. Double-hatted as Commander, U.S. European Command, Azerbaijan fell into his area of responsibility.

Baku sits on a peninsula of land jutting eastward into the oil and natural gas rich Caspian Sea. Azerbaijan lives in a tough neighborhood, with Russia to the north, Georgia and Armenia to the west, and Iran to the south. Like so much of the region, Azerbaijan was incorporated into the Soviet Union in 1920 and gained its independence in 1991. 140 miles east across the Caspian Sea lie Turkmenistan and Kazakhstan. Baku itself had a wild-west feel to it as we drove from the airport to the hotel.

We arrived in Kabul the next day and made the wild ride through the streets to the American Embassy to meet with Ambassador Bill Wood. Loaded into the back of armored Toyota Land Cruisers manned by British Special Forces soldiers, we were required to wear helmets and flak jackets. Each Land Cruiser was equipped with Counter-Improvised Explosive Device (C-IED) electronic jamming equipment and was operated very aggressively on the crowded and disorganized streets of Kabul to minimize the opportunity for an ambush. The streets themselves were crowded with people, cars, donkey carts, and motorbikes that followed no obvious traffic patterns. The roads were potholed, rutted, dusty and dirty, and only partially paved. The poverty was startling, worse than I had seen in Karachi, Pakistan in 1986. The distant scenery however was spectacular. Kabul sits in a flat plain with the snow-capped mountains of the Hindu Kush to the north and lesser mountain ranges in all other directions.

From the Embassy we traveled to ISAF headquarters where we would spend the night and have dinner with the Commander of ISAF, British Lieutenant General David Richards, and his multinational staff. David Richards had replaced the previous American Commander, Lieutenant General Karl Eikenberry. Throughout the American theater of war in both Iraq and Afghanistan, the U.S. military enforced "General Order Number One"—no alcohol. But ISAF was a NATO operation and that rule didn't apply. There was a well-attended bar on the compound and we had wine with dinner.

The following morning, we made the wild ride through Kabul back to the airport and boarded a German C-160 transport for the 180-mile flight north to Mazar-e-Sharif and Regional Command North under the command of a German major general. The German compound at Mazar-e-Sharif was huge, sitting adjacent to a large airfield. In 2007 this region was pretty quiet, with few Taliban attacks. The Germans, adhering to their post-World War II pacifism, did little to encounter the Taliban. They had Tornado multi-role fighter-bombers at Mazar-e-Sharif, but one of the caveats attached to German participation in ISAF was that they would only fly in daylight and only fly unarmed reconnaissance missions. They would provide no air support to troops in combat. They also did not venture much outside the wire. Mazar-e-Sharif was fortress

Germany and the unspoken signal to the Taliban was, "if you leave us alone, we'll leave you alone."

From Mazar-e-Sharif we boarded a Canadian C-130 and flew to Regional Command West, in Herat, about 75 miles from the border with Iran. Herat is the trading capital of western Afghanistan and there was a significant Iranian influence in this part of the country. Regional Command West was, at the time, under Italian command but also with a heavy Spanish presence as they alternated command. We were to spend the night in Herat on the compound and have dinner with the regional command staff. In typical Italian fashion they had constructed an officer's club that looked like a high-end Italian restaurant, complete with a rustic stone façade inside and a salt water fish tank. We had a wonderful Italian meal as you would expect, complete with copious amounts of red wine and finished off with glasses of Lemoncello. How civilized. The Italians and Spanish operated similarly to the Germans. They tended to avoid contact with the enemy, did nothing at night, and had an elaborate and time consuming approval process to render any kind of assistance, to include dispatching a medical evacuation (MEDEVAC) helicopter to recover wounded Afghan soldiers.

The next day they took General Craddock and his team to visit one of their humanitarian projects, the construction of a hospital, and to meet with the local governor of Herat Province. Here I observed a very interesting dynamic as General Craddock and the Governor were escorted around this under-construction hospital. General Craddock traveled with a team of armed bodyguards as did the Italian general. The Governor showed up with his own team of Afghan bodyguards, all sporting AK-47 Kalashnikov rifles, with bandoliers of ammunition crossing their chests and looking like a pretty rough bunch. As we stood in a courtyard while an Afghan translator explained the hospital construction progress to the Governor and General Craddock, I watched the maneuvering of the three different teams of bodyguards; about two dozen in all. They kept shifting positions, each team trying to get behind the other teams in an ever-widening circle. What started as a fairly tight bunch around the three principals gradually expanded outward as the bodyguards continually sought the most advantageous position, should the shooting start. It was fascinating, if a little disconcerting. There was little trust on display.

From Herat we flew in the German C-160 to Farah about 130 miles south where we visited an American Provincial Reconstruction Team (PRT) commanded by a U.S. Navy helicopter pilot. This was a rugged outpost, a small forward operating base with rudimentary plywood and canvas tents and several cinderblock shelters sprinkled around the compound. The PRTs were intended to help with development in the area where they were located and were staffed with military officers from all the services, an Army or Marine Corps detachment for security, and civilian representatives from the State Department, U.S. Agency for International Development, or some other government agency with specific skills for development in the region, such as the Department of Agriculture. In this part of Afghanistan there was usually a Drug Enforcement Agency representative as well. These PRTs were sprinkled all over the country and some were in pretty rough places. The Navy commander told me that they had periodically come under mortar attack by the Taliban, drug lords, or whatever other bad guys were out there.

An American C-130 picked us up in Farah and flew us to Kabul where we spent the night before heading back to Belgium via Islamabad, Pakistan. We had described an arc around the north and west of Afghanistan on this particular trip, General Craddock having made an earlier visit for briefings in the south at Kandahar and the east at Bagram. We flew General Craddock's C-40 to Islamabad where he met with U.S. Ambassador Ryan Crocker and Pakistan's military Chief, General Kayani, to discuss the situation on the border and then back to Cheivres Air Field, near Mons.

I made two more trips to Afghanistan during my time in Brussels, each with the Military Committee. On the first I traveled to Kandahar and Lashkar-Gah in the south, and on the second to the American-run East Region in Bagram. On that second trip we traveled to the far east at the Khyber Pass on the border with

Pakistan and to another PRT, this one commanded by an Air Force lieutenant colonel, at Jalalabad.

The topography of Afghanistan is amazingly diverse, mostly desert, interrupted either by lush green river valleys or the amazingly rugged, steep mountains of the Hindu Kush. On one helicopter flight between Kandahar and Lashkar-Gah, we saw a lone man walking west in the middle of the open desert with nothing around for miles. We wondered where in the world he had come from and where he was headed. Flying in a helicopter gave us an appreciation for the primitiveness of Afghanistan. Although Kabul has high-rise, glass covered buildings in the city center, the outskirts are largely mud huts with small walled in courtyards, usually containing cattle or, more often, goats. The whole country, except in the river valleys, is a dusty gray-brown hue. The further into the countryside you go, the more primitive are the conditions. Most of the country has no electricity and no running water. It is like going back 400 years in time.

The Afghan people are themselves a tough people, scratching out a living in abject poverty and primitive conditions. Most are illiterate and get their news by word of mouth. They could not care less about a central government in Kabul; it has little or no effect on their lives. They are beholden to their families, their tribe, their ethnic group, and their tribal leaders; nothing more. The opium trade and other black market businesses represent the bulk of what passes for an economy in Afghanistan. Corruption is rampant, but corruption is viewed through the lens of western norms and mores. In this part of the world, what we call corruption is normal, everyday business. For these and many other reasons, as time went on I became more and more disillusioned with the prospects for any measurable success for the U.S. and NATO mission in Afghanistan.

In May of 2007, I traveled to the other major NATO operation underway, the United Nations sanctioned peacekeeping mission in Kosovo - KFOR. A small, land-locked country in the Balkans and one of many declaring independence upon the break-up of Yugoslavia, Kosovo is a poor nation, largely populated by Albanian Muslims, which had been subject to brutal attacks by the

Serbian government of Slobodan Milosevic over a border dispute. Traveling to the capital of Pristina, I had meetings with the KFOR Commander, German Lieutenant General Roland Kather, and the Prime Minister of Kosovo, Agim Ceku. A far cry from Afghanistan, Kosovo was, nevertheless, a corrupt and run down country. Possessing little in the way of natural resources, the prospects for Kosovo to emerge as a thriving, democratic and independent country did not appear promising. Perhaps the most striking impression of Kosovo was the almost complete state of disrepair seen everywhere. The country was awash in litter and I don't believe I've ever seen more abandoned, derelict cars on the side of the roads; they were everywhere. Many buildings were either damaged, falling down, or had been started new and the construction stopped. The place was a mess.

The Kosovo War had begun in the early 1990s when Yugoslav President Slobodan Milosevic sharply reduced the autonomy of the Kosovo region. By 1996, the Kosovo Liberation Army, an Albanian guerilla group, had begun armed resistance against the Serbian and Yugoslav armies and thus began the Kosovo War. By 1999, the deaths and refugee situation had motivated the international community to act and the NATO bombing campaign between March and June had forced Milosevic to withdraw his forces. A United Nations resolution (1244) placed Kosovo under UN administration and KFOR was established to maintain the peace. Sponsors of the Serbs, the Russians decried the United States' and NATO's recognition of Kosovo's independence.

In August of 2008 Russia invaded two provinces of the former Soviet Republic of Georgia; Abkhazia in the west, bordering the Black Sea, and South Ossetia in the north, bordering Russia. Both provinces had been seeking to break away from Georgia, inspired in part by the 2008 declaration of independence by Kosovo. Russia charged that the Georgians had initiated the conflict by sending troops into the two provinces to control the factions attempting to break away. The Russians were already unhappy with both Georgia and Ukraine because both were lobbying hard to gain admittance to the NATO Membership Action Plan, or MAP. MAP was a formal process by which a nation wishing to join NATO demonstrated, over time, that it had satisfied the criteria for NATO membership. All of the nations that had joined NATO following the collapse of the Soviet Union had first been in the Membership Action Plan. The United States officially supported the admission of both Georgia and Ukraine in NATO, but most European nations were wary.

The war was a short one, the Georgian military was forced out of both provinces, and NATO did nothing significant to intervene except to express outrage and urge for the restoration of Georgian sovereignty over the two provinces. August is vacation month in Europe and that applies to NATO as well. Virtually everybody goes on vacation and almost nothing gets done. It would take more than a lousy little war in Georgia to bring everyone back from vacation.

Perhaps the bigger impact of the Russia–Georgia war was the sobering effect it had on the idea of inviting either Georgia or Ukraine to join NATO. The key provision in NATO is Article V, which states that an attack on any member nation is an attack on all, and all are obligated to help defend the nation under attack. Article V had only been invoked once in the 59-year history of NATO and that was on September 12, 2001 following the 9/11 attacks in the United States. How ironic; throughout the history of NATO, the assumption had been that if Article V were ever invoked, it would be to defend Europe, not the United States. My colleagues on the Military Committee were quick to ask the question, "What if Georgia was in NATO today? Would we be going to war with Russia?" The answer was no, probably not.

I believe the Russia–Georgia war put the final nail in the coffin of any hopes for either Georgia or Ukraine to eventually become members of NATO. There were other countries in NATO who feared Russian belligerence and also doubted how committed their NATO brethren were to upholding the provisions of Article V. These included the Baltic States and Poland. In private conversation they had expressed to me their doubts that a Russian threat to them would be met by resolve from the likes of Belgium,

France, Germany, Spain and the Netherlands. To that end they began unilateral discussions with the United States, through the U.S. European Command, for the development of contingency plans to assist them should the need arise.

During the course of my time in Brussels I became friendly with the Ukrainian MilRep, assigned to Brussels to keep track of events and attend the occasional meeting while Ukraine lobbied for membership. Major General Petr "Peter" Haraschuk had been a Soviet intelligence officer during the Cold War. I always agreed to see him when he asked for a meeting, and invited him and his wife to dinner at our quarters on several occasions. When the Russia-Georgia war broke out, the Russians claimed that it was a spontaneous reaction to an aggressive action by the Georgians. Petr came to see me to explain that, with his background and understanding of Soviet planning and tactics, this was no spontaneous military response; it was well planned. Having no love lost for the Russians himself, he wanted me to pass this intelligence back to Washington, which I did through my weekly report to Admiral Mullen. It being U.S. policy, I also spoke up in favor of Ukrainian membership in NATO whenever the occasion occurred. For this and other reasons I will never completely understand, Petr lobbied his government to present me with a medal near the end of my time in Brussels. On October 14, 2009, in a small ceremony in our conference room, Petr presented me with the Insignia of the Order of the Ministry of Defence of Ukraine Medal. The citation read:

> *For his personal contribution to the development of military cooperation between the armed forces of Ukraine and the United States of America, for high professionalism and on the occasion of the termination of his tenure at NATO Headquarters it has been ordered:*

> *To award with the insignia of the order of the Ministry of Defence of Ukraine–Medal "for the assistance of the Armed Forces of Ukraine"*

Signed: Acting Minister of Defence of Ukraine, V.V. Ivashchenko

I was very moved by the gesture and got a little choked up when making some brief remarks after Petr pinned the medal on my uniform. My soft spot for these people who had suffered for so long on under the Soviet Union got the better of me.

The other significant NATO operation that occurred in 2008 and 2009 was the establishment of an anti-piracy task force to assist in the multinational fight against piracy in the Gulf of Aden and Indian Ocean off the coast of Somalia. By the early 1990s after the collapse of the Siad Biarre regime, Somalia had become a largely ungoverned country. What began as an attempt by Somali fisherman to deter illegal fishing in their exclusive economic zone, evolved into the capture and holding for ransom of merchant vessels sailing those waters. The international community had begun to mobilize as more and more ships were captured, sailed into Somali waters, and ransomed for millions of dollars, often after their crews had been held for months. An entire piracy industry had grown up along the Somali coast.

Both the European Union and NATO decided to initiate separate counter-piracy missions by deploying navy ships to the region. The European Union, or EU, also has a military committee, headquartered in Brussels, and 22 of my NATO MilRep colleagues were double-hatted as their nation's EU MilRep. Twenty-one of 28 NATO nations were also in the 27 member EU. The United States, Canada, Norway, Iceland, Turkey, Albania and Croatia were not members.

There was a natural tension between the military operations of NATO and of the EU, due in part to the U.S. insistence that NATO be the pre-eminent military organization in Europe. This engendered some resentment, primarily on the part of France and Germany, of the dominant NATO role played by the United States. Occasionally this resulted in subtle competition for preeminence between the two organizations despite the overlapping composition of both. This came to the fore in the establishment of the piracy operations and led to some conflict between me and my French counterpart, and good friend, Lieutenant General Pascal Vinchon. NATO launched Operation Ocean Shield and the EU launched Operation Atalanta, both to patrol the pirate infested waters off Somalia. Naturally there was competition for limited naval resources to conduct meaningful operations, but the French deliberately set out to undermine the effectiveness of Operation Ocean Shield.

NATO is a consensus organization and in order for anything to be decided or accomplished, all 28 nations have to agree. This often leads to some very watered down results as compromise after compromise must be accommodated in order to achieve consensus. Operation Ocean Shield was no exception. Against the objections of me, British counterpart Lieutenant General David Bill, and Canadian Lieutenant General Chris Davis, the rules of engagement for our Ocean Shield ships were very limited. Leading the way in arguing against rules of engagement which would have given more authorities to the commander on the scene was Pascal Vinchon. He invariably was supported by German MilRep Lieutenant General Jurgen Bornemann, Italian Lieutenant General Gian-Piero Ristori, and Luxembourg representative Colonel Mario Daubenfeld. We were all friends; we socialized together often, we were all on a first name basis and knew each other's wives. Pascal and his wife Carine had taken Iris and me on a long weekend driving trip to the French champagne country and to Strasbourg on the German border. But, business was business, and I knew that Pascal was acting on instructions from Paris. Understanding this, we didn't take divergent national positions personally despite the sometimes animated discussion around the table.

On another occasion we were having a lively debate about whether or not to deploy the NATO AWACS to Afghanistan. General Craddock wanted it as an airborne command and control platform. Line of sight radios were ineffective in the mountainous Afghan terrain and an airborne asset could perform a number of valuable functions, such as airborne radio relay and as an airborne battle management platform, re-directing airborne combat air patrol and the like. I was arguing hard for approval of this request and, speaking on behalf of France, Pascal was arguing just as hard against it, saying that there was no air to air threat in Afghanistan so there was no need for AWACS. A fighter pilot himself, he knew damn well that I wasn't making the case based on an air to air requirement, but he had his instructions and he was duty bound to follow them. Earlier that year the French had lost ten soldiers in a firefight in a mountainous area, partially because they were unable to call for air support with their line of sight radios. My British counterpart that day, Deputy MilRep Brigadier Jeremy Thorn, pointed this out to Pascal in a very direct way. Pascal reacted angrily and dug in even harder. That night, coincidentally, we were invited to a dinner party hosted by Pascal and Carine.

As Iris and I were greeted at the door by Pascal, we said pleasant hellos and I said that we were looking forward to a fun evening. As he handed each of us a glass of champagne, Pascal responded that yes, he was too and he hoped it would be more fun than that day. We both smiled and raised a glass together. There were never any hard feelings.

As the 2008 presidential race heated up in the United States, there was great interest among our NATO colleagues. There always is because of the role the United States plays in the world. As the Europeans were fond of saying, "We have to live with the results of your elections."

George Bush had been an unpopular American president in Europe. It was all about the Iraq War and the Global War on Terrorism, Guantanamo Bay, and the Texas gunslinger image. Relations between the United States and France had been particularly strained and Donald Rumsfeld's open hostility to the French had been widely known. One of his early actions had been to downgrade the position of Defense Attache to France from that of a one-star general or admiral to a colonel or Navy captain. At the same time, he upgraded the position in London to one-star from non-flag rank. To the military the paygrade of the Defense Attache says a lot about the relative importance of the host country. His rationale was, "why honor the back-stabbing French with a general officer attache while sending a mere colonel to London, home of our most steadfast allies and friends?"

The primary race between former First Lady Hillary Clinton and Senator Barack Obama was particularly intriguing. A number of times during that 2008 spring and summer I had been asked, "Do you really think Americans are ready to elect a woman or a black man president?"

"It's pretty obvious they are," I would reply, "One of them is going to be the Democratic nominee." Left unsaid was that one of them was most likely going to be the next President. After the unpopularity of the Bush administration and the Iraq war, whoever the Democrats nominated was sure to win.

When Barack Obama got the Democratic nomination the focus turned to race and there was still skepticism on the part of the Europeans with whom we talked. They were solidly behind the candidacy of Barack Obama, fearing that Senator John McCain would be another George Bush. At one dinner party, Georgette Daubenfeld, the wife of the Luxembourg MilRep, asked what the percentage was of the black population in America. I told her it was about 15%. She was flabbergasted. She thought it was about 50%. American television and sports no doubt gave her that impression.

When Barack Obama won the election in November 2008 the Europeans were openly delighted. I received many congratulations the next day at NATO headquarters. I don't think it was because they thought I had voted for him, rather, I believe it was meant as a nation-wide congratulation because we had seemed to have risen above the issue of race in America. No less widely applauded was the selection of Hillary Clinton as Secretary of State. Former President Bill Clinton remained enormously popular in Europe and that extended to Mrs. Clinton. When she made her first trip to Brussels for a NATO Foreign Ministerial, the halls were jammed with people just hoping for a chance to see her as she walked from Ambassador Ivo Daalder's office to the meeting room. Condoleezza Rice had also achieved a certain level of rock-star status during her visits, but nothing compared to that accorded Hillary Clinton.

Two significant NATO events occurred in conjunction with the election of Barack Obama. The first to take effect involved the missile defense plan for Europe. Though not per se a NATO plan, it nevertheless involved NATO for a variety of reasons. In the first place, the plan to install Ground Based Interceptors in Poland and a specially configured missile defense radar in the Czech Republic involved two NATO partners. This was a U.S.–Poland–Czech Republic arrangement, not a NATO arrangement. The NATO nations of Europe were concerned about the reaction of Russia to the plan and the potential implications for them if, someday, the system knocked down a ballistic missile. Where would the debris land? What would be the command and control arrangements? Who gets to decide to pull the trigger? What would be the notification process, and so forth.

The Obama administration removed those concerns in September 2009 when it announced, with little or no consultation with either Poland or the Czech Republic, that it was abandoning the Bush plan for the sites in Europe. My colleagues in Brussels, Polish Lieutenant General Mieczyslaw Bieniek, and Czech Lieutenant General Jaroslav Kolkus, heard it for the first time on the news. When they asked me about it, I had to admit I was hearing it for the first time as well. Both the Polish government and the Czech government had withstood not so veiled threats from the Russians, and domestic unhappiness at home, especially in the Czech Republic. Yet they had steadfastly supported the American plan. I was embarrassed at the way we pulled the rug out from under both countries. Vice President Joe Biden was sent to Brussels, along with Under Secretary of Defense for Policy Michelle Flournoy, to explain the decision to a meeting of the North Atlantic Council. At that meeting the Vice President vaguely outlined the concept for an alternate plan, called Phased Adaptive Approach, which would rely on Aegis guided missile ships at sea and, eventually, a shore based Aegis system. Ultimately, Romania would agree to host the shore based Aegis system.

The second major event concerned the mission in Afghanistan. In June of 2009 Secretary of Defense Bob Gates had relieved ISAF Commander General Dave McKiernan and replaced him with General Stan McChrystal. General McKiernan, an armor officer by training, was reportedly considered too "old school" in his thinking for the combat environment in Afghanistan. Stan, a special operator with considerable counter-insurgency experience, was given 60 days to assess the situation and make a recommendation to the President on what needed to be done to turn things around in Afghanistan. By the summer of 2009 it looked like little real progress was being made, either in defeating the Taliban, or strengthening the Afghan government and security forces enough to stand on their own.

This review underwent several highly secretive iterations and dragged on through the summer and well into the fall. It was a U.S.-only review, despite the fact that ISAF was a NATO operation and, presumably, big decisions on the war would be made in consultation with our NATO allies. In truth, the United States provided two-thirds of the troops, something like 90% of the air support, and 80% of the logistics support. With the exception of a few nations, including Australia who was not even a member of NATO, the bulk of the hard fighting was done by the Americans and the bulk of the financial assistance came from the United States. The joke was that ISAF stood for "I Saw Americans Fighting."

My colleagues on the Military Committee, particularly my close friends like Lieutenant General Jo Godderij, the Dutch Director of the Military Staff, assumed I knew more about it than I did and constantly pressed me for details. At one point I had been emailed a copy of the draft assessment, calling for 40,000 more U.S. troops, over the secure internet system, the SIPRNET. When Admiral Mullen found out that I had it, he directed me to destroy it. It was that sensitive. The backdrop was the belief in the White House that the military was gaming the President by leaking details before a decision had been reached on the final number.

On the 1st of December 2009, President Obama, in a speech at the United States Military Academy at West Point, announced the Afghan surge. I set my alarm for 3:00 AM in Brussels and got up to watch the speech so I would know as much as my NATO colleagues, many of whom, I was sure, had done the same thing. The speech was much anticipated after months of deliberation; some called it dithering. In his announcement, the President split the difference, on the one hand announcing a 30,000 troop surge, three quarters of what Stan McChrystal had asked for, and on the other, announcing the beginning of our withdrawal 18 months later. I found this disappointing and self-defeating. To me, and to many of my NATO colleagues, it signaled that the President felt pressured to "do something," but his heart was not in it and what he really wanted to do was get out. I felt that the announcement would send many of our NATO allies, reluctant participants to begin with, heading for the exits.

When I first arrived in Brussels in December 2006, the U.S. Ambassador to Belgium was Tom Korologos, a political appointee of President Bush. I had paid an introductory call on him early in my tour but he was on the way out and a new Ambassador, Sam Fox, was appointed by the President. A staunch Republican, Sam had been a recess appointee because it was felt that he would never survive the confirmation process. The Senate Foreign Relations Committee, responsible for the confirmation hearings, was led by Senator John Kerry who had run against George Bush in the 2004 election. Sam Fox, a St. Louis-based millionaire, was credited with providing political contributions which, at least in part, provided funding to the "Swift Boat Veterans" who had questioned Senator Kerry's Vietnam War record and run some damaging campaign advertisements.

When Ambassador Fox arrived in Belgium I scheduled an office call and went to introduce myself. It was early 2007. We hit it off, and Sam jokingly made reference to the fact that I didn't tower over him like so many others. I'm five foot six and at least a couple of inches taller than Sam. One of the purposes of my visit was to talk with him about our Memorial Day responsibilities. There are three American military cemeteries in Belgium, two of which serve as the final resting place for World War II American dead, and one for World War I. Each year on the Saturday and Sunday of Memorial Day weekend there is a ceremony at each of the cemeteries and the American Ambassador and American Military Representative to NATO have a speaking and wreath-laying role at each event. For Ambassador Fox and myself, the 2007 events would be our first and we needed to discuss coordination and also make sure that our respective speeches were sufficiently different. We were each briefed by Jim Begg, an American businessman living in Brussels and the Belgium representative of the American Battle Monuments Commission.

When Iris and I first learned that our three-day Memorial Day weekend was going to be filled with official duties we grumbled about it. However, Ed Hanlon had told me that the Memorial Day events were extraordinary and he did not exaggerate. It was an incredibly moving experience all three years we lived in Belgium and one of our most cherished memories.

On Saturday, May 26, 2007 we drove to the small Belgian town of Neupre in the far east on the edge of the Ardennes Forest, the area where the Battle of the Bulge was fought in December 1944. The mayor of Neupre hosted a small breakfast, primarily for the purpose of organizing the car caravan to the nearby Ardennes American Cemetery where the first ceremony was to be held. Ambassador Fox and his wife, Marilyn met us there. I had reconnoitered weeks earlier and knew that the cemetery was an impressive place, but nothing had prepared me for the outpouring of support by the Belgian people. The cemetery itself is at once beautiful and sobering. 5,323 Americans are buried in a spectacular setting. The names of 432 missing are inscribed on the walls of the massive stone chapel. Many of those buried at Ardennes were aviators, and the Eighth Air Force insignia, which Iris's father had been a part of, was prominently displayed on the wall of the chapel. I was amazed at the number of Belgian civilians in attendance, many carrying small American and Belgian flags. Two things in particular stood out. Ambassador Fox, the mayor, and I walked the ranks and shook hands with the "Anciennes Combatantes;" the survivors or descendants of those who fought in World War II.

Many of them wore their old uniform jackets, festooned with patches and medals, and carried full-sized Belgian flags with the insignia of their units sewed on. Some could barely stand, but they all stood and saluted as the American and Belgian National Anthems were played. As part of the ceremony, a class of about 30 Belgian school children, ages seven and eight, sang the U.S. National Anthem—in English. Few Americans who witnessed this display of appreciation for what America had done for Belgium in two world wars could do so without tearing up. I know I did.

After we made our speeches and all the wreath-laying was done, we piled into the cars, went to a fancy luncheon, and then drove to the afternoon ceremony at Henri-Chappelle American Cemetery. Henri-Chappelle lies seven miles from the German border, is the final resting place for 7,992 American dead, and lists 450 of the missing. When the day was done, Ambassador Fox said, "What are your plans tonight?"

"We don't have anything special planned," I said.

"Well come on back to the residence and let's have dinner." We did and that was the beginning of a great friendship. On Sunday the 27th, we rendezvoused at a nice French restaurant for lunch in the town of Waregam before that day's ceremony at the Flanders Field American Cemetery where 368 World War I American dead are buried. Flanders Field is much smaller and more intimate than the other cemeteries, but again the support of the Belgian people is no less amazing.

Each year we looked forward to Memorial Day weekend. It brought home for us the true meaning of Memorial Day in ways that exceeded the impact in the United States. Perhaps it was because we were standing on the soil where these battles were fought, far from home, to liberate people we did not know. Sixty-five years after World War II, and 90 years after World War I, the Belgian people had not forgotten. More importantly, they were passing that appreciation on to their children. It was particularly moving when the mayor of Neupre stood up to make his remarks and said, "Thirty years ago I was one of those school children singing the American National Anthem." All told, there are almost 125,000 American war dead buried in overseas American cemeteries and the names of another 94,000 commemorated on Tablets of the Missing.

As my time in Belgium, and in the Navy, was winding down, I was sitting next to Admiral Mullen at a Chiefs of Defense meeting in Brussels and talking to him about my upcoming retirement. Navy Vice Admiral Dick Gallagher had been named as my replacement and we were in the process of coordinating our turnover.

"What are your plans?" asked Admiral Mullen.

"I think I'll just go back to Washington and quietly retire. We'll move back into our townhouse."

"What about a ceremony?"

"It's too much trouble. And having the CNO retire me over in the Washington Navy Yard in Leutze Park would have no real meaning for me or the family."

"You should do it on a ship in Mayport." Mike knew my background, having once been my detailer, and knew I had spent a total of ten years stationed in Mayport.

I thought about it for a second and then said, "If I do that will you be the speaker?"

"Yes."

CHAPTER 29

Going Ashore

With Admiral Mullen's agreement to be the guest speaker, the die was cast and I began thinking about how to go out in style aboard a Navy ship in Mayport. Having taken part in hosting numerous ceremonies aboard my own ships over the years, I was very cognizant of the workload it places on the ship's crew. I had the additional challenge of pulling it all together without staff support once I left Belgium.

I started by going to my good friend, Rear Admiral Buz Buzby, then stationed at Fleet Forces Command Headquarters in Norfolk, and asking for a list of all the ships stationed in Mayport and the names of their CO's. I was hoping somebody with whom I had a personal relationship would be in command so I wouldn't feel too bad about asking this big favor. Given that my official retirement date had been set as midnight, January 31, 2010, and I was leaving Brussels on December 15th, I also asked Buz which ships would be in Mayport in January. When Buz sent back the list, there were no CO's I knew well. Of the ships in port in January, only two looked like good candidates, *USS VICKSBURG (CG-69)*, an Aegis cruiser like *COWPENS*, and *USS THE SULLIVANS (DDG-68)*, an Aegis destroyer. I canvassed my family, asking the question, should I do it on the cruiser because I had once commanded one, or do it on *THE SULLIVANS* because of the name, even though I had never served in an *ARLEIGH BURKE* class DDG. The vote was almost unanimous: *THE SULLIVANS*. Only Iris raised an objection, saying it was a little too contrived and "hokey" to use *THE SULLIVANS*. On one of the very few occasions in 41 years together, Iris lost.

I had met *THE SULLIVANS* Commanding Officer, Commander Ryan Tillotson, at a ceremony for the unveiling of a

Navy memorial at Utah Beach, site of the D-Day landings in Normandy. *THE SULLIVANS* had been assigned to support the ceremony. I sent him an email and asked if he would be so kind as to let me use his ship for my retirement. He wrote right back with a positive answer. He was due to be relieved before January 2010 so he was volunteering his relief, Commander Neil Funtanilla, for the job.

I took advantage of my staff support in Brussels to get a program put together and, because Admiral Mullen was serving as guest speaker, the Joint Staff took care of having the invitations printed up and mailed stating that Admiral Mullen was inviting the guests to the ceremony. I had picked a Friday, January 15, 2010, for the ceremony and set it up for 3:00 PM so we could roll into a big party at the Mayport Naval Station Club immediately after.

Iris and I left Brussels on December 15th to move back to northern Virginia for my out-processing and retirement from the Navy. Two days before leaving Brussels our phone rang about 9 o'clock the night of the 13th. It was Debbie Dawson, wife of retired Vice Admiral Cutler Dawson.

"Bill, did you hear about Dave Stone?"

"No, what?"

"He died."

Debbie went on to tell me that Dave Stone had been home in Arlington, Virginia from Bangalore, India where he and Faith were living after Dave took a job with Cisco. Just two weeks earlier, I had gone to the Cisco office in Brussels and done a job interview with Dave and his boss from Cisco. Dave had set it up to give me some job interview practice. Dave, who had left the Navy as a rear admiral several years earlier, had gone to work for the Transportation Security Agency as the head man at Los Angeles International Airport after 9/11. He had spent a year in Los Angeles, then come back to TSA headquarters in Arlington, Virginia. When the Director of TSA position came open, Dave was nominated and confirmed. He had left TSA to take the job with Cisco and was back in Washington from India to participate in a TSA event. He had a massive heart attack while sitting at home watching *Sports Center* on television sometime over the weekend. Faith had remained behind in Bangalore. The maid found him when she came to the house Monday morning.

We were shocked; Dave was 57, two years younger than me. We had been close since serving together at Cruiser-Destroyer Group 12 in 1984-1985. Our children, Chris and Amy, were close to Dave and Faith as well. They had no children. When we contacted Faith she said she wanted me to speak at Dave's memorial service at the Naval Academy chapel. She scheduled the service for December 17th, two days after our return to the States.

Vice Admiral Dick Gallagher arrived in Brussels three days before our departure and we conducted a quick turnover. The protocol in the Military Committee was that the incoming and outgoing MilReps were never seen together. The incoming MilRep did not sit in on a meeting with the outgoing MilRep. I attended my last Military Committee meeting and, as was the tradition, I made a farewell speech, got out of my chair, and left the room. My Deputy, Air Force Brigadier General Dave Petersen, slid into my seat for the rest of the meeting. Dick Gallagher would be introduced at the next meeting.

In my final remarks I commented on how remarkable it was that NATO had expanded to include the former Warsaw Pact nations and complimented them on their struggles to gain their freedom and independence from the Communist rule of the Soviet Union. I also complimented them on their ability to listen to arguments in English, formulate their own thoughts, and then make their country's case, also in English.

Around the 7th of January back in northern Virginia with plans well in hand for the January 15th retirement ceremony aboard *THE SULLIVANS* in Mayport, my cell phone rang. It was Admiral Mullen.

"Bill, can you change the time of your ceremony? I have to fly to Australia that day and I can't make it if we do the ceremony at three. Can you move it to ten?"

"Let me get back to you." I talked it over with Iris. One of the advantages of the afternoon ceremony was that many guests, traveling from out of town, could travel that day, a Friday. We decided we couldn't change the time; it would inconvenience too many people. I called Admiral Mullen back and told him I couldn't change it and why. I said I'd ask Admiral Jim Stavridis to substitute; he had RSVP'd that he would attend. A second choice was Marine General Jim Mattis who was now the Commander of U.S. Central Command in Tampa. Jim and I had been National War College classmates and had become close while he was serving a double-hatted position as the Commander, U.S. Joint Forces Command and NATO Commander, Allied Command Transformation. Jim Stavridis is never far from an email machine and he responded right away that he would do it.

I had also decided on my eight honorary sideboys who would pipe Iris and me over the side at the end of the ceremony. In looking around, I realized that virtually all of my contemporaries were either retired or were three or four-star admirals in important jobs. The odds of assembling eight of these senior officers to serve as honorary sideboys were slim. By January of 2010 there was only one naval officer on active duty who had been commissioned before me: Admiral Mike Mullen. Everybody else, from CNO Gary Roughead on down, had been commissioned in 1973 or later. I decided to go with the younger generation, starting with son Chris, now a lieutenant commander and, coincidentally, stationed at Mayport at the Helicopter Maritime Strike Weapons School as the Operations Officer.

I asked Rear Admiral Buz Buzby, a long time good friend who had worked for me in J3 from 1995-1996. I went with Lieutenant Commander Rob Danberg, son of our good friends, Bob and Kathy Danberg. Rob, a LAMPS helicopter pilot was also stationed in Mayport. Sticking with the family friends theme, I asked Lieutenant Commander Kendra Ryan. Kendra, by then a navy reservist, was the daughter of our dear friend Karen Netting from San Diego, and had been assigned to *USS COWPENS* after I had left command. I then turned to my former aides and executive assistants: Commander Andy Fata, my executive assistant at the J5 on the Joint Staff, another helicopter pilot; Lieutenant Commander Pete Kim, a Surface Warfare Officer who had been my last aide at Naval Forces Korea in Seoul. Pete had been working in the J5 in Washington but was slated to become Executive Officer and then Commanding Officer of one of the new Littoral Combat Ships, *USS CORONADO (LCS-4)*. Commander Steve Hoffman, another LAMPS pilot who had been my aide and executive assistant in Brussels and now a student at the Industrial College of the Armed Forces in Washington, D.C. rounded out that category. Finally, I asked Master Chief Chris Adams, the most significant enlisted person in my Navy career who was still on active duty. Chris had been with me in *SAMPSON, COWPENS*, in Korea, and in Hawaii.

Arriving on January 13, we set up camp in the BOQ at Naval Station Mayport. I visited *THE SULLIVANS* and talked over the orchestration of the ceremony with Commander Neil Funtanilla, the CO. He and his crew could not have been more supportive, despite the fact that they were 30 days away from a six-month deployment.

The ceremony on the 15th was well done by the ship and well attended by people from throughout my career, and before. Two Sigma Nu fraternity brothers from Florida State, Bruce and Lorraine Skelton and Rick Beeman were also in attendance. As I looked over the RSVP list, I realized that someone from every single command over the past 37 years was in the audience. Of course, Master Chief Adams checked four of those boxes, Retired Rear Admiral Paul Tobin checked two, as did retired Captain Terry Culton. Rob and Christie Hofmann from *NEWPORT NEWS* came from Pittsburgh and retired Captain Bernie Hollenbeck and wife Sandy from *SEMMES* came up from Palm Coast, Florida. Dave Loy from Navy Recruiting District Atlanta made the trip from Knoxville, Tennessee. There were many other friends, including my CO in *AUBREY FITCH*, retired Captain John Langknecht, who, with his wife, Sandy, had brought Dave Stone's widow Faith. My DESRON 8 buddies, retired Captains Hank and Kate Sanford and Bob and Cindy Sweeney were there along with Cookie Kalleres. Retired Vice Admiral Mike Kalleres was fighting a debilitating bone marrow disease and unable to go aboard the ship.

General Jim Mattis was in the audience, as was Lieutenant General Steve Whitcomb and his wife, Cathy, our friends from Korea. My cousin, Air Force Brigadier General Joe Callahan, who I had promoted to colonel immediately after arriving in J-5, also came. Admiral Jim Stavridis and I met in the wardroom and briefly discussed the sequence of events. He had presided over numerous ceremonies and needed little preparation and no rehearsing.

Of course my entire family was in attendance. I had decided that I wanted to focus on the family, particularly my father, in my remarks. For that reason, I had written a first person account of my career for the official program. In putting together the program before leaving Brussels, I had put pictures on the cover of my son Chris in his flight suit, me on the bridge wing of *SAMPSON*, and a great picture from 1952 of my father climbing out of the cockpit of his AD-4 Skyraider. I wanted to emphasize the three generations of naval officers and the passing of the torch from my father, to me, and now to Chris. My father died in October 2014 at the age of 91. That 1952 picture in his flight suit remains the most appropriate depiction of his life and we used it at the funeral. Almost all of the pictures collaged on the back cover were of me and Iris together at various places and stages of our Navy life.

I also wanted to keep it light. No tears, and no morose stories about how much I was going to miss the Navy. This was supposed to be a celebration, not a wake. I think I succeeded. I introduced every member of my family and said a little about each; saving the most for my Dad and for Iris. I also talked about Iris's parents, by then deceased, especially about her father and his service and POW status from World War II.

When the ceremony was over, the honorary sideboys assembled on the quarterdeck, I took Iris by the arm, and together we walked off the ship arm in arm, leaving the Navy the way we had come in; together.

CPSIA information can be obtained
at www.ICGtesting.com
Printed in the USA
BVHW070251060619
550247BV00002B/167/P